A Guide to the
Helping Professions

A Guide to the Helping Professions

David J. Srebalus
West Virginia University

Duane Brown
University of North Carolina at Chapel Hill

Allyn and Bacon

Boston ■ London ■ Toronto ■ Sydney ■ Tokyo ■ Singapore

Series Editor: *Virginia Lanigan*
Editor-in-Chief: *Paul A. Smith*
Editorial Assistant: *Jennifer Connors*
Marketing Manager: *Brad Parkins*
Editorial-Production Coordinator: *Mary Beth Finch*
Editorial-Production Service: *Modern Graphics*
Composition Buyer: *Linda Cox*
Electronic Composition and Art: *Modern Graphics*
Manufacturing Buyer: *Suzanne Lareau*
Cover Administrator: *Brian Gogolin*

Copyright © 2001 by Allyn & Bacon
A Pearson Education Company
160 Gould Street
Needham Heights, Massachusetts 02494

Internet: www.abacon.com

Between the time Website information is gathered and then published, it is not unusual for some sites to have closed. Also, the transcription of URLs can result in unintended typographical errors. The publisher would appreciate notification where these occur so that they may be corrected in subsequent editions. Thank you.

Library of Congress Cataloging-in-Publication Data
Srebalus, David J.
    A guide to the helping professions / by David J. Srebalus and Duane Brown.
        p. cm.
    Includes bibliographical references and index.
    ISBN 0-205-30844-9 (pbk.)
        1. Mental health services—Vocational guidance. I. Brown, Duane. II. Title.

RA790.75 .S74 2000
362.2'023—dc21

00-044745

Printed in the United States of America

10 9 8 7 6 5 4 3 2 1   05 04 03 02 01 00

To Rosemary and Sandra

CONTENTS

PREFACE

Today helping professionals serve society in many different ways. They continue to provide services that rehabilitate and support troubled and injured individuals. They provide help to tens of thousands coping with the increased stress of modern life. Helping professionals also contribute substantially to human resource development efforts that expand productivity and personnel potential.

While all these roles for helping professionals have been trademarks for a long time, the ongoing demographic changes in the United States and the ongoing globalization of society have created new roles. Multiculturally-trained helping professionals increasingly are called on to be leaders in empowering diverse groups and enabling multicultural communities to succeed.

As society-at-large, in both its public and private sectors, has relied on helping professionals to do so many jobs, there has been a recognition of the power and versatility of the training these professionals receive. Undergraduates have not missed this. Large numbers of them are interested in learning how their baccalaureate degree can merge with other experiences to prepare them for a useful and satisfying career. They do not want to wait to see how their theoretical knowledge of behavior and social issues can be translated into practical, salable skills. This book has been written to help college students see how their education can be combined with a set of attitudes and further combined with additional training that can lead to a career in one of the many helping professions.

In this way this text hopes to empower college students to believe in themselves and their education. This book hopes to demonstrate that what they are learning from their courses in psychology, sociology, criminal justice, social work, and many other disciplines begin to converge, creating a common ground upon which important service to humankind is based. This book celebrates more than one helping profession, it celebrates an entire community of helpers, each providing something special and at the same time sharing common ground. By positioning each helping profession within the community of helpers, each individual profession is further validated as relevant within the collective.

Since job descriptions so often vary in occupations according to local need, rather than profiling specific occupations and professions, this text examines what is common among helping professionals. Whether as a social worker, counselor, probation office, or other helping professional the student has the opportunity examine what it takes as person to qualify and endure as a helper. The early chapters of the book examine personality characteristics, cultural attitudes, and basic interpersonal competencies required in the helping professions. In the middle chapters students get an opportunity to see what it is like to counsel an individual, work with a family, and lead a group. Later chapters begin the process of building ethical decision-making skills and other professional traits as students get direct input on career planning that has as its objectives entry and advancement in a helping profession.

We hope that students reading this book will get more than an intellectual overview; hopefully, they will get a taste of work helpers do. We have tried to achieve this by making the book interactive. Each chapter contains self-assessment exercises to bring out personal preferences and skills to allow for immediate comparison with those of helping professionals. In addition to the many examples embedded in the text, larger case studies are provided to bring the issues under discussion into more vivid focus. The chapter exercises and case studies should also assist the instructor by providing stimuli for class discussion. Most chapters also reference Internet sites that can lead to even more information. Besides these learning aides of a more recent age, traditional aides, such as advanced organizers (chapter objectives) and exit self-tests, also are provided.

We have included the material and features described also because of the many non-traditional students we expect to use this book in both community and four-year colleges. As these students prepare to change or re-enter a career, they depend on cost-efficient experiences that will quickly qualify them for work. Because older students often are more geographically centered, the text can help them see how training for one helping profession generalizes to another, limited though by credentialing standards, also discussed in the book. If opportunities in one helping profession do not exist in their community, others might that require similar skills and provide similar gratification.

Although at present not widespread, there are programs of study in human resources that have an introductory course that will use this book. While these programs do not constitute in most cases a college major, they do certify to graduate programs and employers of entry-level helping professionals that the program graduate has had more applied studies than the traditional psychology or sociology student. He or she has had an opportunity to visualize what a career as a helping professional is like, beyond the common stereotypes. The student is likely further along in the development of a professional identity by more direct exposure to the standards of care for the helping professions.

1 Becoming a Helping Professional

1. The definition of helping
2. Special challenges for helper-trainees
3. The nature and scope of the problems facing clients
4. The strategies used by helpers
5. The career paths that helpers may take

Some of you are embarking on an exciting, challenging journey: You are training to become a professional helper. Others are considering training in one or more of the helping professions. Whether you have decided to be a helper or are considering a helping career as an option, you are probably unsure of all the stops along the way. If you are like most students, the journey to becoming a professional helper evokes a certain amount of anxiety. You probably have many questions, such as, "What will I have to learn?," "What skills will I have to master?," and "What personal changes will I have to make?" As the journey progresses, you will realize that helping is not done *to* people. Rather, helping is a process conducted *with* people in stressful, challenging relationships. The realization about the very personal nature of the helping process will give rise to other questions, such as "What personal demands will be made on me, and how can I deal with them?" Other important questions will emerge, such as "Which helping profession should I enter?" and "What types of people am I most interested in helping?" This book assists you in answering all of these questions. In this chapter, we consider some definitions of helping, special challenges for helper-trainees, the array of problems facing clients in our society, the strategies that helping professionals use to attack these problems, and the career paths that helpers may take.

Helping Defined

It is common in our society to discuss helping others or to make statements such as "I helped Darrell fix his car." Often, when we use the colloquial version of *helping*, it involves providing support to assist friends, neighbors, and sometimes

1

strangers deal with their problems. Helping may involve giving money, volunteering time to help an individual or organization meets goals, or listening to a friend talk about her or his problems. This type of helping is called *informal helping* because it is not systematically planned or carried out. People who are not trained to be helpers and who help on an intermittent basis typically are engaged in informal helping. Informal helping serves a major purpose in our daily lives because it provides us with social support. However, sometimes we need more formalized approaches to helping.

This book discusses formal approaches to helping and therefore defines the term differently. *Helping* is a planned service offered by trained professionals who are governed by a code of ethics to meet the identified needs of clients. The most fundamental ethical principle of professional helpers is to promote the welfare of the individuals and groups served. The two primary objectives of the helping process are (1) to prevent health or psychological problems from arising and (2) to improve the health or psychological profile of the people being helped. Table 1.1 summarizes the differences between informal and formal helping.

When does a person have a mental disorder? Poindexter, Valentine, and Conway (1999) suggest that it is when an individual's thoughts, behaviors, and emotions fall outside the typical societal range and are out of the individual's control. The *Diagnostic and Statistical Manual of Mental Disorders* (4th ed., rev., APA, 1994) (DSM-IV) definition of *mental disorder* is some type of distress (for example, anxiety) or impairment (for example, reduced cognitive functioning). The DSM-IV goes on to stipulate that typical responses to life events, such as feeling grief over a loved one's death or anger over a conflict between individuals, are not considered mental disorders. An individual whose anxiety interferes with sleep, whose motivation to do school work declines significantly, and whose chronic sadness has no precipitating cause has a mental disorder. The person who bombs a federal building as a protest against the income tax does not necessarily have a mental disorder, even though his actions are extreme. People who have cultural beliefs that vary from those in the dominant society (for example, it is possible to communicate with the dead through a shaman) do not have a mental

TABLE 1.1   Informal and Formal Helping Contrasted

Informal Helping	Formal Helping
Unplanned	Planned
Requires no specific training	Offered by skilled helper
Not systematic	Is systematic
Not intentional	Intentional
Impact on client uncertain	Client may get better or worse
Goal is uncertain	Goal is to impact mental health

disorder according to the DSM-IV definition. Common mental disorders include phobias, depression, panic disorders, and alcohol and drug addiction.

Professional helpers offer three types of services. The first is called *primary prevention* and it works to completely prevent the onset of mental illness. Elementary school counselors who work with children to develop assertion skills are practicing primary prevention. The children develop the assertion skills to refuse later invitations to take drugs or participate in other illegal activities. Family therapists and pastoral counselors who conduct marriage enrichment groups also practice primary prevention.

The second type of service that helpers offer is called *secondary prevention.* It helps individuals who have developed a mild form of a mental disorder to reduce the symptoms and effects of their disorder. Secondary prevention also helps to keep mild disorders from becoming more serious. One woman, for example, reported how her untreated social anxiety gradually evolved into agoraphobia, an irrational and often debilitating fear of open spaces that often causes its sufferers to refuse to leave their homes and that requires relatively long-term treatment. Social workers who provide family therapy to abusive families practice secondary prevention. They hope that stemming abusive parenting behavior will prevent the development of mental health problems in the abused members. Probation counselors who work with parolees and probationers on chronic anger issues are also providing secondary prevention services.

Tertiary prevention treats individuals who have serious forms of mental disorders to prevent their problems from becoming life threatening. Therapists who provide psychotherapy and psychiatrists who prescribe medication to the chronically and suicidally depressed practice tertiary prevention. The substance abuse counselor who works with a life-long addict whose life is threatened is also involved in tertiary prevention. And, unfortunately, the acroaphobic who did not receive early treatment now needs this third level care.

Helping, then, is a planned, formal process that is rooted in ethical principles and offered by a trained helper with the intent of preventing mental health problems from arising or keeping them from becoming more serious. As it is discussed throughout this book, helping also involves a human relationship. This might suggest that helping requires helper and client to work face to face, but this is not the case. Helping services are now offered over the telephone and the Internet, a trend that will accelerate as technology develops further. Whether helping is offered face to face or via some medium, the client must appreciate and trust the helper before meaningful outcomes will occur. Professional helpers realize that if helping is not delivered skillfully and ethically, clients may actually get worse as a result of the helping process. Classic studies show conclusively that some clients deteriorate when the helpers are unskilled (Leiberman, Yalom & Miles, 1973; Truax & Carkhuff, 1967). Finally, helping is an intentional process. Intentional helping requires helpers to understand the values and unique communication styles of their clients and to use a helping style that is compatible with them (Ivey, 1994). Intentionality is a particularly important concept in the matter of cross-cultural helping, a topic that is emphasized throughout this book.

Special Challenges for Helper-Trainees

Managing Self-Doubt

Becoming a skilled helper requires trainees to master a number of skills, including the ability to empathize, communicate, diagnose clients' problems, and develop plans for treating those problems. With few exceptions, helper-trainees have difficulty acquiring some of these skills. As trainees understand the array and complexity of the skills they need to master, most enter into a period of self-doubt.

Empathy—the ability to perceive another individual's problem as he or she does—is an essential characteristic of successful helpers. People who enter professional training programs without this trait often become frustrated because empathy rarely can be taught. The self-doubt of trainees who lack empathy arises from their realization of how vital empathy is to successful helping. Often their self-doubt is heightened by feedback from supervisors and others that these trainees are not attuned to the needs of their clients.

Consider too that some helping professionals regularly encounter involuntary clients who are sent by the courts, such as spouse abusers, DWI (driving while impaired) offenders, addicts and alcoholics, voyeurs ("peeping Toms"), and exhibitionists. Other helpers assume responsibility for people with severe and chronic mental health problems, such as schizophrenia and borderline personality disorder. Still others work to rehabilitate criminals who habitually lie and deceive. Given the complexity of the skills needed in these situations, it is understandable that self-doubt results in some trainees.

Self-doubt also arises for many trainees when they realize that helping involves intense, intimate, and sometimes contradictory relationships with clients. A critical moment in many helper-trainees' lives comes when they are lied to the first time. This evokes various responses including anger, doubt about their ability to help the person who lied, and guilt because they have failed the client. Other critical events come when helper-trainees face the dependent client, the client that they genuinely dislike, the excessively emotional client who gets angry at the helper, the cross-cultural client who directly or indirectly calls them a racist, or the client who discloses a sexual attraction to the helper. Any of these anxiety-laden events can lead to self-doubt.

Another major source of self-doubt for helper-trainees is cross-cultural helping. Cross-cultural helping occurs in any situation in which the helper and client hold very different beliefs, values, and worldviews. Cross-cultural helping includes situations involving white, European American helpers working with people of color; straight helpers working with gay, bisexual, or transsexual clients; nondisabled helpers working with disabled clients; and helpers working with clients from different socioeconomic strata. Many helper-trainees believe themselves to be empathic because many of their informal helping experiences have been with people like themselves. When faced with the difficult work inherent in cross-cultural counseling, they begin to question their empathy skills. In some fieldwork sites, trainees confront homeless persons, Hispanic Americans who speak little English, angry workers who have lost their jobs due to downsizing, and individuals who have committed violent crimes. Although the helping professions are specialized because of the diversity of the clients, helpers must have a substantial knowledge base and accompanying skills and attitudes necessary to deal with a wide variety of clients. For some helper-trainees, the prospect of gaining the knowledge and skills needed to deal with diversity is overwhelming and creates self-doubt.

Helper-trainees inevitably experience self-doubts. However, if trainees receive the knowledge they need in their courses and are supervised adequately, typically their fears dissipate as they gain new knowledge and develop new skills. The checklist shown in Exercise 1.1 outlines some of the characteristics of the ideal helper. Compare your characteristics to those listed.

EXERCISE **1.1**

Comparing Myself to the Ideal Helper

I Have This Characteristic

Characteristics of the Ideal Helper	Yes	No	Uncertain
1. Understand their strengths and weaknessess	____	____	____
2. Accept constructive criticism without getting defensive	____	____	____
3. Are naturally curious about people and ideas	____	____	____
4. Are genuine (what you see is what you get)	____	____	____
5. Can accept failure and are not perfectionistic	____	____	____
6. Are comfortable with people who are different from themselves	____	____	____
7. Project warmth and caring	____	____	____
8. Possess a strong sense of their own identity	____	____	____
9. Have high self-esteem	____	____	____
10. Handle stress effectively	____	____	____
11. Are willing to put themselves on the line for others	____	____	____
12. Are highly optimistic about human potential	____	____	____
13. Value diversity	____	____	____
14. Have a high degree of personal integrity and can be trusted	____	____	____
15. Understand their own motivations	____	____	____
16. Take stands against institutional and societal conditions that harm individuals and groups	____	____	____
17. Are sensitive to the needs of others	____	____	____
18. Take care of their own physical and emotional health	____	____	____
19. Understand that they have limits	____	____	____
20. Do not always have to be in control	____	____	____

Maximizing Learning

Ideally, training programs for helpers resemble a Thanksgiving dinner where diners expect to eat hearty portions of all the foods served. However, training programs often look more like buffets where trainees try all the food in smaller amounts, accepting some as palatable and rejecting some as less so. Students may choose their courses in a similar manner. Students perceive that courses have varying degrees of applicability to their careers. Sometimes they base these perceptions on the skill with which the courses are taught, sometimes on what they think they need to know to become effective helpers, or sometimes on how interesting the subjects seem (for example, abnormal versus developmental psychology). However, practitioners often find that their guesses about what material would be most and least useful in their helping roles turn out to be wrong. Therefore, the first rule for maximizing your learning is to suspend your judgement about what is important and consume healthy amounts of each course taken.

The second rule for maximizing your learning is to develop a sense of what you believe as you enter your training program. Begin this process by completing Exercise 1.2. This will allow you to get a sense of your current explanation of human functioning and what you must do to change behavior, thoughts, and emotions. As you receive new information in this book, compare it to what you believe at this time before accepting or discarding it.

Why is outlining your personal explanation of human functioning important? One of the principles of human learning is that we tend to focus on and are more likely to accept information that verifies what we already believe. If you are to maximize your learning as you train to become a helper, you must identify your preconceived notions and open your mind to new ways of looking at people and the change process. If you do not identify your preexisting biases, you may find yourself rejecting ideas and concepts without adequately considering their worth to you as a helper. For example, some helpers believe that they need only one set of helping strategies regardless of the gender and ethnicity of the client in spite of evidence to the contrary.

Maximizing your learning also occurs by practicing what you learn as you learn it. Professors who train helpers smile inwardly when they hear their students practice their newfound communications skills at parties and other events outside the helping process. They recognize that this practice is a sure sign that their students are maximizing their education. Although students need to apply the skills they learn in their lives, there are some exceptions. For example, it is unethical to enter into helping relationships with friends, family members, business associates, and others with whom helpers have preexisting relationships. These *dual relationships* must be avoided. A dual relationship occurs when the helper is involved in a helping relationship and another relationship with the client (for example, a friendship). Well-designed training programs offer students opportunities to take what they learn in the classroom into the field and apply their knowledge and skills in helping relationships with real clients.

EXERCISE **1.2**

My Beliefs about Human Behavior

1. I believe that people are basically:
   a. good
   b. bad
   c. neutral

2. Human functioning can be broken down into behavior, cognitions (thoughts), and emotions. Rank these in terms of their importance. Then write down why you ranked each as you did. Discuss your ratings with a group of classmates.
   Rank (1) _____ (2) _____ (3) _____
   Why did you rank thoughts, feelings, and behaviors as you did?

   _____
   _____

3. Abnormal behavior is caused by

   _____
   _____

4. The primary factors that foster normal behavior are

   _____
   _____

5. I believe that people are motivated by

   _____
   _____

6. What role do inherited characteristics play in the development of behavior?

7. What role do environmental factors, such as family life, play in the development of behavior?

   _____
   _____

8. Are people from all cultures motivated by the same things?
   a. Yes
   b. No

9. The factors that cause people to change are

   _____
   _____

10. To be effective in helping people change the following factors must be considered:

   _____
   _____

Fieldwork

Helper-trainees cannot acquire helping skills solely in a classroom setting just as medical students cannot learn surgery techniques solely from lectures and demonstrations. Ultimately hands-on experiences with clients are required if the knowledge and skills acquisition processes started in the classroom are to be completed. Though the nature and duration of the fieldwork experience varies with the profession, all who educate helpers view fieldwork as being of paramount importance.

A field placement must meet three essential criteria. First, the field assignment must approximate the occupational environment in which you expect to work after completion of your training programs. The fieldwork assignment should require you to assist the same type of clients that you will serve later. Second, the fieldwork assignment must be staffed with good role models. Although much is learned in the classroom, the observation of real helpers performing their jobs is an invaluable source of knowledge and skill. Finally, competent supervisors must carefully supervise fieldwork assignments. From a trainee's point of view, supervision is an anxiety-producing process because it continuously monitors the trainee's work to protect both the student and the client. Supervision also requires face-to-face sessions in which the trainee's work is carefully critiqued. Finally, supervisors provide needed emotional support when the inevitable failures are experienced and the process of acquiring new skills does not meet the trainee's expectations. Trainees welcome the emotional support and appreciate the tutoring that occurs during supervision. Most trainees even welcome negative feedback if it is given in a constructive manner.

Supervision is an unavoidable aspect of training to become a helper. Therefore, trainees must prepare themselves to get the most from their time with their supervisors. Corey and Corey (1998) suggest that trainees must open themselves to learning, say "I need help" in the appropriate situations, interact with instead of react to their supervisors, and take the information they receive from supervisors and integrate it into their own style. To function in this manner, trainees need to assert themselves. They must have a high degree of awareness of what they believe about the nature of helping and human functioning. At this point, you may not have a high degree of understanding of the helping process or of human functioning. However, most trainees have a keen sense of their assertiveness and their willingness to ask for help. Complete the questions in Exercise 1.3 to get an estimate of your readiness for supervision.

If you feel that you are not ready for supervision, take appropriate steps to improve your readiness. You may look at your previous interactions with parents, teachers, employers, and coaches. How willing were you to admit your weaknesses and to ask for help? If your cultural background makes you uncomfortable with the idea of being assertive, you may need to work on other approaches to interacting with supervisors. For example, you could come to supervision with questions, thus setting the agenda for the learning process. By identifying the

---

Readiness for Supervision

Rate yourself on each of the following dimensions using a 1 to 10 scale. A 1 means that you have little confidence in your ability in this area, and a 10 means that you have complete confidence in your ability in the area.

Assertiveness   **Rating**

I am willing to state my opinions even when I know others disagree.   _____
I am not intimidated by instructors or professors.   _____
I am willing to disagree with authority figures when I feel I am right. _____
I am willing to admit that I need help and ask for it.   _____

---

questions you wish to have answered, you demonstrate that you are concerned about learning and aware of your strengths and weaknesses.

Resolving Personal Mental Health Issues

Helper-trainees who enter their training with unresolved mental health issues are almost immediately faced with a dilemma because they realize that their own problems may, and likely will, interfere with their ability to become highly competent helpers. Once this realization dawns, some trainees feel trapped because they fear that when their trainers discover their personal problems it will diminish the trainers' estimates of their potential to be helpers. In fact, they are correct if they allow their problems to go unattended. However, trainees who recognize their unresolved mental health issues and who take action to resolve them typically become highly valued trainees because of their courage. Only those trainees who ignore or attempt to hide their mental health problems become disabled by them. Helper-trainees who have mental health issues should seek help with those problems at the earliest possible time.

Client Needs

Almost all occupational projections, such as those contained in the latest edition of the *Occupational Outlook Handbook,* predict an increased need for helpers at all levels. When the factors that put people at risk of developing mental health problems are examined along with the incidence of mental health problems these predictions are easily understood. For example, Schmolling, Youkeles, and Burger (1997) report that at the time of their study 30% of adults and 17% of children had a mental health problem in need of treatment. They went on to estimate that, at any given time, 13% of adults suffer from an anxiety disorder such as a phobia, 6% are seriously depressed, 5% have a personality disorder, 1% are have schizophrenia, 1% suffer from Alzheimer's disease, and 10% abuse alcohol or drugs. Not all of these people receive treatment, but nationwide studies suggest that more than 16 million people receive treatment for mental health problems each year (Narrow, Regier, Rae, Manderscheid, & Locke, 1993; Regier, Narrow, Rae, Manderscheid, Locke, & Goodwin, 1993).

Schmolling and colleagues' estimate that 30% of adults suffer from some type of mental health problem stands in stark contrast to estimates from 30 years ago that suggested 10 to 20% of the adults in U.S. society suffered from a serious mental health problem. Likewise, their estimate that 17% of all children have serious mental health problems is a marked increase in estimates from three decades ago that 8 to 10% of children suffered from a mental health problem serious enough to warrant professional attention (Joint Commission on the Mental Health of Children, 1970). Part of these differences can be attributed to increased efforts on the part of helpers to identify individuals with mental health problems. It has also been well documented that some of the risk factors associated with the development of mental health problems—for example, abusive situations, unemployment, and poverty—remain high.

Over 28% of all children lived in single family homes at the time of the last census, as opposed to approximately 9% in 1960 (Bureau of the Census, 1991). Children reared in single family homes are more likely to live below the poverty line, lack appropriate role models, and experience less social support because their single parents fill both parental roles (Schmolling, et al., 1997). Children who live in abusive situations may develop aggressive behaviors, low self-esteem, and lowered ability to trust. Helping professionals are needed to help prevent children from developing mental health problems.

In 1998, approximately 5 to 6 million U.S. workers were unemployed, even though the unemployment rate stood at approximately 4.2%, the lowest level since 1958. Unemployed people experience higher levels of depression than do employed people and more instances of family violence. Efforts to return unemployed workers to the workforce can be instrumental in deterring the development of mental health problems.

The 35 to 38 million U.S. residents who live below the poverty level need various forms of assistance from professional helpers. Those facing immediate crisis may need help negotiating the social welfare system or applying for unemployment payments. Some may need help finding a first job. Ultimately, all people who live below the poverty level need help finding better jobs because their incomes are insufficient to provide an adequate standard of living (Schmolling, et al., 1997).

Public employment agencies and social welfare agencies hire thousands of helpers to protect children from abuse, aid the unemployed, and support families in poverty. Public schools also hire helpers such as social workers, psychologists, and counselors. One goal of these helpers is reduce the average school dropout rate, which can exceed 75% for some groups of students in some cities (Brown,

1998). They also institute programs to reduce the 3 million cases of child abuse reported each year, decrease substance abuse, and increase students' acceptance of people with disabilities and those from other cultures (Brown & Srebalus, 1996). Each year, millions of students with potentially debilitating problems receive school services. Students who have problems too serious for treatment in the school setting receive help from professionals outside the school.

Finally, helpers are needed to work with persons convicted in the criminal justice system. Some are incarcerated, some are placed on probation in lieu of incarceration, or and some are paroled after spending time in a correctional institution. Each year, there are more than 100,000 cases of rape, 3 million burglaries, 1 million cases of aggravated assault, and nearly 25,000 murders in the United States (FBI, 1997). The result is a large group of clients, including the criminals and their victims, who require assistance and supervision. Many of these crimes are related to drug and alcohol abuse. One estimate that suggests 100,000 people die each year because of one legal substance: alcohol (FBI, 1997). Treating abusers is a huge industry that requires ten of thousands of helpers.

It was stated at the outset of this section that the demand for skilled helpers is expected to remain high. If Schmolling and his colleagues' estimate that 30% of adults and 17% of children need the attention of professional helper is accurate, 40 to 50 million people need services from a professional helper at any given time. Although this is a staggering figure, it suggests that the predictions regarding the need for increased numbers of helpers are accurate.

Helping Strategies

Helpers must develop a diverse set of helping strategies if they are to deal successfully with the complex problems faced by their clients. Although this book primarily focuses on the skills and strategies needed to perform counseling and psychotherapy, other strategies used by professional helpers are identified and described in this section.

Counseling or Psychotherapy

One of the historic debates in the field of helping has been over the definitions of *counseling* and *psychotherapy,* with some people arguing that they are the same and others indicating that they are different processes. Some people distinguish between the two processes by focusing on the "depth" of change expected. They suggest that counseling is a process that deals with behavior change and psychotherapy is one that focuses on personality change. However, this distinction blurred as long ago as the 1960s, when many psychotherapists began to label themselves as behavioral therapists because they focused primarily on changing behavior. Other people distinguish between counseling and psychotherapy by looking at the clientele served, with psychotherapy being used to describe the helping process for clients with more severe mental health problems. This distinction has blurred as practitioners, realizing that the public holds a more positive view of counseling than of psychotherapy, have labeled their workplaces as counseling centers to escape the negative stereotype often associated with psychotherapy. Other factors have led to a blurring of the distinctions between counseling and psychotherapy, including the fact that many of the theory books are titled theories of counseling and psychotherapy.

Two factors influence what label practitioners choose: the practitioners' training and the settings in which the services are offered. Psychiatrists, clinical social workers, and marriage and family therapists label their services as *therapy* or *psychotherapy* and retain this label regardless of the setting in which they practice. Counseling psychologists, school counselors, mental health counselors, and many others who work in public agencies label what they do as *counseling*. Interestingly, when these groups switch from offering services in public agencies to private agencies they often switch the title to the more prestigious label of *psychotherapy*.

In the final analysis, we believe that counseling and psychotherapy are nearly identical processes. Counseling and psychotherapy are helping services offered by trained helpers that focus on the improvement of the clients' mental health. One or two helpers may conduct the processes, which in turn may involve one or more clients depending on whether the services offered are group counseling or psychotherapy or individual counseling or psychotherapy. The amounts of time required for counseling and psychotherapy vary from single sessions to several years depending on the clients and the helpers providing the services. However, increasingly counseling and psychotherapy are relatively short-term processes. Clients who engage in counseling and psychotherapy experience some or all of the following benefits: improved decision-making, increased self-understanding, improved self-acceptance, altered behavior patterns, reduced debilitation from mental health problems, and improved ability to cope with the people in their lives.

Case Management

Case management is the process of coordinating the delivery of medical, legal, and social community resources so that clients' needs are met (Poindexter, Valentine, & Conway, 1999). Poindexter and her associates suggest that the first step in the case management process is to identify clients, either using the staff of human services agencies or volunteers who go into the community. Once persons eligible for services are identified, the next phase of case management involves conducting a comprehensive needs assessment. Clients who seek assistance often have many unmet needs. The elderly may have chronic medical problems, insufficient income, and few social supports. They may also suffer from dementia that causes difficulties with memory and problem solving. Children in abusive homes may require ongoing supervision to ensure that the abuse does not recur, that adequate food and clothing is available, and that health, dental, and mental health care is provided. On the basis of the needs assessment, goals are established and the helper begins locating community resources that can meet the identified needs. The helper then coordinates the delivery of services and, if necessary, acts as an advocate for the client. Once service delivery begins, the case manager monitors the process to make certain that the services are delivered in an appropriate fashion (Poindexter et al., 1999). In both the examples of the elderly clients and the abused children, case management is likely to be a long-term process. However, in some instances case management is a relatively short-term process. The abused spouse may need immediate placement in a shelter, short-term support to meet needs for food, clothing, and shelter, and placement in a job training program, all of which can be accomplished in a matter of a few weeks.

Advocacy

In many instances, clients do not possess the knowledge or skills needed to deal with educational, governmental, or social service agencies. Newly arrived immigrants face the additional challenge of potential language limitations or cultural differences. *Advocacy* is an empowerment process that acts on behalf of socially disenfranchised clients such as homeless people, the elderly, children, the mentally disabled, chronically ill people, and economically disadvantaged people. It helps them gain those things that are rightfully theirs, including adequate shelter, health care, and clothing. It may also involve promoting organizational and community change (Brown, 1988; Poindexter, Valentine, & Conway, 1999).

Advocates must have a well-developed sense of values. At the core of these values is the basic belief that all people have worth and deserve respect. It is this value that sustains advocates, along with their ability to assert themselves, when they encounter inevitable resistance. Case Illustration 1.1 demonstrates the need for assertiveness and perseverance. According to Poindexter and her associates (1999), advocacy seems warranted if: 1. access to services is impaired, 2. services being provided are inappropriate, and 3. client services are inadequate.

CASE ILLUSTRATION **1.1**

Successful Advocacy

One advocate was attempting to secure vocational rehabilitation services for a client with multiple sclerosis. She was rebuffed time after time with excuses about lack of funding and personnel and with a superficial evaluation of the client that suggested some learning limitations. The advocate paid for an independent evaluation of the client's potential and presented the findings to the agency staff. The results of the evaluation were markedly different than those of the agency's. After weeks of effort, the agency revised their estimate of the client's potential and partially funded an educational program in computer technology. The client finished near the top of her class.

In the 1960s, for example, a group of special educators, rehabilitation counselors, and parents of children with disabilities decided that the services available to persons with disabilities were substandard. They found that the services being provided in schools, organizations, and the community were inappropriate, inadequate, and denied people with disabilities access to many of the things enjoyed by nondisabled people. Their advocacy resulted in the passage of laws, such as Public Law 94-142 and the Americans with Disabilities Act of 1990, that guarantee physically, mentally, and emotionally challenged people receive adequate services. These laws mandate that persons with disabilities receive the least restrictive educational services and improved quality of educational services. They require structural changes to public facilities to allow persons with disabilities greater access, and they mandate increased opportunities for persons with disabilities in the workplace. In the late 1990s, advocacy efforts are aimed at requiring health insurers to cover people with mental health expenses in a similar manner as they do people with physical health expenses. Whether advocacy takes place on the large-scale just described or on a smaller scale, such as in Case Illustration 1.1, it is a vitally important process in helping those who need it.

Consultation

Counseling and psychotherapy are direct services to people who have or may develop mental health problems. Consultation, like advocacy, is an indirect service provided by mental health practitioners aimed at improving the ability of care givers such as parents, teachers, and nurses to deal more effectively with people who have or may develop mental health problems. A social worker who assists a parent to develop strategies to deal more effectively with his or her autistic child is offering consultation services. So is the school psychologist who helps teachers develop effective classroom discipline approaches. The consultation process is shown in Figure 1.1. Finally, consultation services may also be offered to organizations with the managers and employees being the consultees (the recipient of consultation). Organizational consultation is engaged in to improve the organizational climate in a manner that will improve the mental health of individual, as well as improve the organization's overall functioning.

Prevention Services

Although the history of the mental health movement strongly suggests that interventions are provided after mental health problems develop are more common, helpers nonetheless are engaged in many types of preventive services. The best-known prevention efforts involve programs to prevent drug and alcohol use, AIDS and other sexually transmitted diseases, and child abuse. Most communities have one or more systematic programs of this type in operation. Other prevention programs include those designed to prevent problem pregnancies, high school dropouts, family violence, rape (including date rape), and juvenile and adult crime. Programs designed to prevent specific mental illnesses such as depression

Consultant (Helper)

Consultee (Helper or Agency)
(Improved Ability to Deliver Services)

Client with Mental Health Problem
(Improved Mental Health)

FIGURE 1.1   The Indirect Nature of the Consultation Process

and eating disorders such as anorexia nervosa and bulimia are also preventive in nature. Stress reduction programs for employees, career development programs for the unemployed and underemployed, and recreation programs for youth are also primary prevention programs.

Community Programs

There are two types of community interventions: community action programs and outreach programs. Community action programs are designed to mobilize the entire community or a specific subset of it (for example, parents) to deal with a mental health problem such as drug or alcohol abuse. LaFromboise and Young (1996) report that a community action program aimed at reducing alcoholism that was characterized by strong community leadership, a focus on spiritual needs and concern for others, and a dedication to sobriety by core members of the group resulted in a 97% sobriety rate. The elements of this program—strong leadership, focused goals, and dedication by core community members—appear to be the essential ingredients in community actions programs. How can this type of leadership and commitment be developed? Helpers who expect to be successful in designing and delivering community action programs must understand the overall needs of the community, have credibility in the community, have good networking skills, be able to link people together in cohesive units, understand the power structure of the community, be able to identify and mobilize community stakeholders so that they can exert power, and help stakeholders design and implement programs (Corey & Corey, 1998). In addition to the success reported by LaFromboise and Young (1996), community action programs have been successful in reducing violent crime, teen pregnancies, the incidence of AIDS, and abuse in families.

In community outreach programs, human resource agencies take programs into the community to improve access to services. Outreach programs may involve primary prevention educational programs such as those described in the Prevention Services section. They may also involve big brother and sister programs for youngsters who need role models, mentoring programs for at-risk students, and diet and health care programs for pregnant teenagers. Outreach programs could also mobilize business and industry leaders to take their expertise into the schools as a means of orienting students to the world of work and organizing the resources of the educational institutions in the community to expose talented but unmotivated students to educational opportunities. Storefront counseling centers that focus on substance abusers and needle exchange programs designed to reduce the incidence of AIDS are also examples of community outreach programs.

Crisis Intervention

A crisis is an event in the life of an individual, family, or community that, unless managed properly, has the potential to damage the mental health of the people involved. Examples of crises for individuals, families, and communities are shown in Table 1.2.

In the crisis intervention literature, two phases of crisis intervention are routinely identified: prevention and postvention. *Prevention* involves all those efforts employed by helpers to keep traumatic events from occurring. A tornado drill is a prevention effort. *Postvention* involves efforts after a traumatic event has occurred to minimize the negative consequences of the event. A trauma team that helps tornado victims is a postvention effort. As Poindexter and her associates (1999) point out, one goal of postvention is that clients will emerge stronger and healthier. This discussion focuses on the two phases of postvention, the phase that occurs immediately after the traumatic event and the follow-up phase during which the effectiveness of the action taken is monitored. The purpose of both phases of postvention is to prevent the traumatic event from having lasting, negative effects on the mental health on the people who were traumatized.

One way to illustrate the postvention process is to consider a hypothetical process that might have occurred after one of the high-profile shootings that took place in public schools in Mississippi, Kentucky, and Pennsylvania during 1997 and 1998. In a small Kentucky community, two adolescent boys first telephoned a middle school that a bomb had been placed in the school. Then, using hunting rifles, they opened fire on the students and teachers as they congregated outside the school in response to the bomb threat. Two students and one teacher were killed and several others were injured. The primary target of this postvention would be the families and close friends of the people who were killed or injured as well as the witnesses to the event. Students, teachers, and community members would represent a secondary target group. Crisis intervention for the primary groups would include the following:

1. Identify families, close friends, and people who witnessed the shootings.
2. Contact primary group members and invite them to come for assistance. Describe what happened factually.

TABLE 1.2   Types of Crises

Individuals	Family	Community
Sexual assault	Divorce/separation	Natural disaster (for example, hurricane)
Physical assault	Loss of income	Major employer closes
Accident	Murder of or by a family member	War
Death of a loved one		Terrorism
Long-term illness	Abuse of children or other family member	
Suicidal ideation		
Homicidal ideation	Suicide of a family member	
Commission of a crime	Death of a family member	
Being discriminated against		
Loss of a job		
Homelessness		
Diagnosed with terminal illness		
Witness to violent crime		

3. Allow those who come for help to express their feelings in a supportive atmosphere.
4. Identify coping strategies (such as teaching grounding techniques to those experiencing flashbacks to the traumatic event).
5. Treat survivor guilt.
6. Refer individuals who are severely traumatized by the event to mental health practitioners.
7. Follow up and continue to assess the impact of the trauma.

Crisis intervention for secondary groups would include the following:

1. Invite all outside the primary group to come for help.
2. Allow those who come to discuss their feelings in a supportive atmosphere.
3. Make referrals to mental health centers as necessary.

Follow-up involves continued monitoring to ascertain that the individuals involved are not developing posttraumatic stress disorder or experiencing intense survivor guilt. In cases of suicide it also involves making certain that the survivors are not idealizing or glorifying the actions of the person who killed him- or herself. For example, if the suicide is a student, schools are advised to tell students only the facts about the case and to avoid school newspaper articles or assemblies focusing on the deceased student. The reason for this is to avoid "copycat" suicides, which seem to be linked to highly publicized suicides.

Career Paths of Helpers

Later in the book attention will be focused on advancing in one's chosen profession. However, to state the obvious, before you can advance in a helping profession, you must first choose one. Making this choice requires a great deal of careful consideration of the many options available.

You must consider several factors when choosing a helping career, a partial list of which you can find in Table 1.3. The first factor is the amount of education you wish to pursue. Positions as aides typically require one to two years of education in a community college. To be a human services worker, completion of a bachelors degree in psychology, sociology, or social work is normally required. Most counseling positions require a masters degree with a minimum of 48 semester hours of coursework and fieldwork, while social work positions require either a bachelors or a masters of social work (MSW) degree depending on the level of responsibility required. A two-year masters program is required for marriage and family therapists. Psychology positions that allow individuals to function without supervision usually require a doctorate though school psychologists typically complete a two- to three-year masters degree in school psychology. Doctoral programs in psychology require a minimum of five years, and some people take much longer to complete these programs.

A second factor to consider when choosing a career in the helping professions is the clientele with whom you wish to work. What client characteristics most interest you? Do you wish to target an age group, such as the elderly? If so,

TABLE 1.3   Helping Professionals

Art therapist	Occupational therapist
Career counselor	Probation or parole officer
Clinical psychologist	Psychiatric aide
Counseling psychologist	Psychiatric nurse
Credit counselor	Recreation therapist
Dance therapist	Rehabilitation counselor
Employment counselor	School counselor
Gerontological counselor	School psychologist
Human services worker	Social service aide
Mental health counselor	Social worker
Music therapist	Substance abuse counselor

EXERCISE **1.4**

Choosing a Helping Career

1. What level of education do you wish to complete?

   a. No more than two years of post-secondary training.

   Human resources aid

   b. No more than a bachelors degree

   Human resource worker; some social work positions; probation and parole officers

   c. Masters degree

   All counseling and social work positions; school psychology; marriage and family therapist

   d. Postmaster's specialization

   Art and music therapy

   e. Doctorate in psychology

   Clinical and counseling psychology

2. What is the age range of the client group you wish to serve?

   a. Children

   Masters degree in elementary school counseling or social work; doctorate in child clinical

   b. Elderly

   Masters degree in gerontological counseling or social work; doctorate in clinical with specialty in gerontology

   c. Adults

   Masters degree in mental health counseling or social work; doctorate in counseling or clinical psychology

3. What, if any, special modality do you wish to use in helping?

   a. None

   See above

   b. Music, art, or recreation

   Masters degree in counseling, social work with specialized training; doctorate in counseling or clinical psychology with specialized training

4. Are there clients with specialized problems that you wish to help?

   a. No

   See other sections

   b. Substance abusers

   Masters degree in substance abuse counseling or social work; specialized training along with doctorate in counseling or clinical psychology (some states license counselors with a bachelors degree)

   c. People with disabilities

   Masters degree in rehabilitation counseling/psychology; school psychology

   d. People with severe mental health problems

   Doctorate in clinical psychology; masters degree in psychiatric nursing; some specialized masters programs in social work

training programs that focus on children, adolescents, adults, and the elderly are available.

At least two other factors deserve attention when choosing a career in the helping professions. Do you wish to work with persons with severe mental health problems? If yes, consider clinical psychology or social work. If you wish to work with clients who have physical or mentally disabilities, you may wish to consider rehabilitation counseling programs. There are specialized masters programs if you wish to work with probationers and parolees as a part of the corrections system. You may wish to apply music, art, and recreation in your work and thus to seek a specialized training program in these types of therapies. Or you may wish to work in specialized areas such as employment counseling, marriage and family therapy, and career counseling. Begin the process of choosing your career track by completing Exercise 1.4.

Using This Book

This book helps you with many of the issues raised in its introductory Chapter 1. Chapter 2 helps you identify your potential as a helper, including recognizing your personal strengths and weaknesses. Chapters 3, 4, and 5 explain how to become an intentional helper, that is, one who understands the special characteristics of clients and selects appropriate helping strategies for them. Chapter 6 discusses service delivery systems, which are instrumental to providing case management services. Chapters 7–10 extend the discussions begun in Chapter 1. They focus on individual, family, group, and community interventions. The final chapters of the book concern professional issues. Chapter 11 examines the increasing use of Internet helping. Chapter 12 presents the ethical principles that govern the behavior and decision-making of helpers, and Chapter 13 speaks to the issue of gaining employment and advancing in your profession. Chapter 14 focuses on a topic that is often overlooked by people who care for others, maintaining their physical and emotional health. The final chapter, Chapter 15, discusses issues that new helping professionals face as they begin their careers.

Throughout the book there are numerous exercise and quizzes. Completing these exercises will raise your awareness and increase your learning.

Summary

Becoming a skilled helper is both exciting and stressful. Students must acquire a complex set of helping skills, apply these skills to clients in their field assignments, and deal with the inevitable self-doubt that arises while training to be a helper. Perhaps the best way to overcome self-doubt is to become a focused, dedicated student who invests him- or herself in the educational process. Helpers in training must also have a sense of the vast array of problems confronting them as well as the strategies that can use to deal with them. Counseling and psychotherapy are but two helping strategies; others include consultation, advocacy, and crisis intervention. Finally helper-trainees must choose their career path from an array of helping professions. Some of the criteria that may be used in electing a helping specialty should be training required, age of the clientele served, special characteristics of the clientele served, and whether there is a desire to apply a special medium in the therapeutic process.

CHAPTER 1 EXIT QUIZ

Answer each of these questions with a T if the statement is true and an F if the statement is false.

_____ 1. Intentionality and planning are synonymous ideas when defining helping.

_____ 2. Informal helping is of little value because it is impossible to determine its effect.

_____ 3. Primary prevention activities are those activities that helpers engage in to prevent mental health problems from developing in normal people.

_____ 4. Activities that are designed to keep mental health problems from becoming life threatening are called secondary prevention activities.

_____ 5. Counseling and psychotherapy sometimes make people worse.

_____ 6. The ideal helper projects warmth, is willing to take well-reasoned risks, is naturally curious, and is always in control.

_____ 7. People tend to readily accept information that confirms what they already believe.

_____ 8. Outstanding field placements offer trainees the opportunity to practice the skills they will need in their future jobs, are staffed by competent practitioners, and provide ongoing supervision.

_____ 9. Occupational projections forecast a decrease in the demand for helping professionals.

_____10. Estimates are that 30% of all people need mental health services at any given time.

_____11. Research suggests that at least 16 million people engage in psychotherapy each year.

_____12. Counseling and psychotherapy are very different processes because psychotherapy requires more time than counseling and deals with underlying causes rather than behavior.

_____13. Case management is usually a long-term process.

_____14. Although not addressed directly in the chapter, case managers need advocacy skills.

_____15. Advocacy should occur when clients are receiving inappropriate services or are denied access to services.

_____16. Consultation is called an indirect approach to helping.

_____17. Setting up a storefront counseling center in a neighborhood where drug abuse is common is a community action program.

_____18. Crisis intervention can be divided into three phases: prevention, postvention, and follow-up.

_____19. The targets of crisis intervention efforts should be divided into the group who were the victims or who observed the traumatic event and those who were emotionally involved but were not victims or witnesses.

_____20. In the final analysis, the major factor to consider when selecting a helping profession is the amount of training required.

Answers:

(1. F; 2. F; 3. T; 4. F; 5. T; 6. T; 7. T; 8. T; 9. F; 10. F; 11. T; 12. F; 13. F; 14. T; 15. T; 16. T; 17. F; 18. T; 19. T; 20. F.)

SUGGESTED LEARNING ACTIVITIES

1. Divide the class into eight teams. Have each team interview one of the following helpers.
   - Clinical psychologist
   - Counseling psychologist
   - Marriage and family therapist
   - Probation or parole officer
   - Psychiatric nurse
   - Rehabilitation counselor
   - School counselor
   - Social worker

   Include the following interview questions.
   - What types of services were you trained to offerer?
   - What types of helping services do you offer at this time?
   - What client groups do you serve?
   - Do you use any special mediums such as art, music, or recreation in your work?
   - What were the strengths of your training? Weaknesses?
   - What advice would you give to a person who is preparing to enter the helping professions?

2. Form the class into small groups. Have each person write one of their personal doubts about becoming a helper on an index card. Shuffle the cards and then distribute them to people in the group. Have each person read aloud the doubt

written on the card they receive and have people make suggestions about how to deal with it.

REFERENCES

Brown, D. (1998). *Manual: Hanging in or dropping out: What you should know before you leave school* (2nd ed.). Lincolnwood, IL: NTC Publishing Group.

Brown, D. (1988). Empowerment through advocacy. In D. J. Kurpius & D. Brown (Eds.), *Handbook of consultation: An intervention for outreach and advocacy* (pp. 5–17). Alexandria, VA: Association of Counselor Educators and Supervisors.

Brown, D., & Srebalus, D. J. (1996). *Introduction to the counseling profession* (2nd ed.). Boston: Allyn and Bacon.

U.S. Bureau of the Census (1991). *Statistical abstracts of the United States.* Washington, DC: Government Printing Office.

Corey, M. S., & Corey, G. (1998). *Becoming a helper* (3rd ed.). Pacific Grove, CA: Brooks/Cole.

FBI (1997). *Crimes in the United States.* Washington, DC: U.S. Department of Justice.

Ivey, A. E. (1994). *Intentional interviewing and counseling: Facilitating client development in a multicultural society.* Pacific Grove, CA: Brooks/Cole.

Joint Commission on the Mental Health of Children (1970). *Crisis in child mental health: Challenge for the 1970's.* Washington, DC: Author.

LaFromboise, T. D., & Young, K. E. (1996). American Indians and Alaska Native mental health. In P. B. Pedersen & D. C. Locke (Eds.), *Cultural and diversity issues in counseling* (pp. 7–11). Greensboro, NC: ERIC-CASS.

Lieberman, M. A., Yalom, I., & Miles, S. M. (1973). *Encounter groups: First facts.* New York: Basic Books.

Narrow, W. E., Regier, D. A., Rae, D. S., Manderscheid, R. W., & Locke, B. Z. (1993). Use of services by person with mental and addictive disorders: Findings from the NIMH epidemiological catchment program. *Archives of General Psychiatry, 50,* 95–107.

Poindexter, C. C., Valentine, D., & Conway, P. (1999). *Essential skills for human services.* Pacific Grove, CA: Brooks/Cole.

Regier, D. A., Narrow, W. E., Rae, D. S., Manderscheid, R. W., Locke, B. Z., & Goodwin, F. K. (1993). The defacto U.S. mental and addictive services system: Epidemiological catchment area prospective 1-year prevalence rates of disorder in services. *Archives of General Psychiatry, 50,* 85–94.

Schmolling, P., Jr., Youkeles, M., & Burger, W. R. (1997). *Human services in contemporary America.* Pacific Grove, CA: Brooks/Cole.

Truax, C. B., & Carkhuff, R. R. (1967). *Toward effective counseling and psychotherapy training and practice.* Chicago: Aldine.

2 Characteristics of Skilled Helpers

WHAT YOU WILL LEARN

1. The attitudes, personal philosophies, and traits of skilled helpers
2. Whether you have the attitudes and traits of an skilled helper

In Chapter 1 you learned that there are many types of helpers and a variety of ways that help can be provided. Specifically, distinctions were made between informal and formal, intentional helping processes. Formal, intentional helping is engaged in by professional helpers for the purposes of preventing or reducing the impact of mental health problems. This chapter discusses the traits, attitudes, personal philosophies, and skills of the professional helper. As you read, match your characteristics to those of effective helpers and complete the exercises designed to facilitate these comparisons.

Begin your exploration of skilled helpers' characteristics by responding to the statements in Exercise 2.1. As you respond to these statements, try not to think about what others think. If exercises of this type are to be useful, you must be totally honest when you answer the questions.

Perhaps one of the most important characteristics of effective helpers is that they have a positive view of human nature and can bring optimism about the future to the helping process. Being optimistic is easy for most helpers when they deal with clients who are articulate, clean, young, and middle class. However, clients come from all walks of life, from every social strata, and from all ethnic, racial, and religious groups. Clients may not always be clean, may not be very intelligent, and may have some disgusting personal habits. Other clients have committed reprehensible acts against children and adults. It is these types of clients who test the typical helper's positive view of people and their optimistic view of the future. However, if the helping process is to be successful, it is essential that helpers maintain a positive view of their clients' potential and an optimistic view of the future. Admittedly, it is difficult to maintain a positive, optimistic perspective on the future when clients have terminal diseases that will end their lives, mental illnesses that will incapacitate them, or criminal records that will keep them in correctional facilities for the rest of their lives. If pessimistic and negative themselves, helpers cannot imbue clients with hope. Hope is one ingre-

EXERCISE **2.1**

Judging Your Reactions to Different Clients

You are assigned to assist the following people. Check your reaction to each person.

Situation	Positive	Negative	Neutral

1. An illegal immigrant who keeps muttering in her first language, "I hate America"
2. A gay male who deliberately infects three men by having unprotected sex with them
3. A child molester who works as an elementary school bus driver.
4. An 60-year-old male who is diagnosed with early onset Alzheimer's disease
5. A middle-aged male who is trying to get disability payments even though he is in good health
6. A welfare cheater who, after she is caught, is ordered to go to work
7. A drug addict who goes back to drugs after three tries at detoxification and rehabilitation
8. A deserter from the military
9. A highly dependent person who wants you to make all of his decisions for him
10. A lesbian who, after coming out, leaves her husband of 22 years and their three children
11. A 16-year-old who, although she is in the fifth month of her pregnancy, wants an abortion
12. A deadbeat dad who, although he earns a substantial income, refuses to pay his child support, which leaves his wife and children destitute
13. A drug dealer who specializes in getting middle schoolers hooked on crack cocaine
14. A parent who sexually abuses both of her sons
15. A career criminal convicted of murder.
16. A six-year-old who is terminally ill
17. A person of a different race (from you) who you believe does not like you because of your race

dient in the helping process that often must be provided by the helper. Clients often come for help after exhausting their supply of this precious commodity.

Not all of the 17 clients in Exercise 2.1 have committed reprehensible acts or have limited futures. Some are simply in unique situations because of their sexual orientations, their nationalities, or their life experiences. These people are a part of the patchwork quilt of an increasingly diverse demographic landscape. Currently, racial minorities make up about 25% of our population. This percentage of racial minorities is expected to grow until white people of European American descent will be in the minority by the second quarter of this century. But the changing demographics of this country are not restricted to changes in the racial makeup of the population. Our population is aging as the much discussed "baby boomers" pass from middle age, to young-old age (60 to 65), and beyond. Other changes, notably people's willingness to openly own their sexuality, make it increasingly likely that some clients will have a sexual orientation different from that of the helper. Effective helpers must come to grips with their views of people who differ from them in their politics, religious beliefs, lifestyles, and worldviews. If stereotypical views of racial minorities, homosexuals, people with disabilities, older people, and others cannot be set aside, the likelihood that many individuals who come for help can be dealt with effectively is diminished. Effective helpers must learn to celebrate the diversity that exists in our society and revel in the richness that diversity brings to our society. All people have personal power. It is the helper's role to free the potential that resides in clients that come for assistance. Without optimism and a belief in the potential of human beings, helpers may fail to tap the inner resources that clients bring to the helping process.

Characteristics of Skilled Helpers

As noted in Chapter 1, most students who enter the helping professions have doubts about their ability to be effective helpers. One way to explore the validity of these doubts is to compare one's characteristics to those of ideal helpers. Answering the questions in Exercise 2.2 can begin this process.

In 1951, Carl Rogers published his landmark work, *Client-Centered Therapy,* in which he presented an extensive discussion of effective helpers. Five years later, Abraham Maslow (1956) published his research identifying what he termed *self-actualized persons.* Interestingly, many of the traits identified by Rogers were those of self-actualized persons. Maslow identified a number of individuals who seemed to be highly functioning human beings and collected data regarding their traits. The statements found in Exercise 2.2 are based largely on Maslow's findings and represent the characteristics of effective, self-actualizing individuals. Maslow's group of highly functioning people responded positively to most of the statements listed in Exercise 2.2. Subsequent research by people such as Truax and Carkhuff (1967) supported the idea that many of the traits identified by Rogers and Maslow were the characteristics of effective helpers. The paragraphs that follow discuss these traits in more detail.

EXERCISE **2.2**

Comparing Myself to the Ideal Helper

Identifying Your Personal Characteristics	Usually	Sometimes	Rarely

1. I have a "sixth sense" that allows me to spot "phonies."
2. I openly admit my weaknesses.
3. I react to situations spontaneously without worry about what others will think.
4. I have a sense of responsibility to others.
5. I believe that I am a worthwhile person.
6. I am frequently awestruck by human qualities such as tenacity, goodness, forgiveness, and courage.
7. I am compassionate. I feel what others feel.
8. Although people are important, I enjoy time alone with my thoughts and reflections.
9. Although I realize the need for interdependence, I function autonomously. If I had to, I feel that I could "go it alone."
10. I am able to establish deep interpersonal relationships.
11. I do not discriminate against others. I accept others who are from different cultures or have different lifestyles.
12. I am an ethical person.
13. I have a sense of humor that does not involve sarcasm, prejudice, or hostility.
14. I am creative in the sense that I look at problems and issues in new and different ways.
15. I have a great deal of energy.
16. I am a risk taker.
17. I have a high level of tolerance for ambiguity.
18. People who know me trust me.
19. Establishing intimate personal relationships is relatively easy for me.
20. I am self-aware. I understand my values and my prejudices.
21. Others come to me for help.
22. I communicate my thoughts and feelings clearly.

Well-Developed Racial and Cultural Identity

People of all races develop *racial identities.* Pack-Brown's (1999) research studies white race identity. It finds that some white people believe that all races are the same and that they share the same values and worldviews. They may be curious about the differences that exist among the races but are totally unaware of them. Some people never advance beyond this stage of naivete. Persons with a well-developed sense of white racial identity gradually realize that discrimination exists, which leaves them in a state of anxiety. They believe that they must choose between loyalty to their own race and a broader perspective. Their anxiety may lead to what Pack-Brown terms *reintegration.* In this stage, white people idealize their group, believe that white people are superior, and feel angry because they believe they have not discriminated against people of color. This stage in the development of a white racial identity is followed by stages in which white people try to develop a fuller understanding of the meaning of racism and then to rid themselves of it. The final stage in the development of a white racial identity is for people to develop a fuller understanding of what it means to be white, develop the motivation to let go of racism, and to avoid situations that require racism. Though Park-Brown's research focuses on white racial identity formation, the process is similar for all races.

The development of a *cultural identity* requires that an individual become familiar with the beliefs, traditions, history, values, and worldviews of his or her group. To test your cultural identity, complete Exercise 2.3.

E X E R C I S E   **2.3**

Your Cultural Identity

Respond to the statements by checking a yes or no. I can identify:

Item	Yes	No
1. My cultural heritage (for example, I'm Scotch-Irish or Japanese American)		
2. The unique characteristics of my cultural group including its values, beliefs, worldviews, customs, and traditions		
3. The manner in which my cultural beliefs influence the ways I think and act		
4. The manner in which my cultural beliefs influence my beliefs about people from other cultures		
5. The cultural beliefs, traditions, values, and worldviews of cultural groups other than my own		

If you have a highly developed cultural identity, the answers to all the questions in Exercise 2.3 will be yes. How does cultural identity develop? One's overall identity is the sense that we have of ourselves and involves a multitude of factors such as sexual orientation and cultural identity. All aspects of our identity development, including our ethnic, cultural, and sexual identity, develop as we interact with other people. Children begin their lives with no cultural identity, a situation that soon gives way to a perception that the immediate world into which they are born is "the way things are." Early interactions are typically with members of one's own culture, and these serve as the basis for later development. As children and adolescents come into contact with people from other cultures (for some this may not occur until adulthood or not at all), they realize that they are different. For members of minority groups, contacts with members of the majority culture may result in various forms of discrimination. As a result, they may retreat to interacting only with their own group, but this retreat can only be temporary in most instances. For all groups, the ultimate result of interactions is that a cultural identity is internalized. If the identity that is internalized allows people to feel good about themselves, they can move on to two additional stages: integration and transformation (Myers et. al, 1991). In these stages people redefine themselves in broader terms, and cultural stereotypes and barriers that were erected between the person and members of other cultural groups begin to be dismantled.

The result of the process of developing a racial and cultural identity should be the abandonment of racism as Pack-Brown (1999) suggested. Helpers must take one additional step. They must increase their knowledge of cultural groups other than their own. Knowledgeable helpers can contrast the characteristics of their cultural groups with those of other cultural groups. Many helpers have failed to clarify their own racial and cultural identity and gain the information they need to function in cross-cultural helping. As a result, they often fail to recognize the sources of their biases regarding people who come from other cultural groups. You can check your level of awareness by completing the exercise in Exercise 2.3.

Prejudices are negative attitudes unsupported by facts held by members of one race or cultural group about people who belong to a different race or cultural group. *Stereotypes* grow out of prejudices and are beliefs that people from a particular race or cultural group have the same negative characteristics. *Discrimination* occurs when one restricts the opportunities of another race or cultural group or acts to harm them directly because of prejudicial beliefs and stereotypes. Prejudicial attitudes, and the responses growing out of them, occur automatically until they are brought into awareness, examined logically, and changed. Prejudices and stereotypes develop as the result of *cultural conditioning* (Johnson, 1993). Each culture, including the dominant culture in the United States, Eurocentrism, has a set of beliefs and worldviews that are passed on from generation to generation. One result of cultural conditioning is that members of cultural groups are subtlety instilled with beliefs about the superiority of their culture. The result is *ethnocentrism*. Not surprisingly, members of cultural groups often believe that they are superior to people from other cultural backgrounds. For example, many European

Americans hold a future time view, a perspective that believes it is important to dominate time. As a consequence, European Americans wear watches and keep track of time using calendars so they can be on time. Some Native Americans do not share this perspective on time. Instead, they have a view of time that is anchored in natural events such as the changing of the seasons and the phases of the moon. Many adult Navaho Indians report that they do not remember seeing a clock or a calendar in their pueblos when they were growing up. Because some Native Americans hold a different view of time than the one held in the dominant culture, some European Americans judge them as inferior.

Exercise 2.2 asked you to indicate whether you are self-aware, particularly of your biases and prejudices (statement 20). Statement 11 deals with discriminatory behavior. The typical response to these items is, "Of course I'm not prejudiced, and I don't discriminate." However, we live in a society in which discrimination is common place, and many people actively or tacitly condone discrimination. A part of developing a cultural identity, for white people at least, is to acknowledge that European Americans have systematically discriminated against, sometimes in the cruelest ways, Native Americans, African Americans, Asian Americans, and Hispanics Americans, and other minority groups and subgroups. However, much of the racism that is manifested by people in today's society does not come in the form of hate crimes or marches by Ku Klux Klan members. Some common displays of prejudicial attitudes include:

1. *Blaming the victim.* When people assign responsibility to the victimized group they are blaming the victim. For example, some people look at the higher unemployment rate among minorities and conclude that they are unmotivated and lazy, when in fact minorities have been systematically discriminated against in the workplace.
2. *False generalizations.* When individuals read that one person has committed a crime and conclude that all members of the same ethnic group are potential criminals, they are committing the error of false generalizations.
3. *False consensus beliefs.* When individuals assume that everyone in their cultural group agrees with their prejudicial attitudes and stereotypes, they are wrongly assuming that agreement exists within their group. They may make statements about their group's beliefs prefaced with "we" instead of "I."
4. *False, self-serving beliefs.* When individuals decide that they have succeeded and members of other groups have failed because of the superiority of their group and do not consider the impact of discrimination, they are committing this error.

During the last decade much has been made of the failure of white or European American helpers in their efforts to help racial and ethnic minorities (e.g., Sue & Sue, 1990). Some helpers (e.g., D'Andrea & Daniels, 1997) believe that all European Americans, helpers included, have racist tendencies that may manifest themselves in the helping process, and these attitudes have resulted in inappropriate and unsuccessful cross-cultural helping. Although much of the attention of the so-called multiculturalists (e.g., Sue & Sue, 1990) has focused on the prejudices of white helpers, a topic that will be taken up in more detail in Chapter 3, non-white helpers also need to do carefully examine their attitudes toward whites as well as other ethnic and racial minorities. "Hidden" prejudices may manifest themselves in verbalizations and actions that are likely to be interpreted as lack of respect by clients. If this occurs the helping process is unlikely to be successful. It is a well documented fact that minority clients of white counselors discontinue helping prematurely more often than do their white counterparts, a fact that is often attributed to insensitivity by well meaning but culturally unskilled helpers (Sue & Sue, 1990). However, little attention has been paid to the interactions between minority helpers and white clients or cross-cultural helping involving clients and helpers from different minority groups.

At some point in their development, helpers must accept themselves as cultural beings. This does not necessarily mean that they see themselves as European American, African American, Asian Americans, Hispanic Americans, or American Indians. Tiger Woods, a famous golfer, defined his cultural identity in terms of his African American, Thai, Chinese, and Native American heritage. Helpers may develop a bicultural or multicultural identity. As helpers begin to understand their cultural values and worldview of their own culture, the foundation of their cultural identity is established. From this point of self-understanding and acceptance of their culture, helpers can begin to examine the values and worldviews of other cultures. If, simultaneously, there is an examination of the histories of other cultures and how they have interacted, a fuller understanding and appreciation for the beliefs, values, and worldviews of other cultures develops.

The development and evolution of our cultural identity is an ongoing process, particularly for helpers. Gladding, Pederson, & Stone (1997) have provided some guidelines for this process, which will be explored in detail in Chapter 3. However, the process involves a continuous effort to think about one's experiences in his or her own culture and how these impact their own values, attitudes, and behaviors. For example, white professional helpers must give serious consideration of what is termed *white privilege*. White privilege, among other things means never having been stared at because you are a different hue, economic advantages in many instances, and living in a culture where white people make the rules (Ivey & Ivey, 1997).

As noted above, identity development is not restricted to the development of racial identity. As individuals develop they also acquire views about their sexuality, the roles that males and females should take (sex-role orientation), perceptions regarding mentally and physically handicapped people, values that guide their behavior, and so forth. Depending upon the developmental processes that the individuals undergo, prejudicial attitudes can develop regarding women, gays, lesbians, bisexuals, and people who are mentally and physically disabled. It is these biases and stereotypes, as well as those that develop regarding people who are culturally different, that helpers must deal with as they gain a well-developed personal identity.

High Levels of Self-Awareness and Self-Acceptance

In addition to racial and cultural awareness, helpers need high levels of self-awareness and self-acceptance. Figure 2.1 shows a Johari window, a model of personal awareness developed by two graduate students who identified themselves only as Joe and Harry. This model of self-awareness suggests that there are four levels, or windows, of personal awareness. The first level contains those things that individuals know about themselves and that are known to others around them because they share them freely. For example, an individual and his friends, relatives, and acquaintances may know that he is politically conservative, hopes to make a lot of money, admires tall women, and dislikes broccoli and shellfish. Topics known to both the client and the helper are often disclosed in the early stages of helping.

The second window of awareness contains information that individuals do not know about themselves but that is known to others. For example, most people have mannerisms such as fidgeting with their hair or using words such as *so* to "punctuate" sentences when they speak that are out of their awareness. In additional, most people overestimate their physical attractiveness and have "blind spots" in the way that they respond to certain topics. One that is frequently heard is "I'm not prejudiced, but—," at which time the person proceeds to reveal prejudicial attitudes. The friends, relatives, or even acquaintances of these individuals are aware of their mannerisms, are likely to be much more objective about their physical appearance, and are likely to be aware of their prejudicial attitudes as well.

The third level of awareness is information that individuals know about themselves but that others do not know. Often this information is painful in that it is accompanied by emotions such as guilt, anger, or shame, which is why it is not shared with others. Having been sexually molested as a child is one type of information that individuals are reluctant to share.

The fourth level of awareness in the Johari window contains information about individuals that neither they nor the people around them know. An example of this level of awareness is the client who has a number of irrational fears,

FIGURE 2.1   The Johari Window

1 Information Known to Self and to Others	**2** Information Not Known to Self But Known to Others
3 Information Known to Self But Not to Others	**4** Information Not Known to Self or Others

including a fear of flying. During the helping process she remembers a person in a parachute floating to the ground, a previously repressed memory that she could not explain. Further investigation revealed that, as a child, she had witnessed a plane explode over her home and watched as some of the crew ejected from the aircraft and floated to the ground. Unless specific advanced-level helping strategies such as hypnosis are employed to generate information from this fourth window of awareness, it is unlikely to be disclosed.

Awareness of one's cultural and psychological characteristics is not sufficient. Helpers must also accept themselves as unconditionally as they will the people they hope to help. This includes being aware of and accepting one's sexual identity, whether heterosexual, homosexual, bisexual, or transsexual. Helpers whose sexual identity falls into a group not acceptable in much of mainstream society must come to terms with their sexuality and grow to love themselves as they are.

Self-awareness and acceptance extends to one's physical body. The idealized image of the female body in our society is young (less than 30), tall (five feet, seven inches or taller), thin (less than 125 pounds), with high cheek bones, clear skin, shiny long hair, and straight white teeth. The idealized body for males is also young, tall (over six feet) with broad shoulders, athletic and slender build (175 to 180 pounds), with clear skin, straight white teeth, and a full, thick head of hair. Few people fit these images, with the result being that many people develop negative attitudes toward their bodies. All of us have heard individuals apologize for something about themselves, whether it be their looks, their speech, their hair, or some other attribute. Helpers need to come to terms with their strengths and weaknesses and accept themselves fully.

Personal Values of Helpers

Values are beliefs that guide behavior. Helpers hold a unique set of core values include concern for others, belonging, responsibility, and creativity (Brown & Crace, 1997). People who have the value of concern for others gain satisfaction from activities that allow them to make a contribution to the welfare of other people. Individuals with a belonging value are happiest when they feel connected to others, while those with a responsibility value believe that it is important to be dependable and trustworthy. People with a creativity value gain pleasure when they are in situations that allow them to generate new ideas and ways of doing things. Spirituality is another value held by many helpers, particularly those helpers in religious roles. Helpers are much less likely to value financial prosperity than people in other occupations, although some helpers do have this as one of their values. Think about your values by completing Exercise 2.4.

Genuineness

In Exercise 2.2, statements 2 and 3 concern an essential trait of effective helpers: genuineness. Most of us are aware of ingenuineness that occurs in our day-to-day interactions. For example, most people are greeted daily with "How are you

---

EXERCISE **2.4**

Identifying My Personal Values

Read each of the following statements and place a check by the ones that accurately describe your beliefs.

Concern for Others

_____ 1. I gain satisfaction when I know that I have helped others
_____ 2. The prospect of helping others excites me
_____ 3. I spend time helping others

Belonging

_____ 4. I feel most satisfied when I feel others accept me.
_____ 5. I do not like conflict and try to avoid it.
_____ 6. I strive for harmony in all that I do.

Responsibility

_____ 7. Doing things the right way is important to me.
_____ 8. I enjoy assuming responsibility for other people.
_____ 9. I am a dependable person.

Creativity

_____10. I like to think up new ways of doing old tasks.
_____11. I sometimes get bored with repetitive tasks.
_____12. I am always looking for better ways to do things.

Spirituality

_____13. I have strong spiritual beliefs.
_____14. I know that I am part of something greater than myself.
_____15. Having a connection to a higher power is important in life.

If you checked at least two out of three statements as corresponding to your beliefs it is likely that you hold that value.

---

feeling today?" by people who care little about the response. Although ingenuineness of this type typically poses no problem in casual relationships, it can have a debilitating effect on intimate relationships with friends, coworkers, spouses, and significant others. Genuineness involves being spontaneous, avoiding personal defensiveness, being open to feedback, and avoiding "hiding" behind the helping role (Egan, 1994). Being genuine also involves honesty and forthrightness. To be genuine (or, as some people prefer, authentic), helpers must have deep levels of self-understanding and self-acceptance. Without this personal understanding and acceptance, interpersonal interaction in the helping process may create defensiveness, deter spontaneity, and lead helpers to become a caricature of a helping person. Take a moment to write down how you as a helper might respond to the situations in Exercise 2.5.

Although effective helpers are authentic—that is, they are in touch with their feelings and able to communicate them to clients—they also time their responses carefully. Clients often say unexpected things to helpers, things that hurt and anger them. A truly genuine person acting spontaneously might voice that hurt or anger. However, spontaneous, genuine responses sometimes are held in abeyance during the early stages of helping (Carkhuff, 1983; Egan, 1994) so as to facilitate and strengthen the developing relationship. The helping relationship begins as a fragile entity and, if nurtured, grows into a bond that can sustain the stresses of truly authentic reactions. Therefore, early in the helping relationship the effective helper may respond with empathy instead of true spontaneity while avoiding ingenuineness. Should the client ask directly, for example, "Did my statement anger you?," the helper would respond affirmatively if it had. To help explain the difference between an empathic response used early in the helping

---

E X E R C I S E **2.5**

Genuine Helping

African American eight-year-old child to white helper: "I hate you. My parents told me that you can never trust a white person."
Your response: _____

_____

Adolescent female to helper-trainee: "I know you don't care about me. You're seeing me because you have to see so many people to graduate."
Your response: _____

_____

Adolescent male student to juvenile probation officer: "You're just another type of cop. You act like you want to help me, but you're always checking to see if I have been to school or am breaking my curfew."
Your response: _____

_____

Adult male client to female therapist: "I'll bet you secretly want to be a man. Most women hate being women."
Your response: _____

_____

Elderly male to hospice worker: "Get the hell out of here and let me die in peace."
Your response: _____

_____

relationship and a truly genuine one used later, consider the following responses to the clients introduced in Exercise 2.4.

To Child

Early helping: "You really don't like me and can't trust me because I'm white."
Later: "It hurts my feelings that you feel that you cannot trust me."

To adolescent girl

Early helping: "You think that because I'm a student I don't care about you, and you are a bit angry about that."
Later: "Your view of me as uncaring bothers me because I do care. My role as a student is immaterial."

To male juvenile probationer

Early helping: "You think that I'm just the same as every other law enforcement officer, and a phony to boot."
Later: "I can see why you think I'm like other law enforcement officers because I have two roles: one is to check up on you and the other is to help you. It is the helping role that sets me apart."

To adult male client

Early helping: "You seem angry today and are questioning whether I really like being a woman."
Later: "For reasons that I'm unsure of, you are angry, but I can assure you that I very much enjoy being a woman."

To hospice patient

Early helping: "You're pretty upset with the world this morning."
Later: "Telling me to get the hell out hurts my feelings, but I will leave if you wish."

Empathy

Statement 1 in Exercise 2.2 asked you whether you have a "sixth sense about people," and statement 7 asked whether you feel what others feel. Effective helpers, like effective human beings, have the ability to accurately experience the internal frame of reference of others while maintaining their own objectivity. It is this latter aspect of empathy, the ability to maintain objectivity, that differentiates empathy from sympathy. Think for a moment about the internal world of the clients in Exercise 2.6. What do their words suggest that they're thinking and feeling?

EXERCISE 2.6

Empathy

Client to probation officer: "It's just not worth getting out of bed. I'm going nowhere in that dead-end job. I'd be better off back in prison."
Client's thoughts and feelings: _____

_____

Client to hospice worker: "It's not so much dying as is that I won't be able to see my grandchildren grow up."
Client's thoughts and feelings: _____

_____

Client to nurse: "I've been lying here in pain for an hour. Don't people care about the patients in this hospital?"
Client's thoughts and feelings: _____

_____

Client to rehabilitation counselor: "Sometimes I hate this chair and it spills over to other people. I can remember before the accident walking and doing the things others do."
Client's thoughts and feelings: _____

_____

Client to therapist: "That's it then. I'm gay. I've had a lot of trouble saying that, but it's out now."
Clients thoughts and feelings: _____

_____

In some instances, client's thoughts and feelings are fairly transparent, and thus easy to comprehend, as is the case in most of the clients in Exercise 2.6. The parolee is obviously frustrated and perhaps a bit depressed about his situation. The dying hospice resident feels sad, not because of her impending death, but because of the things she will miss. Both the hospital patient and the rehabilitation client are frustrated and angered by their situation. The gay client is relieved because the struggle to come to grips with his sexual identity is finally over. As will be discussed in more detail in Chapter 4, helpers need to be empathic enough to perceive very subtle aspects of clients' internal perspectives.

Respect for Others

Respect for others involves accepting people with different values, religious beliefs, cultural, racial, and ethnic heritages, sexual orientations, lifestyles, levels of intellectual functioning, and varying levels of physical functioning. In its most fundamental form, respect involves a reverence for human beings, not because of their characteristics, but because they are human beings. In Exercise 2.1 several types of individuals were listed, some of which might not seem worthy of respect. However, effective helpers possess contagious enthusiasm and optimism about the potential of all human beings (see statement 6 in Exercise 2.1) and the ability to communicate these attitudes to their clients (statement 22 in Exercise 2.1). Respect, however, should not be confused with acceptance or agreement with every value, attitude, or habit held by the client. For example, no professional helper can agree with or accept the abuse of other human beings.

Capacity for Intimacy

Statements 10, 16, 18, and 19 in Exercise 2.2 focus on your ability to establish intimate relationships. Intimacy involves the ability to comfortably share your innermost thoughts and feelings. Helping, in its most effective form, requires the establishment of nonsexual, intimate relationships with clients. One prerequisite to the establishment of an intimate relationship is trust, and it is often the case that people who come to helpers have a limited ability to trust. To become a trusted person requires that you have many of the traits already mentioned: empathy, genuineness, and respect for others. However, establishing intimate relationships requires more. It requires the ability to share yourself through self-disclosure and to commit your time and energy to the helping process. The capacity for intimacy also requires risk taking (statement 16 in Exercise 2.2) because some clients will resist or reject your overtures to help. Consider the following cases:

1. At 17, Jamarkus already has been in correctional institutions twice, although he has never committed a violent crime. He reveals that he was abandoned as a child and that the Department of Social Services found him living on the street when he was seven. Subsequently, he lived in a series of foster homes "where the people just wanted the money to take care of me." Jamarkus identifies this rule to live by: "Take care of yourself and trust no one."

2. Irene, who was physically and sexually abused as a child, confides to her therapist that she trusts no one except her husband. Later, she admits that she maintains secret checking and savings accounts because she continually fears that her husband will abandon her.

3. Latisha, a 20-year-old college student, is in a rape support group led by a mental health aide. One night a male "friend" drugged and sexually abused her. Her roommate came home unexpectedly, otherwise "You never know. I might have become pregnant or developed a sexually transmitted disease. I don't think I'll ever be able to trust a man again."

In each of the foregoing cases, trust is a major issue. Two of the clients, Jamarkus and Irene, also have very limited capacities for intimacy because their parents' abandoned and sexually abused them. In Latisha's case, her trust has been betrayed, and she needs to relearn the process of trusting. If helpers earn clients' trust and follow the development of trust with the establishment of intimate, caring relationships, the helping process is likely to succeed.

Inviting Interpersonal Style

Purkey and Schmidt (1996) call attention to an aspect of counseling that many helpers overlook. Helpers with an inviting interpersonal style are openly and intentionally caring, accepting, and active in and out of the formal helping relationships. Because actions often are more obvious than the attitudes behind them, actions clearly show an inviting interpersonal style. Here are some examples:

A social worker organizes a community action group to try to get action regarding substandard housing.

A juvenile probation officer organizes a midnight basketball league.

A school counselors organizes a peer helper program.

A psychiatric nurse organizes a support group for cancer patients.

A nursing home aide organizes an animal visitation program for people who are no longer mobile.

The invisible aspects of the inviting interpersonal style are the things that individuals do to promote the welfare of others that do not call attention to themselves. These include writing unsolicited letters of support, donating anonymously to a charity, providing support for a colleague who is being criticized, and encouraging clients at critical points. Helpers with inviting interpersonal styles have a sense of responsibility to others (statement 4 in Exercise 2.2), are continuously amazed and excited at the potential of the people around them (statement 6), are creative (statement 14), have a variety of strategies for helping others, are sought out because of their helping demeanor (statement 21), and manifest the other characteristics identified in this chapter.

Ability to Function Autonomously

Autonomy is defined in this context as *psychological self-sufficiency* and it refers partially to the helper's ability to stand apart from the group. There are times when helpers must take stands against their peers, subordinates, and the policies governing their workplaces if they are to adequately represent their clients. In fact, the ethical codes of many large groups of helpers (for example, psychologists and social workers) require helpers to put the concerns of clients ahead of institutional policies that are not in the best interest of clients. More important, psychological self-sufficiency refers to individuals' ability to enter into what are often ambiguous helping relationships for the sole purpose of facilitating the needs of others. The helper's role is to nurture the personal development of the client, not to satisfy his or her own needs. This is not to suggest that there is no personal satisfaction in helping others, because being an effective helper can be deeply rewarding. However, helpers who are not psychologically self-sufficient tend to talk too much about their own concerns, overcontrol the helping process to deal with ambiguity, and get overly involved in the goal-setting process, often manipulating the process to get the outcomes they deem appropriate. In the worst cases, helpers meet their own needs by establishing inappropriate friendships and even sexual relationships with clients. In these cases, helping becomes destructive to the client. Statements 8, 9, 16, and 17 in Exercise 2.2 are can help you determine your ability to function autonomously.

High Energy Level

Only one statement in Exercise 2.2, number 15, deals with the issue of personal energy level. Helping is a demanding, rigorous process that requires individuals to have great concentration and to expend high levels of mental energy. Although the ability to concentrate and expend mental energy is partially related to physical conditioning, it goes beyond that to include what can only be termed a "high energy level." The helping professions have no room for the so-called morning person who runs out of energy after the lunch hour or the person who is not really sharp until afternoon. Clients require full attention at all times of the day.

High Ethical Standards

Effective helpers must be ethical (statement 12 in Exercise 2.2). All groups of helpers have codes of ethics that they follow, but codes of ethics are based on certain moral principles that some individuals follow and others do not. It is likely that helpers who have little personal integrity and are dishonest in their dealings with people on a day-to-day basis will disregard their code of ethics. Unfortunately, clients and the professional groups to which the helpers belong suffer most when unethical people become helpers. Ethical helpers do not falsify insurance claims, yet there are numerous examples of professional helpers who have ignored their codes of ethics and the law in this manner. Ethical helpers do not manipulate clients into sexual relationships, and yet there are dozens of instances where this has happened. Ethical helpers do not abandon their clients when they cannot pay for services, but more and more people are denied assistance when they most need it because of their inability to pay. Effective helpers are ethical helpers who follow their personal as well as their professional codes of ethics.

Characteristics That Hinder Skilled Helpers

Egan (1994) identifies four characteristics that contribute to what he terms the "shadow side" of helping. These factors retard the helping process:

1. *Rigidity:* the inability to tailor helping approaches to meet the unique needs of the client

2. *Overcontrol:* the use of the helping process to control and manipulate clients

3. *Virtuosity:* when helpers place themselves at the center of the helping process by "showing off" how adept they are at some or all aspects of the helping process and are unable to put the client first

4. *Ineptness:* when helpers are unable or unwilling to learn the techniques and methods of helping

The presence of one or more of Egan's four negative characteristics or the absence of the positive traits and characteristics identified throughout his chapter will severely retard an individual's ability to function as a helper.

Summary

Many people are attracted to the helping process, but not all are initially qualified to take on this role. In almost all instances, people who aspire to be helpers must work to become more fully aware of their personal characteristics, their cultural identities, and any psychological problems that may impair their functioning as a helper. Training programs facilitate development in each of these areas using a combination of didactic and experiential methods; for example, it is possible to raise a trainee's awareness of the differences among cultures by a comparative analysis of the major cultures in this country. However, these differences will take on additional meaning when the trainee interacts informally and in helping relationships with people of different cultures.

Empathy, respect for others, genuineness, the capacity for intimacy, and ethical conduct are also taught in helper training programs, but they are difficult to develop in short-term training programs. Individuals who have deficiencies in these core areas may find that their journey to becoming an effective helper will be difficult at best and may want to rethink their goals.

CHAPTER 2 EXIT QUIZ

Answer each of the following questions with a T if the statement is true and an F if the statement is false.

_____ 1. The characteristics of people who come for help during the next 25 years will be much like the ones coming at this time.

_____ 2. Effective helpers need to recognize that they have prejudices and learn to set them aside during the helping process.

_____ 3. *Cultural conditioning* and *ethnocentrism* are synonymous terms.

_____ 4. People from different cultures tend to judge other groups based on the standards of their own cultural groups.

_____ 5. Cross-cultural helping is restricted to white helpers and nonwhite clients.

_____ 6. To fully appreciate the cultures of others, helpers must understand and accept their own cultures.

_____ 7. *Sympathy* is "helpers jargon" for *empathy*.

_____ 8. Although being genuine or authentic is important in the helping process, there are times when it impossible to be entirely genuine.

_____ 9. Respect for others involves being able to see things from their point of view.

_____10. An example of an inviting interpersonal style would be making anonymous contributions to the senior center.

Answers:

1. F; 2. T; 3. F; 4. T; 5. F; 6. T; 7. F; 8. T; 9. F; 10. T.

SUGGESTED LEARNING ACTIVITIES

1. Survey five of your acquaintances that you trust. Ask them if they are aware of anything about you that you may not be aware of yourself such as mannerisms, beliefs, prejudices (window 2 of the Johari window). Also, ask them if they believe you would make a good helper? Ask them why they do or do not believe you would be a good helper?

2. Identify the most helpful person you have ever known. Place a check by the traits and characteristics of that person in the left-hand column.

_____ 1. Understood the inner world of others (empathy).

_____ 2. Interacted genuinely with others.

_____ 3. Developed successful relationships with people from different backgrounds.

_____ 4. Was creative when it came to solving problems.

_____ 5. Was optimistic.

_____ 6. Had faith in people.

_____ 7. Could function independently.

_____ 8. Didn't demonstrate prejudicial attitudes in his or her speech or behavior.

_____ 9. Demonstrated a great sense of respect for all people.

_____10. Established and maintained intimate relationships.

_____11. Openly admitted his weaknesses.

_____12. Openly volunteered to help others.

_____13. Did things for others without them knowing it.

_____ 14. Had a great deal of personal energy.

_____ 15. Was ethical in all that he did or said.

Now think about yourself. Go back and place an X by all of your characteristics.

3. *Practicing Empathy.* Divide the class into pairs. Make sure that the pairs are as diverse as possible. Have one-half of the dyads think of an emotional experience that they either have witnessed or experienced, preferably one that involved two or more emotions. These are the clients. Have the clients role-play their experiences, reenacting them as accurately as possible. The other half of the dyads, the helpers, tries to identify the emotions the clients are experiencing. Reverse roles and conduct the exercise again. Process the exercise with the entire class. Was it easy or difficult to identify the emotions experienced by the clients? What types of errors were made? What effect might these errors have on real clients?

4. *No names please.* Ask class members to write down a time when they were genuine, that is, they shared their true feelings with another person, but doing so backfired and made the interaction with the other person worse. Pick up the incidents and redistribute them to the class. Then have people read the incidents they received. Ask the class to recommend other things that, while not being ingenuine, might have produced more positive responses from the listeners.

REFERENCES

Brown, D., & Crace, R.K. (1997). *User's manual: Life values inventory.* Chapel Hill, NC: Life Values Resources.

Carkhuff, R.R. (1983). *The art of helping* (5th ed.). Amherst, MA: Human Resource Development Press.

D'Andrea, M.D., & Daniels, J. (1997). Continuing discussion about racism. *Aces Spectrum, 58,* 8–9.

Egan, G. (1994). *The skilled helper* (5th ed.). Pacific Grove, CA: Brooks/Cole.

Ivey, A.E. (1997). White privilege and the need for collaboration: Reflections from New Hampshire. *Aces Spectrum, 58,* 10–11.

Gladding, S., Pederson, P., & Stone, D.A. (1997). Multicultural competencies: A self-examination. *Aces Spectrum, 58,* 4–5.

Johnson, D.W. (1993). *Reaching out: Interpersonal effectiveness and self-actualization.* Boston: Allyn and Bacon.

Maslow, A. (1956). Self-actualizing people: A study of psychological health. In C.E. Moustakas (Ed.), *The self: Explorations in personal growth* (pp. 160–194). New York: Harper & Row.

Myers, L.J., et al. (1991). Identity development and worldview: Toward an optimal conceptualization. *Journal of Counseling and Development, 70,* 54–63.

Pack-Brown, S.P. (1999). Racism and white counselor training: Influence of white racial identity theory and research. *Journal of Counseling and Development, 77,* 87–92.

Purkey, W.W., & Schmidt, J.J. (1996). *Invitational counseling: A self-concept approach to professional practice.* Pacific Grove, CA: Brooks/Cole.

Rogers, C.R. (1951). *Client-centered therapy.* Boston: Houghton-Mifflin.

Sue, D.W., & Sue, D. (1990). *Counseling the culturally different: Theory and practice.* New York: Wiley.

Truax, C., & Carkhuff, R.R. (1967). *Toward effective counseling and psychotherapy.* Chicago: Aldine.

CHAPTER

3

Cultural Diversity and Helping

WHAT YOU WILL LEARN

1. The changing demographics of the U.S. population
2. The differences that exist among the values, worldviews, and communication patterns of the cultural groups in the United States
3. Some of the characteristics of people with disabilities and some of the issues confronting them
4. Some of the issues confronting gay, lesbian, bisexual and transexual people
5. Your cultural values and sensitivity to cultural diversity
6. The implications of differences in cultural values, behaviors, and worldviews for the helping process

The multicultural helping movement has made sweeping changes in the way that many helpers conceive of themselves and the helping process. Perhaps most important, helpers realize that their views of the way people should think and act are often based on erroneous information gleaned from the dominant culture. Helpers also realize that clients who come from different cultural backgrounds have unique perspectives that are often quite different from their own. They have come to understand that their helping strategies must be tailored to the worldviews of their clients. This chapter explores the cultural diversity found in the United States and its implications for helping.

Understanding Culture

Individuals preparing to be helpers often raise two questions when introduced to multicultural helping: "What is culture?" and "What are the unique worldviews I must accommodate in my work?" *Culture* is any given group's values, beliefs, social rules of conduct, symbols usage, and ideologies. Stated somewhat differently, "culture is a way of thinking, feeling, and believing—a stored knowledge that guides people's lives" (Mackelprang & Salsgiver, 1999, p. 21). This stored knowledge is transmitted to children by families, social institutions, the media, and day-to-day interactions with people in their communities. Once adopted, cultural beliefs are powerful influences on behavior and thinking. Jews from countries around the world have maintained their cultural beliefs in the face of unthinkable treatment. Muslims in Eastern Europe are the modern-day victims of ethnic cleansing efforts that have grown out of differences in cultural ideologies. Worldviews develop as a result of the adoption of cultural beliefs and customs. One example of a difference in a worldview concerns the choice of a marital partner. In many parts of the world it is common practice for parents to arrange marriages, a practice that is readily accepted by all parties involved. Though this practice is rejected by most individuals in U.S. society, some nonmainstream cultural groups in the United States do arrange their members' marriages. Helpers need to become aware of the worldviews of their clients regarding marital choices, decision-making, the causes of mental health problems, and other issues.

U.S. Cultural Groups

Because the dominant culture in the United States largely originates from Western Europe, it is referred to as *Eurocentric culture.* However, Native Americans had a culture long before the arrival of Europeans. Many Hispanic Americans had ancestors living in the territory that now makes up Texas, Arizona, California, and New Mexico long before they became parts of this country. Other groups such as the Chinese brought their cultures with them when they immigrated to this country, something that is still occurring. It would be easy to base our classification of cultural groups on skin color or country of national origin, but the classification would be insufficient to explain the diversity of worldviews that exists in this country.

Mackelprang and Salsgiver (1999) make a powerful case that there now exists a culture of people with disabilities partially because these societal members have been isolated, powerless, and have common experiences. Perhaps more important, people with disabilities, like other minorities, are increasingly assuming responsibility for their own lives and rejecting the labels and perceptions of the nondisabled majority. People with disabilities are taking the perspective that disabilities mean diversity, not deficiency, and their lives are to be celebrated, not pitied or mourned. Helpers are very likely to encounter individuals with disabilities. For example, there are approximately 500,000 people who are legally blind, 1.35 million people who are deaf, 2.5 million people with epilepsy, and untold millions with cognitive disabilities such as learning disabilities and attention deficit and hyperactivity disorder (Mackelprang & Salsgiver, 1999). In all, there are probably nearly 50 million people who have some sort of disability in the United States.

Gay, lesbian, and bisexual individuals are now recognized as a cultural group for some of the same reasons just discussed. They have unique experiences, have been systematically discriminated against, and are increasingly assuming responsibility for their lives through political action and assertion of their rights. However, the matter of gay rights is far from settled, and discrimination and abuse against nonheterosexuals is widespread. President Bill Clinton, who was supportive of gay rights, had to settle for a "don't ask, don't tell" stand on homosexuals in the military after armed services leaders balked at his request that gays be allowed to openly declare their sexual orientations. The military leaders were supported by many political leaders as well members of the general public. Gay, lesbian, bisexual, and transgender clients require helpers who can empathize with their worldview. There are no reliable estimates of the number of gay, lesbian, bisexual, and trangender people in our society. However, helpers must be prepared to provide assistance to this group of clients.

Racial and ethnic minorities make up the largest group of multicultural clients. The U.S. population is made up of approximately 75% whites and 25% nonwhites, though the numbers of nonwhites is growing faster than the white population. Projections predict that sometime in the first century of the twenty-first millennium there will be fewer white than nonwhite people in the United States. The major subgroups within the nonwhite category include African Americans, Hispanic Americans, Native Americans, and Asian Americans. Asian Americans may come from China, Japan, Korea, Vietnam, Cambodia, Laos, or India. If, as is sometimes the case, Pacific Islanders are added to this group, people from the Philippines, Samoa, and other islands make the group even more diverse. Similarly, Hispanic Americans come from an array of geographic locations. They may trace their ancestral roots to Cuba, Puerto Rico, Mexico, Central America, or any of the countries in South America. The geographic points of origin of Native Americans are not as diverse as that of Asian Americans and Hispanics, but there are over 500 recognized tribes of Native Americans in this country, many of which vary tremendously in their customs, traditions, and worldviews.

Why this concern about diversity? It has been asserted, and data has been provided to support the assertion, that minorities underutilize helping services. When minorities do come for help, premature termination is often the result (Sue & Sue, 1990). Although the reasons for this underutilization of helping services and premature termination when helpers are consulted are diverse, they fall into two categories: (1) helpers lack sensitivity, and (2) helpers choose inappropriate helping strategies in the helping process. It is the primary aim of this chapter to deal with these issues. However, prior to proceeding with this discussion the matter of politically correct titles for ethnic and cultural minorities will be addressed.

Naming U.S. Cultural Groups

The groups discussed above share several characteristics not the least of which is assuming control of their own fate. One way groups do this is by choosing their own name. For example, since the civil rights movement of the 1950s and 1960s, African Americans as a group have changed their preferred title from *Negro* to *black* and from *black* to *African American*. The most correct and respectful response to adopt as a society is to also use the title *African American*. Calling an African American a *Negro* is now likely to be viewed as insensitive or racist.

At the time of this writing, Native American leaders are considering which title is best for them, *Native American* or *American Indian*. Because this issue has not been resolved, *Native American* and *American Indian* will be used interchangeably throughout this book. There is a similar issue among people who come from countries in which Spanish is the dominant language and culture. To date, both *Hispanic* and *Latino* are acceptable titles for most people in this cultural group, although *Latino* is the more inclusive term because it incorporates Brazilians whose heritage is Portuguese. In the past, the title *Oriental* was used to describe people that are now referred to routinely as *Asian Americans.* Today, referring to a person of Asian descent as *Oriental* is considered derogatory. Persons with disabilities seem to be rejecting titles such as *physically challenged* and *mentally challenged* in favor of *disabled person,* and gays and lesbians made their preferred titles clear two decades ago.

Currently the term *white* is preferred as the title for people of European (not Spanish) descent. However, This book uses the term *European American* in place of *white.* One reason for this substitution is that many people from South American countries are white, view themselves as white, and find the titles *Hispanic* or *Latino* offensive when other white persons refer to themselves as white. A second reason for adopting *European American* is that Eurocentric values and culture dominate the cultural landscape of the United States, a fact that the title *European American* reminds us. Third and finally, the term *European American* is parallel in construction to terms such as *Asian American* and *African American* and thus creates a sense of equal and objective treatment among terms.

Issues in Helping Cultural, Racial, and Ethnic Minorities

Racism and Helping

"Racism is any attitude, action, or institutional structure that subordinates a person because of his or her ethnic background" (Johnson, 1993, p. 377). Many in the forefront of the multicultural helping movement believe that the biggest barrier to effective helping is pervasive racism in our society for two reasons. First, because racism limits the opportunities available to ethnic and racial minorities in our schools, in the health care system, in the workplace, and elsewhere, the results of the helping process cannot be as satisfactory with ethnic and cultural minorities as it is with people from the majority culture. Second, racism often undermines the helping process itself. D'Andrea and Daniels (1997) articulate the position held by many multicultural helpers in the following propositions:

1. Racism continues to be a major problem in this country.
2. Almost all European Americans, including helpers, have racist tendencies, which are regularly manifested overtly and covertly.
3. All institutions in this country foster and perpetuate racism and are the major barriers to social justice.
4. Although people from other backgrounds exhibit racism, it is white people who are primarily responsible for perpetuating it in this country.

5. Given the pervasive presence of racism, it is important that white helpers voice opposition to it and take the lead in discussions regarding racism.
6. Racism is the major reason that social problems, including unemployment and higher mortality rates among minorities, exist.
7. White people are generally uncomfortable and defensive when faced with racism.
8. The use of culturally inappropriate theories and strategies for helping are one of the ways helpers perpetuate racism.

Although we agree with many of the assumptions set forth above, we also believe that they have certain shortcomings in a multicultural society in which individuals from many cultural backgrounds will become helpers. Our assumptions follow:

1. Racism is a fact of life in all cultures, and thus all helpers must be aware of their prejudicial attitudes and any discriminatory practices that grow out of those attitudes.
2. Racial attitudes that are manifested in the form of racial slurs, verbal harassment, and nonverbal communications should not be tolerated, whether they are directed at minorities or the white majority.
3. Discrimination, which is the act of precluding people from various types of opportunities based on their race, ethnicity, age, disability, sexual orientation, or gender, is illegal in this country. Helpers must voice oppositions to all forms of discrimination.
4. The elimination of institutional racism is dependent on placing women and minorities into the power structure of schools, businesses, and public, private, and governmental agencies. Therefore, race, ethnicity, and gender should be considered important credentials in the hiring process of all workers, including helpers.
5. Racism is a difficult topic to address for all people. However, ongoing dialogues that are not precipitated by crises need to occur.
6. Within their agencies, helpers need to take the lead in the elimination of racism and discrimination.
7. All helping strategies used, whether they be theories or techniques, should be culturally sensitive. Therefore, it is incumbent on all helpers, regardless of their race, to develop an understanding of the implications of their clients' cultural background for the helping process.

Unintentional Racism

Sue (1999) and other multiculturalists hold that much of the damage inflicted by helpers is done unintentionally. *Unintentional racists* are persons who believe that they are not racists but who continue to practice or tolerate racism, typically without understanding that their behavior is racist in nature. The questions in Exercise 3.1 provide insight into whether you may practice unintentional racism.

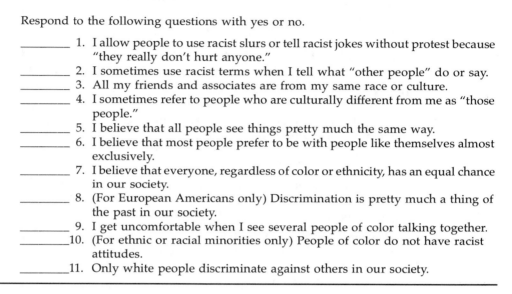

All of the questions in Exercise 3.1 describe people who may practice un-intentional racism. Recognizing this in themselves and in others is very important for helpers to fully meet the challenges of multicultural helping. Moreover, helpers who believe that only white people are racist or only minorities suffer from discrimination may overlook the racist attitudes and discriminatory practices of people from minority groups. Consider the following situations, all of which describe instances of racism or discrimination.

- The executives at a major oil company are audiotaped using racial slurs in their discussions of African American employees.
- In one Native American tribe, children are taught to distrust African Americans because some African American soldiers posed as Native Americans in Europe after World War II.
- A Jewish worker shoots several African Americans because they appear to be "threatening."
- In retaliation for the shooting, a Jewish cab driver is beaten.
- A white realtor shows all Cambodian buyers houses only in a nonwhite neighborhood.

- Japanese students pointedly refuse to associate with Korean students.
- A presidential candidate refers to African Americans as "you people."

Consider the impact of unintentional racism on the helping process when the following worker seeks advice from the helper in the human resource development division of a large corporation.

> **HISPANIC WORKER:** I've been passed over three times for promotion. I believe that I'm not getting the promotion because my supervisor is biased because I'm Hispanic and speak with an accent. My job performance has always been excellent.
>
> **RACIST HELPER:** Our company has made a huge effort at prejudice reduction among our supervisors. I know you are frustrated, but my advice is to keep putting in for promotion. (Helper assumes that discrimination is in the past.)
>
> **NONRACIST HELPER:** Although our company has made a major effort to eliminate discrimination among our supervisors, it's doubtful that we have been entirely successful. Let's look at the facts in your case.
>
> **EUROPEAN AMERICAN WORKER:** I've been passed over three times for promotion. In all three cases less qualified minorities have gotten the promotion.
>
> **RACIST HELPER:** We have made every effort to make our promotion process as fair as possible. Is it possible that you have underestimated the qualifications of the people promoted? (Helper assumes discrimination against whites either is not occurring or is okay.)
>
> **NONRACIST HELPER:** Although our company has made a major effort to make the promotion process as fair as possible, we need to look at the facts in your case.

The brief questionnaire in Exercise 3.1 was designed to help you begin the process of self-examination to determine whether you have racist attitudes that will limit your effectiveness in cross-cultural helping situations. However, simply determining that you do have racist attitudes is not enough. These attitudes must be eliminated. However, even if you take a stand against racism, do not use racial slurs in any context, and work in your school or place of employment to eliminate institutional racism, you are still not prepared to function as a multicultural helper. D'Andrea and Daniels (1997) make a valid point in noting that one of the ways that helpers perpetuate racism in the helping process is through the use of culturally inappropriate theories and techniques. To fully understand the meaning of culturally appropriate helping strategies and theories, helpers must develop an understanding of the cultures from which their clients come. Several multicultural helpers (for example, Gladding, Pedersen, & Stone, 1997) suggest that the point of departure for learning about other cultures is to study one's own culture. By examining one's own culture several things can be accomplished. The most obvious of these is that a fuller idea of the meaning of culture can be developed. The second is that the origin of one's beliefs can be determined and more fully understood. Whether we like it or not, we acquire many of our beliefs from the significant others in our environment. Of course, this does not mean that we retain everything we learn. Most people have seen things in their families that they found objectionable and consciously changed their own perspective. To help you with the process of determining your cultural heritage, complete Exercise 3.2.

Completing the genogram in Exercise 3.2 may heighten your awareness of your cultural heritage and help you identify the sources of some of your racist attitudes if they exist. Developing an awareness of your attitudes and behavior is only the first step. These attitudes must be eliminated by increased contact

---

E X E R C I S E **3.2**

Your Family Heritage

A genogram is a chart or graph that shows the members of your family. The things that are learned from family members and their cultural heritage influence everyone. Provide the information in sections 1–6 and then answer questions 7–15.

1. Maternal grandmother _____   Ethnic and racial background _____
2. Maternal grandfather _____   Ethnic and racial background _____
3. Paternal grandmother _____   Ethnic and racial background _____
4. Paternal grandfather _____   Ethnic and racial background _____
5. Mother _____   Ethnic and racial background _____
6. Father _____   Ethnic and racial background _____
7. Based on the information provided above, what is your racial and ethnic heritage?
8. What are the unique traditions and customs of your racial and ethnic groups, if any (for example, Scotch-Irish or Hispanic)
9. What are the unique beliefs of your racial and ethnic groups, if any (for example, some Indian Americans believe in arranged marriages)?
10. What are the stereotypes that others have of your racial and ethnic groups (for example, Italians are passionate)?
11. Have you incorporated any of these stereotypes about your group into your own belief system or behavior?
12. Are there any historical ethnic or racial issues within your racial and ethnic groups (for example, Protestant and Catholic disputes in Northern Ireland)?
13. Have you incorporated any of these beliefs or prejudices into your belief system?
14. Did any of the people in section 1-6 overtly or subtlety display racist attitudes in the form of stereotyping other groups, insinuations that other groups are inferior, concerns about people who are different moving into their neighborhood, remarks about school integration, racial jokes, and so forth?
15. Do you occasionally find yourself displaying some of the racist attitudes of your relatives?

with people who come from cultural backgrounds different from your own and by increasing your knowledge of these groups. Exercises at the end of this chapter will help you identify ways to increase your contact with people from different cultural groups. The process of increasing your knowledge base about cultural difference is taken up in the next section.

Racial, Cultural, and Ethnic Differences and the Helping Process

Before embarking on a discussion of cultural differences in the helping process, it may be useful to paraphrase an Apache story about the insensitivity of white people (Basso, 1979).

> WHITE MALE GREETS AN APACHE: Hello my friend. How are you feeling? You feeling good? (He then slaps the Apache on the shoulder.)
>
> APACHE AND WHITE MAN ENTER WHITE MAN'S HOUSE: Look who's here everybody. It's Little Man. Come on in and sit right down. (Faces Little Man.) Sit right here. Are you hungry? You want some food? Crackers? How about a beer? If you don't eat, you are going to get sick.

What errors do you see in this brief conversation? Consider the following:

- "Hello my *friend*" is a presumption, one that is deemed irresponsible.
- "How are you feeling?" is viewed as an intrusive statement.
- Touching is viewed as inappropriate in public, particularly among Apache men.
- Using an Apache's name is like borrowing a personal possession without asking.
- "Come on in and sit right down" is viewed as bossy.
- Direct eye contact is viewed as aggressive, as is moving a person from one place to another.
- Repeating a question is seen as rude, particularly when a person isn't given time to respond.
- Rapid-fire talking too much may be seen as a sign of foolishness.
- Talking about illness may cause it to happen.

The point of the story is obvious. Helpers should not make assumptions about communication with people from cultures different from their own based on their own cultural experiences.

Acculturation and Helping

Acculturation is the process by which individuals from one cultural group adopt the values and worldviews of another cultural group. In the United States, the most likely scenario is that individuals from minority cultural groups will be acculturated, that is, they will adopt the values and worldviews of the dominant culture. However, it is possible that European Americans will adopt the values and worldviews of one of the minority cultures. Moreover, acculturation is a reversible process. For example, a Native American who has adopted European American values and worldview may decide to return to the traditions and beliefs of his or her tribe.

Acculturation occurs as a result of two processes (Rokeach, 1973). One of these is conflict. Individuals from minority groups are subjected to the cultural beliefs and expectations of the dominant culture in almost every phase of their lives, including watching television, learning in school, and engaging in their day-to-day interactions with others. Independence is one of the primary values in European American culture. Movies and television programs glorify independent decision-makers who put their own beliefs and ideas ahead of those of their peers and often their families. Students are expected to work independently in most public schools, and independent workers are more likely to be promoted in the workplace. However, the concept that people should function independently from their families is contrary to the beliefs of many Asian Americans, Hispanics, and Native Americans who subscribe to a collateral value. Individuals who hold a collateral value believe that they should place the wishes and welfare of the group ahead of their own. Because people who believe in collateral values are constantly bombarded with information that contradicts their beliefs, internal conflicts may develop. To resolve this conflict, they may adopt an independence value, in which case acculturation has occurred. They may also decide to maintain their collateral value.

The second process that contributes to acculturation is contemplation. Sometimes people change their values and worldviews because they carefully consider the options and make a conscious decision to change. For example, some people question some of the implications of an independence value in a world that increasingly calls for collaboration to solve problems such as global warming, energy shortages, and economic crises. One result of the acculturation process, whether it be the result of resolving conflicts or thoughtful consideration, is that acculturated individuals feel more comfortable with the values and traditions of the dominant culture than the culture into which they were born. Thomason (1995) reports the results of a study of African American and Native American college students that found that 10% of the Native Americans and 75% of the African Americans studied considered themselves to be acculturated.

Because acculturation results in basic changes in the beliefs and worldviews of individuals, it is inappropriate for helpers to make assumptions about clients on the basis of race, ethnic group membership, and any other external characteristic. Skilled multicultural helpers become familiar with the "internal culture" of the client, that is, their beliefs and worldviews. Stereotyping—making assumptions about the client based on external characteristics—is avoided.

Can the degree of acculturation be determined by a skilled multicultural helper? Yes, there are sophisticated inventories that helpers can use to measure the extent to which a minority group member has been acculturated. However,

Thomason (1995) and Garrett and Pichette (2000) suggest that the degree of acculturation may be ascertained through an informal interview that elicits the following information:

Cultural Group Affiliation
How does the client perceive himself or herself?
What is his or her cultural identity?

Language Spoken
What is the preferred language of the client?
Does he or she prefer the language of his or her cultural group or English?

Cultural Group Affiliation of Parents
What is or was the cultural identity of the parents of the client?
If the individual was raised in a foster home, what is or was the cultural identity of the foster parents?

Influential People Other Than Parents
What is or was the cultural identity of people other than parents who influenced the client's development?

Friends
Are the individual's friends largely from one particular cultural group?

Current Associates
With whom does the client associate currently?
What are their cultural identities?

Traditions or Religion Practiced
What religious or national holidays are observed?
What is the client's religious affiliation?

Acculturated clients may have difficulty describing their cultural identity. They are likely to speak English and may have forgotten how to speak their native language. Their parents may have been unsure of their cultural identities, or the client may have rejected his or her parents' cultural identity. The associates of acculturated clients are either acculturated members of their own cultures or members of the dominant culture. Finally, if they honor the traditions of their culture of origin, they may also honor the traditions of the dominant culture.

Exploring Cultural Groups

The point of departure in cross-cultural helping is learning about different cultural groups. This requires that helpers explore these groups' history, traditions, religious beliefs, worldviews, and values. In the case of gays, lesbians, and bisexuals the history to be explored deals with the systematic discrimination that has occurred, the stands taken by religious groups, and the public policies that limit people who do not have a heterosexual identity. Similarly, when looking at the history of people with disabilities in the United States, it may be useful to look at the historical practice of isolating people with disabilities and systematically discriminating against them. Kiselica (1991) suggests three ways by which this might be accomplished: readings, seminars, and direct discussions with the client groups. Providing an in-depth view of the cultures that exist in our society is outside the scope of this discussion. However, some of the variations among ethnic and racial cultures are addressed with particular emphasis on values and communication. In the sections that follow, some of the salient characteristics of the major cultural groups are compared and contrasted. The final section of this chapter explores some of the implications of the cultural differences identified for the helping process.

Values. Values are beliefs that are experienced as "oughts" and "shoulds." They are the standards that we use to judge ourselves and others. When we act in ways that are at odds with our values, we perceive ourselves as acting in an unacceptable fashion. When others act in ways that are not in keeping with our values, we judge their actions as inappropriate or, worse, inferior. Because the beliefs held by cultures vary, one result of interactions among people from different cultures is that each group will conclude that the other acts and thinks in an inappropriate manner. Cultural values are the basis for ethnocentrism, which is the belief that one's culture is superior to others. Table 3.1 shows some values belonging to certain cultural groups in the United States (Ho, 1987; Ibrahim, 1985; Kluckhorn & Strodtbeck, 1961; Sue & Sue, 1990). The values are defined below.

Moderate Self-Control. Although it is okay to show emotion and to let people know what you are thinking it is inappropriate to lose total control of one's emotions.

It Is Very Important to Maintain Self-Control. Controlling one's thoughts and emotions is of utmost concern. Showing emotion is a sign of weakness.

Future Time Orientation. It is important to look ahead and plan for the future. Keeping track of time by mechanical means and making things "run" on time is important.

Present Time Orientation. What is happening at this time is more important than what happens in the future. (Note: Many African Americans have adopted a future time orientation.)

TABLE 3.1   Traditional Values of Major Cultural Groups in the United States

Group	Importance of Self-Control	Time	Activity	Social Relationships	Relationship to Nature
European American	Moderate	Future	Doing	Individual	Dominate
American Indian	Very	Circular	Being-to-becoming	Collateral	Harmony
Hispanic	Moderate	Present	Being	Collateral	Harmony/subjugation
African American	Moderate	Present	Doing	Collateral	Mixed
Asian American	Very	Past-future	Doing	Lineal	Harmony

Circular Time Orientation.   Time is related to natural events such as the changing of the seasons or the phases of the moon. Keeping track of time mechanically is unimportant.

Past-Future Orientation.   Although it is important to plan for the future, the traditions and lessons of the past should not be forgotten.

Doing Activity Orientation.   It is important to tackle problems and deal with issues when they arise. Activity is undertaken for the purpose of individual gain or enhancement.

Being Activity Orientation.   Problems, including wrongful acts against you, are meant to be and cannot be resolved. Being and experiencing is more important than doing something. Activity is undertaken for the purpose of improving family or group.

Being-to-Becoming Activity Orientation.   Inner fulfillment, thoughtful contemplation, self-control, and feeling as one with the tribe and the universe are most important. Noninterference with the affairs of others is an important guideline, and thus problems may not precipitate activity. Activity, when undertaken, is for the benefit of others.

Individual Orientation in Social Relationships.   The individual is most important in social relationships, and individualism is to be encouraged and nurtured.

Collateral Orientation in Social Relationships.   The group is most important. (Note: Many African Americans have adopted individual orientation social relationships.)

Lineal Social Relationships.   Social relationships are hierarchical with people who are older or in positions of authority deserving respect.

Worldviews.   Not surprisingly, each of the major cultural groups listed in Table 3.1 have somewhat different worldviews that are based on their values. The worldview of American Indians probably diverges most markedly from that of European Americans. Thomason (1995) summarizes the worldview of American Indians as follows:

> Humans are a part of a larger unity, and humans are not separate from nature. All of creation is alive and whole. Nature is structured and follows laws of cause and effect, but not necessarily in ways we can understand. Time is not rigidly linear, so causation can flow backward as well as forward. Time is circular, based on the seasons of the year, and since time is eternal there is never a lack of time. Events begin not at a rigid clock-time, but when everyone is present and everything is ready.

On the other hand, most European Americans believe that events should start on time, that human beings have a special place in nature, that time moves forward, and that cause and effect relationships are rather easily determined. In sharp contrast to European American views, many American Indians believe that health, particularly mental health, is related to maintaining harmony with nature. Mental illness occurs whenever taboos are violated or from witchcraft (Thomason, 1995). One final difference between the worldviews of American Indians and European Americans rests with their activity orientation. European Americans believe that, when problems arise, they need to be solved. American Indians are much more likely to take time to consider the nature of the problem before taking action. See Case Illustration 3.1.

Hispanics also have a worldview that contrasts rather dramatically from that held by the dominant European American culture. See, for example, Case Illustration 3.2. Hispanics may want to enjoy the moment instead of looking ahead to the next day and may feel that they have limited ability to influence the future because

CASE ILLUSTRATION **3.1**

Native American Children Teach the Expert

In the late 1960s, I was asked to direct a project for middle school children on the Sac and Fox settlement in Tama, Iowa. The purpose of the project was to promote career exploration and cultural pride. Because the project was well funded, we established a behavior modification program that rewarded the highest achieving children with silver dollars. When the rewards were passed out, many of the children threw their coins into a nearby woods. Earlier, I had observed that when the children played ball they did not keep score. I had also noted that when they chose sides for softball they did not necessarily choose the most athletic first. After consulting with the children, teachers, and some of the tribal elders, I changed the behavior modification program to reward cooperative behavior.

Source: Duane Brown.

of their perceptions about the impact of nature on human functioning. They may therefore refrain from action taking. Moreover, because of their collateral values, Hispanics are likely to depend on their families in the decision-making process more than European Americans do. European American helpers may perceive American Indians, Hispanics, and Asian Americans as dependent because of their reliance on their families and or tribal affiliation. This error in judgment represents a classic case in unintended racism growing out of cultural values.

Two values held by Asian Americans are probably the basis for worldviews that set them apart from other groups. First, they have a past-future time orientation, which is most similar to the circular time orientation of American Indians. However, Asian Americans take a linear view of time and of cause and effect relationships. Many Asian Americans view the traditions of the past as lessons that guide the future. Perhaps more important, maintaining traditional views and ways of doing things are likely to be seen as more important by Asian Americans than it is for any other group except American Indians. The second value that distinguishes the worldview of Asian Americans from others is their concept of lineal social relationships. Many Asian families tend to be patriarchal, which means that the father is viewed as the authority figure. Asian American children are often expected to follow the wishes of their parent when they make important decisions such as the choice of an occupation and, in some instances, when they choose a spouse. One implication of this lineal value for helpers is that they may be placed in a position of authority and treated with more respect than is the case with many clients.

The worldviews of African Americans may be similar to that of European Americans because of acculturation. However, because of their African heritage they may be more inclined than European Americans to hold a collateral social relationships value, a present time orientation, and the belief that people are dominated by nature.

Verbal and Nonverbal Communication

Cultural values influence all aspects of behavior of clients, including their verbal and nonverbal behavior. However, communications researchers (see, e.g., Brasso, 1990; Kim, Shin, & Cai, 1998) believe that the primary reasons for the differences in communication styles may rest with the individual versus the collective social relationship values. Regardless of the source of the differences, many aspects of verbal and nonverbal communication vary among cultural groups. It is important for helpers to understand the variations in communication styles that exist and learn to adapt their own styles to those of the clients. Tables 3.2 and 3.3 summarize some of the major cultural differences in verbal and nonverbal communication styles.

Clearly, verbal and nonverbal behavior occur together in the helping process. The overall communication style of European Americans is open and direct. Unless they are shy they have few compunctions about immediately initiating a conversation with a stranger. This idea is contrary to that held by most Native Americans and Asian Americans. Under conditions of ambiguity, the preferred communication style is silence. Moreover, they do not feel compelled to provide

---

CASE ILLUSTRATION **3.2**

A Fearful Flyer Workshop and Time

I was conducting a workshop for 12 fearful fliers in San Juan, Puerto Rico. The schedule for the workshop was set for 7:00 A.M. to 6:00 P.M. on day one and from 7:30 to 1:30 on day two. The "graduation flight" for the group was scheduled for 2:00 P.M. on the second day. On day one, everyone was in attendance by 8:30 and the workshop went well. At the end of the day, many people stayed to chat and we ended our informal discussions about 7:30. On day two, three people were in attendance at 7:30. One member of the group, who was aware of my time orientation, kept reassuring me that the group would arrive and told me numerous stories about events she had scheduled that started very late. The group trickled in until everyone was present at 10:30. They all took the graduation flight to the Virgin Islands.

Source: Duane Brown.

---

answers if they believe the answer is understood. Helpers need to learn to provide structure by explaining the purpose of the helping interview. They also need to be more patient, expect more silences, and see less direct approaches. For example, an Asian American who wishes to make a request may initially hint at the request as opposed to asking for it directly as would be the case with European Americans (Kim, et al., 1998). African Americans, like European Americans, tend to be more direct. This exaggeration is not done to mislead, but it may be an approach that grows out of a genuine desire to make a positive presentation of their characteristics. Although initial interactions with Hispanics may mirror those with Asian Americans and Native Americans, it is likely that Hispanics will become more animated, both verbally and nonverbally, as the helping process grows. However, they are likely to be indirect in making requests.

Adapting the Helping Process

The helping process must be tailored to the unique characteristics of the client. What follows is a discussion of the helping process and some suggestions for making it culturally sensitive.

Identifying the Helper. You are reading about the process of becoming a helper and may have aspirations to enter the helping field as a mental health aide, counselor, psychologist, a hospice worker, nurse, or some other type of helper. If you fill one of these roles you would expect to be the helper. This may not be the case. In the worldviews of some Native Americans and others (see Case Illustration 3.3), mental health problems are often viewed as a result of witchcraft or being out of harmony with nature. None of the formal training programs for helpers prepare

TABLE 3.2 Nonverbal Communication Styles among U.S. Cultural Groups

Group	Preferred Style in Helping	Implications
European Americans		
Eye contact	Maintain eye contact during conversations at least three-quarters of the time	Eye contact is a sign of respect, and lacking eye contact may be interpreted as sign of dishonesty.
Interpersonal space	Prefer 36 to 42 inches interaction space	Closer interaction space may be seen as invasion of personal space; farther away may be equated to withdrawal.
Nods; Facial expressions	Smiles and head nods sign of interest	Failure to smile or nod head may be seen as a sign of disinterest.
Handshake	Firm	Weak "dead fish" handshake may be interpreted as lack of enthusiasm or weak personality
American Indians		
Eye contact	Indirect	Direct eye contact may be viewed as disrespectful
Interpersonal space	Respectful distance initially; later much closer distances are okay	Initially, close interpersonal distances may be viewed as invasion of personal space
Nods; Facial expressions	Few smiles and head nods	Until client knows helper, smiles and head nods may be seen as a lack of self-control or foolishness
Handshake	Soft and pliable	Firm handshake may be viewed as aggression
Hispanics		
Eye contact	Indirect eye contact, at least initially	Uncomfortable with eye contact; sign of intimacy
Interpersonal space	24 to 36 inches with no barriers	Larger distances and barriers may be interpreted as aloofness
Nods; Facial expressions	Initially reserved; smiles and head nod may occur frequently later	Lack of smiles may be seen as lack of interest or enthusiasm
Handshake	Firm for males; soft and pliable for unacculturated females	For males weak handshake may be viewed as lack of enthusiasm
African American		
Eye contact	May look away when helper is speaking; can show disrespect in same manner	Lack of eye contact is seen as disrespectful

Interpersonal space	36 to 42 inches preferred	More tolerant of closer distances than European Americans
Nods; Facial expression	Expressive; nods and facial expression common	Prefer helper to smile and exhibit warmth
Handshake	Firm; males may use "brother's handshake" (greeters tap each other's fist vertically)	May consider weak handshake as lack of enthusiasm

Asian Americans

Eye contact	Indirect	Direct eye contact may be seen as aggression or sign of unwanted affection
Interpersonal space	Prefer respectful distance: 36 to 42 inches okay	May interpret closer interactions as aggression or unwanted affection
Nods; Facial expressions	Few smiles; head nods may be used to signal respect	Smiles from client may convey negative feelings such as embarrassment
Handshake	Soft and pliable	Firm handshake may be viewed as aggression

TABLE 3.3 **Stylistic Differences in Verbal Communication among U.S. Cultural Groups**

Group	Self-Disclosure	Loudness	Rapidity	Interruptions	Pauses	Directness
European American	acceptable; content-oriented	moderate	moderate	acceptable	yes; may make uncomfortable	direct; task-oriented
American Indian	unacceptable; seen as loss of control	soft	slow; controlled	unacceptable	yes; comfortable with	indirect
Hispanic	acceptable	moderate	varies	unacceptable	comfortable with	indirect
African American	acceptable; expressive	moderate acceptable	moderate uncomfortable	acceptable initially	yes; may make uncomfortable	indirect initially
Asian American	unacceptable; seen as sign of weakness	soft	slow	unacceptable	yes; comfortable	indirect

CASE ILLUSTRATION **3.3**

A Shaman at Work

Vang was a Laotian Hmong freedom fighter who escaped from Laos and settled in Chicago. As a soldier he had seen his comrades and relatives tortured and brutalized. His abrupt move from one culture to another seemed to induce culture shock that made matters worse.

After a few months in the United States, Vang began to have problems sleeping. When he did sleep he had horrible dreams, typically of a dog or cat sitting on his chest making it difficult for him to breathe. However, he had one dream that was even more frightening that involved a female who would lie on top of him and keep him from breathing. He often awoke screaming. A young bilingual Hmong was concerned about Vang because several newly arrived Hmongs had died of what was termed Hmong Sudden Death Syndrome. Victims of this syndrome displayed symptoms similar to Vang's prior to their deaths, and autopsies failed to reveal any problems. Traditional methods failed to provide relief for the problem.

After consultation with the elders of the Hmong community, a shaman, Mrs. Thor, was contacted to help Vang. She consulted with Vang and concluded that she could help. In the presence of Vang's family, Mrs. Thor lit candles and began a chant that Vang and others knew was used to communicate with spirits. After one hour Mrs. Thor announced that the souls that lay on Vang's chest and made it hard for him to breathe were those of the former tenants of the apartment, who had moved so quickly they left them behind. Mrs. Thor then cut a cloak out of newspaper for Vang to wear. She then cut the cloak in two and burned it. She related that the souls that had been left behind went away with the smoke. Vang was also asked to crawl through a hoop and between two knives. Mrs. Thor told Vang that this would make it difficult for spirits to follow. Vang's nightmares have not reoccurred since the ceremony.

Abstracted from D. W. Sue (1999, March). Advocacy and indigenous methods of healing. *Counseling Today*, 30–31. Used by permission of the publisher.

helpers to deal with witchcraft, the feelings associated with violating taboos, or being out of touch with nature. Neither are they qualified to initiate the rituals associated with the healing process such as interpreting the dreams and visions of the client (Herring, 1996). The "training programs" for this type of helping occur in many Native American tribes. Aspiring medicine men and women and other tribal healers apprentice themselves to people who occupy this position and learn the skills of the craft. Helpers who are trained in helping based on European American approaches may find that it is necessary to become a cofacilitator with the tribal healers when dealing with Native Americans (Herring, 1996).

Past Discrimination and Helping. Sue and Sue (1990) conclude that many Hispanics, African Americans, and Asian Americans view European Americans as racists because they have been discriminated against in the past by members

---

CASE ILLUSTRATION **3.4**

Two Consequences of Past Discrimination in Helping Relationships

Vignette 1

In my role as supervisor of counseling interns, I frequently sit in on their small groups so that I can better assess their skill development. The intern, who was African American, had told the children I would be in attendance, and when the group began I was sitting in the circle. A nine-year-old African American male took his customary place in the group, looked at me, and said, "I hate you!" I responded, "I don't dislike you and I'm wondering why you hate me." He responded, "Because you are white." I left the group.

Vignette 2

I was leading a group of nine- and ten-year-old African Americans who had been victimized by violence. One of the boy's closest relatives, a cousin, had been killed by a white man in a drug deal. Although the boy had volunteered to be in the group, initially he would make only minimal eye contact, and then out of the corners of his eyes. When I told the children I was from the University of North Carolina at Chapel Hill, he immediately said in a loud voice, "I'm for Duke!" As the group progressed, Jamarcus began to make more and more eye contact, and I occasionally received an approving smile. On the next-to-last session, he came to the group wearing a tattered sweatshirt with the emblem CAROLINA on it. I cried.

Source: Duane Brown.

---

of this majority culture. Whether their statement is supportable by data is unclear, but it is true that some clients will not trust helpers because they have been discriminated against in the past. See Case Illustration 3.4. Therefore, it is important, particularly for European American helpers, to ask clients if they believe that they can enter into a successful helping relationship with them. If the response is negative, a different helper should be found.

Identifying the Client.   Normally speaking, the persons who present themselves to the helper will be the client. This might include the student who goes to the school or college counselor, the parolee who presents himself to the court counselor or parole officer, the client who seeks assistance in choosing a new career from a rehabilitation psychologist, or a mother who seeks assistance from the department of social welfare. However, when clients have a collateral or lineal value, others may need to be included in the helping process. For example, with Asian American clients career counselors report that students who come for help with their choice of a career may be accompanied by one or more parents. Family therapists find that instead of working with the nuclear family (wife, husband,

and children), it is necessary to work with the extended family, which may include grandparents and other relatives. In Hispanic families, parents and godparents may both be influential caregivers and thus may need to be added to the client list. Finally, when dealing with Native Americans, the family network may extend into tribal relationships.

Scheduling Appointments.   If clients do not have a future time orientation, the scheduling of appointments requires flexibility. As noted earlier, the idea of being on time in the European American meaning of that phrase has little meaning. Clients who believe that they are "on time" at the moment they arrive may not understand the exasperation experienced by a helper who is accustomed to telling time with a watch or clock.

Establishing the Helping Relationship.   Processes that seem simple, such as identifying the helper and client and scheduling appointments, can become quite complex in cross-cultural helping. This rule extends to the most critical aspect of helping, establishing a helping relationship. Cross-cultural helping is fraught with potential problems for the uninformed helper. The following guidelines may be helpful in crafting a strategy for establishing a relationship in cross-cultural helping.

1. Ask the clients whether they would prefer a helper who shares their cultural background if one is available.
2. Make sure that clients have sufficient understanding of English to understand the concepts that need to be discussed. If they do not, they should be referred to a helper who speaks their language and dialect or a translator should be used. Even when cross-cultural clients appear to have a command of English, make frequent checks to make certain they understand your comments.
3. Match nonverbal approaches such as eye contact and use of interpersonal distance to the cultural norms of the client.
4. Avoid asking for disclosure of personal information from Asian Americans and American Indians because of their concerns about self-control.
5. Avoid using reflection of feeling with unacculturated Asian Americans and American Indians because they may be embarrassed by the emphasis on feelings.
6. Be prepared to accept the role of the authority figure with clients who hold lineal value or clients. In this same vein, be prepared to be an advice giver for clients who have lineal social relationship values.
7. Be modest. Admit that you may not have all the correct approaches and invite assistance.
8. Adopt a style that is more reserved and less talkative when dealing with Native Americans and Asian Americans. Brasso (1990), who examined the communications patterns of Navajo and Western Apaches, found that they were suspicious of people who quickly launch into conversations. The Taoist

religion holds that is against nature to talk all the time, and Confucius was against eloquent speech (Kim, et al., 1998).

Identifying the Problem and Crafting Interventions. Helpers have different underlying theoretical beliefs about the way people function. Some believe that all behavior is learned, while others believe that personality, which is formed by age five or six, dictates how people function. Some of the theoretical approaches to helping require extensive amounts of information gathering, some of which is highly personal. For the most part, it is acceptable to ask European Americans about their relationships with their parents, the nature of their sex life, whether they have irrational beliefs, and so forth. These same questions may not be acceptable to Asian Americans and American Indians. Fortunately, there are approaches to helping that require little probing for personal information. For example, the "magic question" posed by practitioners of solution-focused helping is as follows, "If you woke up one day and your problem was solved, what would your world look like?" As the title, *solution-focused,* and the question used suggest, the emphasis in this approach to helping is to have clients identify the solutions to their problems and begin to work on approaches to the problem immediately.

Behavioral approaches to helping can be initiated without asking probing, personal questions about thoughts and relationships. They focus on behavior, the antecedents to and consequences of it, and ways of changing the environment to alter what the client has learned. However, behavioral approaches to learning illustrate other problems with helping strategies that have grown out of European American values. Behavioral techniques such as contracts are often individually oriented, are future oriented, and are based on the concept that events should occur on time as measured by a clock or calendar. Behavioral approaches can be altered to be based on group activities and natural events, but helpers need to be fully conversant with the values and worldviews of their clients for this to be done successfully. See Case Illustration 3.5 for an example.

To summarize, the problem identification and intervention phases of the helping relationship need to be reconceptualized so they match the values and worldviews of the client. To do less is to condemn the helping process to failure. Helpers must abandon the idea that there is a universal approach to helping in favor of a more pragmatic view of applying what works.

Helping Persons with Disabilities

The foregoing section paid much attention to the importance of avoiding stereotypes in the helping process. Helpers who expect to work with people with disabilities must also conduct an assessment of the beliefs they have developed about this population. Exercise 3.3 contains a brief self-assessment device that can help to identify the misperceptions that you may have developed about people with disabilities.

CASE ILLUSTRATION **3.5**

Changing an Intervention to Match the Collateral Value of a Client

"I" messages are often used as portions of interventions, particularly in assertion training, self-esteem development groups, anger and fear management groups, and so forth. I was leading a group to help college students overcome their fear of public speaking. As a part of the group, students were asked to use self-talk in which they reassured themselves that they could conquer their fear. The self-talk was, "I can conquer my fear when I speak." One of the students, a Japanese American, asked to speak to me after the group. He confided that he was very uncomfortable when he said, "I can conquer my fear when I speak." After some discussion, I asked him if he would be comfortable saying, "We can conquer our fears when we speak" as a way to reassure himself. He answered affirmatively, and the saying became a part of his intervention.

Source: Duane Brown.

If you are like most helpers in training, and probably most practitioners, you answered no to all the questions in Exercise 3.3. Only a few special educators and most rehabilitation counselors and psychologists could answer yes to all of the questions in Exercise 3.3. The following sections discuss the answers, beginning with question 5.

Philosophy of Helping People with Disabilities

The philosophy behind helping people with disabilities bears strong resemblance to those underlying all helping: Helpers must see strengths before limitations and must see as their primary goal the empowerment of the client. Persons with disabilities, like all oppressed minorities, need to be able to take care of themselves, advocate for their political and personal rights, and find joy despite the limitations imposed by their disabilities (Mackelprang & Salsgiver, 1999).

Major Categories of People with Disabilities

People with disabilities are often grouped into six categories:

1. Mobility disorders: any congenital or acquired problem that limits movement
2. Deaf and hard of hearing: hearing disorders that limit or preclude hearing all together
3. Visual impairment and blindness: visual disorders that limit or preclude vision

EXERCISE **3.3**

Test Your Information about People with Disabilities

Respond to each of the following statements with a yes or no.

_____1. I can identify the major categories of people with disabilities.

_____2. I am aware of the major provisions of the Americans with Disabilities Act of 1990.

_____3. I am aware of the types of assessment strategies used in helping people with disabilities.

_____4. I can identify at least four helping strategies that can be used to facilitate the development of persons with disabilities.

_____5. I am aware of the current philosophical position regarding providing assistance to persons with disabilities.

4. Developmental disabilities: mental and physical limitations such as mental retardation, Down syndrome, autism, and epilepsy that limit the ability of the person to conduct routine activities

5. Psychiatric disabilities: psychological problems that impair normal functioning

6. Cognitive disabilities: disabilities such as learning disabilities that limit the acquisition or processing of information

Provisions of the Americans with Disabilities Act of 1990

The Americans with Disabilities Act of 1990 (ADA) is in fact a statement that prohibits discrimination against people with disabilities in any setting and imposes penalties for those who do. Title I of the ADA focuses on employment. For example, employers must make certain that job notices are sent to organizations that can bring them to the attention of disabled. Employers must also take reasonable steps to accommodate people with disabilities, including assigning them to jobs commensurate with their skills or modifying jobs so that people with disabilities can perform them. Title II of the ADA requires that public agencies eliminate access barriers to public buildings and transportation, make information about the ADA available to all employees, designate a compliance officer to ensure that the provisions of the ADA are met, and establish grievance procedures. Title III focuses on the civil rights of disabled persons. Commercial enterprises such as restaurants, public agencies such as museums, and organizations such as health insurers are forbidden to discriminate against the disabled by this section of the ADA.

Assessment Strategies

Typically the assessment process focuses on the identification of the interests, values, attitudes, and aptitudes—the traits—of the individual. (Chapter 6 takes up the matter of assessment generally.) This same model applies to some degree to the assessment of the individual with a disability. However, even the assessment of traits becomes more complicated because of the range of problems. For example, take the matter of determining whether an individual has a developmental disability such as mental retardation or a cognitive disability such as a learning disability. An accurate diagnosis is required to determine the most appropriate. Moreover, there is often the matter of determining physical characteristics such as the degree of mobility, the extent of the visual impairment or hearing disorder, or the eye–hand coordination of the client. Here again the assessment must be accurate to choose an appropriate job or educational placement for the client. Although there are parallels between assessing the traits of people with and without disabilities, the two processes diverge to some degree in area of assessing clients' environments. The ADA and other legislation, such as the Individuals with Disabilities Education Act of 1990, impose conditions that must be met by schools, employers, and others. One question that often arises in the assessment of disabled clients is, "Does the environment provide the opportunities to succeed specified by law?" This question may have to be answered by examining policies and practices of schools, employers, and agencies that provide services to disabled people.

Helping Strategies for People with Disabilities

For the most part, the strategies used to help other clients will be employed when helping clients with disabilities. However, they may have to be modified in several respects, depending on the nature of the disability. Clients who have visual impairments may need reading material presented orally, in Braille, or through the use of a computer that has voice capability. Children who have attention deficit hyperactivity disorder (ADHD) may need medication before they are able to sit and talk to an adult for 20 to 30 minutes. Mentally retarded clients may need helpers to simplify their vocabularies or, if profoundly retarded, may need strategies that do not involve conversational approaches to helping at all. Although there are differences in the approaches to helping, the one constant in the helping process is the human factor. Warmth, empathy, caring, and patience works universally with all clients.

Helping Gay, Lesbian, and Bisexual Individuals

All minority groups are characterized by negative stereotypes, and gay, lesbian, and bisexual individuals are no different in this regard. What may be different is that several major religious groups view them as "sinners." Unfortunately, some people use the "antigay" stand on homosexual relationships taken by these churches to legitimize discrimination in everything from parents' rights to em-

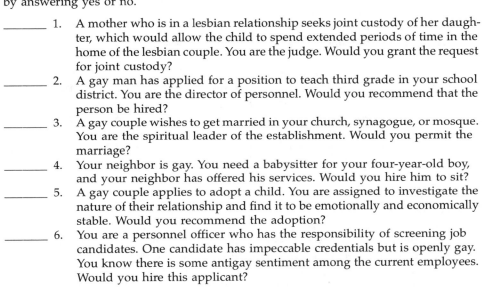

EXERCISE **3.4**

Identifying Your Attitudes toward Homosexuals and Bisexuals

You have been put in a position of great power to control the lives of people. What follows is a series of decisions that must be made regarding the lives of several gay, lesbian, and bisexual people. Indicate how you would handle each of these situations by answering yes or no.

_____ 1. A mother who is in a lesbian relationship seeks joint custody of her daughter, which would allow the child to spend extended periods of time in the home of the lesbian couple. You are the judge. Would you grant the request for joint custody?

_____ 2. A gay man has applied for a position to teach third grade in your school district. You are the director of personnel. Would you recommend that the person be hired?

_____ 3. A gay couple wishes to get married in your church, synagogue, or mosque. You are the spiritual leader of the establishment. Would you permit the marriage?

_____ 4. Your neighbor is gay. You need a babysitter for your four-year-old boy, and your neighbor has offered his services. Would you hire him to sit?

_____ 5. A gay couple applies to adopt a child. You are assigned to investigate the nature of their relationship and find it to be emotionally and economically stable. Would you recommend the adoption?

_____ 6. You are a personnel officer who has the responsibility of screening job candidates. One candidate has impeccable credentials but is openly gay. You know there is some antigay sentiment among the current employees. Would you hire this applicant?

ployment. Antigay feelings have also been fueled by the AIDS epidemic, even though the group with the fastest growing number of new cases is heterosexuals. It is not unusual for helpers to have unconsciously adopted some of these negative feelings toward homosexuals and bisexuals. Like all prejudices, the first step toward ridding ourselves of them is to identify them and examine them logically. Use Exercise 3.4 to start this process.

If you answered no to any of the situations in Exercise 3.4, you may want to explore your attitudes in this area further. The issues identified are the issues confronting our society and may very well be brought to you by a gay, lesbian, or bisexual client. Even more to the point, as you advance through your career as helper, you may actually be the decision-maker.

Guidelines for Helping Gay, Lesbian, and Bisexual Clients

Poindexter et al. (1999) offer six guidelines for providing assistance to gay and bisexual clients.

- Be nonjudgmental.
- Do not assume that every client who comes to you is heterosexual.
- Validate the client's experiences of discrimination and the stigma attached to homosexuality in all forms.
- Work with clients to identify rules regarding disclosure of their sexual orientation that will safeguard their best interests.
- If the client has internalized shame and guilt because of his or her sexual orientation, develop interventions to rid them of their negative feelings about themselves.
- Make referrals and engage in advocacy that will open opportunities to gays, lesbians, and bisexuals that may have been closed to them, such as couples counseling.

Poindexter and her associates do not suggest that helpers need to alter their helping styles to accommodate gay, lesbian, and bisexual clients. Awareness of one's own biases and of the unique experiences and needs of this group should be sufficient, with one exception. Just as was the case with cultural and ethnic minorities, helpers need to do in-depth study of the homosexual culture to prepare themselves to work in this arena.

Summary

Being an effective cross-cultural helper requires knowledge and skills beyond those needed when dealing with typical clients. First, it is important to come to terms with the possibility that you as a prospective helper have developed prejudices and habits that will interfere with the helping relationship. Second, it is important to understand the cultural backgrounds of your clients, particularly those aspects of their backgrounds that might play a prominent role in the helping process. To develop this understanding, the cultures of ethnic and racial minorities, person with disabilities, and people with homosexual or bisexual orientations should be studied in depth. Third, it is important to understand and be able to assess the degree of acculturation when ethnic and racial minorities are clients. Fourth, most clients have experienced discrimination in the past that may influence the helping process. Helpers must be sensitive to this reality and be prepared to deal with it. Fifth, and finally, helpers must be prepared to change both the helping process and the techniques used to facilitate it as they work to assist clients.

CHAPTER 3 EXIT QUIZ

Place a T before the statement if you believe it is true and an F before it if you believe it is false.

_____ 1. Stereotyping ethnic and racial minorities is one form of unintentional racism.

_____ 2. Many multicultural helping leaders believe that most helpers engage in unintentional racism.

_____ 3. Acculturation is the process by which members of the majority culture impose their values and beliefs on minorities.

_____ 4. Evidence supports the idea that more Native Americans are acculturated than African Americans.

_____ 5. Of the cultural groups discussed in this chapter, the two with the most similar values are Hispanics and European Americans.

_____ 6. It seems likely that the two values that most clearly influence divergent behavior among ethnic groups are individualism and collateralism.

_____ 7. One principle of cross-cultural helping is to match the helper's communication style with that of the client.

_____ 8. Generally speaking, helpers have been as successful when helping ethnic minorities as they have when helping European Americans.

_____ 9. The indirect communication style of Native Americans can best be described as emanating from their being-in-becoming activity orientation.

_____10. When working with Asian Americans, verbosity may be looked on as inappropriate.

_____11. European Americans and African Americans have similar communications styles in that they are direct as opposed to indirect.

_____12. Intense eye contact may be seen as aggression among Asian Americans.

_____13. There are more than 45 million people with disabilities in the United States.

_____14. There is very little difference between the assessment process for people with disabilities and persons who have no disabilities.

_____15. The Americans with Disabilities Act of 1990 addresses dual standards in the educational process.

Answers:

1. T; 2. T; 3. F; 4. F; 5. F; 6. T; 7. T; 8. F; 9. T; 10. T; 11. T; 12. T; 13. T; 14. F; 15. F.

SUGGESTED LEARNING ACTIVITIES

1. Spend at least one-half day with a person who is a member of a racial or ethnic cultural group different from your own. At the conclusion of your visit with this person, reflect on the following:
   a. Were there any differences in our communication styles?
   b. Were there any discernible differences in our values? Beliefs? Customs? Traditions?
   c. Were there any discernible differences in preferences for food? Music? Use of leisure time? Importance attached to school? Dress?

Report the findings along with your conclusions to a small group or to the class. Discuss the issue of helping: If a someone with the same background of the person being discussed came for help, what changes would need to be made in the helping process?

2. Make four signs labeled as follows: Hispanic Americans, Asian Americans, Native Americans, and European Americans. Form into groups of six students and choose one to be the leader. One person stands behind the leader with the signs. Select a topic such as friendship. The person standing behind the leader signals the group which cultural group they will be. As they talk, it is up to the leader to determine which cultural group he or she is working with (he or she does this verbally) and to use culturally appropriate helping techniques. Group members **should switch roles every five minutes.**

3. Identify the major holidays of one of the following countries. What do they commemorate? How are they celebrated?
   a. Mexico
   b. Japan
   c. Vietnam
   d. Iran
   e. Spain
   f. Brazil
   g. Iraq
   h. India
   i. Pakistan
   j. Cambodia
   k. Korea
   l. The Philippines
   m. Israel
   n. Argentine
   o. Colombia
   p. Peru

4. Identify the courtship habits of people in the countries listed above. How do these habits reflect their values?

5. Develop a class of people with disabilities. Have each person in class assume a mobility, visual, hearing, developmental, or cognitive disability for 24 hours. Form groups and discuss what was learned from this experience.

6. Invite a gay, lesbian, and bisexual individual to the class to discuss their experiences in their families, churches, schools, and workplaces.

REFERENCES

Basso, K. H. (1990). To give up words: Silence in Western Apache culture. In D. Carbaugh (Ed.), *Cultural communication and intercultural contact* (pp. 303–327). Hillsdale, NJ: Lawrence Erlbaum.

Basso, K. H. (1979). *Portraits of the "Whiteman": Linguistic play and cultural symbols among the Western Apache.* New York: Cambridge University Press.

D'Andrea, M. D., & Daniels, J. (1997). Continuing the discussion about racism. *Aces Spectrum, 58,* 8–9.

Garrett, M. T., & Pichette, E. F. (2000). Red as an apple: Native American acculturation and counseling with and without reservation, *Journal of Counseling and Development, 78,* 3–13.

Gladding, S. T., Pederson, P., & Stone, D. (1997). Multicultural counseling competencies: A self-examination. *Aces Spectrum, 58,* 4–5.

Herring, R. D. (1996). Synergistic counseling and Native Americans. *Journal of Counseling and Development, 74,* 542–547.

Ho, M. K. (1987). *Family therapy with ethnic minorities.* Newbury Park, CA: Sage.

Ibrahim, F. A. (1985). Effective cross-cultural counseling and psychotherapy: A framework. The *Counseling Psychologist, 13,* 625–683.

Johnson, D. W. (1993). *Reaching out: Interpersonal effectiveness and self-actualization* (5th ed.) Boston: Allyn & Bacon.

Kim, M., Shin, H., & Cai, D. (1998). Cultural influence in the preferred forms of requesting and rerequesting. *Communications Monographs, 65,* 47–82.

Kiselica, M. S. (1991). Reflections on a multicultural internship experience. *Journal of Counseling and Development, 70,* 126–130.

Kluckhorn, F. R. & Strodtbeck, F. L. (1961). *Variations in values orientations.* Evanston, IL: Row Paterson.

Mackelprang, R., & Salsgiver, R. (1999). *Disability: A diversity model approach in human service practice.* Pacific Grove, CA: Brooks/Cole.

Poindexter, C. C., Valentine, D., & Conway, P. (1999). *Essential skills for human services.* Pacific Grove, CA: Brooks/Cole.

Rokeach, M. (1973). *The nature of human values.* New York: Free Press.

Sue, D. W. (1999, March). Advocacy and indigenous methods of healing. *Counseling Today,* 30–31.

Sue, D. W., & Sue, D. (1990). *Counseling the culturally different: Theory and practice* (2nd ed.). New York: Wiley.

Thomason, T. C. (1995). *Introduction to counseling American Indians.* Flagstaff, AZ: American Indian Rehabilitation and Training Center.

Thompson, M., Elis, R., & Wildavsky, A. (1990). *Cultural theory.* Boulder, CO: Westview Press.

4 Professional Helping Skills and Techniques

W H A T   Y O U   W I L L   L E A R N

1. Verbal and nonverbal relationship development skills
2. How to use relationship development skills in a culturally appropriate fashion
3. The types of interventions used by professional helpers

As noted in earlier chapters, professional helpers are increasingly involved with clients from different cultural backgrounds. As a result they must adjust their helping style and the techniques they use to the unique perspectives of each individual. They must also be sensitive to the unique needs and perspectives of lesbian and gay clients, clients who have physical and mental disabilities, clients of different ages ranging from 5 to 105, and clients from different socioeconomic backgrounds. In short, the art of helping has become increasingly complex, and helpers who take a "one size fits all" approach to helping is not likely to be successful. This chapter discusses the basic skills needed by effective helpers. Included in this discussion are suggestions for using these skills in a culturally appropriate fashion. Although many prospective helpers are interested primarily in the skills needed to be successful counselors or therapists, helpers must develop the ability to use a wide array of interventions because of the diversity of their clients. Almost all of these interventions require the counselor to apply the skills discussed in this chapter. Specific interventions used by helpers are discussed in later chapters.

Foundational Skills

Before proceeding complete the pretest shown in Exercise 4.1. The pretest is based partially on material found in Chapter 3. You may wish to review that chapter before continuing. The answers are discussed at the end of the chapter.

EXERCISE 4.1

Pretest

Assume that in your work as a helper you deal with many people from cultures other than your own. Answer each statement to the degree that it applies to you using the following key:

1 Strongly disagree
2 Disagree
3 It depends
4 Agree
5 Strongly agree

_____ 1. I can usually tell when something is bothering the people I interact with because they will usually display a sad or depressed manner.

_____ 2. I can usually tell how other people are reacting to me from their facial expressions.

_____ 3. When a person responds to my question with silence, it usually indicates that the person has not understood what I said but does not want to cause embarrassment to either of us by asking me to repeat the question.

_____ 4. What is not said in a conversation is often more important that what is expressed directly.

_____ 5. Laughter indicates that a person is happy and comfortable.

_____ 6. A person who does not maintain eye contact with me is not paying attention or may be showing lack of respect.

_____ 7. The external characteristics (such as skin color or clothing worn) of a person from another culture is not an important factor in what I think of her or him.

_____ 8. When talking with people whose first language is not English, I use lots of gestures and emphasis in my voice because these nonverbal clues will help me to be understood.

_____ 9. I usually try to keep the conversation active and lively because people will think I am not interested in them if I am silent.

_____10. I sometimes interrupt people in conversations to make sure I understand the point they are trying to make.

Adapted from Singelis, T. (1994). Nonverbal communication in intercultural interaction. In R.W. Brislin and T. Yoshida (Eds.), *Improving intercultural interaction: Modules for cross-cultural training programs* (pp. 269–270), Multicultural Aspects of Counseling Series 3. Thousand Oaks, CA: Sage. Used by permission of the publisher.

Foundational skills are those skills required for all types of interventions including individual, group, and family helping as well as consultation and collaboration with others. These skills can be divided into several categories:

1. attending skills;
2. reflection of verbal and emotional content;

3. structuring skills;
4. information eliciting techniques, such as asking questions;
5. summarization and transitional skills;
6. confrontational skills;
7. social influence skills, including the use of expertise, self-disclosure, warmth, and reinforcement;
8. diagnostic skills;
9. goal-setting skills;
10. skills that facilitate action taking, including intervention design and implementation, reinforcement and encouragement, facilitative self-disclosure, and feedback; and
11. evaluation and termination skills.

Before launching into a discussion of each of these categories of foundational skills, two important principles of helping must be introduced. The first relates to the comment in the first paragraph of the chapter regarding the necessity to avoid a "one size fits all" approach to helping. Helpers must learn that not all of the foundational skills discussed in this section are used with all clients or in all helping processes. It is the helper's responsibility to select and use those skills that facilitate, the helping process with each client (Ivey, 1994). Diller (1999, p. 19) sets forth this principle by stating, "Culturally skilled helpers are able to engage in a variety of verbal and nonverbal helping responses. They are not tied down to only one method or approach to helping but recognize that helping approaches are culture bound."

The second principle relates to the discernible stages that helping moves through. These typically called *relationship development* or *entry, assessment* or *diagnosis, goal setting, intervention selections and implementation,* and *evaluation and termination.* The second principle that helpers must recall is that not all foundational skills are appropriate for use at each stage of the helping process. It may be helpful for prospective helpers to conceptualize helping relationships using a dating metaphor. First dates are often uncomfortable for both parties. Certain rules apply if one wishes the dating relationship to continue, such as you do not criticize the clothing your date is wearing or complain because he or she is 15 minutes late for the date. As the dating process continues and the relationship between the dating couples is strengthened, the rules of dating change, including the rules that govern communication. For example, it may become permissible to suggest to one's date that he or she would look better in green than in red and that punctuality is expected.

Dating relationships are complex, but not nearly as complicated as helping relationships. Helpers who consider the unique characteristics of their clients and are sensitive to the status of the helping process are much more likely to succeed.

Attending Skills

Attending skills can be divided into two categories: nonverbal and verbal skills. Nonverbal attending skills include eye contact, the use of interpersonal space, body posture, and body movement such as head nods and hand gestures. The following guidelines for the use of nonverbal techniques in the helping process are based on literature reviews and research by Diller (1999), Okun, Fried, and Okun (1999), Kim, Shin, and Cai (1998), Lauver and Harvey (1997), Basso (1990), Sue and Sue (1990), Ho (1987) and the authors' experiences with clients from different cultures.

Verbal helping techniques include minimal encouragers such as *um-hmm;* brief nonjudgmental feedback such as *I understand, I see,* and *tell me more* (Lauver & Harvey, 1997); verbal tracking, which involves staying on the same topic as the client without interruption; and supportive silence (Ivey, 1994). Each of these nonverbal and verbal skills are discussed next.

Eye Contact.   Among white European Americans, it is expected that direct eye contact will be maintained, although intense eye contact is not considered appropriate. Among Native Americans, Hispanic Americans from lower socioeconomic groups, and Asian Americans, indirect eye contact is preferred. Hispanic Americans from middle- to upper-class backgrounds and African Americans also may engage in direct eye contact, although African Americans may avoid eye contact when the helper is speaking.

Recommendation.   If clients from other cultural groups avoid eye contact, respect their preference. Never maintain intense contact with any client, particularly Asian American and Native American clients who may consider this aggressive.

Interpersonal Space.   When conversing white European Americans and African Americans typically maintain a space of 36 to 42 inches. People from the Middle East (for example, Iran) and many Hispanic Americans are comfortable with closer interactions. Native Americans and Asian Americans prefer interaction distances that are somewhat farther apart than those that are standard among white European Americans.

Recommendation.   People adjust the interpersonal space by forward or backward body movement, moving their chairs forward or backward, or by turning to the side. If you observe that your client is working to adjust the interpersonal distance, do not counter by trying to restore the distance originally established.

Body Posture.   The traditional recommendation regarding body posture is that helpers should assume a SOLER position (Egan, 1994). This acronym stands for facing the client squarely (S) and openly (O), leaning (L) toward the client, maintaining eye contact (E), and assuming a relaxed (R) posture. As was just discussed, maintaining eye contact must vary with the cultural background of the client. However, the remainder of Egan's recommendations appears to be appropriate.

Recommendation.   Assume a relaxed, open posture, with a slight forward lean that maintains the appropriate interpersonal space between yourself and the client.

Body Movements and Gestures.   In white European American conversations, hand gestures, head nods, and smiles or other facial expressions are used frequently in day-to-day conversations. African Americans and some subgroups of Hispanic Americans are more animated in their use of gestures and expressive in the use of head nods and smiles. Generally speaking, Native Americans and Asian Americans are less expressive than other groups, but there are individuals who vary from this general rule. Among Asian Americans, smiles may signal discomfort rather than warmth or amusement.

Recommendation.   Limit hand gestures, smiles, and head nods until you get to know your clients.

Minimal Encouragers.   Minimal encouragers are used to convey to clients that the helper listening attentively and that they should proceed with whatever they are disclosing. Lauver and Harvey (1997) suggest that minimal encouragers should be brief and neutral. They recommend that minimal encouragers be brief so that they can be inserted into the helping conversation while clients are speaking. Although we agree that minimal encouragers should be brief, we recommend that they not be used while Asian Americans and Native Americans are speaking because these cultural groups view interruptions as rude. However, we do agree that minimal encouragers should be neutral. Examples of brief, neutral minimal encouragers include *I see, tell me more,* and *um-hmm.* Minimal encouragers that should be avoided, at least in the initial phases of helping, include value-laden comments such as *that's too bad, great, good,* and *that's terrible* (Lauver & Harvey, 1997).

Recommendation.   Verbal minimal encouragers that are neutral in nature can be used with most clients regardless of their cultural background. Because Native Americans and Asian Americans are less expressive it may be a good idea to use them sparingly and, as noted above, they should not be used with these groups while they are talking. Nonverbal minimal encouragers such as head nods can be used instead.

Tracking.   Verbal tracking involves staying on the client's topic (Ivey, 1994), which requires helpers to listen very carefully to what their clients are saying. Tracking also requires helpers to pay close attention to the nonverbal behavior of their clients. Professional helpers soon learn that clients may begin the helping conversation with one topic and abruptly shift to another topic once they become comfortable. For example, clients who come to university counseling centers may begin by discussing a relatively safe issue such as choosing a major or making a career choice and shift, sometimes without warning, to topics involving mental health or relationship concerns. Cues that clients have problems that are not routine can often be found in their nonverbal behavior. For example, clients who are anxious may clinch their fists, grip the arms of their chairs, kick their feet, tap their feet, or wrap their arms around their bodies in an attempt to control their nonverbal behavior. Many clients are anxious at the beginning of the helping process. If this anxiety does not dissipate, it may very well be the case that a shift in the presenting problem is about to occur.

Recommendation. Tracking what the client is saying verbally and nonverbally is an essential skill for helping all groups.

Supportive Silence. There are times in all helping relationships when clients need time to think or to deal with emotions such as sadness and anger. As Ivey (1994) notes, helpers must allow clients to gather their personal resources so that they can continue during these times. However, if the client becomes uncomfortable with the silence, as indicated by their nonverbal behavior, it is time to break the silence and move on.

Recommendation. When using supportive silence with white European Americans, African Americans, and middle-class Hispanic Americans, helpers should be alert to nonverbal cues such as shifts in posture and questioning looks that clients are uncomfortable with the silence. With all clients, it is appropriate to ask if they are ready to continue the helping interview.

Reflection of Verbal and Emotional Content

It is important to do more than simply listen and observe the client. Helpers must master techniques that allow them to convey that they have heard and understand what their clients have said. The ability to understand the internal frame of reference of a client is known as *empathy*. The technique that allows helpers to communicate their empathy is known as *reflection*. Reflection has two components: the paraphrase of the verbal content of what was said and the identification of the emotions underlying the verbal content. This technique is illustrated below.

> CLIENT: I'm so mad I could kill someone. I worked around the clock on that job and when they found out I've been in prison they canned me.
>
> HELPER: Because you have a prison record you feel that you have been treated unfairly, and that makes you very angry.
>
> CLIENT: You're damn right. (Sighs and drops his head. Voice trembles.) I just wonder if I'll ever get a break.
>
> HELPER: You're angry because of the way you have been treated, but you are also frustrated and maybe a bit scared because you are not sure whether things are going to get better.

Reflection, like many helping skills, was developed for use with white European Americans, African Americans, and Hispanic Americans. These groups are less concerned about self-control over their thoughts and emotions. Native Americans and Asian American clients, however, are generally very concerned with maintaining self-control, and reflecting feelings may embarrass or alienate them (Sue & Sue, 1990). When dealing with Asian Americans or Native Americans, use only reflection of content. Reflection of verbal and emotional content can be used with other groups as long as it appears to be acceptable. You can try your hand at reflecting content and emotion by completing Exercise 4.2.

Structuring Skills

Structuring skills include making preinterview contacts and completing "house-keeping chores" such as setting the time and place of the helping sessions, ascertaining clients' expectations about the nature of the helping process and the roles helpers and clients will have during helping, establishing confidentiality, setting initial goals, explaining techniques that will be used, and planning for emergencies that may arise during the process (Hutchins & Vaught, 1997).

Preinterview Contacts.   Preinterview contacts are not always made by helpers, particularly if they work in a community mental health center, a large private practice, a university counseling center, or in another large agency. Typically, clients telephone receptionists in these agencies to set up appointments. The

E X E R C I S E   **4.2**

Practicing Reflection of Verbal Content and Emotion

Complete this exercise by first identifying the verbal content in the each client's communication and then identifying the emotional content of what is being communicated. After completing the exercise, compare notes with one of your classmates.

Client: This chemotherapy is nasty stuff. I'm here in the hospital for 24 hours while they pour some stuff into my veins that the doctors say will burn your skin if it touches it. Then I have a radiation treatment. Then I'm sick for a week, and all I have to look forward to is coming back here. (Sighs.) Sometimes I wonder if it is worth it.

Verbal Content: _____

_____

Emotional Content: _____

_____

Client: It has been a long time since I have had that much fun with a man. You know how I have struggled since, well you know—the rape. I never thought that I would ever trust another man. God! It feels good to relax and just enjoy myself.

Verbal Content: _____

_____

Emotional Content:_____

_____

exception to this is when these agencies accept walk-in clients who are experiencing emergencies. In these cases, there is only minimal preinterview contact because the people who are in crisis are placed in the care of a helper. Helpers who work in social service agencies are more likely to make their own preinterview contacts, particularly if they are scheduling a home visit.

Regardless of who makes the preinterview contact, the structuring process should be started. During the first contact, the date, time, and place where the first meeting will occur should be established. Concerns about confidentiality preclude the collection of other types of information if the contact is with a receptionist. In those cases in which helpers contact clients to set up an initial interview, clients should be told the [reason for the information request] and then date, time, and place of the interview should be established.

Helpers often work in agencies such as schools, universities, and community mental health centers and, as result, schedule their helping sessions in their offices. While this may be efficient, it is not always the best setting for helping interviews, particularly when families are involved. Many clients do not have their own transportation. This may not pose a problem in cities in which public transportation is readily available, but in rural areas, clients who have no transportation are dependent on friends or family for transportation. Further, many clients have had negative experiences with schools or community agencies and may not wish to schedule sessions in them. Finally, people who have immigrated to this country have differing perceptions of the role of governmental agencies and schools and may be very uncomfortable with the idea of having a session in these offices. Since the first interview is crucial to the outcome of the helping enterprise, every effort should be made to insure that clients are comfortable with the setting. In many instances, this means meeting in client's homes or in neutral sites such as churches or community centers.

Although the matter of setting times for helping sessions seems like a routine matter, it is only routine if clients monitor time using watches and calendars and have the same personal rules regarding punctuality as the helper does. Many Native Americans, African Americans, rural white European Americans, and Hispanic Americans do not operate on the basis of these assumptions (Carter, 1991; Thomason, 1995; Sue & Sue, 1990). Therefore, when scheduling clients their time orientation should be taken into consideration.

Recommendation. Space the schedules of clients who may not operate on the same assumptions about punctuality as those of the broader society so that if they are late it will not interfere with other appointments. If possible, follow up after appointments are made with telephone reminders to clients about the time and place of their helping sessions.

Ascertaining Expectations about the Helping Process and Establishing Confidentiality.
Determining clients' expectations about the nature of helping and the roles of the helpers and clients in the process typically occurs during the first interview. Helpers should try to ascertain clients' expectations before sharing

their views regarding the nature of helping because some clients, such as recent immigrants to the United States from Southeast Asia or Mexico and some Native Americans, may accept helpers' views because they believe it is inappropriate to disagree with people in positions of authority (Attneave, 1969; Herring, 1996; Kim, Shin, & Cai, 1998). If clients' expectations can be ascertained, helpers' responsibilities lie with crafting a helping process that is culturally sensitive. If clients are from cultural groups that expect the helper to "be the authority" and explain the process to them (Sue & Sue, 1990), helpers should explain that helping is based on the unique needs of clients and is conducted in a manner that is respectful to their beliefs, customs, and traditions. Clients should also be told that they have the right to reject any of the approaches that may be used during the helping process.

Explaining confidentiality is an important part of setting expectations and the developing the helping relationship. All clients must be told about the helper's ethical obligation to keep information in confidence and the legal and ethical exceptions to keeping information confidential. For example, clients should be told that helpers are legally obligated to report child abuse and that they are ethically bound to break confidentiality when clients may harm themselves or others. In groups, clients need to be aware that only helpers are obligated to keep information shared by clients confidential, and thus confidentiality cannot be guaranteed (ASGW, 1989). It is particularly important to tell and then reinforce the concept with Asian Americans (Kim, 1996) because they may be more fearful than most clients that information will be disclosed.

Recommendation. Prepare a written statement that outlines the helping process, the roles of the helper and client, and confidentiality policy. If clients from different cultures are seen routinely, different statements may be used for each group, although issues of confidentiality should not vary in these statements. Prepare these statements in both English and the native languages of the clients who come for assistance.

Setting Initial Goals. Establishing the initial goals of the helping process begins when clients are asked to indicate what they expect to accomplish during the helping process. Helpers may wish to comment on the appropriateness of the goal if it does not correspond to their expectations. Clients should also be apprised of the cost of the helping process if fees are involved.

Recommendation. In so far as possible collect as much information about the clients as possible prior to the initial interview. By knowing the client's background helpers may be better able to assist them in goal setting.

Explaining Techniques and Strategies. From an ethical standpoint, clients have a right to know what they will experience during the helping process. From a practical point of view, it is unwise to surprise clients with strategies that may make them uncomfortable or, worse, alienate them and cause them to terminate the helping process. Intrusive techniques such as guided imagery that require clients to imagine a series of scenes that are suggested by the helper, dream analysis, hypnosis, and any technique that requires a great deal of disclosure about self or family members should be avoided. So should techniques that require clients to identify their thoughts if the clients have a high level of concern about self-control. Asian Americans and Native Americans especially may fall into this category. Confrontive strategies such as challenging irrational beliefs (Ellis, 1995) should probably be avoided with these groups as well as with many Hispanic American clients (Altaribba & Bauer, 1998). However, if these strategies are to be used they should be carefully explained and the client's permission obtained before using them. Group helpers also need to make clients aware what techniques will be employed in the group as well as the expectation that the group members will self-disclose.

Recommendation. Prepare a handout to give to clients that describe the techniques that will be used in the helping process. Like the disclosure statement just described, this statement probably should be individualized for different clients.

Planning for Emergencies. Clients come to the helping process with problems that vary tremendously in their intensity and seriousness. Families may be experiencing minor childrearing problems or may be abusive. Individuals may be suffering from mild psychological discomfort because of an immediate problem or they may be suffering from severe psychological distress because of chronic psychological problems. Between sessions, problems may worsen and emergencies arise. Therefore, a part of the structuring process should be to make clients aware of the steps that they should take if emergencies arise. Some agencies have a person on call at all times so that clients have access to round-the-clock assistance. Other agencies advise their clients to report to the emergency room of a local hospital when emergencies arise. In any event, for both ethical and legal reasons, clients need to be apprised of the steps to take if an emergency arises.

Recommendation. Include directions for getting help during emergencies in the disclosure statement given to clients. Review those directions and check for understanding in the initial interview. For those clients who seem likely to require emergency help, such as clients with suicidal ideation, review the steps to take should a need for emergency services arise on a continuing basis.

A sample of an initial helping interview follows. As you read the interview, note the structuring statements made by the helper. Also note the use of attending skills.

> HELPER: (Gets up from seat.) Good morning. I'm delighted to see you this morning. Please come in and have a seat. That chair is quite comfortable. May I get you something to drink? It's a hot day, and I know you came in on the bus.

CLIENT: (Sitting down.) No, thank you. It is hot, but the receptionist gave me a drink when I came in.

HELPER: We have 45 minutes together today, and I want to start by telling you about my policy regarding confidentiality (Helper explains confidentiality and checks for understanding. She also gives the client a copy of the policy.) Now, what brings you to see me?

CLIENT: I'm not sure. I know things aren't going so well in my life. I seem to have no energy and all I want to do is sleep. It was a struggle getting up this morning to come to see you, and some of the thoughts that I have been having worry me.

HELPER: Life is a bit of a struggle for you right now. Tell me about the thoughts you are having.

CLIENT: Well—(Hesitates.)

HELPER: Take your time. (Silence.)

CLIENT: (Tears begin to flow.) I'm thinking I should just give up. I'm never going to get what I want out of life.

HELPER: It makes you sad when you think about your future, and there are times when you think it may better to give up. (Helper conducts a suicide assessment at this point and, because the client has active thoughts about suicide, asks her to sign a contract in which she agrees not to take her own life.)

HELPER: I am confident that if we work together we can deal with your problem. Let me tell you what I propose. First, I would like to refer you to a psychiatrist so that we can get you on an antidepressant.

CLIENT: I don't like the idea of taking medicine.

HELPER: Taking medicine for problems such as yours bothers a lot of people, but I hope you will agree to do it. It will speed the process of making you feel better about yourself and allow us to be successful in a shorter period of time.

CLIENT: (Nods assent.)

HELPER: I also want to propose that the next time we meet we begin to look at your thoughts about your future, yourself, and why you think things aren't going to change. I'll also want you to keep a daily diary of some of your negative and positive thoughts. These strategies are explained in this brochure. (Hands her the brochure.) I don't want to do anything that will make you uncomfortable, so I hope you will read these so that we can discuss them next time.

CLIENT: I think it will be a relief to talk to someone about my thoughts.

HELPER: Yes, I think it will too, and I look forward to talking more about it next time. I propose that we meet once a week on this same day and at this time. I anticipate that it may take seven or eight months to complete our work, but that is only if we both work very hard.

CLIENT: That sounds fine.

HELPER: Finally, I want to review how you can get help if your problem begins to feel like it is overwhelming you and you need immediate help. (Explains procedure and gives client directions for getting help in an emergency.)

Information Eliciting Techniques

Many helpers use a cliché that states the obvious: You cannot solve problems that you do not understand. To understand a client's problem, the helper must know the *what* (the problem), *why* (the factors that motivate the client to act as he or she does), *when* (time that problem occurs), *where* (place that problem occurs), and *with whom* the problem occurs (the people involved). Unfortunately, few clients are able to provide the information that helpers need without assistance. Providing this assistance requires helpers to elicit information if the clients' disclosures do not allow them to understand the problem. Once again, the helper's choice of which information eliciting techniques to use depends on the cultural background of the client. Techniques that require clients to discuss their thoughts and feelings should not be used with unacculturated Asian Americans and many Native Americans (Sue & Sue, 1990). However, it is appropriate to ask what they did, that is, to focus on their behavior in most instances. The types of information gathering techniques that helpers must master include the use of open and closed questions, open-ended leads, and some specialized techniques such as play strategies when dealing with children.

Questions.   Closed questions require one-word or very short answers. Use only closed questions only when ascertaining specific information. Some examples of closed questions are:

> How old are you?
> Where were you born?
> How many brothers and sisters do you have?

Open-ended questions require clients to provide longer, more thoughtful answers and are generally preferred because they require less effort by the helper and because they place the onus of providing information on the client. Most helpers also prefer them because they provide a stimulus that allows the clients to respond by giving the information that is most important to them. Some examples of open questions are:

How have you tried to adapt to the loss of your spouse?
What are the most important things that have happened to you in your life?
If you could change your life, what changes would you make?

Open-Ended Leads.   Open-ended leads, like open questions, prompt clients to provide more information, but provide less specificity about the nature of the information to be provided. Some examples of open-ended leads are:

Tell me about yourself.
Tell me about your family.
Tell me about your plans for the future.

Specialized Information Gathering Techniques.   Helpers who work with children often need to use specialized information gathering strategies such as play media. Very shy children may talk to the helper using a toy telephone when they will not disclose information in face-to-face conversations. Some children can be prompted to disclose information through drawings, particularly when the helper models what is expected. A helper may ask a child to draw a picture of his or her home and family while completing the same exercise alongside the child. After the drawings are complete, the helper may begin the information gathering process by telling the child about his or her own picture. The child is then asked to tell about his or her picture. The use of play techniques as a tool to collect verbal data should not be confused with play therapy. Art therapists look for patterns such as the size of the drawings and the spatial relationships of the figures in the drawings as a way of understanding children. There are many other specialized information gathering techniques that can be used with children and adults such as role-playing psychodrama, which describes interpersonal interactions on a scene-by-scene basis to provide structure for the information gathering process.

Recommendation.   Be careful about using intrusive information gathering strategies with clients who will be offended or alienated by them. In the event the helper is uncertain about the use of a strategy, he or she should ask the client if the techniques would make them uncomfortable.

Summarization and Transitional Skills

Helping moves through overlapping and, in some instances, recurring stages beginning with relationship development. Helpers must be able to bring closure to topics and facilitate the transition to the next stage. This is typically done using summarizations and transitional statements. Some immature helpers worry that they will try to push the helping process too quickly and alienate the client. Although this is a possibility, most clients take their cues from the helper. Additionally, helpers have limited amounts of time with clients because of their workloads, agency policies, and the fact that some health insurers will pay for only a limited number of sessions. If the helping process has time limitations, these should be made clear in the structuring that occurs early in the helping process.

Summaries and Transitional Statements.   Ivey (1994) indicates that summaries are attempts on the part of helpers to communicate to clients they have been heard and understood. Although this is an accurate description of the role of summaries in helping, it is too limited. Summaries are tentative statements made by the helper about some aspect of the *what, why, when, where,* and *with whom* nature of the client's problems. When summaries are used, helpers expect the client to agree or disagree, with silence usually being interpreted by the helper as assent if the client is African American, white European American, or middle-class Hispanic American. With other groups of clients, the helper should check the accuracy of their summaries by asking if they represent the client's view of the situation. When there is agreement between helper and client, the team can explore the next area or pursue the next phase of helping. The following are examples of summaries that might be used at different stages in the helping process with the client in the sample initial interview on pages 83–85. The transitional statements included might be used to facilitate movement toward problem resolution.

Summary 1 Nearing the End of the Relationship Stage. "It sounds like you had a very turbulent childhood and some of that turbulence has continued into your adult life. You have had one marriage fail, you cannot get a job in your preferred field, and your current relationship isn't working out very well either. I'm wondering if you would share when you first began to have these feelings of depression."

Summary 2 At the End of the Assessment Stage. "Thank you for sharing with me your thoughts about yourself, about your future, and the people around you. Let me see if I can capture what you have said. First, you cannot shake the idea that you are worthless because in your mind you have failed repeatedly. The future seems gloomy because you see yourself as powerless to change either yourself or the partners that you seem to attract. (Pause) How would you like to change some of your thinking?"

Recommendation. Do not assume that silence means that the client agrees with the summary. Ask if the summary is accurate, particularly when dealing with Asian American, Native American, and recently arrived or lower socioeconomic Hispanic American clients. Even when clients in these groups agree with the summary, be alert for evidence such as nonverbal cues that the summary was incorrect.

Confrontational Skills

Confrontation is the process of pointing out discrepancies in clients' behavior. These discrepancies may involve either verbal or nonverbal behaviors. Discrepancies occur in the following situations.

1. The client tells two different versions of an event. Example: In the first session, client reports that her mother often yells at her. In the second session, she tells how well her mother treats her.

2. The client states one thing and does another. Example: A probationer tells how important it is to do well in school and then cuts school three days in a row.

3. The client states one thing and subtle nonverbal behavior suggest otherwise. Example: The client tells how happy she is to be caring for her elderly mother, but both fists are clenched, indicating that the idea makes her anxious.

Confrontations should always be done tentatively and with caring and respect. Aggressive statements about the discrepancies in client behavior that helpers observe should be avoided. Helpers may directly identify the discrepancies they observe so long as the statements are buffered by tentativeness, as an hypothesis about the discrepancy. Helpers may also engage clients in self-confrontation, a technique that is illustrated later. Another type of confrontation that can be used is to point out the discrepancy along with an interpretation of why the discrepancy is occurring. Of these approaches, directly and aggressively pointing out the discrepancy and interpreting why the discrepancy is occurring have the greatest potential to negatively impact the helping relationship. Carkhuff (1984) notes that confrontation is a risky technique and suggests that helpers who use it be prepared to rebuild their helping relationships if clients respond defensively. Although Ivey (1994) rightly notes that confrontation is one of the techniques that can assist clients in beginning the process of identifying their own incongruities, it can also alienate them. When clients are defensive, helpers should allow them to vent their feelings and use reflective techniques to communicate to them that they are being heard and understood. This is not a time for probing questions such as, "Why are you angry?" It is a time for helpers to reassure their clients that they care. Later, the helper and client can explore together the reasons for the defensive reaction.

The following confrontational statements contrast the use of tentative, caring statements with direct, more aggressive statements.

- *Direct Statement:* In the last two sessions, you have presented two views of your mother. One view is that she is a "bitchy woman," and the other is that she is loving and caring.
- *Tentative Statement:* You seem to be ambivalent about your mother. You have described her both as a "bitchy woman" and as a caring mother.
- *Direct Statement:* On several occasions you have told me that you know school is important. However, I received a call from your school telling me that you had cut classes the last three days.
- *Tentative Statement:* I'm a little confused about your feelings about school. On one hand, you tell me that you want to do well in school, and on the other, I get a report that you missed three days of school. Help me straighten this matter out.

Engaging clients in self-confrontation can also be used to point out discrepancies in behavior. The following vignette illustrates the use of self-confrontation. *Vignette 1:* Client is a parent who wants her children to grow up to be responsible, caring, and organized, but because of guilt growing out of her failed marriage, she is inconsistent in her behavior with her children. She "lays down the law" but then feels bad and picks up the children's clothes, makes their beds, and generally relaxes her expectations for them. *Self-confrontation:* You have said that your guilt results in some inconsistent behavior when it comes to disciplining your children, but you have also said that you want your children to grow up to be mature, responsible adults. How do you think your inconsistent behavior is influencing your children?

The third type of confrontation involves direct labeling of the basis for the discrepancies that occur in the client's behavior. The following confrontation illustrates this approach.

Helper: In some sessions you talk about how little attention your husband pays you, and in others you seem to have decided that he isn't that inattentive after all. It seems to me that you vacillate between these two positions because you are afraid of being on your own.

Recommendation. Directly pointing out discrepancies in behavior or pointing them out with interpretations should not be used with Asian Americans, most Hispanic Americans, or Native Americans unless they are fully acculturated. Direct confrontation is for the most part unacceptable in these groups. Although there is no empirical support for its use, the less direct approach of engaging clients from these groups of clients in self-confrontation can be tried sparingly as a last resort if confrontation is required.

Social Influence Skills

Helping is first and foremost a process involving social influence, that is, it is a process that requires helpers to use their interpersonal and helping skills to influence their clients to explore and deal with their concerns. Although the basis of helpers' social influence can be thought of in several ways, we prefer to think of it as the exercise of two types of power: referent power and expertise power. *Referent power* develops as a result of two interrelated factors: the personal characteristics of the helper and the ability of the helper to communicate with the client in a meaningful fashion. Many of the helping skills already discussed, such as attending skills and the use of reflective techniques, are important in the development of referent power. Helpers' warmth, that is their ability to communicate through their nonverbal behavior that they are genuinely concerned about the client, also plays a role in the development of referent power. Helpers who are ready to greet their clients, attend to them in a culturally appropriate fashion, use reflective and other helping techniques appropriately, and show respect for the background of their clients are likely to develop the form of social influence described here as referent power.

Another type of power needed by helpers is expertise power. Helpers, depending on their roles, need different types of knowledge. Social workers need to understand the laws governing areas such as child abuse and how clients qualify for Medicaid, affordable housing, and Aid for Dependent Children. Rehabilitation counselors need to be familiar with the types of aid available for students with different disabilities, ways of assessing disabilities, and how to set up structured work experiences for clients with mental disabilities. Parole and probation officers must be familiar with the penal codes as they relate to children and adults. Substance abuse counselors must be familiar with the physiological and psychological impact of drugs on the body, how illegal and prescription drugs interact, and penal codes pertaining to the use and possession of illegal substances. Clients are unlikely to be impressed or influenced by helpers who do not have the knowledge needed to assist them with some of the technical problems they bring to the helping process.

Helpers must be aware that, beginning with the first contact with their clients, they are involved in a subtle process that is aimed at persuading clients to change. Being skilled in the use of helping techniques is only one aspect of the process. Helpers who have the technical expertise needed to assist clients to deal with their concerns have the other component of social influence.

Diagnostic Skills

Chapter 5 is designed to assist prospective helpers begin the process of learning how to distinguish between clients who have mental disorders and those who do not. Clearly, a single chapter will not provide the background needed to fully understand human behavior. Helpers need to complete the process by studying a wide array of additional material including abnormal psychology, developmental psychology, family functioning, and objective and projective personality assessment to hone their diagnostic skills. The objective of this training is to assist helpers develop clinical judgment. Helpers use their clinical judgment to collect, interpret, and ultimately to draw conclusions about the functioning of their clients. In this process, they draw on their training and experience as well as information provided by diagnostic tools such as the *Diagnostic and Statistical Manual of Mental Disorders* (4th ed., rev., 1994) (DSM-IV-R) to diagnose clients' problems. This diagnosis provides the basis for the treatment that will follow. Consider the following clients.

- Matt, a 4-year-old, started wetting the bed after the birth of his sister.
- Chevette, a 10-year-old girl, has started having nightmares. When she wakes up, she "sees" eyes looking at her from the wall and ceiling.
- Janet, 24, recently gave birth to her first child. She has found herself avoiding elevators and experiencing unexplainable anxiety.
- Gerrard, a 60-year-old retired pilot, became impotent a few weeks after his retirement.

■ Callie, a 51-year-old career woman, cannot seem to get herself motivated, and her performance ratings at work have fallen to the point that she is in danger of losing her job.

The helper's responsibility is to make sense of these presenting problems and work to eliminate them or to reduce the suffering that results. As noted above, helpers may use information that requires extensive training to interpret, such as the results of projective assessment such as the Rorschach or objective personality inventories such as the Minnesota Multiphasic Personality Inventory. However, most helpers rely on one or more of the following sources of data to diagnose the nature of the problem: thoughts, behavior, emotions, and background information. Consider the data that you already have about the clients just described plus the information presented in Table 4.1.

As can be seen in Table 4.1, different pieces of information provide varying perspectives regarding clients' problem. Since it is next to impossible to ascertain clients' thoughts before the age of seven, the helper must make a decision about Matt based on his behavior and some rudimentary data about his feelings. This information can be ascertained by interviewing Matt directly or by interviewing his mother. It seems clear that Matt's bed-wetting is due to the fact that he was poorly prepared for the birth of a sibling, and perhaps partially the result of receiving less attention from his parents and others who come to the house to see the new baby. Chevette's problem is more complex, but both her current behavior and a past event, sexual molestation, provide clues that she may be suffering from posttraumatic stress disorder. Additional data collection about her behavior and thoughts would be needed before drawing a final conclusion about

TABLE 4.1 Diagnostic Information for Five Clients

Client	Behavior	Thoughts	Emotions	Background
Matt	Bed-wetting	Not discernible	Does not like baby	Only child before birth of baby; not prepared for event
Chevette	Nightmares; sees things	Does not understand why	Afraid to go to sleep	Sexually molested when she was seven
Janet	Avoids elevators	Life is too good; something bad will happen	Fearful, anxious	Mother had same problem
Gerrard	Impotent	Can't explain why; never had problem	Depressed	Little preparation for retirement
Callie	Poor work habits	Work has lost its meaning	Depressed	Always wanted children; entering menopause

her problem. Janet is fearful her happiness will be interrupted by a tragic event, a superstitious belief that she probably learned from her mother. Gerrard's identity was tied to his work role as an airline pilot, which is one reason he failed to prepare himself for retirement, which is mandatory at age 60. His reaction, impotence, is not altogether uncommon. Finally, Callie had largely suppressed her dreams of having children as she pursued her career. The onset of menopause was a signal that she could no longer have children and that her long-suppressed dream would never be fulfilled.

Ultimately, helpers' theoretical orientations to helping determine what types of data are used in the diagnostic process and whether a diagnosis is needed at all. In a few instances, such as person-centered approach to counseling and psychotherapy (Rogers, 1951), the helper does not diagnose. In other approaches, such as traditional psychoanalysis (Freud, 1949), helpers rely extensively on historical information and material evoked from the client's unconscious to make their diagnoses. Other helpers, particularly those operating from a behavioral theoretical orientation (e.g., Kazdin, 1994), use observable behavior as the basis for their assessment of their clients' problems.

The Cultural Context of Diagnosis.   Regardless of helpers' theoretical orientations, the diagnosis of their clients' problems must take their cultural background into consideration. In the dominant culture, the common belief is that mental health problems are the result of the twin influences of nature and nurture. Natural influences stem from genetically predisposed factors that increase the likelihood that clients will develop problems such as depression or schizophrenia. Nurture or environmental variables are also viewed as factors that influence mental health problems. For example, childhood abuse has been linked to a variety of mental health problems including becoming a serial killer, but not all children who are abused develop mental health problems.

We have cultural beliefs about the causes of mental health problems. We also have cultural views about what constitutes a mental health problem, the stigma associated with having a mental health problem, and the way people with these problems should be treated. Beliefs about what constitutes a mental health problem at this time are codified in the DSM-IV-R. It is noteworthy that this manual is being revised on a more or less continuous basis. During revisions mental health problems are redefined, new ones are added, and problems deleted because they are no longer viewed as mental health problems. Homosexuality was once classified as a mental health problem, and psychotherapists actively engaged in conversion therapy designed to cure the "problem." Not only has homosexuality been deleted from manuals such as the DSM-IV-R, it is now viewed as unethical to engage in conversion therapy by almost all groups of professional helpers.

Although the stigma placed on people with mental health problems has lessened over the past two hundred years, people with mental health problems are still stigmatized to varying degrees. Similarly, the treatment of people with mental health problems has evolved from the "snake pits" of the nineteenth century where people were confined in dreary institutions with little hope of release to a situation where most people with mental health problems are treated on an outpatient basis. However, the treatment of mental health problems is rarely given the same priority as the treatment of physical ailments. Probably the best support for this point can be found in the policies of many health insurers, who place severe limits on the amount of money they will pay for mental health services.

Clients from other cultural groups who are unacculturated, that is, have not adopted a Western European perspective, are unlikely to share the views of mental health just outlined. For example, some Korean Americans and Native Americans may attribute the development of mental health problems to supernatural forces, while other Native Americans may believe that people with mental health problems are out of touch with nature (Herring, 1996; Kim, 1996). Further, the stigma attached to people associated with mental health problems is likely to vary among cultural groups. Asian American families may feel shame because a family member has a mental health problem, and members who have strong feelings and emotions that might bring shame to the family are expected to restrain those feelings (Leong & Chou, 1996). Because of the shame associated with having a mental health problem and cultural beliefs about the importance of self-control, Asian American clients who do ask for help are more likely to discuss their symptoms in terms of bodily complaints than they are to talk about their thoughts and feelings (Draguns, 1990). Many Native Americans also may be hesitant to report their thoughts and feelings, making it more difficult for helpers who are unfamiliar with their culture to accurately diagnose their mental health problems. Finally, clients from different cultures will have varying perceptions of the treatment of mental health problems. Although there is evidence that some minority groups are increasingly turning to professional sources for help with their mental health problems (LaFromboise & Young, 1996), some Native Americans may wish turn to tribal healers and rituals such as sand paintings in an effort to regain their connection to nature. Others may wish to pursue nontraditional helping strategies by communicating through a third party instead of face to face (Kim, 1996).

Recommendation.   Helpers should develop assumptions about the causes, perceptions, and treatment of mental health problems based on the cultural background and current values of their clients.

Goal-Setting Skills

Assisting clients to set goals begins with an accurate assessment of their mental health problems. Once the problem assessment is complete and the helper and client agree on the nature of the problem, goal setting can begin. However, the use of goals in the helping process is not restricted to theoretical approaches that engage in formal assessment of diagnosis. Some of the brief approaches to helping begin the process by asking the client, "What would your life be like if the problem you just presented to me was solved?" The vision of a life free of the presenting problem then becomes the goal of the helping process.

As during diagnosis, the extent to which helpers from different theoretical orientations engage in goal setting varies widely. Person-centered helpers do not engage in formal goal setting, while behavioral helpers establish very specific goals for the change of observable behavior. Goals should have two characteristics: they should be attainable within certain practical time limits and their attainment should be measurable. If more than one goal is to be pursued, goals should be prioritized.

Long-term helping relationships—that is, relationships that last more than a few months, are increasingly rare. It is difficult to imagine a brief helping strategy that is not predicated on practical goals. Moreover, there must be some relatively simple way to measure goal attainment. Counselors who work in employment agencies usually have the same goal: to find their clients jobs. Measuring the success or failure to attain this goal poses no problem. On the other hand, whether the goal of increasing the self-esteem of clients has been attained is more difficult to measure, although it is not impossible. Other common goals of helping that can be measured include reducing anxiety, increasing the quality of the relationship between partners, decreasing depression, increasing grades, and decreasing aggressive behavior.

Clients often have a number of issues, and therefore a number of goals, that need to be addressed during the helping process. For example, a parolee may need to learn anger management skills, develop better work habits, and become more assertive so that he or she can resist peer pressure to commit crimes in the future. Once the client and helper identify the areas that need to be addressed, they should establish the order in which to address them. The exception to this rule occurs when one of the areas the client needs to address has immediate, critical consequences. In the case of the parolee, work habits might be addressed first solely because he or she is about to lose employment or is violating parole requirements.

Recommendation.   Helpers should aid clients to establish specific, attainable goals and, if necessary, to assist them in prioritizing those goals.

Skills That Facilitate Action Taking

To be successful, clients usually must take action to solve the problems that brought them to a helper in the first place. To facilitate this process, helpers must help clients design interventions, prepare them to act on them, and provide the support they need as they move forward with the interventions chosen.

Designing Action Steps and Preparing Clients.   As would be expected on the basis of the earlier discussion in this chapter, two major factors play an important role in the design of interventions: the theoretical orientation of the helper and

the cultural background of the client. Table 4.2 presents guidelines for preparing culturally sensitive interventions.

The information contained in Table 4.2 should make it clear that helpers cannot use one theoretical orientation as the basis for the design of interventions. Clients may be alienated by interventions that include confrontive strategies, intrusive strategies that require them to disclose thoughts and feelings, or assertive strategies that require them to deal directly with problems.

Recommendation. An eclectic approach, that is, an approach that relies on a number of theoretical perspectives, should be adopted by helpers who expect to be successful with a multicultural clientele.

Providing Reinforcement and Encouragement. Once clients are engaged in the change process, helpers may use a variety of supportive strategies including

TABLE 4.2   **Designing Culturally Sensitive Interventions**

Group	Interventions
White, European Americans	Interventions requiring disclosure of thoughts and feelings, confrontive interventions, assertion training, time-oriented interventions such as behavioral contracts, and interventions that require independent decision-making are acceptable.
Native Americans	Focus on behavior change that is oriented more to events than to specific times (Brown, 1997). Involve entire extended family, including tribal members, in the process if possible (Herring, 1996). Avoid affective interventions and those that require independent decision-making, assertiveness, or the disclosure of thoughts and feelings.
Hispanic Americans	Family interventions can be used successfully with Hispanic Americans. Interventions that increase harmony and connectedness are likely to be more successful. Interventions that focus on thoughts and feelings can also be used successfully. Avoid assertion training and interventions that require independent decision-making. Also avoid confrontive interventions such as those requiring the labeling of irrational thoughts (Altarriba & Bauer, 1998).
African Americans	The interventions typically used with white, European Americans can be used if a sound relationship can be established.
Asian Americans	Focus on behavior change that is oriented to time and that calls little attention to the client. Also, family interventions can be used, but helpers should recall that many Asian American families (for example, Korean) families have a hierarchical power structure. In these cases, use interventions that defer to the hierarchy. Avoid interventions that require democratic action, assertiveness, independent action, or the disclosure of thoughts and feelings (Kim, 1996)

many of those already discussed. However, helpers should also encourage and positively reinforce clients as they move through the change process. Encouragement is the process of expressing confidence in the ability of clients to perform certain tasks. A helper who uses encouragement might say to a client, "I'm sure you will be able to deal with your anger the next time somebody calls you a name." "I know that you have had a difficult time communicating with your father, but I am confident that you can improve your relationships." Encouragement takes place before action-taking and focuses on the individual's potential. Positive reinforcement praises the effort and outcome. For example, a helper might say, "I'm very proud of you for going home when your friends wanted you to stay out after your curfew." Helpers use both of these supportive mechanisms, but encouragement is likely to be more acceptable to Native Americans and Asian Americans because it focuses on potential and not individual accomplishment (Brown, 1997). Of course, encouragement can be used with groups and families. For example, an entire family could be told, "I have great faith in your ability to come together and work out your problems" or "I think that what you have accomplished as a family in a short time is terrific."

Recommendation.   Supportive strategies such as encouragement and reinforcement should be used only if they are acceptable to the client.

Facilitative Self-Disclosure.   In this context, facilitative self-disclosure means self-disclosure by the helper that facilitates action-taking on the part of the client. Helping conversations usually focus on the thoughts, behaviors, and emotions of the client. However, when helpers have had experiences that parallel those of the client, they may wish to share their thoughts and feelings about the situations that they encountered and the actions (behaviors) they took in response. Self-disclosure usually begins with the personal pronoun *I* and continues as the helper tells about his or her thoughts, feelings, and actions. For example, a client who is trying to decide what to do with a child who acts out might be told, "I had the same problem with my oldest child and found it very upsetting. I found that the best thing that I could do was to set rules with him before the behavior occurred so I did not have to get involved in discipline when I was frustrated or angry."

Recommendation.   Facilitative self-disclosure should be used sparingly and should be used only when the disclosure is directly related to the issues being faced by the client.

Feedback.   Feedback is information regarding the helper's perceptions of the client. Feedback should focus on strengths, be specific, and be as nonjudgmental as possible (Ivey, 1994) and should be positive to increase its acceptance. Often feedback is provided at the request of the client. An example of feedback might be, "Based on my observation, you can be quite abrasive. Sometimes you are pretty loud and you make remarks about things such as people's weight that makes them defensive. I wonder if that accounts for your inability to maintain friendships." Negative feedback in individual helping either should not be used or should be made as positive as possible for clients, who otherwise may feel that they have lost face with the helper because they are viewed negatively. Negative feedback should never be used in groups or families with this type of client.

Recommendation. Feedback may begin by asking clients to tell what they think about their thoughts, feelings, and behavior, particularly if there is a concern about the clients' willingness to accept negative feedback. Also, use the positive, negative, positive approach to providing negative feedback. Say something positive, then provide the negative feedback, and end with something positive. Do not provide negative feedback to clients who may perceive that they have lost face if they are perceived negatively by you.

Evaluation and Termination Skills

Helping processes are terminated by helpers under three conditions. First, helpers are ethically obligated to terminate their efforts when clients' problems require the use of skills that they have not mastered. This does not mean that these clients should be "abandoned" because this is also unethical. Helpers who find that the challenges presented by their clients exceed their skills should find other helpers who can provide the needed assistance and make referrals. Second, referrals may also need to be made when agency policy or other factors limit the number of sessions that clients can be offered and forces termination before a client's problems has been resolved. As shown in Case Illustration 4.1, failure to make an appropriate referral can have legal consequences for the helper. Third, helping is terminated when clients have attained their goals.

The skills required at the termination of helping are (1) to identify the progress that has been made by clients (evaluation), (2) to identify individuals and agencies that can continue the helping process that that the helper has begun, and (3) to facilitate the transfer of clients to referral resources. Skill one, evaluating the clients' progress toward the goals that have been established, requires helpers to devise strategies to evaluate goal attainment. After the intervention is implemented, helpers and clients continue to meet to monitor and reinforce the clients' progress, redesign the intervention as necessary, and evaluate the outcome. They may also agree on what constitutes success or failure.

Probably the single most controversial issue regarding the outcome of helping is the selection of criteria to be used to determine the success or failure of the process. Behavioral helpers (for example, Kazdin, 1994) use elaborate research strategies to evaluate the outcomes of their work. Their designs begin with using an observational system to determine how often a behavior is occurring, implementing the intervention, and continuing to collect data about the behavior. Their designs usually are referred to as *single-subject designs* (Heppner, Kivlighan, & Wampold, 1999). Once the target behavior is reached, the intervention is withdrawn and helping is terminated. The result of this empirical approach to evaluation is a numerical description of the outcome of helping. Unfortunately, many types of helping do not lend themselves to the type of quantification called for in single-subject evaluation designs. A quite different approach to evaluating consultation is qualitative research. "Qualitative research involves understanding the complexity of people's lives by examining individual perspectives in context" (Heppner et al., 1999). Qualitative research typically is not concerned about cause and effect relationships. Rather, it focuses on reality as it is constructed by the helper and client and may involve strategies that require both people to write a description of their views of the helping process. Qualitative research results in a verbal description of the process and the outcomes of helping.

Referral resources, which are identified on an ongoing basis, include individuals such as physicians, members of the clergy, and helpers in private practice and agencies such as departments of health, shelters for battered women, abortion clinics, charitable organizations such as the Salvation Army, facilities that specialize in treating alcoholics and substance abusers, and law enforcement agencies. Facilitating the transfer of clients to referral resources may be as simple as providing a telephone number and an address or as complex as making the appointment and providing transportation.

Recommendation.   Helpers should prepare clients for termination during the early phases of helping and should terminate as soon as they and the clients believe the goals that have been established have been attained. For example, if the number of helping contacts is limited by agency policy, clients should be told this at the outset.

CASE   ILLUSTRATION   **4.1**

The Consequences of Failing to Terminate Properly

Mr. Z was a law student at a major university. He was being treated for paranoid schizophrenia by a psychiatrist in the University Health Service who retired at the end of the spring semester. During the subsequent summer, Mr. Z stopped taking his prescribed medication, which controlled his delusions that he could read people's minds and his paranoia that certain people were out to get him. A few weeks later, he armed himself with a rifle and walked from his apartment to the center of town, shooting people as he went. He killed one person and wounded two others. He was tried for murder and found not guilty by reason of insanity. Consequently, Mr. Z sued his psychiatrist for failing to adequately inform him of the seriousness of his problem and failing to refer him to another mental health practitioner. The jury found on behalf of Mr. Z and awarded him $500,000 in damages.

Return to the Pretest

Early in this chapter you were asked to complete a pretest regarding your helping style. The questions included in that pretest follow, along with some brief discussion of the appropriate answers.

1. I can usually tell when something is bothering the people I interact with because they will usually display a sad or depressed manner. **Answer:** People from some cultures do not readily show their emotions. If they do, it may be inappropriate to recognize them.

2. I can usually tell how other people are reacting to me from their facial expressions. **Answer:** Not all people show how they react to other people.

3. When a person responds to my question with silence, it usually indicates that the person has not understood what I said but does not want to cause embarrassment to either of us by asking me to repeat the question. **Answer:** Clients from different cultures may be simply contemplating the nature of the questions and thus do not respond immediately. Repeating a question is viewed as inappropriate in some cultures.

4. What is not said in a conversation is often more important that what is expressed directly. **Answer:** Hopefully you strongly agreed with this statement. Clients from some cultures do not communicate directly and may not disclose intimate details about themselves or their families.

5. Laughter indicates that a person is happy and comfortable. **Answer:** This statement is false. For example, Asian Americans may laugh when they are uncomfortable, and white European Americans and others laugh nervously at times.

6. A person who does not maintain eye contact with me is not paying attention or may be showing lack of respect. **Answer:** This statement is false. Only white European Americans are apt to maintain a high level of eye contact.

7. The external characteristics (such as skin color or clothing worn) of a person from another culture is not an important factor in what I think of her or him. **Answer:** Hopefully you strongly agreed with this statement.

8. When talking with people whose first language is not English, use lots of gestures and emphasis in your voice because these nonverbal clues will help yourself to be understood. **Answer:** Gesturing and talking with emphasis do not make your words easier to understand. If you are worried about being understood, get an interpreter.

9. I usually try to keep the conversation active and lively because people will think I am not interested in them if I am silent. **Answer:** If you strongly agreed with this statement, reread this chapter and Chapter 3. This type of behavior is inappropriate for most clients.

10. I sometimes interrupt people in conversations to make sure I understand the point they are trying to make. **Answer:** Although interruptions are acceptable to many groups, they are seen as rude by many Asian Americans and Native Americans.

Summary

Helping is a complex process that requires helpers to master a wide range of skills. These foundational skills, which include the use of nonverbal and verbal communication, have been set forth in this chapter. However, as has been emphasized throughout this book, skilled helpers select and use techniques and strategies that are appropriate for their clients. This is particularly true in the diagnosis of problems and in the design of interventions. Further, helpers apply techniques based on their understanding of where they are in the helping process.

CHAPTER 4 EXIT QUIZ

Answer each of the following questions by writing T if you believe the statement is true and F if you believe the statement is false. The answers to the questions are provided on the next page.

_____ **1.** The typical interaction distance in U.S. culture is from 36 to 42 inches.

_____ **2.** The *L* in the acronym SOLER stands for learning from the client.

_____ **3.** Minimal encouragers that are provided while the client is talking should probably not be used with Native Americans.

_____ **4.** Minimal encouragers such as *I see* should not be used with most minorities.

_____ **5.** Normally speaking, the receptionist will try to ascertain the purpose for the visit to a helping agency.

_____ **6.** Because immigrants may have negative reactions to government agencies, it may be a good idea to schedule meetings in their homes or in the community.

_____ **7.** Establishing a time to meet is rarely a problem with unacculturated Hispanic Americans.

_____ **8.** Informing clients about confidentiality should be done in the same way regardless of their cultural backgrounds.

_____ **9.** Minorities have about the same concern as white European Americans regarding confidentiality.

_____ **10.** Play techniques and play therapy are different phrases for the same thing.

_____11. Generally speaking, it is a good idea to check out whether clients agree with summaries of their disclosures of information.

_____12. Referent and expert power are essentially the same type of power.

_____13. The two major factors involved in the design of interventions are the cultural background and age of the client.

_____14. Definitions of what constitutes a mental health problem may change over time.

_____15. Facilitative self-disclosure is sometimes used to move the client toward action-taking.

Answers:

1. T; 2. F; 3. T; 4. F; 5. F; 6. T; 7. F; 8. T; 9. T; 10. F; 11. T; 12. F; 13. F; 14. T; 15. T

SUGGESTED LEARNING ACTIVITIES

1. Divide the class into two groups, helpers and clients. Have the helpers conduct an interview that is devoid of any type of interruption. Process both the clients' and the helpers' reactions to the interview. Reverse the roles and try this exercise again.

2. Divide the class into two groups, helpers and clients. Have helpers conduct an interview in which there is little direct eye contact. Process the reactions to the interview and then reverse the roles and conduct the exercise again.

3. Divide the class into triads made up of helpers, clients, and observers. Ask clients to take the role of an unspecified person who has a problem and has come to the helper for assistance. The helper's role is to practice providing encouragement and positive reinforcement. The person in the observer's role should make a notation each time one of these techniques is employed. At the end of a five- to seven-minute role play, the triad should process how often each technique was employed. The role play should continue until each person has assumed each role.

4. Divide the class into triads comprised of helpers, clients, and observers. Clients should assume the role of a troubled client who has many emotional problems. Helpers should reflect both the verbal and emotional content of what is said. The observer should make notes about the accuracy of the reflections. At the end of a five- to seven-minute role play, the accuracy of the helper's reflections should be discussed. The role playing should continue until all students have practiced each role.

5. Divide the class into two groups comprising helpers and clients. Have the clients assume roles that are fraught with contradictions in their verbal behavior. Have helpers use self-confrontation and direct confrontation with the clients. Reverse the roles and repeat the exercise.

6. Divide the class into small groups and ask them to write goals for Tim, whose profile follows. What goals should be set for Tim, assuming that he is agreeable?

Recall that goals need to be easily measured measurable and realistic in the short term. Have groups compare the goals that they have written.

Tim's profile: Tim has been anxious all of his life. He really never felt that he fit in when he was in high school and still feels that he is not well liked at work. He admits that his anxiety keeps him from meeting new people and that he is nervous around people that he has known for several years. He only feels comfortable with his parents and one friend. His anxiety has kept him from dating and making new friends.

7. Once small groups have presented their goals to the remainder of the class, have them discuss the basis of Tim's problems. Should the intervention for Tim focus more on thoughts, feelings, or behavior? Would it matter if Tim were a Native American? A Hispanic American? An Asian American?

REFERENCES

Altarriba, J. & Bauer, L.M. (1998). Counseling the Hispanic client: Cuban Americans, Mexican Americans, and Puerto Ricans. *Journal of Counseling and Development, 76,* 389–396.

ASGW (1989). *Ethical guidelines for group counselors.* Alexandria, VA: Association for Specialists in Group Work.

Attneave, C. (1969). Therapy in tribal settings and urban networks. *Family Process, 8,* 192–210.

Basso, K.H. (1990). To give up words: Silence in Western Apache culture. In D. Carbaugh (Ed.), *Cultural communication and intercultural contact* (pp. 303–327). Hillsdale, NJ: Lawrence Erlbaum.

Basso, K.H. (1979). *Portraits of the "Whiteman": Linguistic play and cultural symbols among the Western Apache.* New York: Cambridge Press.

Brown, D. (1997). Implications of cultural values for cross-cultural consultation with families. *Journal of Counseling and Development, 76,* 29–35.

Carkhuff, R.R. (1984). *The art of helping* (5th ed.). Amherst, MA: Human Resources Development Press.

Carter, R.T. (1991). Cultural values: A review of the empirical research and implications for counseling. *Journal of Counseling and Development, 70,* 164–173.

Diller, J.V. (1999). *Cultural diversity: A primer for the human services.* Pacific Grove, CA: Brooks/Cole.

Draguns, J.G. (1990). Applications of cross-cultural psychology in the field of mental health. In R.W. Brislin (Ed.), *Applied cross-cultural psychology* (pp. 302–324). Newbury Park, CA: Sage.

DSM-IV (1994). *Diagnostic and Statistical Manual of Mental Disorders* (4th ed.). Washington, DC: American Psychiatric Association.

Egan, G. (1994). *Exercises in helping skills: A manual to accommodate the skilled helper.* Pacific Grove, CA: Brook/Cole.

Ellis, A. (1995). Rational-emotive therapy. In R.J. Corsini & D. Weddings (Eds.), *Current psychotherapies* (pp. 162–196). Itasca, IL: Peacock.

Freud, S. (1949). *An outline of psychoanalysis.* New York: Norton.

Heppner, P.P., Kivlighan, D.M., & Wampold, B.E. (1999). *Research design in counseling.* Pacific Grove, CA: Brooks/Cole.

Herring, R.D. (1996). Synergistic counseling and Native Americans. *Journal of Counseling and Development, 74,* 542–547.

Ho, M.K. (1987). *Family therapy with ethnic minorities.* Newbury Park, CA: Sage.

Hutchins, D., & Vaught, C.C. (1997). *Helping relationships and strategies* (3rd ed.). Pacific Grove, CA: Brooks/Cole.

Ivey, A.E. (1994). *Intentional interviewing and counseling: Facilitating client development in a multi-cultural society.* Pacific Grove, CA: Brooks/Cole.

Kazdin, A.E. (1994). *Behavior modification in applied settings* (5th ed.). Pacific Grove, CA: Brooks/Cole.

Kim, B.S.K. (1996). The Korean Americans. In P.B. Pedersen & D.C. Locke (Eds.), *Cultural and diversity in counseling* (pp. 47–50). Greensboro, NC: ERIC-CASS.

Kim, M., Shin, H., & Cai, D. (1998). Cultural influence in the preferred forms of requesting and rerequesting. *Communications Monographs, 65,* 47–82.

La Fromboise, T., & Young, K.E. (1990). American Indian and Alaska Native mental health. In P.B. Pedersen & D.C. Locke (Eds.). *Cultural and diversity issues in counseling* (pp. 7–12) Greensboro, NC: ERIC-CASS.

Lauver, P., & Harvey, D.R. (1997). *The practical counselor: Elements of effective helping.* Pacific Grove, CA: Brooks/Cole.

Leong, F.T.L., & Chou, E.T. (1996). Counseling Chinese Americans. In P.B. Pedersen & D.C. Locke (Eds.), *Cultural and diversity in counseling* (pp. 25–28). Greensboro, NC: ERIC-CASS.

Okun, B.F., Fried, J., & Okun, M.L. (1999). *Understanding diversity: A learning-as-practice primer.* Pacific Grove, CA: Brooks/Cole.

Rogers, C.R. (1951). *Client-centered therapy.* Boston: Houghton-Mifflin.

Singelis, T. (1994). Nonverbal communication in intercultural interaction. In R.W. Brislin and T. Yoshida (Eds.), *Improving intercultural interaction: Modules for cross-cultural training programs* (pp. 269–270). Multicultural Aspects of Counseling Series 3. Thousand Oaks, CA: Sage.

Sue, D.W., & Sue, D. (1990). *Counseling the culturally different: Theory and practice* (2nd ed.). New York: Wiley.

Thomason, T.C. (1995). *Introduction to counseling American Indians.* Flagstaff, AZ: American Indian Rehabilitation and Training Center.

5 Understanding and Assessing People

1. Strategies for assessing clients' problems and strengths
2. Important examples of problems and strengths for clients of different ages
3. How the *DSM-IV-R* is used in the helping professions
4. The similarities and differences in diagnosing problems among children, adolescents, and adults

People who enter the helping professions have a keen interest in people. Besides enjoying the company of others, they often like to watch people. With such high people interests, future helping professionals often come into contact with a wide variety of people, many of whom show both the strengths and the problems of future clients. For example, you may know a person with great physical beauty who seems to lack self-confidence, and you wonder how someone that good looking can be insecure.

To begin reflecting on people and on their strengths and weaknesses, complete Exercise 5.1., p 105.

Your interest in people is put to good use in a service-oriented career. First, it often will allow you to work more easily with difficult people. Second, it lightens the burden of paying careful attention to people; and third, it seems to shorten the long hours spent exploring peoples' strengths and problems.

Identifying Problems and Assessing Strengths

Both problem identification and strengths assessment are central to conducting case histories on clients. And, in most medical and human service settings, workers continually write reports and maintain records built around case histories. Sometimes problem identification results in a formal diagnosis, such as the ones used in mental health facilities. While this is becoming more common, many helping professionals concentrate less on learning the technical aspects of a diagnostic system and more on sharpening their ability to convey in everyday language the meaning of those diagnoses to clients and their significant others.

EXERCISE **5.1**

Client Characteristics

Listed below are characteristics often found in client groups. Rate on a 10-point scale (1 = lowest, 10 = highest) both your prior experience with people showing each characteristic and your interest in learning more about people with the characteristics listed.

Description of Characteristic	Prior Knowledge	Future Interest
1. Frightened people with bizarre thoughts who seem to be out of touch with reality.	_____	_____
2. People who have suffered physical or emotional injuries at the hands of partners or family	_____	_____
3. People who abuse or are addicted to alcohol or drugs.	_____	_____
4. People who violate the rights of others through violence or deception.	_____	_____
5. People who are lonely and isolated, and who have a very low opinion of themselves.	_____	_____
6. People who have mental or physical disabilities.	_____	_____
7. Children who have difficulty learning in school, relating to peers, or calming themselves down.	_____	_____
8. People with serious illnesses who have little hope of recovery.	_____	_____
9. People facing a crisis as a result of an accident or natural disaster.	_____	_____
10. Adults who seem to be immature and impulsive and whom others find difficult to like.	_____	_____

Let us begin a more detailed exploration of some ways to understand problems and strengths by first directing our attention to several examples of people experiencing difficulty. Read the brief descriptions in Case Illustration 5.1; a little later you will be asked to identify some of the problems that each person exhibits.

Listed below are some, but not all, of the factors that might explain the problems Mary, Arthur, and Martin, as well as other people, have:

Factors

1. Organic or physiological problems
2. Substance use
3. Conflict within important interpersonal relationships
4. Membership in a dysfunctional group, family, or community
5. Victimization from physical, sexual, or emotional abuse

C A S E   I L L U S T R A T I O N   **5.1**
Mary, Arthur, and Martin

Mary, age 84, is taken to the emergency room by her son. She appears confused and frightened. Her son says she has not been recognizing family members. The psychiatrist on call asks how long she has been this way and whether she takes any prescription medicines or other drugs. Later, he hopes to give her a brief memory test.

Arthur, age 14, was referred by juvenile justice after he was caught killing a cat. Numerous pets in Arthur's neighborhood have been reported missing over the past several months. When Arthur is interviewed, he is very angry and threatens several staff members.

Martin, age 44, had worked as a machine operator for 21 years at the company before the plant closed. Out of unemployment benefits, Martin is feeling very low and is worried about the increasing tensions in his family. Martin learned that another plant in town was closing, one where he had hoped to find a job.

---

6. Facing a difficult but typical challenge of a life phase
7. Being victim to an unforeseen hardship that could happen to almost anyone

When we conclude that one or more of the factors listed may apply to someone we are trying to help, we must also assess the consequences that result. The impact of these factors may result in one or more of the following conditions.

Conditions

a. Emotional distress: anxiety, depression, or hostility
b. Impaired functioning: becoming unable to perform in an area of previous competence
c. Internalized blame resulting in lowered self-worth
d. Externalized blame resulting in aggression toward others

The extent to which these factors and conditions exist vary. They may be temporary or long-lasting. We may understand them as *acute*—they seem to be of recent onset with no prior history—or *chronic*—more or less constant with a long prior history.

To apply the factors and conditions we are discussing to the three individuals introduced earlier, complete Exercise 5.2., p 107.

When we assess the situation of someone we are trying to help, it is important to assess strengths and resources as well identifying problems. Let's introduce you to the individuals in Case Illustration 5.2., p 108.

EXERCISE **5.2**

Applying Factors and Conditions

Jot down below for each individual the numbers of the factors and the numbers of the conditions that were listed earlier. Get feedback on your answers at the end of the chapter on page 124.

Individual	Factor(s)	Condition(s)
Mary: elderly woman in the ER	_____	_____
Arthur: angry teenager	_____	_____
Martin: unemployed father	_____	_____

Resilience

You may know people who have faced difficult circumstances that most of us think would defeat ordinary individuals. Instead, these people not only cope with their disadvantages, they even seem to thrive. Considerable attention has been directed toward young people, whom we call "at risk" because they are at risk for any of a number of negative future outcomes. For example, they may be at risk for becoming drug addicted or incarcerated. The strengths of these individuals and the supportive resources behind them have been described under the concept of *resilience* (Rak & Patterson, 1996). Resilience equals successful adaptation despite risk and adversity. It is the ability to thrive, mature, and increase competence in the face of adverse circumstances, whether they are biological or environmental. Resilient persons can achieve favorable outcomes besides being at risk, sustain that competence under threat, and recover from traumatic or abusive situations more easily.

Protective Factors

Risk factors and stressors affecting children and adolescents have given rise to an interest in understanding protective factors that serve to fortify the resources of individuals. They are divided into internal and external factors. Here are some of the internal protective factors that researchers have identified so far.

Temperament. Resilient children seem to be "easy going" or mild mannered from birth. They tend to elicit more positive responses from caretakers. These children develop greater social skills as they mature, being more competent in interpersonal situations. This is in contrast to "difficult" children, ones with a

---

CASE ILLUSTRATION **5.2**
Cindy, Jason, and Carla

Cindy, age 34, is a widow finding it difficult to support herself and two children with her salary as a case manager for mentally ill patients. While she is working on a graduate degree in public administration, her father watches his grandchildren while Cindy takes evening and weekend classes.

Jason, age 12, is in foster care. He spent his early years with his mother, who is now in a drug rehabilitation program. At school he is well liked by his teachers for his sense of humor. He is an honor student with a measured IQ of 130.

Carla, age 27, received a spinal cord injury in an automobile accident seven years ago. She is now confined to a wheelchair. Every day Carla uses public transportation to get to her job as a dispatcher for a rescue squad. She played varsity basketball in high school and now, during work breaks, shoots hoops with the ambulance crew.

"chip on their shoulder" who prompt anger and the lack of empathy from caretakers.

Intelligence.   Resilient children have higher intelligence, more advanced problem-solving skills, and greater cognitive-integrative abilities.

Self-Esteem.   This is the most important internal factor; resilient children maintain a high level of self-esteem, a realistic sense of personal control, and a feeling of hope.

Here are some examples of external protective factors.

Family Climate.   Homes characterized by warmth, affection, emotional support, and clear-cut and reasonable structure and limits are more likely to produce resilient children. Homes riddled with family discord, hostility, and a lack of warmth are less likely to achieve this.

Social Climate.   Grandparents, other extended family members, friends, and community groups and agencies can provide support if it is absent at home. In particular, schools that offer experiences to enhance self-esteem and competence reinforce resilience. The impact on the life of child by a single adult should never be underestimated.

We find it helpful to view every person in need of help as resilient in some way, not just at-risk youth. In some cases, we think that a protective factor may be dormant but with nurturing may become active. Finding them sometimes demands following very faint clues. Go back and reread the descriptions of Cindy, Jason, and Carla in Case Illustration 5.2. What protective factors can you identify for each one? Feedback on these protective factors can be found at end of the chapter on pages 125 and 126.

Locating the Source of Problems

As practical people, helping professionals make the most of their effort at problem identification when the assessment and a possible diagnosis points to promising treatments. We will see in later chapters that helping professionals have access to a wide variety of treatments or interventions. However, different treatments work better for different problems with no one intervention being universally applicable.

We have modified an approach to locating the source of different problems that was developed by Frances, Clarkin, and Perry (1984). Table 5.1 shows a hierarchy of problem levels along with an example of each.

The *DSM-IV*

This chapter is intended to introduce you to assessment issues in the helping professions and to help you begin to look for important information that will help you understand how you can serve people. Future training will increase

TABLE 5.1 Locating the Sources of Problems

Source of Problem	Example
Society / government	No governmental programs to support access to education, such as federal college loans. Career opportunities are based on personal resources. Only people with wealth can access higher education and advanced career training.
Community	Public services restricted to programs funded by the government. For example, local employers do not financially support local causes, such as parks and recreation. Volunteers for public service are not supported by training and support programs.
Peer group	Strength and athletic ability are supremely valued in a high school. Diversity is not valued; it is not "cool" to be a musician or a scholar. Many students are bullied, intimidated, and afraid of injury.
Immediate family	Children never invite friends home, fearful that others may learn of their mother's alcohol problem.
Partner / significant other	Both partners find their sexual relationship unsatisfying. They do not talk about it for fear of hurting the other partner's feelings.
The person	A person is unhappy about his low salary in spite of good feedback about work performance. He is afraid to ask for a raise; he does not know how to be assertive.
Body systems / physiology	An elderly person periodically has difficulty recognizing family members. This person also finds the loss of bladder control embarrassing; she avoids being around her grandchildren.

your technical grasp of assessment issues and will build your skills in doing assessments. Already, some using this text have had a course in abnormal psychology. Today most abnormal courses introduce students to psychopathology, following the framework of the *DSM-IV.*

DSM-IV stands for the *Diagnostic and Statistical Manual of Mental Disorders* (4th ed., rev., 1994). This book is published by The American Psychiatric Association (APA) and reflects a system of classifying psychiatric problems that is used worldwide. Because many readers will need to use this classification system in their professional work, we will overview the *DSM-IV* system briefly.

Historical Background

For the first half of the twentieth century, the diagnosis of emotional and behavioral problems was not well standardized. Mental health professionals used a variety of theories about psychopathology, the most common coming from psychoanalysis. These differences created confusion. Following both World Wars, thousands of returning military created a large demand for mental health services, and with it a demand for a common nomenclature, that is, a vocabulary that everyone could understand and use. The Veterans Administration, the World Health Organization (WHO), and the APA began to work on this common language for mental disorders.

In 1952, the *DSM-I* was published; it received a better reception than the *International Classification of Diseases* (6th ed.) (*ICD-6*) that was published around the same time by the WHO. Refinements to these classification systems followed with ever closer agreement. In 1968, the *DSM-II* was published, followed in 1980 by the *DSM-III.* With the publication of the *DSM-III, Revised* (1987) the classification system broke with older theories of psychopathology and began to rely only on a list of symptoms, most observable, to set the criteria for various disorders. They came to be known as *criteria sets* to reflect this result. The current *DSM-IV* has continued the evolution of the system, making it even more objective. There is close agreement between the *DSM-IV* and the *ICD-10* in the description of mental disorders. However, each system uses a different numeric code to represent the same disorder.

How *DSM-IV* Defines Mental Disorders

When many hear the words *mental disorders* they are inclined to think that reference is being made only to problems in cognitive or intellectual functioning. In fact, *mental disorders* is a broad label used in medicine and mental health to signify overall adaptive functioning. It includes problems in cognitive, emotional, and behavioral areas.

A mental disorder crosses a boundary we imagine between normality and pathology. A disorder, first of all, must be *clinically significant,* that is, beyond the range of differences found in ordinary people. A *mental disorder* is a behavioral or psychological pattern of symptoms (a *syndrome*) that is distressing and disabling with risks attached. A mental disorder is associated

295.30 Schizophrenia, Paranoid Type, Single Episode in Full Remission

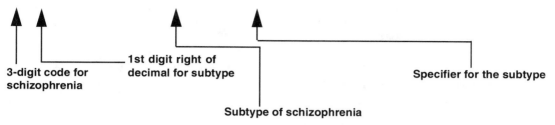

FIGURE 5.1 **Example of DSM-IV-R Type, Subtype, and Specifier**

with emotional suffering, impairs important functioning in intimate relationships or work, and brings with it the risk of death or more suffering with an important loss of freedom.

Within the *DSM-IV* sixteen different diagnostic *classes* are listed. Within each class or category are *types* of disorders. Some disorders also have *subtypes* in the system. Finally, types and subtypes may be further grouped according to *specifiers*. Figure 5.1 gives you an example of how the *DSM-IV*, along with its numeric codes, divides disorders into classes, types, subtypes, and specifiers for a disorder.

From Figure 5.1 you can see that the codes for any of the subtypes of schizophrenia will have the first three digits of its numeric code as 295. *Schizophrenia* is a type within the category of "Schizophrenia and Other Psychotic Disorders." Different subtypes of schizophrenia receive the same first three-digit code, but a different code for the first digit to the right of the decimal point. The specifier for the subtype of *paranoid* indicates the duration and where the patient is in the course of the disorder. This specifier means that the patient has had only one episode instead of repeated ones, and there are no longer any symptoms or indications of the disorder, so it is considered to be "quiet" or in remission.

The Effectiveness of the *DSM-IV*

While the *DSM-IV* is an improvement over earlier versions, it is not without limitations. The categories of disorders in its system are not mutually exclusive, that is, if a person has one disorder he or she can have others as well. Also, the symptom lists (criteria sets) used to diagnose a disorder are not independent or exclusive. Different disorders will contain some of the same symptoms. For example, grandiosity is a symptom of mania, which is part of bipolar disorder, and a symptom of narcissistic personality disorder. Even for one disorder, a person need not show all the symptoms in the criteria set, so in some instances one person gets the diagnosis with a different symptom picture from another person with the same diagnosis. All these features complicate the use of the *DSM-IV*.

In understanding how mental disorders are distributed among the population, knowledge of cultural factors is important. A behavior that one subculture considers very odd another subculture may consider fairly ordinary. Thus, to use the *DSM-IV*, you must understand the cultural context of the people you are trying to help. Many of us wish there were some absolute rules we could apply in our work as helpers. However, much is relative, based on culture and circumstance.

In learning how to apply the *DSM-IV*, more than intensive study of the system is required. Its use is based on what is called *clinical judgment*. This means that a helping professional gets specific training in the *DSM-IV-R*, then adds to it more training and experience at a clinic. This experience demonstrates exceptions to rules and how the variances among people must be taken into account in making diagnoses. The *DSM-IV* cannot be used in cookbook fashion.

Learning More about the *DSM-IV*

At the end of the chapter, in the learning activities, are several suggestions for learning more about this diagnostic system. Check with your instructor for other ideas to expand your knowledge of the *DSM-IV*. You can buy condensed versions that include just the criteria sets for the disorders. These are intended for professionals who are very familiar with the system and need only to refresh their memories about specific criteria while using the system in clinical settings. Students need to study the full version. The American Psychiatric Press, which publishes the *DSM-IV*, also markets other training materials. Call 1-800-368-5777 or fax requests to 1-202-789-2648.

How to Do an Initial Assessment

Helping professionals, regardless of work setting, need skills in assessment as part of gathering necessary information to compile clients' case histories. This section suggests some important principles that will make you better at assessment and better at completing case histories. The skills you will learn are related to clinical interviewing. Think about what an initial interview with a client might be like, how you might feel, and what you might expect to be problems you need to solve. The following suggestions will help you to conduct an interview that flows easily while it gathers enough information for a balanced and complete written record.

Practice Using Empathy and Compassion to Put the Client at Ease

Use the characteristics of skilled helpers that you read about in Chapter 2 to help you develop a nondefensive relationship with the client. Through such a relationship you are more likely to get accurate information. It may take a while for the individual to warm up to you, but if you encourage the individual to take the lead in offering information, you will feel less on the spot than if you think you have to bombard the person with questions. Make any questions open-ended ("Would you tell me more about that?"), rather than "yes" or "no" questions. Summarize frequently, which prompts the client to add to or correct your summary. Stay relaxed because you will cover more ground that way. If you follow these suggestions, your interviews will be less tiring. Try taping interviews with the client's permission to see what the talk ratio is between you and the client. If you seem to be doing all the talking, say 80%, you need to use more open-ended questions, reflections, and summaries to get the client to shoulder more of the responsibility for getting important information. Try to get the talk ratio down to where you do about half the talking.

Separate Present Functioning from Past History

In doing an initial assessment, you want to learn most of all how the individual is doing right now in the present. Try to ignore past history in the beginning. After you learn about the present and draw some conclusions about it, past history will be valuable as a means to confirm those conclusions.

One of the things clinical interviewers try to ascertain very early in an interview is the "chief complaint," which is not usually difficult to do. You could ask "What is bothering you exactly?" or "How did you get to be here?" The second option is a good one if you are interviewing someone in a prison or in a hospital. You will want to write down the exact words people use when they respond. Hopefully, you will learn about the person's symptoms, the severity of his/her symptoms, and the course his/her condition followed.

Pay Attention to the Circumstances Surrounding the Individual

As you begin to develop impressions of what the person thinks, feels, and does, you will also get information about the person's environment. Again, the emphasis is on the present, in this case the present environment. Conditions that challenge the person's ability to cope and that cause stress are called *stressors*. Sometimes these stressors are so powerful that adapting to them is outside the range of most people. Sometimes people respond adaptively to their home environment, but behave inappropriately outside of it. For example, in high crime neighborhoods, higher levels of aggressive behavior are adaptive, where in low crime areas the same level would be considered excessive.

Learn How to Conduct a Brief Mental Status Evaluation

A mental status examination is a very important tool in emergency psychiatric evaluations. This procedure has been used for decades. The material in the evaluation has even been converted into brief rating scales that you can check and score (Overall & Gorham, 1962). However, most experienced clinical interviewers follow an outline or protocol to investigate areas of functioning. Below are ten areas to explore in assessing a person's present functioning. For each area are suggestions on what to look for.

> Appearance: Note the person's dress, his or her hygiene, and mannerisms. Is there anything alarming or unusual about any of these?
>
> Activity: Look at motor activity including indications of excitement, agitation, jitteriness, dizziness, or slowed responses. Activity often gives clues to emotions, which we will discuss later.
>
> Speech: Speech is a clue to how the person is thinking. Look first at quantity of speech and then content. Is the person so talkative that he or she is difficult to interpret? Is speech limited or sparse? Is the content of speech coherent or is it strange?
>
> Attitude: How does the individual handle talking to others, including you? Does the person seem withdrawn or uncooperative? Is he or she highly sensitive, distrustful, or manipulative? Your feeling during the interview may shed light on the person's attitude.
>
> Thought process: How well organized do the person's thoughts seem? Can you follow them? Are there logical conclusions to be drawn from what is said?
>
> Thought content: Are the topics offered by the person strange? Does the individual seem preoccupied by certain things? Is content marked by excessive suspicion or by exaggeration of things?
>
> Perception: Are sensations and perceptions within the range of everyday experience? Does the person see, hear, or smell things that are not present?
>
> Emotions: Look for indications of anxiety, depressed mood, or hostility.
>
> Orientation, recall, and memory: Does the person seem to know who he or she is, where he or she is, and when the interview is happening? Can they recall some information immediately? Is their memory functioning, both short- and long-term?
>
> Insight and judgment: Does the person have a reasonable explanation of what might be behind his or her problems? Can the person understand relationships and draw conclusions? How well can he or she make a decision?

If you can create an informal atmosphere in which the person can talk freely without you controlling what is said by pointed questions, you will get a better impression of the individual. Your impressions are very important. If you are an open and tolerant person, yet find the content of the interview and the manner of the person you are interviewing to be strange, that suggests the presence of more serious problems.

Remember, though, that you are interviewing the person to discover not just problems, but strengths as well. And strengths can be understood as both internal and external protective factors, the way they have been described in this chapter.

If, during an interview, you become unsure of the meaning of something, in all but the most desperate of situations, you can excuse yourself and seek consultation with a supervisor or colleague. It is never a good idea as a professional to work in total isolation.

Following Up Initial Impressions

Once you believe that you have a good grasp of the present situation and have an idea of what is behind it, past history can be gathered as a means of confirming your hunches. Besides the person's own background, you can look at family history as well. In some situations, you may be conducting the assessment interview to formalize your impressions with a *DSM-IV* diagnosis. This depends on where you work.

A complete assessment may involve talking with other key persons in the life of your client. Mental health counselors working with children, for example, may contact the child's natural parents, foster parents, probation officer, social worker, classroom teacher, and school counselor. That is a lot of permissions to get, but each individual can offer an important perspective on the situation and on how the child can be helped.

Important Areas to Investigate

There are circumstances that every helping professional should be alert to. These include:

- dangerousness to self (suicide risk),
- dangerousness to others (homicide risk),
- alcohol and drug use (adds to dangerousness), and
- victimization through abuse or neglect (adds to dangerousness).

The first two areas often constitute what is called a *risk assessment*. It is absolutely necessary to protect the people we work with from any known danger or risk. Since the use of substances tends to intensify other risks, assessment of substance use goes hand in hand with the assessment of danger. Finally, because unattended abuse and neglect are often life-threatening, they constitute an important element in risk assessment.

To gain an understanding of how risk assessment occurs, several illustrations follow that demonstrate the four factors listed above. Each illustration represents different age levels: a child, adolescent, young adult, and older adult.

Illustrations of Assessment in Action

Assessment of Children

Abuse and neglect have been selected for illustration with children. The incidence of abuse and neglect among children is alarming. In 1994, there were 3,140,000 suspected cases of child abuse with 1,036,000 confirmed. Of these abuse cases, 1,200 children died (National Committee to Prevent Child Abuse, 1994).

Abuse is divided into three parts: physical, emotional, and sexual. We will give examples of each type of abuse and the signs that point to them.

The first people to uncover physical abuse of children are usually educators and medical personnel. Infants and children brought to a hospital emergency room for an atypical injury raise the suspicion of physical abuse. It is easy to imagine the difference between treating a youngster in a football uniform with a dislocated shoulder and a broken arm of an infant not old enough to walk. The vast majority of abusive injuries to children occur as a result of beatings either with an instrument or by hand (U.S. Department of Health and Human Services, 1992). The most common injuries are:

- bruises and welts;
- abrasions, contusions, and lacerations;
- burns and scalding; and
- bone fractures.

Most of the physical injuries children receive are easily recognizable through a routine medical examination. When abuse is suspected, attention to behavioral indicators further the suspicion of abuse. Battered children are often wary of physical contact, may seem constantly alert for danger, and seem to show no expectation for being comforted when sad or hurt. They may become apprehensive when other children cry and become very uncomfortable when an adult approaches that crying child.

Parents are the most common perpetrators of physical abuse. They tend to have personal and marital problems. They are often isolated from others and have no apparent support system. Their expectations of their children often are excessive. The parents' fearfulness and suspicion may even extend to their children, who are seen as judgmental.

When interviewed about their children's injuries, abusive parents are often evasive and contradictory. The parents do not seem able to be soothing to their youngsters and may seem uncomfortable when left alone even briefly with their children.

Physical neglect occurs through the failure to provide necessities for health and development. The child may be exploited, like Cinderella, by having excessive responsibilities. Their hygiene and nutrition needs are neglected.

Emotional abuse and neglect often centers around denying the child the experiences that lead to feeling loved and wanted. Children abused emotionally are often yelled at, blamed for problems, and constantly criticized. They are neglected through being left alone for long periods of time. Sadly, emotional abuse and neglect often leads to the child becoming a discipline problem. This results in further rejection by the community, even by some professional helpers.

Sexual abuse is discovered through injuries, pregnancy, and venereal disease. Many delinquent and aggressive youngsters have been sexually abused. Parents involved in incestuous relationships often are extremely protective; the family in general is secretive.

The consequences of childhood abuse often last a lifetime. The sooner the abuse is discovered and treatment begins the better the chances are for recovery. The victim must talk about the abuse; the victim will not forget about it or eventually outgrow it (Herman, 1992). For this reason, assessment of abuse and neglect is of supreme importance among everyone, but especially helping professionals.

Assessment of Adolescents

The most common *DSM-IV* diagnosis found among adolescents is conduct disorder (APA, 1994). Its most distinctive feature is a pattern of behavior that violates the rights of others, including acts of aggressive conduct toward others, destruction of property, theft and deceit, and serious violations of rules. This feature often makes assessment of conduct disorder complicated. Because what the youth says often cannot be trusted, assessing the situation involves contact with others who know about circumstances involving the juvenile. Since aggression is so much a part of conduct disorder, learning how to assess violence or aggression is important for professionals working with youth.

Teenagers in the United States have the highest risk of nonfatal assault of any age group (U.S. Department of Justice, 1991). Violence affects adolescents at home, in school, and in the community. Adolescents not only receive violent injury, but injure others. Because it is so common and so important, let's increase our ability to assess violence risk.

Affective versus Predatory Aggression. There is a long-standing view of aggression that divides it into two forms, affective or predatory (Eichelman, Elliott, & Barchas, 1981). *Affective aggression* is the result of arousal; something stimulates it. For example, an event (for example, name calling) provokes anger, and the person retaliates with violence. Before the assault, an observer could see the violent person develop signs of anger arousal, such as taking an attack posture, even growling. In another example, a perpetrator may describe after the attack how she became frightened of being hurt and, to avoid the expected injury, struck first with a knife. Affective aggression is not planned. It often results from poor impulse control. The perpetrator regrets the act after it is over.

By contrast, *predatory aggression* is much more difficult to predict, often because of the absence of advance signs. This violence is planned and purposeful; it is usually a sign of an antisocial person, one with little regard for others. In the past, these individuals were called psychopaths or sociopaths. Because they do not bond with others and cannot empathize, they can be sadistic in their actions.

A lot of people admit to at least mild acts of affective aggression, times when they let their emotions get the best of them. We hope with some education or training mild violence can be reduced. Changes in predatory violence may be more difficult to achieve, since we consider them to be more imbedded in the character of the individual.

Aggression Risk Factors.   The potential for violence is based on both the characteristics of the individual and the characteristics of the environment within which the person lives. To begin examining some of these characteristics, read the cases in Case Illustration 5.3, p 119. Take notes on what you think each individual portrays that increases the risk for becoming violent.

Which of the following risk factors for violence do you think apply to the individuals just described?

Violence Risk Factors

- Disturbed thinking with possible delusions, hallucinations, and fantasies to harm others
- Brain diseases (for example, Alzheimer's, tumors, temporal lobe epilepsy, head injury, viral encephalitis)
- Alcohol and drug use, diminishing impulse control
- Personal values that endorse violence as a solution to problems
- Peer group affiliation that endorses and uses violence
- A victim of abuse, resulting in long-standing anger and resentment
- Lifestyle disruptions resulting in sleep loss, hunger, or personal hygiene problems that affect self-control
- Previous rewards for using violence as a means to solve problems
- Limited opportunities to learn nonviolent ways to solve problems
- Availability of weapons and victims

These factors demonstrate how any of a number of situations that make it difficult to "think before you act" increases the chances of affective aggression. In our case examples, Herbert seems to have a serious thought disorder requiring emergency psychiatric treatment. He has serious distorted beliefs (delusions) and serious perceptual distortions (hears voices). Tammy is at risk for using violence since she has herself received so much of it. Nathan lives in an environment that seems to require aggressiveness for survival. Joe is in some ways like Tammy,

CASE ILLUSTRATION **5.3**

Herbert, Tammy, Nathan, Joe, and Gene

Herbert firmly believes that he is an angel sent by God to avenge evil in the world. He hears a voice that tells him to kill sinners so the earth can be saved for the righteous.

Tammy has just run out of her house after being slapped again by her drunken mother. She is planning to run away for good. Not only is she angry about the way her mother treats her, but she is furious about being fondled and talked to sexually by her mother's boyfriend.

Nathan has had his lunch money taken from him every day this week. On the way home from school he has been pushed and intimidated. He is seriously thinking of accepting membership from one of the gangs in the neighborhood. He believes this will provide him with the protection he needs.

Joe thinks a lot about how much he hates his father for the harsh punishments and restrictions he receives. At school one of the coaches unconsciously reminds Joe of his father because they look and act much the same. Another student writes an obscene note on the blackboard. When the coach comes in the room, he immediately grabs Joe by the shirt and yells at him for the message on the board.

Gene admires his father. Gene has been taught by his Dad that you don't get anything for nothing; you have to earn everything, including respect. To be sure you get respect, you don't take anything off of anyone. Someone hits you, you hit back, only harder.

but may in his own mind transfer his resentment toward his father to the coach. Finally, Gene may have internalized his father's values that endorse violence.

If you go to the list above, you can see how other individuals with violence risk may appear. For example, can you imagine the violence potential of a college student who has not slept for several days in order to study for exams. The student has been using a lot of amphetamines to keep awake. He becomes bothered by some noise down the hall and, in anger, picks up his softball bat. He wants to confront whoever is making the noise. The college student's violence potential has been increased through the use of drugs, irritability caused by sleep loss, and the availability of a weapon.

Assessment of Younger Adults

Our illustration of assessment of younger adults involves the use and abuse of alcohol and other substances. It is the third "must" area for risk assessment mentioned earlier.

Substance abuse is defined as a maladaptive pattern of use leading to a significant inability to meet obligations with resulting physical danger, legal problems, and interpersonal difficulties (APA, 1994). Dependence or addiction to a substance has the same problems and dangers as abuse, but also involves physical and psychological dependence. The history of substance use for the addict includes greater tolerance for the drug with the need for larger doses, withdrawal symptoms if use is abruptly stopped, repeated unsuccessful efforts to stop use, and a general lifestyle centered around obtaining and using the substance (APA, 1994). Case Illustration 5.4 shows two examples.

Assessing substance use involves an awareness of the signs of both intoxication and withdrawal. People under the influence of substances (intoxication) often show belligerence, quick mood changes, impaired intellectual functioning, impaired judgment, and problems in their social and occupational relationships. Professional helpers often find that knowing these signs helps them avoid the futility of trying to work with a person who is intoxicated. Whatever is accomplished is unlikely to be remembered and retained.

Signs of substance withdrawal include coarse tremor of hands, tongue, or eyelids; nausea or vomiting; anxiety; general weakness (malaise); irritability or depressed mood; rapid heartbeat (tachycardia); and sweating. Withdrawal from many substances can be life-threatening; people in withdrawal can stop breathing. They may need emergency medical attention.

Assessment of Older Adults

Our last illustration of assessment is devoted to depression. The *DSM-IV* estimates that the lifetime risk for contracting a major depressive disorder is from 10 to 25% for women and 5 to 12% for men. Because of depression, billions of dollars a year are lost in lowered work efficiency and medical expenses, not to mention the thousands of lost lives. While a big and costly problem, it is estimated that 80 to 90% of those people who suffer from major depression can be successfully treated (Regier, Hirschfeld, Goodwin, Burke, Lazar, & Judd, 1988).

C A S E   I L L U S T R A T I O N   **5.4**

Virginia and William

Virginia is having problems with her girlfriend. Often, after a fight, she drives to a nearby bar where she becomes intoxicated. Hangovers the following day make it difficult to work. One time she made a bookkeeping mistake that almost got her fired. After the last fight, she received a DUI driving home drunk. Virginia seems to be abusing alcohol.

William's wife left him because of his drinking. For years he tried to hide his drinking from her. He hid bottles in different places so he would not run out but would seem to be drinking less he than was. He has begun to develop tremors in his hands. He was hospitalized twice for alcohol use. This history suggests alcohol dependence.

Depressed people are potentially dangerous to themselves. Depression dramatically increases the risk of suicide. Thus, we will overview both how depression and suicide are assessed.

At one time or another, most of us feel sad, begin to lose hope, and think things are unlikely to get better. Moods rise and fall. We feel "low" when someone has rejected us or when a loved one has died. Mood disorders such as depression begin where normal grieving and loss end. Let us look at some of the important symptoms of depression.

Some of these symptoms have to do with biological processes; in the past they were called the *vegetative signs* of depression. They have to do with eating, sleeping, and activity or fatigue. Other symptoms are more cognitive, having to do with self-esteem, concentration, and the report of feelings. Read Case Illustration 5.5, which describes many of these symptoms.

Suicide Risk. The DSM-IV estimates as many as 15% of those troubled with a major depression may commit suicide. The risk of suicide with depression is

---

CASE ILLUSTRATION **5.5**

Elizabeth

Elizabeth is a frail-looking, 72-year-old widow, living alone but near to her daughter. During her interview at the clinic, she looks very sad and drawn. Indeed, her overall mood seems depressed. She complains about her memory, but tests show that her short-term and long-term memory are fine. She does have problems in concentration. She "drifts off" for periods of time. For example, if she is watching a TV program, she remembers the first part of the program, but then misses a part, so when her attention returns to the show, she has difficulty following what is happening.

Elizabeth is accompanied by her daughter, who expresses concern for her mother's weight loss of approximately 15 pounds during the past month. Elizabeth says she is not dieting; she just does not have an appetite. When asked about her sleep habits, Elizabeth says that she falls asleep, but often awakens at 2:00 or 3:00 A.M. and cannot get back to sleep. When she does get out of bed, she feels very low in energy. As the day progresses, Elizabeth feels a little better but still does not get much done.

When asked about her thoughts, Elizabeth says that she often believes that she would be better off dead. At least then she could be with her husband. She expresses hopelessness about the future. Even doing a small thing, such as going to get a few groceries at the store, seems almost impossible to do. She admits to crying often. When asked why she does not spend time with her family and friends like she used to, she says that they would not want to be around someone like her (showing her low self-esteem). In addition, even though it is spring and many flowers are blooming, Elizabeth does not enjoy being in her garden, even though it was once her most proud possession.

serious. Elizabeth at first may seem to have some suicide risk because she thinks and talks about death. But these alone do not predict suicide risk. Any depressed person who talks about "resting in peace" or dying should be given a quick suicide assessment by checking the following:

Suicide Risk Assessment

■ Does the person have the *intent* to commit suicide?
■ Does there exist a specific *plan* to complete the suicide?
■ Are the *means* to be used in the plan *available?*
■ Have there been *previous attempts* at suicide?

If any one of these conditions is present, steps need to be taken to protect the individual. Additional indicators of suicide risk and factors that may increase the lethality of an attempt, that is, the chances that the suicide attempt will be successful (from Fujimura, Weis, & Cochran, 1985).

Factors Increasing the Potential for Successful Suicide.

■ Client has a history of severe alcohol or drug abuse
■ Client has a history of previous psychiatric treatment, especially hospitalization
■ Client's suicide plan uses means that do not allow the attempt to be reversed
■ Client begins settling personal affairs or giving away possessions, showing the plan is final
■ Client has no access to a support system or helpful resources
■ Social support system encourages suicide

CASE   ILLUSTRATION   **5.6**
Janet

Janet has been suffering severe and chronic back pain for many years following an automobile accident. She is considered permanently disabled by the Social Security Administration and is receiving benefits. Just sitting creates the most pain; she cannot work or enjoy the leisure activities that had always been part of her life. With such physical pain and feelings of uselessness, Janet often thinks about suicide. Because she loves her husband and children very much, she decides her suicide would be too dreadful for them and she never attempts to do it. Janet knows from her reading about suicide that family members often blame themselves for the suicide, feeling that if they were better people, the deceased would have had something to live for. Janet does not want her loved ones burdened by such self-blame.

Suicide is more likely if the attempter has lowered impulse control through the use of substances, severe loss of sleep, or the activation of a severe psychiatric condition that lowers contact with reality. Also, suicide is more likely if the client plans to use a method that produces rapid harm, such as a gun. A slower-acting method such as a drug overdose leaves a chance that the attempter will be discovered and saved. Finally, a client who has no connection with loved ones or who feels certain that no one will care if he or she died has a powerful risk factor for suicide. Read Case Illustration 5.6 for someone at risk for suicide.

Standardized Assessment Techniques

This chapter has focused on the assessment of strengths and problems that might surface during a face-to-face interview. Helping professionals, especially those in education and mental health, often use standardized assessment techniques in the form of tests and inventories, available from reputable publishers. An intelligence test is considered to be a form of standardized assessment because its use allows for consistent results, provided those giving the test follow the directions for administration of the instrument. Graduate school training in such programs as clinical psychology and special education provides the background and credentials required for use of standardized test and inventories. Skill in the use of these instruments can add to your understanding of people.

Summary

The genuine interest and concern professional helpers have in people enables them to go far beyond the norm in trying to understand the behavior and circumstances of those they are trying to help. This understanding results in the assessment of problems and strengths that in turn define the goals the helping relationship will have. In this way, assessment guides the professional helper in planning interventions.

Both the personalities and the environments of clients influence how well they are able to cope with circumstances in their lives. The source of a person's problems can range from chaos in his or her social system to diseased cells in the body. Depending on the location of the problem, the intervention to solve it will be different.

The capacity of individuals to resist being affected by negative conditions varies as well. Some people are surprisingly resilient; based on their circumstances, they should have more problems than they do. From them we have learned how people are protected from psychological injury.

In many professional settings, problem identification results in a formal diagnosis. Use of the *DSM-IV-R* and its diagnostic system is the most common example of this in hospitals and clinics.

Following the outline given in the chapter, assessment during an interview should cover important areas of functioning and should avoid confusing past problems with current ones. Assessment should never ignore any potential for danger, either danger to the person being helped or to others.

CHAPTER 5 EXIT QUIZ

Answer each of the following questions with a T if the question is true and an F if the question is false.

_____ 1. Writing case histories of clients requires the careful assessment of problems and strengths.

_____ 2. Resilience is successful adaptation in spite of adverse circumstances.

_____ 3. For a child to develop successfully, no one can replace the child's parents as a source of support.

_____ 4. The *DSM-IV* is of limited use because it describes problems only of U.S. citizens.

_____ 5. Mental disorders in the *DSM-IV* have both distressing and disabling symptoms.

_____ 6. An assessment interview will achieve better results if the interviewer practices empathy and compassion.

_____ 7. When assessing problems it is important to first identify past problems, then current ones.

_____ 8. The risk of harm is higher if drug abuse is involved.

_____ 9. There is a strong link between major depression and the risk of suicide.

_____10. Assessment of problems and strengths is effective if it points to treatment.

Answers:

1. T; 2. T; 3. F; 4. F; 5. T; 6. T; 7. F; 8. T; 9. T; 10. T

SUGGESTED LEARNING ACTIVITIES

1. Imagine yourself in a job interview with an employer or in a graduate degree program admission interview. Describe the interviewer and the way he or she might get information from you in the least stressful way. Write a two-paragraph description of this individual. What is it about you as an interviewer that you need to work on to have this description fit you?

2. Visit a nearby clinic, correctional facility, or mental health facility. Ask to see a blank information form that is completed for clients. Review the information gathered and how assessment is used.

3. In many states, laws exist that require previous child molesters to register with the authorities when they move into a community. In many cases, the individual has paid for the crime through a prison sentence. Some argue that registration laws violate the rights of the individual. Others argue that such laws are needed to protect the community. Divide the class into two groups to debate the pros and cons of such laws. What conditions need to exist to make such laws needed, and what conditions need to exist to make them unconstitutional? Identify spokespersons to debate these issues in front of class.

4. Divide into groups of three for brief role plays of problem assessment interviews. Have one member be the interviewer, another the interviewee, and the third the observer. The observer should act as a referee to make sure that immediate and current problems are fully explored before past history is gathered.

5. Research the DSM-IV-R on the Internet. Use one of the popular search engines, such as Excite.com to get started. Review at least one positive and one negative reference.

6. Check the audio-video library on campus for training materials on the DSM-IV.

CASE ILLUSTRATION 5.1

- **Mary.** *Factors 1* and *2* and *Condition 3* seem to be the best to explain the brief information provided. Mary seems to be showing some attention or memory problems. At her age this may be a sign of dementia or senility. Her memory may be changing. Like our memory, hers used to be like a videotape that stores experiences. When those experiences are recalled, it is like playing back the tape; the experiences are sequenced and connected, like scenes of a video. Now Mary's memories may be more like a stack of snapshots that were sorted in a sequence but got dropped, so that the "pile of memories" became mixed up. When she tries to recall family members and experiences, she becomes confused because her memories don't make as much sense as they used to. This worries and frightens her.

- **Arthur.** While all of the factors listed may apply, *Factors 3, 4, and 5* often lead to *Conditions 1 and 4* among youngsters in the juvenile justice system. We would want to check on substance use as well, but the brief picture of Arthur does not suggest this factor at this point.

- **Martin.** *Factor 7* and *Conditions 1* and *3* are the best bets in beginning to explore this individual's situation.

CASE ILLUSTRATION 5.2 FEEDBACK

- Cindy. She is being supported by her father, who cares for the children so Cindy can advance her education. This is an external protective factor.

- Jason. His intelligence and engaging interpersonal style are internal protective factors.

- Carla. Her sense of personal responsibility and history of previous successes seem to act as internal protective factors. Her supportive and friendly work colleagues supply an important external protective factor.

REFERENCES

American Psychiatric Association. (1994). *Diagnostic and statistical manual of mental disorders* (4th ed). Washington, DC: Author.

Eichelman, B., Elliott, G.R., & Barchas, J.D. (1981). Biochemical, pharmacological, and genetic aspects of aggression. In D.A. Hamburg & H.B. Trudeau (Eds.), *Biobehavioral aspects of aggression* (pp. 51–84). New York: Alan Liss.

Frances, A., Clarkin, J., & Perry, S. (1984). *Differential therapeutics in psychiatry: The art and science of treatment selection.* New York: Brunner/Mazel.

Fujimura, L.E., Weis, D.M., & Cochran, J.R. (1985). Suicide: Dynamics and implications for counseling. *Journal of Counseling and Development, 63,* 612–616.

Herman, J.L. (1992). *Trauma and recovery: The aftermath of violence—from domestic abuse to political terror.* New York: Basic Books.

National Committee to Prevent Child Abuse. (1994). *Current trends in child abuse reporting and fatalities.* Chicago: Author.

Overall, J.E., & Gorham, D.R. (1962). The brief psychiatric rating scale. *Psychological Reports, 10,* 799–812.

Rak, C., & Patterson, L. (1996). Promoting resilience in at-risk children. *Journal of Counseling and Development, 74,* 368–373.

Regier, D.A., Hirschfeld, R., Goodwin, F., Burke, J.D., Jr., Lazar, J.B., & Judd, L.L. (1988). The NIMH depression awareness, recognition, and treatment program: Structure, aims, and scientific basis. *American Journal of Psychiatry, 145,* 1351–1357.

U.S. Department of Health and Human Services. (1992). *National child abuse and neglect data system: Working Paper 1.* Publication No. (ACF) 92-303661.

U.S. Department of Justice. (1991). *Criminal victimization in the United States.* Washington, DC: Author.

6 Service Delivery Systems

1. How human services and health services are provided.
2. The features of various service delivery strategies and how they affect you.
3. How to use information on service delivery to make your own career decisions.
4. Career options in human services agencies.

Where might there be sources of help for the people in the following situations?

- An elderly couple without insurance and living on a small pension, who lost their home in a fire.
- A family trying to cope with a physically abusive child.
- A parolee who wants to avoid a return to drug use.
- A middle-aged worker with a recent spinal cord injury from an auto accident.
- A high school senior from a poor family who wants to attend college.

In these examples and in millions of others, human resource workers have the opportunity to reduce human suffering, contribute to people's feelings of self-worth, and enrich society through the delivery of needed services. Collectively, human services agencies are meant to provide a safety net that guarantees people that their basic needs will be met, but this guarantee is not always kept. The issue facing helpers who are confronted with helpees such as those described above is to find agencies and people within them who can address the identified problems.

In virtually all our lives, problems and setbacks arise that disrupt our ability to care for ourselves and contribute to the common good. The better helpers are in assisting people help themselves, the more productive a society becomes. This is why highly successful societies, like ours, view investments in services to preserve the physical and mental health and well-being of people as very cost-effective. Without human services agencies and the helpers in them, acute problems could become individual and social catastrophes. Without prevention efforts and strategic interventions by helpers in the community, small outbreaks of disease would become epidemics, substance abuse problems would skyrocket, and homeless individuals and the poor in general would be without food and shelter.

Overview of the Human Services and Health Care System

Our current human services system has its roots in the small community in which people worked together to provide support to individuals in need. With the growth of large cities and the loss of the closeness of the small community, supporting the needs of people became increasingly more difficult. Moreover, as our society has become more diverse and advanced technologically, it has become increasingly difficult for unorganized individuals to meet the needs of people in their communities. People need many physical and mental health services provided by hospitals, clinics, and outreach programs. They also need to apply for unemployment benefits, housing assistance, or disability benefits. People may wish to rely on an adoption agency to help them achieve their dream of becoming a parent. Families may require the emotional support provided by a hospice as a loved one slowly dies of a degenerative disease such as cancer or Alzheimer's. Human services helpers and their agencies provide care during hard times.

In response to the diverse needs of people within our society, organized charities such as the Salvation Army and the Red Cross began to deliver assistance. The help provided by these organizations was, and still is, largely delivered by volunteers. However, advocates for the poor, sick, aged, and other disadvantaged people were politically active and lobbied for social change. The principles of these individuals eventually resulted in legislation that made the provision of human services primarily the responsibility of publicly supported agencies. Aid for Dependent Children, Social Security, Medicare, and Medicaid are a few of the high-profile sources of public support for needy people. Although there have been public outcries regarding the cost of human services programs, the cost of government-sponsored human services continues to be small compared to expenditures for military defense, subsidies to business, infrastructure and public facilities improvements, and payments on the national debt, a debt that developed largely because of expenditures other than human services.

Today, there are both public (government) and private (charitable) programs that help insure that basic needs for food, shelter, and clothing are provided to everyone. In addition, assistance is provided to enhance the potential of individuals. Such programs include welfare to work, job placement via Employment Security, and Pell Grants for people who desire postsecondary education but cannot afford it. Programs to meet people's basic needs and to enhance their potential are offered in combination with efforts to ensure the health of individuals. Examples of these combinations include prenatal care programs, childhood immunization programs, and Medicaid, which covers a full range of health care for people who are unable to pay for these services. When injury or sickness occurs, the health care system often provides treatment to both lessen the life risk and speed recovery. Immediate, acute care for accident victims or people who have experienced life-altering health problems such as strokes may be followed by rehabilitation programs to return the individuals to their level of functioning prior to the sickness or injury.

In the latter part of the twentieth century, as health care costs began to approach one-fifth the entire gross national product, strong measures have been enacted by both government and business agencies to slow the rising costs of health care. Just as corporations have had to control costs to be competitive, human service agencies have had to cut costs. Over the last decade and a half, there has also been an effort to lower management costs in human services by bidding services to private companies. The privatization of human services lessens the bureaucracy in government and the cost of services to taxpayers.

One cost-cutting trend of particular interest to people entering the helping professions is the greater standardization of treatments, allowing professionals with less training to be the primary caregivers. For example, many hospitals employ helpers with bachelor's degrees to treat people suffering from various addictions. This has resulted in many career opportunities for individuals with bachelor's degrees.

Bachelor's-Level Professionals

Bachelor's-level graduates work in many different settings, including community agencies, clinics, correctional facilities, and hospitals. Opportunities exist for graduates with degrees in psychology, sociology, criminal justice, public administration, social work, nursing, and many others. In many states with licensing laws, a master's degree is usually attached to the job title of "counselor." However, in some public agencies, some workers at the bachelor's degree level are referred to by that name. Some job titles, but certainly not all, are listed in Table 6.1.

Often, bachelor's-level workers, especially in areas such as mental health, need to advance their careers via graduate degrees in counseling, psychology, and social work. Being licensed by the state in which one works in a discipline allows the employer more latitude in billing for services. Most licensing of mental health professionals, especially those with the title of counselor, requires at least the master's degree. Thus, incentives are often offered to become a licensed professional counselor (LPC), licensed clinical social worker (LCSW), or licensed psychologist. We will talk more about how one can advance in a career in Chapter 13.

TABLE 6.1 Selected Bachelor's-Level Positions in the Human and Health Services

Addictions counselor	Drug rehabilitation aide	Parole / probation officer
Behavioral skills assistant	Evaluation officer	Physical therapist
Case worker / case aide	Group leader	Psychological assistant
Community worker	Intake worker	Recreational therapist
Correctional counselor	Nurse	Social worker
Counselor	Occupational therapist	Unit manager

Utilization of and Need for Human and Health Services

The demand for services and the opportunities to work in the helping professions can be reflected by what extent services are needed and used within our communities. In 1970, it was estimated that 3% of the children in this country were living in poor neighborhoods with large unemployment and single-parent families. In 1990, the estimate of children in the same situation rose to 17% (Annie E. Cassie Foundation, 1997). It is estimated that in 1997 more than 16 million households were headed by a single parent (Bureau of the Census, 1998). Also in 1997, over 8 million adults had the marital status of divorced (Bureau of the Census, 1998). In June 1997, the total number of individuals incarcerated in the United States was more than 1.7 million (Bureau of Justice Statistics, 1998). There were over 1.5 million arrests for drug abuse violations in 1996 (Office of the U.S. President, 1998). In 1996, an estimated 6.4% of the U.S. population age 12 and older (13.9 million citizens) were users of illicit drugs (Department of Health and Human Services, 1998).

In 1996, one in seven children in the United States had no health insurance (Bureau of the Census, 1998). The unemployment rate in 1997 was 4.9% (Sahr, 1998). In the beginning of the twenty-first century an estimated one in five Americans will have some kind of disability, and one in ten will have a severe disability. Already about 9 million people of all ages have disabilities so severe that they require personal assistance to carry out everyday activities (Bureau of the Census, 1997).

In our educational system, there were almost 500,000 high school students who dropped out of school in 1996 (Bureau of the Census, 1998). Also in 1996, many of 11 million undergraduates attending college (Bureau of the Census, 1998) were not prepared for college. A strong need exists to maximize educational opportunities in both public and private education.

With all these needy people requiring educational and human services, what is the employment outlook in the helping professions? According to researcher Jessica L. Kohout, even the U.S. government does not know exactly how many helping professionals will be needed to meet the need for human services (Clay, 1998). In 1996, Kohout estimated that managed care companies identified the need as only 70 behavioral health practitioners per 100,000 citizens, while there already existed 113 per 100,000. This suggests an oversupply of helping professionals. However, when looking at the prevalence of mental and emotional disorders, an oversupply of helpers does not exist. To meet the real need for services, it is estimated that 250 practitioners are needed per 100,000 citizens, which is two times the current average (Clay, 1998). If society makes a commitment to meet the human service needs that exist, the job market for graduates of programs in the helping professions looks very good.

Problems in Service Delivery

Services delivery is based on the ability of the client or patient to access those services. People with strong financial resources are often able to travel long distances and stay long periods for medical and mental health treatments. A wealthy person from Alabama could conceivably seek medical treatment at the Mayo Clinic in Minnesota. But less fortunate clients likely could not consider a treatment center away from the neighborhood or a bus route. Disadvantaged community members often feel uncomfortable in public schools, clinics, and other agencies. Prior experiences with helpers in these facilities may not have made them feel welcome, especially if the facility's delivery system was based on the ability to pay for services. Because of this, the establishment of elegant clinics have been supplemented with outreach programs that bring the services to the consumer, be they at home, in the school, or in the neighborhood. In this way, many needy individuals may access those services, even if they are afraid to enter the clinic.

Colleges often recognize the importance of this. Many college campuses have an extensive array of health clinics, remedial educational services, and career planning and placement centers. Often, however, services such as learning centers that help with improving reading and study skills have more clients if they are inside the residence halls instead of in a building away from student life. Tutoring programs in student living centers work better because of easier access.

Close proximity of services, however, is not always welcome in a community. For example, a neighborhood might fight the placement of a homeless shelter or a treatment center for troubled youth, seeing their presence as a safety risk. Also, if accessing services is too public, prospective consumers may decline to protect their privacy.

Physical facilities may also pose a barrier to the delivery of human services in the community. Storefront operations in the community can provide drug counseling to street people, but some health services may require a large space, involve many types of equipment, and need personnel trained in different disciplines. A small community-based center, even a community hospital, may not be able to accommodate the needs of all people who come for services, so a facility such as a university medical center with its equipment and laboratory facilities may be required.

Sometimes "small and nearby" is better, but at other times "bigger" is better. Service delivery does become a system where small, medium, and large elements are combined, hopefully in a way that they work together, each performing functions appropriate for it.

Designing Service Delivery Systems

Better system design decisions can be made if they are based on objective evidence. Thus, many of the research skills students learn in college and graduate school have practical application in designing service delivery systems. For example, government and private agencies employ epidemiologists, scientists who study the incidence, distribution, and control of disease. Most of the recent studies of the impact of smoking have been epidemiological studies. Although these studies cannot determine cause and effect relationships, they can be used to identify trends and potential relationships. The Center for Disease Control and Prevention, located in Atlanta, is the best known agency that employs epidemiologists.

When social and health problems have been objectively studied or researched, we all have a better idea about how society should invest its resources in correcting existing problems and preventing them in the future. This enables us to make decisions on what kinds of treatments and programs to develop to protect the health and well-being of people.

Social and life scientists apply the same objectivity and methods they used to identify problems in the formulation of treatments. For example, research-oriented clinics begin to assess current treatments and formulate new ones that will also be researched and evaluated. Western Psychiatric Institute and Clinic in Pittsburgh has a long history of working closely with the National Institute of Mental Health (NIMH) in studying mental illness and in developing new mental health interventions. Western Psychiatric was one of a number of research sites to evaluate special therapies targeted for depression (Elkin, et al., 1989). These therapies have since been "manualized," that is protocols providing clear instructions on how to use the therapy have been written. Today, many clinics throughout the world use the treatments first developed in research settings such as Western Psychiatric under the sponsorship of NIMH. Table 6.2 lists Web sites for government and volunteer agencies that employ researchers to study health and social problems and develop programs to treat those problems.

Working in the Public Sector

The vast majority of employment in the helping professions and in public safety occurs in government agencies. Schools, county health clinics, mental health agencies, state divisions of vocational rehabilitation, and social service and welfare

TABLE 6.2   Web Sites for Social Research-Oriented Agencies

Name of Agency	Internet Address
American Public Health Association	*http://www.apha.org*
American Red Cross	*http://www.redcross.org*
Center for Disease Control and Prevention	*http://www.cdc.gov*
Consumer Products Safety Commission	*http://cpsc.gov*
Department of Education	*http://www.ed.gov*
Department of Justice	*http://www.usdoj.gov*
Environmental Protection Agency	*http://www.epa.gov*
National Institute of Health	*http://www.nih.gov*
U.S. Department of Health and Human Services	*http://www.os.dhhs.gov*
U.S. Public Health Service	*http://phs.dhhs.gov/phs/phs.html*

agencies are some of the best examples. The expansion and contraction of employment in these agencies is usually based on funding from Congress and state legislatures. When tax burdens are believed to be high, especially when it limits the ability of business or the private sector to expand and create jobs, less funding becomes available for social programs. However, if the economic conditions turn for the worse, unemployment increases, and more people are less able to pay for services. In response, Congress often increases funding for social programs to reduce suffering and to provide low-cost services to people without means.

It is seldom the case that radical and unanticipated cuts occur in the funding of governmental programs. For this reason, employment in the public sector is often secure. Reductions in programs occur in phases. Personnel are seldom let go in large numbers. However, funding can become inadequate, leaving workers without needed resources, supplies, and equipment. If an agency is forced to limp along with a low budget but high workload, employee morale can decline. Some workers may resign in order to work in the private sector, which at the time may have more resources to devote to the same work.

Working in the Private Sector

Working for a private company that offers health or social services can be attractive. In many cases, fewer laws apply to managing personnel. This could result in greater flexibility to reward effective employees and reduce the number of ineffective ones. In a small company, employees in work groups that supply their own supervision may be able to respond to client needs more quickly, innovate practices more rapidly, and terminate practices that no longer seem to work. These groups of employees do not need to go through layer after layer of administrators to get something changed.

Private companies increasingly are hired to provide social services, the expectation being that these companies will deliver services at a lower cost while still maintaining a profit that will pay dividends to its stockholders. For example, over the past several decades private-for-profit rehabilitation agencies have hired large numbers of rehabilitation counselors. Insurance companies contract with these private rehabilitation agencies, often to help injured employees more rapidly return to employment, saving the insurance companies large sums of money in health and disability benefits.

If the private-for-profit rehabilitation agency has strong contracts with the insurance industry, counselors in the agency may earn high salaries and have job security. This does not always happen, leaving some companies to close the business, laying off employees. Many rehabilitation counselors believe the risk of this is worth the high salaries and benefits they earn from the private versus public agency.

To see what working environment might suit you best, complete Exercise 6.1. Take a few minutes to discuss your responses in Exercise 6.1 with other class members. Did varying opinions show how one work setting might be preferred

EXERCISE **6.1**

What Is Your Ideal Working Environment?

Think about what might be important to you in a work environment by answering the following questions. Indicate whether the factor is important to you, you are neutral about it, or it is unimportant.

Item	Important	Neutral	Unimportant
1. I like to be my own boss; the fewer people I have supervise me, the better.			
2. I would rather have job security than anything else.			
3. I like to have a work area that is all my own; I do not like sharing a desk.			
4. I like to be on the move; I would not like having to work in one small space.			
5. I like my salary to be based on merit or performance; I don't mind competing for raises.			
6. I think I will move from working directly with clients to administration.			
7. I like being affiliated with a large organization with many employees.			
8. I like a casual work setting with few rules, such as a dress code.			
9. Status is important to me; I want to be affiliated with a prestigious organization.			
10. I like the challenge of working with very difficult clients.			
11. Besides serving clients directly, I want to be involved in research.			
12. I want a job that is not too stressful; I want something left over for other pursuits.			
13. I like to be able to work closely with others on the job and to get to know them.			
14. I like working for a large organization because more promotions are possible within the organization.			
15. I prefer being cross-trained in a variety of skills than being highly specialized.			

by some, but not by everyone? Because of the varied opportunities within the helping professions, individual preferences for work environment characteristics usually can be satisfied.

Service Delivery Strategies

Delivering services to clients fundamentally gets down to either having them come to you for services where your offices and equipment are or going yourself to clients where they live or spend most of their days. There are advantages and disadvantages to both basic strategies in terms of the quality of service provided and of how it impacts the career and well-being of the helping professional. After we explore several examples in some detail, we will look across the work settings common in the helping professions.

The Mental Health Clinic

Congress passed the National Mental Health Act (Public Law No. 79-487) in 1946 to create the National Institute of Mental Health (NIMH). One month before his death, President Kennedy signed the Community Mental Health Centers Act (Public Law No. 88-164). Remnants of the system of mental health care centers or clinics built by this legislation remain today. Since the 1960s, the country has been divided into "catchment areas." Each area comprises a population of 50,000, who can receive services from the mental health center in the area.

Today, many of the mental health facilities created during the 1960s are private, nonprofit corporations that serve the chronic mentally ill and their families, the developmentally disabled, people in crisis, and individuals troubled by the stresses of everyday life.

A center often has a so-called partial care or day hospital program in which individuals with severe, debilitating mental illness can come for group recreation, group therapy, and monitoring several times a week. These programs provide relief for the clients' families, who often must provide most of the care. A center provides familiar surroundings and usually has large rooms for group activities and a kitchen for light meals and refreshments. Offices of mental health professionals—including psychiatrists, psychiatric nurses, social workers, psychologists, and mental health counselors—may be located in the center, making a variety of services available. These different mental health professionals can collaborate to assess mental health needs and design programs.

Suites of offices for therapists in a mental health center provide the privacy needed for counseling. Costly equipment, such as testing kits and biofeedback equipment, can be shared by the staff. Mental health centers receive public funding to provide mental health services mandated by law. Their personnel will often complete the evaluations required to involuntarily commit an individual to a hospital or other facility that can provide 24-hour supervision and protection.

Today, many mental health centers also operate what are called *short-term recovery units.* These facilities are somewhere between a hospital and an outpatient center. They may have four to eight beds and offer shelter and crisis intervention. Clients often are the chronic mentally ill who lose control of managing their lives. A brief stay of several days helps avoid longer, more costly hospitalization. Short-term recovery units usually have a nurse, a caseworker, and a mental health counselor. Psychiatrists or psychologists may be on call.

While services are provided to the chronic mentally ill in the main offices of the mental health center, other, better functioning members of the community can attend classes and receive individual, couples, family, and group counseling on an outpatient basis. Because of the diverse clientele and staff size, mental health centers are excellent placements for students. Psychology, counseling, and social work students get a chance to work with clients who function at many different levels. Students are exposed to different programs and differing points of view on how to best serve clients.

For mental health centers to work, clients must be able to access them. They need transportation to and from the center. Effective routing of clients, combined with a record-keeping system that also tracks clients, is essential in a moderate to large-sized clinic. Case conference meetings in which several staff can contribute ideas to a treatment plan augments assessment of progress of individual clients.

The advantages of working in a mental health clinic begin with opportunities to learn from other staff from many different disciplines. In the beginning of one's career, it is important to begin early supervision for a professional license. Potential supervisors for licensure are easy to find in a sizeable clinic. Later in one's career, the other side of this relationship also is available. As a senior staff person, a mental health worker can mentor newer members. In a larger clinic, the chances of promotion may be greater. One also has an opportunity to network widely with other professionals in the community with the potential of enhancing one's professional reputation.

The disadvantages of working in mental health centers begin with often below-average salaries, especially at entry level positions. There is considerable paperwork, and the offering of services almost around the clock may require some to have irregular work hours. More economically disadvantaged clients and clients with more severe problems are likely to be on one's caseload, making the work difficult and stressful. Professional burnout is a strong risk. The prestige of working in a mental health clinic is not as high as working in a hospital or in private practice.

Especially for the young professional, the benefits of beginning one's career in a mental health center probably outweigh the disadvantages. Thus, this work setting is one to consider while you are still in training.

Home-Based Services

Home-based services have attracted considerable attention in recent years. A 15-year follow-up evaluation of home interventions with low-income mothers showed reduced pregnancy rate, use of welfare, child abuse and neglect, and criminal behavior (Olds, et al., 1997). Helping parents develop health habits, parenting skills, and birth control planning are effective when offered in the home. Low-income families are often the target of home-based health and social programs.

Home-based treatment for behavioral disorders among children and adolescents also has become popular. For example, a juvenile who has broken the law by breaking into a neighbor's home to steal money may not be prosecuted for the offense if he or she agrees to see a caseworker to help correct the behavior. Casework involves determining the juvenile's needs, identifying human service agencies that can meet those needs, and coordinating the delivery of the services. This process may begin when the juvenile is referred to a clinic for evaluation and treatment plan development. The treatment plan may include counseling at the clinic, home-based parent education, and a mentoring program. The juvenile may be referred to a clinic for evaluation. When treatment is provided to the individual and family, it is sometimes called providing "wraparound" services. Wraparound services are very popular in helping juveniles and their families.

We can see how helping parents learn more effective discipline or child management practices can help support positive changes that the child may be making in individual counseling. The Washington family, described in Case Illustration 6.1, p 138, demonstrates how in-home parent education can work.

Amos and the Washington family will continue to work together on other discipline issues. The plan Amos follows in the home is part of a larger treatment plan designed by Charles's therapist, who consults regularly with Amos. The two work to keep the individual counseling and the in-home parent training consistent and connected.

There are some risks to home-based services. The worker is less protected from potential harm from a client. The home must be safe to work in. Judging this is often best done initially by a team of human service workers. In-home services are also costly because workers are likely to spend considerable time traveling to client homes. The benefit of working with clients in the home is being able to deal more directly with the real problems that arise in the family. Immediate attention and immediate action can be given to an issue to reduce tensions and problems.

School-Based Services

Providing services to youth can be costly, both in terms of time and money. If a child needs to see a health professional, it is common to have his or her parent take off from work, travel to the school to pick up the child, transport the child to the medical office, wait until the treatment is over, and then transport the child back to school. In the meantime, the child may have missed a considerable number of classes, now has makeup work to do, and may have difficulty learning in the next class because he or she is now behind in the material being studied. One of the authors recalls working in a mental health clinic where one of the social

CASE ILLUSTRATION **6.1**

Charles Washington

Charles Washington, 10, was picked up on two different occasions by the police for being on the streets past the city's evening curfew for juveniles. Charles also has been suspended from school for insolent behavior, using bad language toward teachers, and refusing to do school work. His mother reports similar "oppositional" behavior from Charles and admits that she feels helpless to correct his behavior. The juvenile judge referred the Washingtons to the juvenile probation office, who arranged for group counseling at the mental health center and in-home parent education, also offered through the mental health center.

Amos, a caseworker, goes to the Washington home two afternoons a week to work with Mrs. Washington, Charles, and the other two children in the home as soon as they arrive from school. Amos observes how the children are disciplined and offers suggestions to make the process more effective. Here are some of Amos's observations and recommendations:

Observations

- Charles seems to have a "chip on his shoulder" when at home. He arrives sullen and noncommunicative. He usually does not instigate trouble with his brother and sister
- Mrs. Washington often commands the children to do chores or homework. When they hesitate, she repeats her commands with increasing anger in her voice. Threats of punishment often follow as well.
- If the conflict continues, Charles usually will say something disrespectful, followed by more conflict, followed by him often leaving the apartment without permission.

Recommendations

- Amos tape-recorded the exchanges one day right before Charles refused to sit at the kitchen table and do part of his homework. Amos helped Mrs. Washington begin to understand that her own angry voice may trigger increasingly hostile behavior from Charles. She is beginning to learn that trying to subdue a defiant child rarely works; it usually increases the child's resistance and disobedience.
- Amos helped Mrs. Washington to reduce her tendency to make numerous threats to her children for not doing as told. Amos and she are working with the concept that "actions do speak louder than words." Especially with a defiant child, actions that create a positive relationship while working toward personal needs are more effective than threats and punishment.
- With the help of Amos, the Washingtons are now talking about what would make after-school time and the evenings enjoyable while completing basic chores and homework. Already there is less shouting in the home. Charles is beginning to smile more as well. These are positive signs.

workers for child protective services would transport four of her children at one time to the clinic from three schools. The children would spend most of the morning in the clinic, usually waiting for some of the other children to be seen before everyone was taken back to school. The heavy caseload of the social worker forced her to combine her effort to find services for several children at a time. The child the author was seeing in therapy attended a nearby school. He found that in the hour set aside to see the child at the clinic, the author could drive over to the school for the appointment and be back in time for his next client. By going to the school the child missed one class instead of three.

The Full-Service School

Dryfoos (1994, 1995) documents the first appearance of the title "full-service schools" in Florida's legislation to integrate education, medical, and human services to benefit youth and their families on school grounds or locations with easy access to nearby schools. Our example of the full-service school is Fienberg-Fisher's Elementary in Miami, Florida.

In 1993, Fienberg-Fisher's received a $475,000 grant for constructing a 4,200 square-foot building that included a child care center and offices for several social service agencies (Lim, 1993). A health clinic was the first to open, providing much-needed services to students, their families, and the community. The child care center accepted infants to three year olds with other preschoolers enrolling in Head Start and a prekindergarten program. Following the ideas of James Comer, a noted educator, home-school services teams were organized including teachers, principals, and human service workers. They were supported by parents working as *paraprofessionals,* that is, individuals without formal training and degrees who work as aides under the supervision of professionals.

Students at Feinberg-Fisher are referred to the professionals and paraprofessionals for assessment and intervention. Attention is given to learning disabilities, behavioral problems, and other mental health needs. Early intervention, at the first sign of difficulty and before problems become serious, is emphasized to cut off declining school performance and social adjustment.

Fienberg-Fisher is located in the South Beach area of Dade County, Florida. In South Beach, people from 50 countries are represented. Students in the attendance area are from extremely transient families who live mostly in rental apartments and hotels. Most students live within a two-mile radius of the school and must find their own way to school.

Without many resources, the children and their families need services extended to them. The school fills this need. The Bright Horizons Parent-Student Resource Center at Feinberg-Fisher provides training in child discipline, family literacy, and computer utilization. The Center provides a wealth of materials that parents and children can check out for home use. This resource center is open from 9 A.M. to 9 P.M. during the week and 9 A.M. to 1 P.M. on Saturdays. Physical education teachers focus on health as physical fitness, working toward the goals of the President's Council on Physical Fitness, while other teachers work on nutrition. A program called "Psycho-Emotional Pathway" works toward student self-confidence. The "Do the Right Thing" program builds self-esteem as well by recognizing exemplary behavior. The school counselor and outside agencies provide individual and small group counseling at the school.

The Mobile Clinic

Imagine the difficulty elderly individuals have traveling long distances to receive medical treatment. The number of persons living in a rural area may be too small to support even a modest hospital or clinic. Just as services are brought to children via the full-service school, basic medical screening and treatment can be provided to residents in small communities by equipping a van or similar vehicle to serve as a mobile clinic. Stops could be scheduled across a broad area, allowing patients to travel shorter distances to receive treatment.

A mobile medical unit could use technology to increase its diagnostic capability. The unit could be electronically linked to a university medical center, taking advantage of its instruments and personnel. Medical center specialists could help interpret test results and recommend treatment. Besides the advantages of the mobile unit, in an era of managed care, often special funding is required for a mobile unit program.

Working on a mobile unit would have some advantages. Small teams would work closely together in a small space. If compatible, members of the team could experience a closeness with colleagues not possible in most work environments. Combined travel and patient contact may seem more like an adventure. In addition, consumers of the services provided may be more appreciative, recognizing that a special effort was made to serve them, to consider their needs and their convenience. Mobile units may also provide helpers who live in cities opportunities to avoid some of the negative aspects of city life. The beauty of nature would be closer, and the less hectic pace of country life may generalize to a more peaceful approach to serving patients. It may enable the helping professional also to live in the service delivery area, enjoying the enrichment that results from a lower cost-of-living community. With lower prices for property, the beginning helper may more quickly be able to afford a home.

However, if the mobile unit crew must travel long distances from their headquarters to the people they serve, the workday lengthens, and so does the possibility of burnout. If some piece of equipment breaks while "on the road," a technician usually is not on hand to fix it. If conflict develops among workers, avoiding one another is next to impossible.

Work Settings for Professional Helpers

We now review many of the traditional work settings that employ professional helpers. Selected elements associated with each work setting will be discussed to provide contrasts among the work settings.

A Medical Center

A medical center that is part of a university or other organization is often a referral source for other medical facilities. It expects patients to come to the center for services. A mission of service is combined with teaching and research. Special clinics that treat specific, sometimes rare, conditions are more likely to be present in a medical center receiving money to conduct research. Employees range from world-renown experts to minimum wage blue-collar workers. Considerable status differential could exist among employees.

Medical centers, with their many employees and programs, can be very bureaucratic and have many rules and regulations. Also, the combined goal of training and research can lower the quality of care given individual patients. Students in training are not as skilled as fully trained professionals, and most medical centers have numerous stories of near disasters involving students. Similarly, a research protocol may dictate that treatment be administered in a certain way, and not necessarily the way that the practicing professional endorses. Professional advancement in these centers may require more than time in service and performing one's job well. The next level of promotion may require another degree or certificate. Thus, one usually resigns from the job, gets the necessary credentials, and applies for the higher level position at another medical center. Promotions often do not go to internal candidates.

The variety of services at the medical center include both inpatient and outpatient services. Helping professionals may have a position in which they provide both services. This variety, and the fact that training is so much a part of the medical center mission, makes a medical center a frequent choice for student field placements.

The Community Hospital and Clinic

Today, many health care systems link the large medical center with the general hospitals and clinics in the community. General hospitals have surgical, obstetric, and emergency units to care for the illnesses and accidents common among residents. Inpatient stays at the hospital are increasingly of shorter duration. Some hospitals have diversified as a result. For example, they may have turned a unit of the hospital into a hospice care center.

The hospital is also likely to provide outpatient services. These may include such things as outpatient surgery, physical therapy, coronary rehabilitation, well-baby clinics, and so forth. Physicians practicing in the community have hospital privileges and come and go from it. Primarily, administrators and nursing staff manage the community hospital.

Today, tight budgets require hospital staff to be cross-trained and able to fill in and provide a variety of procedures. The reputation of the community hospital results from the quality of individual care—as in *caring*—provided the patient. Most medical problems benefit from well-known treatments applied in a caring manner. The community hospital can excel in doing this.

Residential and Correctional Facilities

Within our service delivery systems, there still exists a need for long-term place-ments. Because of the cost of long hospital stays, other less restrictive and less expensive strategies are tried first. The mentally ill who have committed violent crimes are an example of a population that may be treated in a long-term, resi-dential facility.

With the exception of a small number of private hospitals for the affluent, residential treatment facilities have had a history of being understaffed and un-derfunded. The reason for this lies in the preference today to spend money for the brief, least restrictive alternative. Many state mental hospitals across the United States have large campuses with many dilapidated buildings, now closed. At the edge of the grounds, one often finds smaller, newer hospitals that house a fraction of the patients once living in the closed buildings. The residential hospital, espe-cially if it is in a small community, is a major employer for the area and thus essential to its economy. Generations of local residents are likely to have worked at the hospital. Specialists and administrators stay for much shorter periods.

Prisons share some of the same features just discussed. In recent years, rural areas suffering from the lack of jobs have been anxious to attract a new correctional facility. The risk to the community is outweighed by the jobs created.

Prisons and other residential facilities may not be attractive as work envi-ronments, but the patients and inmates may be central to the interests and pro-fessional commitment of the helper. For example, the special challenge of working with antisocial character traits may draw one to a career in corrections.

Finally, nursing homes are residential facilities of smaller size with a spe-cialized purpose. Most communities now have higher percentages of elderly among the population than at any other time in their histories. Forms of dementia or senility, such as Alzheimer's, often require a family to seek 24-hour care for their elderly member. Chronic diseases such as arthritis can impair all forms of movement, and advanced cases of diabetes can cause blindness or limb ampu-tation. Nursing homes for chronically ill seniors provide residents with comfort-able environments and social support rather than complete recovery and release. Other types of nursing homes are designed for more active, healthier seniors who need limited assistance but 24-hour medical supervision. One of the newest de-velopments in senior care is offering staged assistance starting with independent living and ending with what seniors in one nursing home called "the other side." The "other side" is for terminally ill residents who require high levels of care and medication designed primarily to ease their suffering.

Employees who work in nursing homes must understand the goals of these facilities and accept the realities of aging. Helpers who are devoted to the idea that the last stages of life should be lived with dignity and comfort are ideal em-ployees. Moreover, helpers must understand that the stereotype of the cheerful senior is not an accurate picture. Residents with certain diseases, such as Alzhe-imer's, often pass through a stage in which they are verbally and physically aggressive. Other residents who were unpleasant in their younger years will not change magically because of aging but will still be unpleasant as seniors.

Community Outreach Programs

Serving the elderly also includes many programs intended to provide support for needy citizens to remain in their own homes. Meals-on-Wheels is an example of this. Outreach may be coordinated at a center, be it for seniors, juveniles, or the community in general. The senior or youth center provides space for professional services, recreation, and planning.

Outreach programs are often funded by special grants from government and private foundations. Unless they become part of a permanent agency in the community, they will exist for the funding period and then disappear. This is to be expected if the program is intended to meet a particular need that is not expected to last. If the need is lasting, then the initial program hopefully demonstrates how the need can be met. Success doing this increases the likelihood that the program will continue, maybe under the sponsorship of another agency.

Community outreach workers need to be comfortable working for a project that may not last. They must also do well where there is not much structure or direction. Planning and operating such programs require one to be a self-starter and good at working without a lot of supervision. At the same time, the outreach worker also has to be good at being accountable to generate records and data to show that the program works.

Community outreach programs often combine paid professionals and volunteers. This adds a special dimension to the work. Often the professional helper needs additional leadership skills to focus the effort of volunteers. However, sometimes this is reversed. The American Red Cross, for example, operates largely as a volunteer organization, with paid staff being a very small part of its human resource. In the Red Cross, the staff person most often takes direction from a coordinating committee or board of volunteers. It is the case that most community programs have citizen boards establishing policy and evaluating the performance of program administrators. Getting along with a citizen board of directors requires very good public relations skills.

The potential for large numbers of outreach programs operating in a community exists. Later, in Chapter 10, we will look at programs intended to serve the community and how such programs can be designed and linked together.

Private Practice

Having trained hundreds of professional helpers, we very often hear our graduates say that establishing a private practice in counseling or some other human service is their ultimate objective. It is indeed appealing to think of being one's own boss, maybe even becoming so successful as to require hiring others to handle all the business.

You may recall from an earlier section of this chapter, to achieve success in the private sector, the emphasis has to be both on being a competent practitioner and a businessperson. Case Illustration 6.2 shows some important aspects of opening a private practice.

Evaluating Service Delivery Systems

After reviewing several different approaches to service delivery and some of the many different settings in which professional help is offered, we now are at the point of examining the best ways to serve the needs of people. To do this, we must consider what criteria to use in evaluating service delivery. Stroul and Friedman (1986) recommend using the following criteria: how accessible the services are, how restrictive the services are (that is, do they avoid violating clients' basic rights), and how cost-effective the services are. We also believe that the best system provides a full continuum of services, is coordinated under a unified management system, and uses interdisciplinary treatment teams, thus offering coordinated services among various agencies within a community.

This assumption was tested when an $80-million project, called the Fort Bragg Demonstration Project, was compared to a standard fee-for-service program

---

C A S E   I L L U S T R A T I O N   **6.2**

Chwee

Chwee's live-in partner received an excellent job offer in a different city, too good to turn down. Since Chwee was a licensed psychologist and had seven years of mental health experience, she decided that the move to the new community would be an opportunity for her too to begin a private practice. After six months, Chwee was barely making rent payments on her office. She closed her practice and took a position in an agency.

Later Chwee realized that prior to starting her practice, she had not done a market analysis of what services existed and what services were needed in the area. She thought that if she charged a lower fee than other practices, she would get business. Chwee put little thought into the location of her office, selecting it primarily because of the low rental fee. Her attempts to network with other mental health professionals was not sufficient, it seemed, to compensate for her being unknown in the community. Her out-of-the-way office did not help generate business either. Chwee realized that her business skills did not equal her counseling skills.

Three years later, Chwee was better known in the community. She joined an established group practice with a good reputation and many contracts for ongoing services with agencies and businesses. She was able to set her own work hours and specialize in services she enjoyed providing. The group practice has an office manager and secretary that take care of billing and records, helping her to avoid that kind of paperwork and to concentrate on her therapy.

covered under CHAMPUS, the medical insurance program for military personnel. The Demonstration Project provided continuous and coordinated services to children and adolescents from military families. The CHAMPUS program provided quality services, but the services were not coordinated and they often had gaps or interruptions in service. When evaluated a year later, both service delivery systems resulted in high client satisfaction. The Demonstration Project, while more costly, did not show improved mental health outcome or quicker recovery (Bickman, 1996). The researchers concluded that delivery system design is not as important as the quality and potency of the treatments within the system. Since both the Demonstration Project and CHAMPUS often used the same treatments, differences in outcome were minimal. The delivery system does not reform the treatment; it merely insures that clients receive it. Service delivery systems improve outcome if they insure that needed services are provided.

Summary

Providing services to persons in need requires the building of a system that allows consumers access to those services while the costs of those services are kept as low as possible. Some needed services can only be provided by a large facility, sometimes distant from consumers. Other services are effectively delivered by small facilities located close to clients. A combination of delivery strategies is often needed to provide comprehensive service. Still, research shows that the quality of individual services is more important than the design of the system in determining the results obtained.

Service delivery systems take advantage of both government-sponsored programs, and services delivered by private agencies and companies. The many different services needed by people and the variety of means used to deliver those services creates many career options for helping professionals. It makes it possible to match one's own preferences for a work environment with the most desirable alternatives available.

CHAPTER 6 EXIT QUIZ

Answer the following questions, writing "T" for true and "F" for false in the spaces provided.

_____ 1. Social services today are delivered increasingly by private agencies contracted by the government.

_____ 2. Many career opportunities exist in the helping professions for individuals with a bachelor's degree.

_____ 3. Citizens always welcome the placement of social and health services in close proximity to where they live.

_____ 4. Public or governmental human services agencies have the disadvantage of low job security for their employees.

_____ 5. Because of fewer regulations governing their services, private agencies often can respond more quickly to new client needs as they arise.

_____ 6. Remnants of the mental health system designed in the 1960s still exist.

_____ 7. Wraparound services are very popular in helping juveniles and their families.

_____ 8. Schools are not suitable places to offer social and health services.

_____ 9. Hospitals also coordinate outreach services to patients in addition to the treatments offered inside the hospital.

_____10. Research has shown that the quality of individual services being offered is more important than the way in which they are delivered.

Answers:

1. T; 2. T; 3. F; 4. F; 5. T; 6. T; 7. T; 8. F; 9. T; 10. T.

SUGGESTED LEARNING ACTIVITIES

1. Review your answers to the questions in Exercise 6.2. Select the five most important items for you. Review the different service delivery settings in the chapter. List three settings that best satisfy your five most important answers to Exercise 6.2.

2. List the human and health services in your community. (Your community may have a directory of services to help you.) What appear to be strong service areas? What gaps appear to exist?

3. Divide the class into groups of five students. Assign to each member one of the following: the local hospital, the public assistance and welfare office, the largest local mental health facility, a private practice therapist, a local charity (for example, the Salvation Army), or private nonprofit organization (for example, the American Red Cross). Have each group member contact a representative from each setting or agency. Have the group members report back to the class what they learned about the services their contact provides and how their contact cooperates with other agencies in the community.

4. Arrange a debate in class with one point of view representing the public sector and another representing the private sector. Have each side present a beginning argument that their sector can provide services better than the other sector to the community. Allow for each side to make a rebuttal. Have the class vote on which side provided the most persuasive arguments. Discuss the results in class.

5. Health Maintenance Organizations (HMOs), Preferred Provider Organizations (PPOs), and some health insurance companies now limit the number of psychotherapy sessions that can be provided to people with various types of mental

health problems and the amount paid for those services. Divide the class into teams to debate the pros and cons of limiting sessions and the amount of funds spent for mental health services.

REFERENCES

Annie E. Cassie Foundation (1997). *City kids count*. Baltimore: Author.

Bickman, L. (1996). A continuum of care: More is not always better. *American Psychologist 51*(7), 689–701.

Bureau of Justice Statistics (1998). *Nation's prisons and jails hold more than 1.7 million*. Washington, DC: Department of Justice.

Census, Bureau of the (1997). *Disabilities affect one-fifth of all Americans: Proportion could increase in coming decades*. Washington, DC: U.S. Department of Commerce.

Census, Bureau of the (1998). *Annual high school dropout rates*. Washington, DC: U.S. Department of Commerce.

Census, Bureau of the (1998). *College enrollment of students*. Washington, DC: U.S. Department of Commerce.

Census, Bureau of the (1998). *Children without health insurance*. Washington, DC: U.S. Department of Commerce.

Census, Bureau of the (1998). *Households by type*. Washington, DC: U.S. Department of Commerce.

Census, Bureau of the (1998). *Marital status of the population*. Washington, DC: U.S. Department of Commerce.

Clay, R. (1998). Psychologists, social workers and psychiatrists: Too many or not enough? *APA Monitor 29*(9), 20.

Department of Health and Human Services (1998). Annual national drug survey results released: Overall drug use is level, but youth drug increase persists. Washington, DC: Department of Health and Human Services. 1998.

Dryfoos, J.G. (1994). *Full service schools: A revolution in health and social services for children, youth, and families*. San Francisco: Jossey-Bass.

Dryfoos, J.G. (1995). Full service schools: Revolution or fad? *Journal of Research on Adolescence 5*(2), 147–172.

Elkin, I., et al. (1989). National Institute of Mental Health treatment of depression collaborative research program: General effectiveness of treatment. *Archives of General Psychiatry 46*, 971–983.

Lim, G. (October 7, 1993). Feinberg-Fisher, Beach High getting clinics. *The Miami Herald*, pp. 4, 26.

Office of the U.S. President (1998). *Social statistics briefing room*. Washington, DC: Office of the U.S. President.

Olds, D.L., et al. (1997). Long-term effects of home visitation on maternal life course and child abuse and neglect. *Journal of the American Medical Association 278*, 637–643.

Sahr, R.C. (1998). *Welfare and jobs, project vote smart*. www.vote-smart.org/issues/1998rsb/welfare.html. Accessed on September 22, 1998.

Stroul, B.A., and R. Friedman (1986). *A system of care for children and youth with severe emotional disturbances*. Washington, DC: Georgetown University Child Development Center, CASSP Technical Assistance Center.

7 Counseling Individuals

WHAT YOU WILL LEARN

1. How to describe the general process of individual counseling as it progresses step by step.
2. Examples of approaches that work well with different types of clients.
3. Where you can go to learn more about counseling individuals.

Working face to face with an individual is our most common image of a helping relationship. We think of helping professionals as good interviewers and good relationship builders. We often entrust to the helping professional the challenge of engaging a troubled or suffering individual that others with less training are unable to reach. Even if our efforts to be helpful extend to working with a person's family or helping the individual within a small group, in between family or group meetings individual contacts with clients often are used. The "one-on-one" time provides the opportunity to establish closeness and confidentiality, and to work through issues very relevant to the individual, but not relevant for discussion in a family or group session.

As a person begins training for a helping profession and learns how to interview, many of the attitudes and skills mentioned in earlier chapters become part of his or her repertoire. As educators of helpers, we have seen how quickly our students learn and demonstrate the individual skills described in Chapter 4. In a very brief period of training, a helper can become effective in conducting an initial counseling session. More difficult is understanding how to connect what occurred in an initial interview with a series of sessions that follow. How can 6 or even 15 interviews comprise a coherent process of helping?

In this chapter, we look at the helping process as it extends over time. In the future you may work with an individual over many months. For some clients you may schedule weekly sessions. Your direct contact with other clients may be more irregular. At times you may believe that a client should be seen on a regular basis for a long time, but the reality of the situation, because of a court order or because of insurance coverage, only allows you a fraction of the time you believe is needed. You feel pressured to squeeze all the elements of the more long-term process into the brief time you have.

Helpers work under these different circumstances that affect the time allocated for the helping process. The next section of this chapter provides a map of the helping process from the beginning to its end. Each different time in the process has different issues and different objectives.

After a general overview of the individual counseling process, we present three popular approaches to helping. These approaches contain ideas that help us grasp important issues and goals. The ideas also show how we can adjust helping so it fits the needs of clients with very different problems and personalities. The material that follows should make it easier to combine a series of client contacts into one coherent sequence.

Process of Individual Counseling

The Beginning Phase

The immediate goals in the counseling process are: (1) to establish a positive working relationship and (2) to explore the reasons the client sought help. These two goals are accomplished by creating an interpersonal atmosphere characterized by empathy, respect, and genuineness (Rogers, 1957). Empathy was discussed earlier in Chapter 2. Important in establishing an empathic relationship is the counselor's ability to overcome self-consciousness and pay complete attention to what the client says. Getting to know clients and appreciating their circumstances makes it possible to respect them, even some that others find difficult to like. It also makes it easier for the helper to separate the actions of the client from the person. Our clients may do things that we do not condone, but because they do them does not prohibit us from accepting and respecting them as individuals.

As noted in Chapter 4, listening is an absolute requirement for knowing the client. If counseling begins well, clients will feel supported and encouraged and will begin to become active participants in the process. Helpers can tell if a partnership is developing if the talk ratio between helper and client is around 50:50. The helper encourages client participation by asking open-ended questions mixed with comments that reflect and summarize the content and sentiments of the client. The client's opinions are shown to be important by the helper soliciting them. A question such as "What do you make out of what we have been talking about?" may be used for this purpose.

Early in the helping process, the emphasis is on the helper understanding the internal frame of reference of the client. To do this, the helper listens. A good rule of thumb for helping people is to listen for at least one-half of the time you have to help. If you only have 20 minutes to help someone, spend 10 minutes listening before you do anything else. As discussed in previous chapters, helpers are involved in "active listening" that uses reflections, open-ended questions, and summarizations to show understanding.

In listening, it is important for the helper not to prejudge because doing so cuts off avenues of exploration. The cooperation between helper and client keeps the discussion focused and meaningful. Chit-chat is kept to a minimum. The helper demonstrates leadership not by overcontrolling, but by remaining the most flexible member of the relationship. Helpers who demand that clients conform to their wishes and ideas do not show flexibility or strength. The helper shows strength through character, sensitivity, and good timing. Timing is displayed by often waiting to make a point when the client is ready to deal with it, not when the counselor is ready. For example, coming out as a gay or lesbian person or acknowledging sexual abuse are issues that require timing.

Telling people how they should be resembles teaching. It is important to understand that there are some similarities between teaching and counseling, but many differences. In both, learning occurs, but the process is different. The counseling process is based much more on cooperative learning. Instructing, training, educating, and lecturing are all synonyms for teaching. In later phases of counseling, teaching may be relevant, as we shall see, but in the beginning listening is more important. Cavanagh (1990) thinks that new counselors attempt to reduce their anxiety by lecturing in counseling sessions. In one session they may give a seminar on anger, the next may be on communication, and a third on sexuality. Teaching may give beginning counselors the impression that they are "doing something." Cavanagh says that counseling is more than passing on to the client one's own class notes on behavior and emotions.

Avoiding the lectures to achieve the early objective of a working relationship is essential for later stages of helping. Trust is necessary for clients to reveal their most sensitive concerns. Many clients need a relationship with a professional helper because the attempts of others to help have failed. Clients may have had a series of unsuccessful relationships. For example, a teenager referred for counseling by the courts may have had many painful experiences at home with parents. The juvenile adds to this conflict other painful experiences in school with teachers and the principal. In the community, additional negative experiences occurred with the police. This youngster more than likely will bring into counseling the expectation that the new "authority figure," the helper, cannot be trusted any more than the police, the principal, or parents.

The distrust of helping professionals carried by clients to counseling is based on past experiences and has nothing to do with the counseling relationship just beginning. The client has transferred to the helper feelings generated from the past. Because of this, the helper may not deserve the negative treatment the client gives. Eventually, if a working relationship does develop, these feelings of distrust, of being misunderstood, and of being mistreated can be discussed. In the beginning, the counselor first must recognize the situation and show self-discipline by setting as a priority the client's need for trust.

Clients need a trusting relationship, but helpers need not be naive to the troubles many clients have caused for themselves and for others. They have learned distrust from their negative experiences with others, but sometimes clients respond to their own hurt by striking back at innocent people or by isolating themselves from people who deserve their trust.

As a trusting relationship develops, exploration of problems occurs. Clients begin to make progress by being able to tell their story. At first it is limited to their frame of reference. It will likely contain their narrow view of the situation that does not permit them to see alternatives, different ways of solving their problems that might be more successful than the ones they have tried.

While establishing a working relationship and exploring problems, the helper must remain sensitive to cultural issues. In earlier chapters, we discuss how respect is conveyed in different cultures. Listening is often conveyed by our nonverbal behaviors. Direct eye contact, leaning forward, and intense facial expressions may be too intrusive. Self-disclosure, especially with regard to personal weaknesses, is valued differently in many cultures. While we encouraged the helper to involve the client in a working partnership, many cultures expect the helper to be an expert who will provide information and advice.

The Middle Phase

In the middle phase, the emphasis is on clients gaining a new frame of reference that helps them better cope with their circumstances. Providing a different frame of reference is possible for the counselor because of careful listening throughout the process. Counselors listen to more than words: they listen to the meaning of words and to body language, taking what they hear to begin to make inferences. This leads to a new way to interpret events, resulting in new strategies and options to improve both how the client feels and how the client responds to everyday situations.

In the middle phase, helpers begin to share their understanding of the situation to increase client understanding. This is sometimes called *insight.* Not all approaches to counseling believe insight is necessary for the client to begin behaving differently, but some do argue that insight comes before changed behavior. Successful counseling usually accomplishes both increased understanding and more effective behavior. Read Case Illustration 7.1, p. 152, for an example of how a helper balances insight and behavior change.

Clients often search for a new understanding of their problems in the middle phase of helping because without it, they would have no reason to behave in a different way. For example, in the beginning it is common for clients to believe that their problems are caused by others. If only their parents were different or their friends were different, they would be all right. From this perspective, clients believe that the problem can be solved by others changing but by the clients remaining the same.

Clients learn to "personalize" the problem by seeing how they contribute to the situation. This opens the door for self-change, the real focus of counseling. Changing ourselves is never easy, but it becomes possible in a supportive, trusting relationship. The helper's acceptance makes it easier for the client to accept ownership for at least part of the problem.

CASE ILLUSTRATION **7.1**
Albert and Alisa

Albert, a second semester college sophomore, comes to the counseling center because he wants to overcome his uneasiness with women. Albert has not dated since he began school the year before. He has met several women in class, at church, and at campus social functions. He would like to begin dating one or more of them. In all other aspects of his life, Albert is satisfied. He is getting good grades in school, has many male friends, and is on good terms with his family.

Alisa is assigned to help Albert. She is a staff counselor at the center. Alisa has an initial interview with Albert, learning about his concern. As she plans how to help Albert, Alisa is faced with several questions. How much should she go into Albert's past, his heterosexual experiences in particular? How important would it be to explore in detail Albert's self-image? Could an exploration of the past provide an explanation for why Albert seems to be shy or at least uncomfortable asking a female out for a date? And would this understanding of how the past influenced the present help Albert to become more comfortable dating women in the future?

As Alisa ponders these questions, she also considers other options. Could she take a here-and-now view of the situation? Could she ask Albert, "What would immediately help you feel more comfortable about asking someone out?" If Albert could answer the question, would it make sense to simply work on the behaviors that might enable Albert to call someone for a date and increase the likelihood that she will accept? If Alisa takes this straightforward approach with little emphasis on insight into the reasons 'behind' Albert's shyness, would Albert be successful? Or might it be necessary to explore even further some not-so-obvious reasons for his inability to feel comfortable around women? For example, does he see women as more threatening than men and, if so, why? If this hypothesis proves correct, will it explain some of his discomfort?

Alisa realizes that many clients are searching for a framework that put old problems in a new light. She also realizes that clients do not want to wait long for change. She needs to formulate a balance between the achievement of new understanding of problems and working on immediate behavior change.

Egan (1994) notes that coming to grips with one's own involvement in the problem situation becomes a motivator to change. The helper uses confrontation, that is mirroring back to clients aspects of themselves that are contradictions, areas that have been disowned but that lurk under the reality of the situation. From this a new honesty can emerge, and clients can work toward realistic changes while they gain acceptance of things they cannot change. We have already noted in earlier chapters that care should be taken in the use of confrontations. One that sounds more like the counselor is thinking out loud to get feedback usually works better than a confrontation that seems like an accusation. Case Illustration 7.2, p. 153, is an example of how this happens.

This case of Karen shows how many clients begin counseling with one agenda that they eventually abandon to work on the underlying issues. The

CASE ILLUSTRATION **7.2**

Karen

Karen had been through a very difficult divorce that involved a bitter custody battle over her two sons. In the final judgment, Karen's husband received primary custody of the boys and she ended up paying both child support and alimony. Her visitations were limited to two weekends per month and alternating holidays.

For months Karen resisted counseling, but after considerable coaxing from her brother she finally sought professional help. At first in counseling all Karen could talk about were her former husband's faults and how he had cheated her out of her children. Her anger was overwhelming during the first weeks. Her counselor was able to tolerate its expression while being supportive of Karen without joining into the contempt for Karen's former husband.

Gradually Karen became more willing to explore feelings besides the anger directed toward her former husband. She began to realize that she had much anger left over from her unhappy childhood, and her difficult early years as an overweight, self-conscious adult. With gentle confrontations from her counselor, Karen began to realize that she also had a great deal of anger toward herself. How could she have been so concerned about her career that she spent little time with her sons, that everyone, including the judge, recognized that her husband was the primary caretaker of the boys?

With a more personalized view of the custody situation that no longer disowned her involvement in the outcome, Karen was able to grieve not only the loss of primary child custody, but her wished-for image of herself as an all loving mother. Rather than crushing her, this realization enabled her to be more tolerant of her sons' fighting and arguing when they visited. She began to be more able to relate to them than to focus on how uncomfortable she was when they fought. Her increased self-acceptance in counseling led to greater acceptance of her sons. The best consequence was a growing closeness to them after the divorce. No small additional benefit was a new emotional freedom from the hate she had had toward her former husband. Being able to personalize her problem had helped her.

---

middle phase of counseling often ends with a reformulation of goals. This permits clients to work on the real problems.

In getting to the real issues, especially with the use of confrontation and interpretation, careful understanding should be given to cultural differences. Recall from earlier chapters that some cultural groups would see a direct confrontation as disrespectful. Interpretations that call for a deeper exploration of hidden motives and emotional blind spots may be viewed as insensitive.

The Late Phase

If the early and middle phases of counseling have been successful, clients will feel better, have more self-confidence, and have a stronger commitment to change their situation. These feelings of empowerment increase the desire to act. Whether the client's life improves depends on this action.

The action phase of counseling may not occur without the relationship-building and self-confrontation that was described earlier. Many clients do not have the resilience to persevere in their actions without support and a revised, more realistic view of their situation. A person who acts on what he/she knows has to be done and who can do that without excessive dependence on others usually does not need counseling.

During the middle phase, the helper may have been very active in formulating a revised understanding of the client's situation. The helper may have interpreted new meaning to situations and human actions, confronted the client's self-deception, and drawn comparisons among events and people. This activity may begin to decline as the focus turns more and more toward what the client does between counseling sessions.

The between-session work of the client is reported during sessions that follow. It may be analyzed to determine why it succeeded or failed. Together the helper and client plan, revise strategy, and consolidate gains. The support of the helper enables the client to maintain energy and determination. Roger Banister, the first human to run a mile under four minutes, was once asked what enabled him to push himself to achieve this record. He said that he ran hard because he did not want to disappoint his coach. Clients first may try something new that they were afraid to try before simply because they do not want to disappoint their counselor. Afterward they can continue to do it because it works. Read Case Illustration 7.3, p. 155, for an example.

Working relationships between helpers and clients do not always result in all initial goals being accomplished. However, if the client seems to be headed in the right direction and is motivated to keep working on problems, the helping process has succeeded.

The degree of emphasis on action-taking is influenced also by culture. We know that differences exist regarding the value of long-range planning. Planning and breaking down complex tasks into more easily achievable small steps is not common to all cultures. Skill mastery, for example, is considered by some as more a "male" priority. Fitting in and being part of a relationship or group may be of higher value than succeeding, especially if being masterful and successful is based on competition. Sometimes these themes intertwine, as in the case of Raymond. For him, success in counseling was to meet his goal of fitting in and being part of relationships consistent with his sexual orientation.

Types of Individual Counseling

During all parts of the helping process—beginning, middle, and late—the process must be adjusted to meet the needs of the client. For example, a client may seek help for a problem that is immediate and pressing. In this case, a solution must occur quickly. Another client may be troubled by a different problem, one that he or she has struggled with for years. No one would expect that the resolution

Raymond

Raymond went to the student counseling center because he was feeling lonely and depressed. In counseling he learned to trust his counselor and reveal his painful shyness. Since a child he had been teased and bullied because he was thin and small for his age. Finally, in high school, Raymond found a degree of peer acceptance by joining the cross country team at the repeated urging of a kind teacher.

As a runner Raymond did well enough to letter three years. He gained some friends from the team and recognition in school. Raymond still felt unattractive physically; he was too self-conscious even to ask girls to the school dances. During high school he did not have one date or one outing with a female that was private and personal. In this respect, he was much like our earlier example, Albert.

In college, Raymond became increasingly anxious about his lack of contact with women whom he found attractive. While in counseling, he was able to confront his shyness and his tendency to expect rejection before he had any reason to expect it. His counselor helped him to understand how he mentally talked himself out of meeting women.

At first, his counselor offered a different view of success and failure in dating as the necessary but often painful process of learning compatibility with others. Raymond's counselor used humorous stories to defuse the tension of asking someone out. For example, the counselor encouraged Raymond to greet a woman in class, saying, "If you say hello, you might think next you could ask her out for coffee, but please don't propose marriage over your first expresso." Raymond began to realize that a turndown by a woman would not destroy him.

A few days after he chatted with a woman in his Spanish class, she asked him if they could study together. Would that have happened if counseling had not helped Raymond to be more communicative in small ways?

of that problem would occur quickly. Clients need the helping process to be tailored to their unique situations.

Crisis Counseling

One type of counseling that is short-term and solution-focused is crisis counseling. It is based on some of the same principles listed in Chapter 1 when crisis intervention was discussed. Things happen to people that are disruptive. These events create a sense of imbalance and a loss of control. In times of crisis, clients feel a great deal of emotional turmoil and are disorganized intellectually as well. Loss of control in some cases can result from an overwhelming experience that has traumatized the individual. A string of disappointments can begin to eat away at the ability of the client to adapt, eventually resulting in an emotional breakdown. Here are some situations that could lead to a state of active crisis:

- Getting the results of a blood test and learning that you are HIV positive.
- Discovering that your partner has been sexually active with your friend.
- Having a loved one die suddenly.
- Being accused of cheating and threatened with expulsion from school.
- Being arrested for driving under the influence and realizing the possible penalty of jail time besides the loss of your driver's license.

Crisis counseling clearly differs from other types of counseling by its limited objectives. The goal for the client is to regain equilibrium at least to the level that existed prior to the crisis. If clients remain in a state of crisis, the risk increases for damaging, long-term consequences such as violence toward self, violence toward others, depression, or shock. Here are some real-life traumas encountered by one of the authors:

- A woman and her fiancee were driving across country in separate cars to their new home. As she watched in her rearview mirror, the rear axle from a tractor-trailer came across the median of the interstate, crushed her fiancee's car, and killed him. She stopped trusting all mechanical things.
- A child's house was destroyed by a tornado while he and his family huddled in the basement. He had nightmares and startle responses to loud noises, particularly trains.
- A man was flying across the Pacific Ocean when the cargo door on his plane gave way and ripped a large hole in the side of the plane. More than half a dozen people were swept out of the plane by the decompression. He thought he was next. Ten years later, he still refuses to fly.

So how does a counselor work with a crisis when the time available may range from one to six sessions? The helper focuses only on the current crisis, maybe noting but not dealing with more long-standing problems. The helper may also be more active than previously described. This may involve being more direct, suggesting actions, and even intervening with others for the welfare of the client. These interventions could result in referrals to other helping professionals. For example, a teenager on probation had been involved in a hit-and-run fatality. He had not been driving. A social worker for the project in which he lived contacted the youth's probation officer. The youth was then able to discuss with the probation officer his fear of identifying the driver and his own remorse for the death of the pedestrian. When the driver was arrested for another offense and linked to the hit-and-run fatality, there was no penalty for the youth who contacted the social worker.

In the situation just described, the social worker decided to help the youth act decisively in response only to the hit-and-run incident. Later, the social worker and the teenager could examine more closely the attitudes and relationships that put the youngster at risk. They could examine his response tendencies that invite trouble. In the heat of the crisis, the goal was to help him deal with his mounting fears and his need to confront the problem with action that reduced the threat of even more serious consequences.

When the situation is not quite as urgent and the goal is to help correct ongoing problems, helping will follow more closely the process described earlier. The process may be different depending on an analysis of what the helper can use that most likely will reach the client. Here are just a few factors that may influence the approach a helper may take:

- The client thinks very concretely and cannot easily understand abstract concepts.
- The client is suspicious of people in authority and resists being influenced by them.
- The client is demoralized, has extremely low self-esteem, and has very low expectations that he or she can influence what happens.
- The client has prior experience with counseling that was negative.

To provide just a sample of the many different directions counseling can take, we will describe three contrasting approaches. We selected reality therapy, rational emotive behavior therapy, and client-centered therapy. These three approaches emphasize different dimensions of a person: the first focuses on behavior, the second on cognitions, and the last on emotions. All three approaches are commonsense in nature. They are easy to learn and have a large following among helping professionals.

Reality Therapy

This approach to counseling was originally proposed by William Glasser (1965) and further developed and simplified by Robert Wubbolding (1986). Both authors have combined their efforts to provide a recent statement on this therapy (Glasser and Wubbolding, 1995). The part of this approach that describes the reasons why people behave as they do is called *control theory,* and the part that describes how people are helped to change is *reality therapy.* These theories have been applied to a wide variety of settings, including correctional centers, schools, and mental health clinics (Parrott, 1997). Let us take a look at some of the basic ideas in control theory.

Control theory hypothesizes that people are motivated by both needs and wants. Needs are universal to all; they include the need for survival, belonging, power (achievement, self-worth, and recognition), fun, and freedom.

Exercise 7.1, p. 158, should help you understand the universal needs of human beings. Individuals attempt to fulfill needs by their specific wants. For example, to desire a car is a want. One person may want to own an automobile so he can go out for a drive any time. He may fantasize about the open road with the windows down and the wind blowing through his hair, seeing the sights, and being able to go wherever he wants. For this person, the want of a car is to

EXERCISE **7.1**

Life Complaints

On a blank sheet of paper make a numbered list from 1 to 20 down the left margin of the paper. What you will be asked to write, you will not have to share with anyone unless you want to. With this in mind, list all the complaints you have about your current life situation. What is going on right now that you don't like? Be completely honest. Try to list at least 10 complaints. They can be little things or big things.

After you have listed your present complaints, try to determine if the item has to do with belonging (a problem with relationships), power (having to do with feeling worthwhile or valued), fun (you know what that is), or freedom (not enough opportunities to be who you are). In class your instructor may want to discuss the control theory set of needs and have students provide examples of each need. You have the option to share one of yours or make one up.

satisfy a freedom need. Another individual may desire her own automobile so she can go home to visit family and friends, to be able to go on more dates, or to drive to her friends across town to get together. For this individual, an automobile is an important tool in satisfying belonging needs. Certainly a car can satisfy other needs as well. It can get individuals to a concert or a ballgame and satisfy their need for fun. According to control theory, every person has the same needs, but individuals satisfy those needs in different ways.

Reality therapists use wants and needs as ways to understand their clients. From the moment they begin working with someone, they interpret what the person says in terms of needs that are and are not being satisfied. Not having needs and wants met will produce specific behaviors. Sometimes these behaviors backfire; they do not produce positive results but create even worse circumstances. The goal of counseling is to find ways for clients to better satisfy their needs and get what they want. Read Case Illustration 7.4, p. 159, for an example.

Another important idea in control theory has to do with what constitutes "total behavior," which is composed of doing, thinking, feeling, and physiologic behaviors. Again, the goal of behavior is to satisfy needs and wants. Any change in one part of total behavior results in changes in the other parts—maybe not immediately, but eventually. For example, if a person begins to feel depressed, his or her thoughts are likely to become less optimistic, motivation lessens, and bodily functions may slow as well. The unity of behavior composed of doing, thinking, feeling, and physiology can be used to help a person. A helper can assist a client to make positive changes in one, and improvements in all the rest will follow. Control theory teaches that the easiest part of total behavior to change are actions or doing. Doing exercises the most control over total behavior, followed by thinking.

CASE   ILLUSTRATION   **7.4**
Arnold

Arnold feels his parents are too strict. They require him to be home on weeknights at 9:00 and 11:00 on weekends. He envies his friends, who can stay out longer. On several occasions, Arnie broke curfew. In return, his parents grounded him. While grounded, he tried to sneak out. He was caught again and grounded for a longer time. He then argued with his parents, who then would not allow his friends to visit Arnold. Regardless of how we may feel about the actions taken by his parents, it does seem clear that the behaviors Arnie has chosen to satisfy his needs are not working. He may require help in finding more effective ways to satisfy his needs.

The final part of control theory that we will describe has to do with perception. There are two different levels of perception, low and high. If you simply have knowledge of an event, it is a low level of perception. If your perception not only gives information but provides value to the situation, then you have a high level of perception. You perceive the meaning of the event. Many people who do not do a good job in satisfying their needs and wants operate too much with only a low level of perception. They act and can tell you what happened, but they have not evaluated or valued the act. People can satisfy their needs better with higher levels of perception.

Let us begin reviewing reality therapy. We will discuss how helping progresses from this approach by looking at the kind of relationship the helper establishes, how client change is encouraged, and how planning helps the client to satisfy needs.

Creating a Therapeutic Environment. The goal of this approach, like most others, is to develop a supportive, nonthreatening atmosphere. The counselor makes an effort to be friendly, both through verbal and nonverbal behavior. Listening is important, but the counselor tries to keep the client in the present, rather than focusing on the past. Reality therapists tend not to reflect feelings, preferring to use "probes." Probes are questions, the best of which are open-ended so they cannot be answered by a "yes" or "no." However, helpers following reality therapy show understanding by frequently summarizing what has been said. Their interview style is a combination of probes and summarizations. The probes enable the client to investigate how things are and how they would like them to be. Summarizations assist the helper in showing acceptance and understanding.

The helper, besides making the sessions safe, attempts to meet the needs of the client, using humor to make parts of the process fun and engaging. Helpers make every effort to show confidence that the client can find ways to deal with past difficulties. This is intended to empower the client. Accepting no excuses for irresponsible behavior is part of this demonstration of confidence. The "Deadly C's" are avoided: control, criticism, and conflict.

Setting the Stage for Change.   Reality therapists see the basis for change coming from evaluating the behaviors that have not worked in the past, those things that do not meet needs. The following questions are asked repeatedly:

- What do you really want?
- What are you doing now?
- Does what you are doing get you what you want?

Eventually, variations of these questions will be directed to more long-term goals:

- What direction do you want to take?
- Is what you are doing going to get you where you want to be?

Helping the Client Change through Better Planning.   Assuming clients are able to honestly evaluate their actions in the way described, they see that more effective behavior must be developed. Since no one does everything all right or all wrong, planned changes include doing some things different, but repeating those that work.

The plan the client develops should be simple and the goals attainable. Long-term goals are worked toward in steps, progressing from the simple to the more complex. In line with the principles of reality therapy, valued procedures attain goals without violating the rights of others.

In planning, the reality therapist tries to get the client to offer suggestions first by saying something similar to "What do you think you can do?" The helper may ask clients if they know anyone else who has solved the same problem and, if yes, what they did. If helpers offer suggestions, they limit the number and keep the emphasis on the client working on solutions.

When a plan is finally developed, the counselor tries to get a commitment from the client to follow it; it can be a verbal agreement, a handshake, or a written agreement. Reality therapists are taught to accept no excuses ("I'm more interested in what you can do than in what you can't do.") They remember that their job is not to criticize or punish. They try to understand that changes in total behavior are difficult, and that circumstances often make satisfying wants and needs difficult. Thus, reality therapists are good at tolerating frustration. One of the most important principles of reality therapy is not to give up easily on a client.

Reality therapy has become popular because it is straightforward and understandable. It is one of the preferred approaches to use with troubled youth because its direct methods and supportive relationships tend to produce less resistance. These clients are very suspicious about being "conned," and any counseling approach that appears to be full of "tricks" is not well received.

Rational Emotive Behavior Therapy (REBT)

Albert Ellis is the founder of rational emotive therapy (RET). In the 1960s, when Ellis first wrote about RET (Ellis, 1962), an approach like it—straightforward and emphasizing reasoning and logic as the primary means of solving emotional problems—was unusual. Today, many of the most popular approaches to counseling rely primarily on cognitive interventions. In general, there appears to be sufficient evidence that cognitive approaches such as RET are effective.

A word of caution, though, in considering any theory as purely cognitive. Ellis was one of the early proponents of "homework" as an important part of the helping process. He strongly encouraged clients to practice actions discussed in counseling sessions in their daily lives. He assigned them tasks to do between sessions. The active nature of this approach has led to it now being called rational emotive behavior therapy (REBT) (Ellis, 1995).

While attention is given to behavior in REBT, a client's belief system is the target for change first. Ellis proposes that clients seek help because they feel terrible. Most clients seem to think that they feel bad as a result of unfavorable events in their lives. However, Ellis believes that it is not the event that produces the anxiety, depression, or anger, but a belief or thought that intervenes between the event and the emotional consequence. REBT (Ellis and Grieger, 1977) proposes the A-B-C theory: There is an activating event (A), usually some kind of setback such as being dumped by your girlfriend. Such an event no doubt would lead to hurt feelings. However, clients seek help because the emotional consequence (C) is of much greater proportion than need be because in between being dumped and becoming depressed, there is a belief or set of beliefs (B) that dramatically increase the intensity of the emotion. In our example, the beliefs that may apply are "If I get dumped, it proves that I am totally no good, and I may never have another girlfriend again."

REBT proposes that humans can be both rational and irrational. When they are rational, they feel better and act more effectively. When they are irrational, their biased, nonobjective beliefs create psychological disturbances. Regrettably, from childhood we learn all sorts of irrational beliefs. For example, two of the most common irrational beliefs are that we must be loved and accepted by everyone, and that we must be perfect. If everyone does not love us and our imperfections become evident, not only is that unfortunate, but it is a catastrophe! The REBT counselor tries to help someone identify the irrational beliefs that intervene between the activating events and the painful emotional consequences. Complete Exercise 7.2, p. 162, to identify some possible irrational beliefs.

Because humans communicate so much with words, it is easy to accept the REBT position that we talk with ourselves too. We have internal dialogues in which we say things to ourselves. This self-talk can be based on objective evidence and logic or on mistaken beliefs. The REBT counselor helps clients by

EXERCISE **7.2**
REBT Exercise

Below are listed situations or activating events followed by an emotional consequence. On a blank piece of paper, write down what you think might be an irrational belief that might lead to the exaggerated emotional consequence.

1. In class while the instructor is writing on the board someone in the back of the room snickers. The instructor turns around, throws the chalk in the wastebasket, and yells "What is wrong with all of you? Don't you have any common courtesy? If I ever hear anyone laughing out loud again, I will reduce everyone's class participation grade by 5 points."
2. A student has been trying to get up his nerve to call someone he chats with in class for a date. Every time he picks up the phone his hearts begins to pound, his hand shakes, and he breaks into a sweat. The fear of being unable to talk once the phone is answered prompts him to put down the phone.
3. Stella enrolls in a course only later to learn that one of the requirements was a verbal presentation in front of the class. Her anxiety continues to increase as the date for her presentation approached. The week prior to her presentation, she drops the class.
4. A student applies for a supplemental scholarship recently offered by a new foundation. The competition is stiff, and she does not get the scholarship. Her mood continues to drop following the rejection. Her friend suggests she go to the health center to get some antidepressant medication.

helping them change their self-talk. In this dialogue, words such as *terrible*, *should*, and *must* are replaced by less damaging words such as *unpleasant*, *desirable*, and *preferred*.

So how is this done? The user of REBT is very active in challenging the irrational beliefs of the client once they are uncovered. The goal is to teach clients how to analyze and correct their beliefs. In this way, undesirable emotions can be reduced. This leads to adding some steps to the A-B-C theory, making it an A-B-C-D-E-F theory. The counselor will dispute (D) or challenge the mistaken belief (B). This is done using the scientific method and logic. This disputing or attacking the belief will lead to recognition of effects (E), namely emotions and behaviors that were not previously evident. Finally, the ultimate result will be a new, more comfortable feeling (F) for the client.

The key to the process just described is the disputing. It can be done in a less harsh manner if humor is used. Also, if the homework assigned the client proves the value of a new set of beliefs by feeling better and by behaving more effectively, then the clients are less likely to revert back to their old beliefs. Sadly, it seems there is a tendency to revert back to irrational thinking. Thus, the REBT therapist works also to teach clients how they can dispute their own beliefs. In this way, clients walk away from counseling with tools to combat their tendencies to make themselves miserable. Read Case Illustration 7.5, p. 163, for an example of how REBT works.

Person-Centered Therapy

Person-centered or client-centered therapy is one of the first modern, short-term approaches that has been proven effective (Smith et al., 1980). Its founder, Carl Rogers, believed that it was primarily the relationship between the helper and client that contributed to improvement (Rogers, 1951). The relationship was the impetus for releasing an inborn actualizing tendency of the client. Rogers believed that clients could make effective decisions and act in an effective manner if they could overcome the anxiety and the distorted beliefs they had in themselves. Clients were vulnerable because they had lost faith in themselves as a result of not being accepted for what they were. In a sense they led false lives as a result of others having placed conditions on their worth. If they experienced a release from this conditional worth, the actualizing tendency in them would be released.

Person-centered counselors accomplish this by offering the important therapeutic conditions of empathic understanding, acceptance, and congruence. On

---

CASE ILLUSTRATION **7.5**

Judy

Judy was 25 years old. She was a full time student in a competitive graduate program, worked 20 hours a week, was writing her masters' paper, was interviewing for jobs with leading accounting firms, and was attempting to carry on a serious relationship. On her way to school, she had a panic attack characterized by sweating, shortness of breath, dizziness, and other symptoms that terrified her. Like many people who have panic attacks, she thought she was having a heart attack. When she discovered that she was physically healthy, she sought help from a REBT therapist.

Her primary irrational thoughts had to do with perfectionism. She had become more and more anxious because her heavy schedule precluded her from devoting as much attention to each task as she would like. For example, she was devastated when she learned that she had turned in a paper with a typographical error. Additionally, when she did something that was "substandard," she felt intensely guilty because she believed she was letting down her parents. Her therapist told her she was "shoulding" on herself.

She was taught to combat her irrational thoughts of perfectionism and to stop living up to her imaginary expectations of others. After four weeks (eight sessions), the panic attacks subsided. She attended four more sessions spaced over six weeks. Eight years later, she still uses the strategies learned from her REBT therapist to dispute any irrational thoughts that reoccur.

experiencing these conditions, clients feel safe to drop their defenses and honestly evaluate their experiences. They become energized by the acceptance of the counselor. Clients are not able to work toward change if they do not have the energy to do so. A counselor could assign the most effective "homework" imaginable, but a low-energy, demoralized client simply will not have the fuel needed to complete the tasks.

As clients become more open to their experiences within the safety of the helping relationship, they are able to see for themselves new options for solving problems. The counselor helps clients evaluate their experiences by reflecting feelings and attitudes. The emphasis in what counselors say is to share their understanding of clients' experiences. In doing so with empathy, often the clients' understanding is deepened. An important outcome will also occur; self-acceptance and increased feelings of worth will result. Besides having the energy to work on changes, clients also have the self-acceptance to tolerate things they cannot change, especially about themselves.

Comparing Counseling Approaches

Reality therapy, REBT, and person-centered therapy are only three of many different approaches to counseling. Other popular approaches include cognitive-behavioral therapy, existential therapy, Adlerian therapy, and psychoanalytic therapy. Earlier we noted some of the research support for the effectiveness of the three approaches we described. Each has been shown to be effective. Typically, the research does not report much on the cultural background of clients. How applicable are these approaches to today's culturally diverse client populations?

All three are examples of approaches that have a following in many different countries. Person-centered therapy is used successfully in Japan (Hayashi et al., 1992). Of all the creators of modern therapies, Carl Rogers was the first to significantly address interracial and international problems. The Institute for Reality Therapy offers programs in at least ten different countries from Korea and Hong Kong to Norway and New Zealand (Glasser and Wubbolding, 1995). The Institute for Rational-Emotive Therapy has similar international ties.

Earlier in this text we noted that many minority cultures have the expectation that an expert such as a counselor is expected to have a directive style. In research, this directive style usually demonstrates few reflections of feeling and more questions, including closed-ended questions. Research on international students in the United States shows a preference for such a directive style (Idowu, 1985; Yuen and Tinsley, 1981). This may favor an approach such as REBT. However, at the same time we cautioned you earlier about the use of confrontation with individuals from cultures that would consider direct challenges to their beliefs as rude and disrespectful. Cross-cultural research using international students in the United States does not always show a preference for a directive style when compared to a more feeling-oriented, nondirective one (Yau et al., 1992).

Counseling approaches that have emerged specifically for women have emphasized a democratic, interactive process (Enns, 1993). At the same time, it is recognized that women, through gender socialization, have learned many cognitive injunctions that limit their development. Thus, more directive cognitive-behavioral techniques are seen as useful in changing those limiting beliefs (Enns, 1992).

As we go back and forth noting the advantages and disadvantages of different counseling approaches, we are reminded that not only does one approach not fit all clients, we know that the same client may benefit from different approaches for different problems. Fassinger (1991) demonstrates this with gay and lesbian clients. Cognitive approaches like REBT may be useful in overcoming negative thinking and self-talk about sexual orientation, while client-centered approaches may be useful in encouraging repressed feelings about being gay and the treatment received from others as a result.

Summary

In this chapter we described individual counseling as one of several different interventions. Circumstances that suggest individual counseling as the most appropriate intervention were discussed. We then attempted to describe the counseling process by dividing it into three phases from early to late. How the counseling relationship changes, how the counselor might respond differently at different times, and how the expectations for client participation change were discussed. To show that there are exceptions to the process, we described crisis counseling and how its process adjusts to the urgency of the situation. Finally we presented three approaches to counseling. These approaches were selected because they are fairly easy to learn, they are popular among helping professionals, and they put different emphases on actions, thoughts, and feelings.

CHAPTER 7 EXIT QUIZ

Answer each of the following questions with a "T" if the question is true and "F" if the question is false.

_____ 1. Individual counseling should be used with every client, especially in the beginning.

_____ 2. If a client is verbal and intelligent, counseling is not as difficult.

_____ 3. An important early objective of counseling is the establishment of a working relationship.

_____ 4. The actions clients take between counseling sessions is very important for the success of the process.

_____ **5.** The goal of crisis counseling is to help the client return to the state of equilibrium that existed before the crisis.

_____ **6.** Reality therapy holds that ideas are the easiest part of total behavior to change.

_____ **7.** REBT holds that people feel worse about bad experiences than they need to because they tell themselves things that intensify negative feelings.

_____ **8.** Person-centered therapy emphasizes the healing nature of the counseling relationship.

_____ **9.** Research has proven the superiority of directive counseling approaches with lesbians and gay men.

_____**10.** The counselor adjusts the approach to counseling according to the background and needs of the client.

Answers:

1. F; 2. T; 3. T; 4. T; 5. T; 6. F; 7. T; 8. T; 9. F; 10. T.

SUGGESTED LEARNING ACTIVITIES

1. After reviewing the three approaches to counseling described in this chapter, which approach do you like? What are your reasons for preferring it?

2. Here are some of the most popular search engines on the Internet: _www.altavista. digital.com, www.excite.com, www.yahoo.com, www.hotbot.com, www.infoseek.com, www.lycos.com, www.webcrawler.com_. Research client-centered therapy, REBT, and reality therapy to see what you can find.

3. Check with the audio-visual library at your school to see if there are films or videos of different counseling approaches. If so, view one and report back to the class what you observed.

4. Debate the issue of whether thoughts or actions are more important in determining total behavior, especially feelings.

REFERENCES

Carkhuff, R.R. (1983). _The art of helping._ Amherst, MA: Human Resources Development Press.

Cavanagh, M.E. (1990). _The counseling experience: A theoretical and practical approach._ Prospect Heights, IL: Waveland Press.

DiGiuseppe, R.A., et al. (1979). A review of rational-emotive psychotherapy outcome studies. _Theoretical and empirical foundations of rational-emotive therapy._ A. Ellis and J.M. Whiteley (eds.). Monterey, CA: Brooks/Cole.

Egan, G. (1994). _The skilled helper: A problem-management approach to helping._ Pacific Grove, CA: Brooks/Cole.

Ellis, A. (1962). _Reason and emotion in psychotherapy._ New York: Lyle Stuart.

Ellis, A. (1995). Rational emotive behavior therapy. In R. Corsini and D. Wedding, *Current psychotherapies* (5th ed.) (pp. 162–197). Itasca, IL: F.E. Peacock.

Ellis, A., and R. Grieger (1977). *Handbook of rational-emotive therapy.* New York: Springer.

Enns, C.Z. (1992). Toward integrating feminist psychotherapy and feminist philosophy. *Professional Psychology: Research and Practice 23*(6): 453–466.

Enns, C.Z. (1993). Feminist counseling and therapy. *The Counseling Psychologist 21*(1), 3–87.

Fassinger, R.E. (1991). The hidden minority: Issues and challenges in working with lesbian women and gay men. *The Counseling Psychologist 19*(2): 157–176.

Freeman, S.C. (1993). Client-centered therapy with diverse populations: The universal within the specific. *Journal of Multicultural Counseling and Development 21*, 248–254.

Glasser, W. (1965). *Reality therapy: A new approach to psychiatry.* New York: Harper & Row.

Glasser, W., and R.E. Wubbolding (1995). Reality therapy. In R. Corsini and D. Wedding, *Current psychotherapies* (5th ed.) (pp. 293–321) Itasca, IL: F.E. Peacock.

Goldstein, A.P. (1971). *Psychotherapeutic attraction.* New York: Pergamon Press.

Hayashi, S., et al. (1992). The client-centered therapy and person-centered approach in Japan: Historical development, current status, and perspectives. *Journal of Humanistic Psychology 32*, 115–136.

Idowu, A.I. (1985). Counseling Nigerian students in United States colleges and universities. *Journal of Counseling 63*, 506–509.

Parrott, L.I. (1997). *Counseling and psychotherapy.* New York: McGraw-Hill.

Rogers, C.R. (1951). *Client-centered therapy.* Boston: Houghton Mifflin.

Rogers, C.R. (1957). The necessary and sufficient conditions of therapeutic personality change. *Journal of Consulting Psychology 21*, 95–103.

Smith, M.L., et al. (1980). *The benefits of psychotherapy.* Baltimore: Johns Hopkins University Press.

Wubbolding, R.E. (1986). *Using reality therapy.* New York: Harper & Row.

Wubbolding, R.E. (1991). *Understanding reality therapy: A metaphorical approach.* New York: HarperCollins.

Yau, T.Y., et al. (1992). Counseling style preference of international students. *Journal of Counseling Psychology 39*(1), 100–104.

Yuen, R.K., and H.E. Tinsley (1981). International and American students' expectancies about counseling. *Journal of Counseling Psychology 28*, 66–69.

CHAPTER

8 Working with Families

W H A T   Y O U   W I L L   L E A R N

1. The diverse way helping professionals come into contact with families
2. The stages of development families go through
3. The typical problems families have
4. Special concepts that help to explain family problems
5. Approaches used to help families

No matter where you work as a helping professional, it is certain that you will have to deal with families. Your contact may begin with only one member, but in the end you will be working with the entire family unit. Here are some examples of how it may begin:

- Felicita has not been in school since the term began. When her mother was contacted, she said she had tried to get Felicita to go to school, but her daughter refuses. The mother said that she does not know how she can make the child go.
- It is certain that the bone marrow transplant did not work, and Mrs. Warnick will die soon. Her husband is emotionally devastated, and the family has been ruined financially by medical bills. Marvela, the hospital social worker, already has had two sessions with the children, who show signs of depression.
- Juvenile protective service workers have responded to the second complaint by neighbors for child neglect. The children said their mother had left for the weekend and forgot to leave any food in the apartment.

Family life has undergone so many changes during the last four or five generations. Just think of the differences today compared to 25 years ago on just one change: access to information. In the 1970s, parents could control much more of what their children were exposed to. TV had only the major networks. The Internet did not exist. Censors carefully screened movies and television programs.

One thing that hasn't changed is the tendency to see family life as the cause of many individual problems. This is particularly true when it comes to children and adolescents. But today it has become increasingly more difficult to diagnose family problems because there seem to be so many different kinds of family units.

Family Patterns

Two important family patterns will be discussed, nuclear and extended families. The classic family pattern in sociology is the *nuclear family*. In this arrangement, we typically find two different generations living together with one parent working inside and the other working outside the home. Today, we often have both partners working outside the home. In some cases, this may be a dual-career couple in which each ascribes a great deal of importance to his/her career or work. Other dual-working couples do so more out of economic necessity. One member may prefer to stay home but works primarily to supplement the family's income.

There are also *extended families,* an increasingly common family pattern. An extended family is composed of members beyond one household. Many important family influences for Asian Americans are the result of closely knit extended families. The family may also be *intergenerational,* that is, it is composed of several generations of offspring. Families define themselves differently, one difference being how many generations are considered to be part of the family and whether they live under the same roof. Many families are both extended and intergenerational. With our increasingly diverse society, stereotypical family patterns, such as the nuclear family with the husband–father as the sole breadwinner, apply to fewer and fewer families.

Today, there are many other family combinations because of personal choices previous breakdowns. Very common is the single parent family. Divorced parents with children may remarry other divorced parents. They form a blended family with a household that contains two sets of children from previous marriages. However, one does not have to have children to have a family. Never-married individuals can form families with other never-married. Unmarried individuals can adopt a child, often from South America, China, or Eastern Europe, to form a family.

While we have not exhausted all the possible combinations, the diversity of family patterns is evident. One additional pattern is lesbian and gay families. The way a family operates is influenced by the larger contexts in which it exists, starting with the community. The patterns of interactions in families differ dramatically if they are in geographically isolated areas, crowded urban areas, or communities with high racial and ethnic diversity. Communities, even nations, can be supportive of or hostile toward different family patterns. For example, many groups hold negative attitudes toward families headed by gay and lesbian partners.

Types of Family Problems

Like all social units, families exist to serve a purpose. They help insure survival of their members, provide social support, and help meet other important needs.

Basically, a family is functioning adequately when it succeeds in solving problems faced by the unit and its individual members. Professional helpers consider a family to be in trouble when it cannot solve those problems.

When families are viewed as a problem-solving unit, it is important to observe both their success rate and the process used. A troubled family often seems stuck in a pattern that fails to address an important problem or repeatedly fails to solve it. Such a family cannot seem to break its pattern, to examine new options or strategies, and actually try one or more of them. The pattern in which the family communicates is one of the best examples of how a process succeeds or fails.

Several years ago, an international endurance race took place in the Australian Outback. One of the new teams to enter the event was one of the favorites. They were a group of Navy Seals. Everyone thought they had the edge because of their training and physical ability. As the event progressed through the dessert, down gorges, and on raging rivers, the Navy Seals steadily lost ground to the leaders. People began to realize that one secret to success in the race was communication, the verbal support team members gave each other as each experienced extreme exhaustion. When the going got tough for the Seals, they did not talk. Their inability to share their pain may have cost them the victory.

There is a parallel between the Seals and many families. Families that do not communicate well and do not emotionally support members do not take advantage of all the resources available in the unit. Problems are more difficult to solve. If failure to deal with problems continues, the family becomes increasingly discouraged. As the discouragement mounts, the tendency increases for family members to free themselves of the guilt for the failure by blaming someone else. This can lead to scapegoating. Several discouraged and frustrated family members can identify one other family member as the reason for everyone's discomfort. The scapegoated member is sometimes referred to as the *identified patient* because it is this person's problems that lead the family to ask for professional help.

Professional helpers face a significant challenge when they begin working with a troubled family. The family unit that begins working with the helper is usually discouraged, blaming, and caught in patterns in which they often repeat behaviors that continue to fail in solving problems. Added to that are the normal tensions among different generations. Each generation may value different things, based on different patterns of socialization. For example, a Latino family that has immigrated to the United States may have parents and children at different levels of acculturation. These differences may add to the normal conflict that would occur when adolescents are striving for their independence. The parents may continue to hold the common Latino value of strong family solidarity and strict parental control. The teenagers in the family may have adopted more of the individualism promoted in the dominant U.S. culture.

Some family conflicts may be the result of gender socialization differences. One of the authors recalls numerous conversations at the end of the workday with his partner that started fine but became tense. If his partner would complain about something that happened to her at work, he would automatically adopt the "male" attitude that somehow he had to find a way to "fix it." Finally his partner got through to him when she said "When I'm bothered by something that doesn't involve you, I don't expect you to fix it. All I want you to do is listen and understand." This was very liberating and very helpful to family dialogue.

Developmental Stages of Families

Each of us as individuals will evolve from birth to death through a series of stages that help describe our growth, our formation as individuals. The same is true of families. Families as they first form will be different from what they become later. At each stage of its life, the family faces different problems and has different goals. Let's look at some common stages in a two-generation family.

The family typically begins with a marriage. The first stage of its life often extends to the birth of the first child. Family life significantly changes with the presence of children. The workload is increased with added responsibility for the safety and growth of the children. Often we think of the childrearing years as being different stages, one involving infants and preschoolers and another involving children in school. A new stage with new issues emerges as the children become teenagers. At this point, the family has to begin negotiating greater autonomy for the adolescent, while maintaining some order to relationships in the family. Eventually the adolescent will begin the actual separation from the family, maybe first leaving home to attend college or the military. At first time away is mixed with long periods of returning to the family home. Later absences lead to the establishment of one's own home. If children have difficulty separating, tensions can develop. If the children succeed in separating, parents of the children eventually will have an "empty nest" with all their offspring gone. After decades of defining their relationship around childrearing, the couple now must renegotiate their relationship. Other changes, such as retirement from work, may add to the adjustments the couple must make.

At each stage of family development, there will be many differences in circumstance that will affect how the stage progresses. Some of these differences will have to do with who the people are, others with the conditions surrounding their family at the time. History, especially with their family of origin, will also influence the challenges to be met. Explore differences in a family by taking a closer look at the first stage of family life by completing Exercise 8.1, p. 172.

The situations described in Exercise 8.1 were intended to explore differences in the early life of a family. They were cast as issues confronting individuals who were partnering in marriage for the first time. However, today with divorce rates being high, there is a strong likelihood that individuals will have more than one marriage. The previously married person will first have to adjust to separation and divorce, followed perhaps by becoming a single parent. Later, the individual may attempt to remarry, first by reentering the dating scene, followed by a new marriage. Let's examine some differences that may face the remarried family. How might the following situations affect the remarriage?

EXERCISE **8.1**

Issues in Family Development

Read over the following issues and make written notes. Later, your instructor may want the class to discuss the possible meanings of each. What do you think it might mean if you observe the following in a young couple? How might the family develop in a special way because of what you observe?

1. The couple definitely does not want to have a formal wedding ceremony. They elope and make sure their parents are not present at their wedding.
2. The couple marries and does not plan to have children.
3. The couple lives in the home of one of the member's parents.
4. The couple has known each other since preschool. They lived in the same neighborhood and attended the same schools. They had the same friends. Their parents are friends.
5. Both partners are in their late 30s before they marry. This is their first marriage.
6. Both partners come from families that broke up. There was a great deal of conflict in each family of origin.
7. The couple has known each other for only a month before getting married.
8. The female of a heterosexual couple was pregnant before they decided to marry.
9. The partners are from different social classes and ethnic backgrounds.
10. The partners are forming an interracial marriage.

- Lesbian partners were previously in heterosexual marriages.
- One partner with two young children was recently divorced; the other divorced ten years ago and has lived a single lifestyle since then.
- The cultural background of one partner places great value on extended family relationships. The same cultural heritage has low tolerance of divorce and even less acceptance of remarriage. The other partner's background shows weak extended family ties. Divorce and remarriage are accepted.
- One remarried partner stills retains contact with his or her former spouse.

Strengths of Families

We have noted a number of problems families experience and how different problems emerge at different stages. It is important to note that strengths in the family unit emerge across stages as problems are met and challenges answered. Earlier in Chapter 5, we discussed the concept of resiliency, the fact that people against seemingly impossible odds not only cope but thrive. The same can be true of families. Later in the chapter, we will build on this idea by giving some examples of how helpers use a competency-based approach to families that helps build their skills to cope with the challenges they face. Case Illustration 8.1, p. 174, is an example of a closely knit family that consolidated its resources across generations to cope with the problems it faced.

As in any interpersonal situation, conflict will arise in families, especially when they must deal with difficult situations. These tensions will be real, but may not negate the loyalty and support that exists. The family can remain cohesive, combining effort to solve both common and uniquely individual problems.

Ideas to Deepen Our Understanding of Families

This section is based on many of the concepts that have emerged over the last five or six decades from couples and family therapists. Ministers, social workers, and counselors had practiced marriage or couples counseling since the 1920s. Until the 1950s, work with the entire family in which all members were interviewed at one time was largely underground (Nichols and Everett, 1986). Treating the family together is called *conjoint family therapy*. Since the 1950s, interest in families has increased considerably, in part because of the useful and creative ideas that are the basis for family work.

Understanding Family Structure

Salvador Minuchin was one of the first family therapists to draw attention to ways in which a family is structured or organized (1974). He thought a family could be helped if attention was paid to the way members interact both inside and outside the family. The way the family was structured would be revealed by these interactions. For example, if a child has difficulty learning math at school, who does he or she discuss the problem with? How many family members eventually know about the problem? How do the parents respond to messages about the problem from the school?

The family structure may contain various hierarchies. In one family, authority could be a vertical hierarchy. Older children can tell younger children what to do about minor matters; the mother may be able to make modest decisions, for example, the kind of laundry detergent to use. However, final authority on most issues rests in the hands of the father. He decides the family budget on his own. He controls who visits the home. He even dictates when dinner will be served.

In another family, no line of authority may be evident. If the parents argue, the teenage daughter reprimands them. She in turn cannot find a way to keep her little brother out of her room, even by enlisting the help of her parents. The little brother has difficulty depending on other family members. He had to quit Little League because he could not rely on his sister or his parents to drive him to practice. In another family, a different kind hierarchy seems to exist. Whenever someone has a complaint, it always is directed toward the mother. In all these examples, there is regularity to the interactions, suggesting that something is organizing them.

CASE ILLUSTRATION **8.1**

The Caggiano Family

The Caggiano family lives in Elizabeth, Pennsylvania, a town located in the Monongahela Valley, a once thriving center for steel production. Now if you travel up and down the river valley you see mostly rusting and abandoned steel mills that once employed thousands of workers. Gene Caggiano ran the restaurant he inherited from his father. For years the restaurant featured hearty pasta dishes that appealed to the many ethnic groups that worked and lived in the valley.

With unemployment reaching almost 25% in the valley and with changes in the tastes of especially younger generations, the business at the restaurant declined. Jaco Caggiano and his brother Al have taken over the business. Gene hurt his back several years ago and now has a chronic pain condition. Jaco and Al were working in New Jersey, but they saw the difficulty their father was having and how the stress of filling in was also affecting their mother. They moved back to help their parents and to revitalize the family business.

The menu for the restaurant has changed since "the boys" took over. There is much more emphasis on lighter dishes with seafood headlining the menu. The building has been renovated with new wedding and banquet rooms. The restaurant is doing very well, receiving awards from the Pittsburgh food magazine, and showing a healthy profit. Gene still greets customers for several hours each evening. You might even see him in the kitchen making his original pasta sauce. Later in the evening, some of his old friends may join him for dinner. Gene's wife Christiana might bring the grandchildren to see their fathers and grandfather.

Gene will be quick to tell you that his sons run the restaurant and how proud he is of what they have done. Al's oldest daughter is studying at the Pittsburgh Culinary Arts Institute and plans further study in Europe. She wants to work as a chef in Italy before she too comes "home." On Sunday, you often see four generations of Caggianos attending church together.

Many helpers understand family structure by seeing the family as a system. Think of a system as a group of elements that stand in a regular relationship with one another. The elements or units of the system influence one another by consistent interactions that help to regulate the entire system. For example, the heating system in a building is composed of the furnace connected to one or more thermostats. The heating system is self-regulating. When the temperature in the building is too low, the thermostat, sensing the temperature, signals the furnace to turn on. When enough heat is generated, the desired temperature is achieved and the thermostat turns off the furnace.

A family needs a system to regulate its interactions as well. For example, the expression of anger becomes regulated. Unpublished rules about how feelings are expressed apply to the expression of anger in the family. Helpers may run into mostly silent families in which considerable anger among members may be present, but there is an unwritten rule that forbids expressing it.

A family system can differ according to how open or closed the system is. Our earlier example of the heating system was an example of a closed system, because regulation was internal to the system. Imagine a person coming into a cold room and turning up the thermostat. The heating system of thermostat and furnace has been regulated from a force outside the system. Most family systems are open to some degree, being regulated by forces outside the family. If this were not the case, a helper from outside the family could not assist a troubled family.

Within the family system may be subsystems. There may be the parental subsystem that is governed by patterns of behavior that apply to the spouses and how they relate to each other, but do not apply to the way they relate to their children. There may be a sibling subsystem with its own rules. If the rules that govern the family system and its subsystems are strict, then firm boundaries exist. The boundaries may limit the ability of members to interact with others outside the family. The boundaries may create distance among family members themselves. Here are some examples of system and subsystem boundaries:

- The children cannot invite their friends to the house without first having the approval of a parent.
- It is OK for the mother to go out with friends as long as they are female.
- When the parents argue, the children know to stay out of the conflict.
- When the helper asks one of the children a question, he or she looks to the father to see if it is all right to answer.

Sometimes the boundaries are loose or what family specialists call *permeable.* For example, it may be difficult to tell the difference between subsystems. Who are the parents and who are the children? In a family with one or more alcoholic parents, it may be one of the children who manages the daily operation of the family. When we see a child or teenager assuming many of the duties of a parent, we view the child as having been *parentified.* Later in life, this same person may find it difficult to enjoy life. In part, not having had the opportunity to be a child has limited the degree of playfulness this person exhibits as an adult. They get stuck in always being a parent because they know nothing else.

Boundaries in a family are influenced by the degree to which alliances are formed among members, sometimes in opposition to other members. These alliances or coalitions may unite one parent with a child to isolate the other parent. The isolated parent may be perceived as not assuming his or her proper share of household responsibilities. The opposing coalition may exclude the outsider from conversations, from private jokes, and so forth. This is a good case of a family wanting more participation from a member but dealing with it in a way that creates the opposite effect.

The coalitions that develop in a family and the boundaries that form can affect the individual identity of members. Besides solving mutual family members' problems, the value of a strong family is the support members receive to be themselves. Tight boundaries and rigid rules within coalitions and subsystems can deprive members of personal autonomy. Assigned roles can have the same effect. Someone may be the "good child" who always is expected to be compliant and hard working, while the "bad child" always is expected to get into trouble. When individual differences are not respected and when member's behavior is narrowly defined, the family unit becomes *enmeshed*. It is hard to tell who are the "real" people in the family. Case Illustration 8.2 offers an example of an enmeshed family.

In this example, Marsha no doubt is enmeshed with her mother. Her mother may be living through her, being able to do the things she wants through Marsha. Part of the situation allows Marsha to obtain privileges and avoid many of the hardships students face in most high schools. The relationship between mother and daughter feels restrictive to Marsha, who repeatedly tries to break away. It may be that Marsha's father could be more involved but feels unwelcome. From

---

CASE   ILLUSTRATION   **8.2**
Marsha

Marsha Spencer had been home-schooled by her mother from the seventh to tenth grades. Marsha's mother believed that the local school system in their small town offered too limited a curriculum, especially in foreign languages, and was too devoid of enrichment experiences. Thus, she had a homebound educational plan approved that included numerous field trips to museums in large cities, outdoor activities, strenuous instruction and practice in piano, and travel abroad. Marsha's father was not involved in her schooling. He operated a retail business that was open seven days a week. Since Marsha's parents had been married, her father was rarely at home. If not at work, he was playing golf with his male friends. When she was still a baby, her mother had nearly divorced him.

At the end of the tenth grade, Marsha enlisted her aunt and minister to discuss a transfer to a boarding school that was noted for its music program. Marsha argued that her career ambition as a musician would be served by this change. Her mother reluctantly agreed. Marsha knew that her mother always wanted to be a performing artist herself and used that knowledge as part of her persuasion.

As Marsha was about to graduate from boarding school, her mother became intensely involved in helping Marsha select a college. Applications were sent only to expensive, private schools. Marsha did receive partial tuition scholarships to several of these schools, but even with this support the schools remained very expensive. In the end, her parents decided that their financial situation would only permit Marsha to attend the local university while living at home. Marsha did so for two years. She then, on her own, arranged to study for a semester in London. While abroad she met a student who helped her relocate to another city. Marsha worked in that community in retail sales for 18 months. She turned 21 and applied for financial aid on her own to attend the university in the city where she lives.

a family perspective, we would not blame any one person in this family for what we might see as a problem. We see that a family structure has evolved. It seems at this point that the departure of Marsha will so disrupt the structure of the past that her parents will now have to renegotiate their relationship. For the most part, the people will be the same, it is the pattern of their interactions that will change. Some of the changes eventually observed may be consistent with our expectations for the new developmental stage of the family.

Societal Influences on Families

Our understanding of family systems is more complete if we see it as more than a system operating on its own, being regulated only by internal influences. A family and the patterns it exhibits can be seen as a subsystem within a much larger social system. A family's ethnic heritage has transmitted through many generations the norms and values from which the family unit operates. Already in this book we have seen many examples of extended family closeness in ethnic families, the most recent being the Caggianos in Case Illustration 8.1. Imagine what it would be like for Al Caggiano's partner, who may have come from an extended family with distant relationships. For her, there were no large-scale family gatherings. A close family meant a close nuclear family. Would this increase the possibility that she would perceive the extensive involvement with grandparents, aunts, uncles, and cousins as an intrusion into what was her "family?" Could Al's extended family become a source of friction?

In this section of this chapter, as we look at concepts therapists have formulated to understand family life, it is clear that the emphasis has been on understanding nuclear families. Extended families and their influence are beginning to receive more attention. Better knowledge of extended families, especially from a cross-cultural perspective, provides a more complete picture of family relationships.

Earlier in the chapter we provided examples of communication differences that result from differences in gender socialization. Relationship problems between males and females commonly are seen as created by the social roles each sex is expected to fulfill, not by biological differences (Tannen, 1990). We see a similar situation for sexual orientation socialization.

Chapter 3 identifies homophobia as a dominating influence today, affecting attitudes toward nonheterosexual individuals and their partnerships. Reinisch (1989) reviews studies in which gay men report their sexual experiences with women. It is estimated that 4 to 5 million gay or bisexual U.S. men will marry women at some time in their lives. Gochros (1992) argues that homophobia explains why gay men enter into heterosexual marriages and why their wives avoid the reality of the situation. Both the men and their wives have difficulty accepting a gay sexual orientation because of internalized homophobia. Socialization experiences that degrade gay, lesbian, bisexual, and transgender persons force the formation of families, like these which often experience enormous hardship once the truth of sexual orientation is known. They are also less likely to receive family acceptance or support. For example, it is common for a partner to receive substantial support from family and friends after a separation from an unfaithful partner. However, this is more true if the infidelity involves heterosexual partners (Gochros, 1992). If the partner was unfaithful in same-sex liaisons, the other partner commonly is blamed or at least seen as so foolish as to deserve the outcome. Thus, families are strongly influenced by the way the larger society responds to different sexual orientations.

By recognizing social influences and how they affect our beliefs and actions, we are forced to go beyond the family structure concepts we have been discussing when we try to help families. If a people's belief systems drive much of their behavior, as many helping professionals believe, then aid to families can occur by helping them explore beliefs and behaviors that impact the health of the family unit. Together with the family, helping professionals can experiment with strategies to change those cognitive and behavioral elements that disturb the family's health.

Helping Families

A quick review of the last several pages suggests that professionals can help families function better by first analyzing how they are structured. Based on this understanding, steps can be taken to alter the interactions that create the structure. Since communication is the basis for members' interactions, if communication can be improved, the family can better use its resources to solve problems. Finally, if beliefs and actions that create conflict and distance in the family can be replaced with ones that increase cohesion and respect, the family will function better.

The strategies just listed can become the basis of an intensive helping relationship such as family therapy. We will give an example of this soon. The same strategies can be the formula for less expensive and less intense forms of help. For example, these ideas can be the basis for a family education program. In this more structured, time-limited environment, several families together can understand dysfunctional family patterns. They also can examine and change attitudes, beliefs, and behaviors that inhibit family togetherness and restrict individual development.

Family Therapy

There are many diverse points of view and many different approaches to conjoint family therapy. Structural family therapy already has been mentioned (Minuchin 1974). Strategic family therapy (Haley, 1973; Madanes, 1981), transgenerational family therapy (Bowen, 1978), and experiential family therapy (Satir, 1967; Satir, 1972) are other approaches. Some approaches that began more as individual therapy have been adapted for family work. Some examples are behavioral family therapy (Jacobson and Weiss, 1979) and object relations therapy (Scharff & Scharff, 1987).

Just as it is true for individual counseling, family helpers tend to integrate different approaches, finding that a blend of approaches more often satisfies their need to understand the many different ways families are able to solve their problems (Brown & Christensen, 1999). With this in mind, we will present a blended view of family therapy. In doing so, a few major differences in style will be noted in the process.

Family therapy often begins with the helper's effort to make each family member feel respected and accepted. The helper makes an effort to be genuine, attempting to promote better communication within the family by modeling it for them during the sessions. The effort of the helper to engage the family is based on a genuine respect for the family. Making sessions inviting to the family and demonstrating respect and understanding is called *joining*. The helper clearly demonstrates a desire to participate in the family problem solving. In the process, it may be important to the helper that family members work on their own self-esteem because their capacities to be intimate and to let others into their private worlds are strongly related to how they feel about themselves.

While this relationship-building effort is taking place, the helper is carefully observing how the family interacts. These interactions reveal family structure. To promote meaningful interactions, the helper is careful not to dominate the conversation. Rather, the helper tries to promote interchanges among family members.

As the family begins to interact, the helper may observe the dominance of some family members and the isolation of others. If the distribution of power seems to be too lopsided, the helper may work to redistribute power by supporting weak members. This is often done indirectly. The helper may sit next to a powerless member to increase that member's status. As the helper enters into and observes family interactions, there is an effort to respect cultural differences influencing those interactions.

If the family engages with the helper and trust begins to develop, the helper's contact allows the family to redirect its effort at solving ongoing problems with the helper offering a new, sometimes novel understanding of the problem. A new view of this kind applies a different interpretation to the problem. In family therapy this is often described as *reframing* the problem.

Sometimes the helper will be more active and directive. The helper may appear at times like a director of a play or movie. The family may be asked to demonstrate something that they allude to in their conversation. These are sometimes called *enactments*. For example, if the parents refer to an episode that occurred the previous week in which they attempted to discipline one of the children for misbehavior, the helper may ask them to enact or demonstrate the episode right in the session. At the end of the enactment the helper may point out the strengths and weaknesses of the discipline attempt. The active helper might also listen to the complaints or symptoms mentioned by family members, pointing out exceptions or noting how the symptom has positive consequences. For example, a spouse continually complained of her fear of intruders in the house on the evenings her husband was away at lodge activities. The helper noted that being fearful and needing the protection of her husband had resulted in him attending fewer lodge functions and spending more time with her. The fear she expressed served the purpose of increasing time together.

In family therapy, just as in individual therapy, the homework the helper may give family members to do between sessions can be important practice; it can solidify what the family learned in a session. Helpers do not always expect full compliance with homework assignments. The family may resist the homework in part because they do not want to give too much power or control to the helper. A very daring strategy to counteract this resistance is called a *paradoxical directive* (Haley, 1976). A paradoxical directive is a form of reverse psychology. The helper tells the family or a family member to do something that the helper expects will be met with aversion or resistance. Often the paradoxical directive prescribes a symptom of the family problem that originally motivated the family to seek help. The helper commands the persons involved to do something that they will resist by doing the opposite of what they were instructed. If it is the symptom, they will resist the symptom. For example, if the symptom is bed-wetting, the idea is to have the family member resist wetting the bed. Of course, what the family ends up doing by resisting is what the helper wanted in the first place: reduce bed-wetting episodes. Case Illustration 8.3 offers an example of this theme described by King, Novik, and Citrenbaum (King et al., 1983). It is a variation of the "good guy, bad guy" scenario. It shows how some family therapy techniques have application in other situations as well.

Many of the techniques used in strategic family therapy, such as paradoxical directives, require extensive training. Also, many family situations do not lend themselves to strategies that may provoke anger or the belief that members are being manipulated. For example, families in which there is confusion, in which even the adult members are immature, or in which suspicion and distrust are

---

CASE ILLUSTRATION **8.3**

Family Therapy Technique

A young man was in the hospital following a motor cycle accident. He was depressed and had resisted going to physical therapy. This therapy was absolutely essential if the patient was to walk again. The patient seemed to like the physician who has prescribed the treatment but disliked the head nurse, whom he had already complained about as too stern and rigid.

To capitalize on this situation the doctor and nurse agreed that she would go in to talk to the young man. She would say that she disagreed with the doctor, that it was too soon for the patient to try physical therapy. The next time she discussed physical therapy she would say that she was sure the young man could not do it, and if he tried he would just worry the doctor needlessly. It was hoped that the young man would want to resist the orders given by the nurse. Her paradoxical directives hopefully would motivate him to make a strong effort during his physical therapy sessions.

prevalent would make poor settings for techniques such as paradoxical directives (Weeks, 1991).

In many cases, helping families is straightforward and clear. The open approach of the helper reduces suspicion about being "tricked" or unfairly manipulated. The Walker family in Case Illustration 8.4, p. 182, is an example of a clear and direct approach.

Family Education

After our brief look at family therapy, we are now ready to examine some illustrations of family education. Because of the many common problems families share, several families can work together in a class on common problems. A helper can structure the classes and repeat the entire process with additional families. Parent education often follows a curriculum. It is flexible so meetings can be adjusted to address the unique aspects of the problems. The family educator combines some teaching via mini-lectures, the use of handouts with discussion, and at times activities that insure participation from everyone. Here some examples of what might be included in a family education program.

Identifying Beliefs that Affect Family Life. Family members can benefit from understanding how their beliefs and values affect the quality of family life. The family educator may explain "self-talk" just as we did in the previous chapter when we discussed Rational Emotive Behavior Therapy (REBT). A sentence completion exercise could be a useful to personalize this concept. Participants could be given sentence stems that point to their expectations for others in the family. For example, they may be asked to complete "My husband should . . ." "Good children are . . ." A class discussion would follow examining how different responses may affect family interactions.

A follow-up to the exercise and discussion of expectations might be an opportunity for family members to reframe common complaints they have of one another. For example, a "procrastinator" could be reframed as "thoughtful." Instead of "wasting time watching TV" the family member could be seen as "recharging personal energy." The helper could solicit a list of common complaints family members have of one another. After the complaints are written on the board, the reframed view could be written next to them.

Family Problems as Messages. During a family education class, a helper could explain that many of the complaints of families can be understood as ways family members transmit important messages to one another. The helper may give an example of a "good boy" who gets into trouble for something that seems really odd to his parents. The helper may explain that this could be a message that the boy feels too constrained by the role he believes he must play, that he is afraid his acceptance from his parents is conditional, based only on "good" performance. He is testing this belief by misbehaving, seeing if he can still gain acceptance from his parents. In this class the helper may have written on a flip chart several

---

C A S E   I L L U S T R A T I O N   **8.4**

The Walker Family

Cindy Walker has been a single parent for the three years. Since her divorce, her law practice has grown considerably, forcing her to take work home and spend more time away from her children, one in the sixth and the other in the eighth grade. Tensions have increased at home. Cindy has taken to more yelling about the house being messy. She argues with the children about homework. The children fight with each other over TV programs.

When Cindy and the children met with the helper, Cindy was quick to share her belief that much of the family conflict was related to her increased work demands. She confessed that she felt bad about her shouting at the children and at times being overly critical of them "just being kids." The children acknowledged that they were angry and sometimes intentionally provoked their mother because she spent so much time with her work. Both Cindy and her children agreed that she may be perfectionistic, especially about keeping the house tidy.

The helper assisted all three family members to verbalize how close they wanted the family to be. She helped all of them agree that anything that might reduce the conflict was worth trying. The helper described "time out" techniques or simply requesting that an argument be stopped until everyone calmed down. When the issue behind the argument could be discussed calmly, then it would be addressed. A second ground rule was set to avoid personal criticism of another. Rather than accusing someone, everyone was taught how to make "I statements." By this a person would convey to another how they felt. For example, Cindy might come home and say, "It really bothers me when I get home to see today's mail spread out all over the dinner table." The helper encouraged each person to avoid deciding who was right and who was wrong in a dispute. Rather, each individual might work simply to understand the other person's point of view.

During the next meeting, the helper and the family discussed different ways to spend quality time together. The idea was to replace tense times with relaxed, enjoyable ones. Other alternatives were explored. The family budget was discussed and revised to hire someone to clean the house every two weeks. The weeks in between everyone agreed to share housekeeping chores. The evenings Cindy needed to work would be days either the family ate out or had pizza or some other low effort dinner. Cindy and her children agreed that it was helpful to have a third party, the helper, mediate some of their disagreements, offer suggestions, and keep everyone focused on solving problems.

---

common problems. Family members are then divided into groups with members from other families to discuss what message may be given by those problems.

Learning Creative Solutions through Brainstorming.   To encourage families to learn from other families in the class, the helper may encourage brainstorming solutions to common problems. In brainstorming the goal is to arrive at as many solutions to problems as possible without evaluating the solutions. The fun of brainstorming is to create a list of solutions that are unusual, interesting, even humorous.

Writing down a list of criteria to judge the solutions often follows brainstorming. Before the solutions are evaluated, the criteria are weighted according to their importance. Weighted criteria will give a more accurate evaluation of each solution's value. Brainstorming and other problem-solving exercises allow families to observe others trying to cope with the same issues they must confront. They have the opportunity to have modeled for them tolerance of differences.

Internet Resources for Families

The Internet contains many resources for families. Helpers can use these resources to educate themselves to optimize the face-to-face contact they have with family members. Families can be referred to Web sites to search for helpful information. Family issues frequently addressed on the Internet include adoption, day care, divorce and custody, domestic violence and missing children, family planning, home schooling, and parenting. Here are several Web sites with numerous links to other family resources:

- *http://family.com*
- America Online *keyword:* family
- *http://www.parenthoodweb.com*
- *http://www.parentsplace.com*
- *http://www.familyinternet.com*
- *http://parent.net*
- *http://www.familyweb.com*

Summary

In this chapter we have sampled some of the many ways that helpers contact families, learn about their problems, and try to help them. We have emphasized understanding families as a social system that exists within other social systems. Families have a developmental history with stages in that development that offer new challenges. Specialists in family work have developed approaches with many useful concepts to deepen our understanding of family life. These concepts are useful helping families solve their problems. The assistance helpers provide to families can use a variety of techniques. Help can occur within the context of conjoint family therapy, something requiring extensive training and experience. Other approaches can use educational practices already familiar to the reader.

CHAPTER 8 EXIT QUIZ

Answer each of the following questions with a "T" for true and "F" for false.

_____ 1. Extended and intergenerational families are often the same.

_____ 2. Communication is often the key to the problem-solving ability of a family.

_____ 3. When children begin school is often the beginning of a new stage in family life.

_____ 4. For a family to exist there must be children who are part of the family unit.

_____ 5. Family structure differs according to how power is distributed.

_____ 6. A family with diffuse boundaries may have difficulty controlling negative behavior of its members.

_____ 7. The relationship the helper establishes with a family is important to the helping process.

_____ 8. Reframing a family problem is similar to interpreting it in a different way.

_____ 9. Family education addresses some of the same problems as family therapy, but in a more structured way.

_____10. Counselors adjust their approach to families according to the background and needs of family members.

Answers:

1. T; 2. T; 3. T; 4. F; 5. T; 6. T; 7. T; 8. T; 9. T; 10. T.

SUGGESTED LEARNING ACTIVITIES

1. To learn more about the intergenerational nature of families, interview your parents and an aunt or uncle about their experiences growing up in your grandparents' household. If possible, interview one of your grandparents regarding their experiences growing up in your great grandparents' household. Compare their experiences to yours.

2. Identify what you think are three of the most common problems families face. Research them on the Internet. Begin with the Web sites listed in this chapter.

3. Have the class develop a list of services provided to families in the community. Have class members review the local newspaper, a local radio station with frequent public service announcements, and the announcements on cable TV.

4. Have a professional therapist who works extensively with families come to class as a guest speaker.

REFERENCES

Bowen, M. (1978). *Family therapy in clinical practice.* New York: Aronson.

Brown, J.H., & Christensen, D.N. (1999). *Family therapy: Theory and practice.* Pacific Grove, CA: Brooks/Cole.

Gochros, J.S. (1992). Homophobia, homosexuality, and heterosexual marriage. In W.J. Blumfeld, *Homophobia: How we all pay the price* (pp. 131–153). Boston: Beacon.

Haley, J. (1973). *Uncommon therapy: The psychiatric techniques of Milton H. Erickson, M.D.* New York: Norton.

Haley, J. (1976). *Problem solving therapy.* San Francisco: Jossey-Bass.

Jacobson, N.S., & Weiss, R.L. (1979). *Marital therapy: Strategies based on social learning and behavior exchange principles.* New York: Brunner/Mazel.

King, M. et al. (1983). *Irresistible communication: Creative skills for the health professional.* Philadelphia: W.B. Saunders.

Madanes, C. (1981). *Strategic family therapy.* San Francisco: Jossey-Bass.

Minuchin, S. (1974). *Families and family therapy.* Cambridge, MA: Harvard University Press.

Nichols, W.C., & Everett, C.A. (1986). *Systemic family therapy: An integrative approach.* New York: Guilford.

Reinisch, J. (1989). The prevalence of AIDS risk related to sexual behaviors among white middle-class urban American adults: A survey of research from Kinsey to the present. Montreal: Fifth International Conference on AIDS.

Satir, V. (1967). *Conjoint family therapy.* Palo Alto, CA: Science and Behavior Books.

Satir, V. (1972). *Peoplemaking.* Palo Alto, CA: Science and Behavior Books.

Scharff, D.E., & Scharff, J.S. (1987). *Object relations therapy.* Northvale, NJ: Jason Aronson.

Tannen, D. (1990). *You just don't understand: Women and men in conversation.* New York: Ballantine Books.

Weeks, G.R. (1991). *Promoting change through paradoxical therapy.* New York: Brunner/Mazel.

9 Helping in a Group Setting

W H A T   Y O U   W I L L   L E A R N

1. The different types of groups that helpers can employ with clients
2. The advantages and disadvantages of using groups in the helping process
3. The factors that make groups effective
4. The factors that may cause groups to be harmful to group members
5. The skills and characteristics of effective group helpers

A *group* is two or more people who have common goals, a communication system or network, rules regarding the behavior of its members, and some type of leadership system in place. This definition rules out groups of people who appear at a bus stop for the purpose of catching a bus to different destinations. This type of group has no communication network and no leadership system in place. One of the best ways to begin the process of exploring helping in a group is to think about the groups to which you belong using this definition. All students belong to a family group and attend classes with other students. Many students belong to clubs, play on athletic teams, and participate in community organizations.

Families have one or more people who are recognized as the "heads" of the families, have loosely defined purposes, and have an established communication system. The major purposes of families generally involve nurturing and supporting each other, but other purposes may evolve including helping family members economically. At first glance, the communications networks in families may be hard to discern, but on exploration it is generally the case that communication flows through certain channels (people) and are relayed in specified ways. Family members may call each other on certain days of the week, and one person may be "responsible" for communicating bad news to family members. Families may also have informal rules regarding communication such as those related to Uncle Charles's drinking problem. His obvious alcoholism may be off limits when conversations occur among family members, although most family members think it is perfectly legitimate to talk to people outside the family about Uncle Charles's "secret."

Classes usually have easily identified purposes and rules that are spelled out in the course syllabus. Also, the leader of a class is easily identified. The communication patterns in classes may be one way if a lecture format is used (instructor to class), two-way if a lecture-discussion format is employed (instructor to class and back to instructor), or multidirectional if small group or cooperative learning approaches are used.

The remainder of this chapter will be spent examining the characteristics of the groups employed by helpers. What differentiates helping groups from family groups is that they are deliberately formed for the purpose of assisting clients with their concerns. However, like most family groups and classes, helping groups have leaders and discernible patterns of communication. Moreover, helping groups that are successful have unique characteristics that are the result of leaders' decisions. The decision-making processes that go into the formation of groups, the stages through which groups pass, and the techniques needed to facilitate successful groups will be examined.

Group versus Individual Helping

Before pursuing a full-blown discussion of helping groups, the matter of group versus individual helping will be addressed. When comparing helping modalities, three questions typically surface. The first of these is "Which approach is most effective?" Helpers wish to select the approach to helping that will most effectively ameliorate the concerns of clients. When researchers have compared individual versus group approaches, the usual finding is that no significant differences exist. As we shall see, there are clients who cannot be incorporated into group approaches to helping. However, for those clients who can benefit from individual or group treatments, the most likely outcome is that they will benefit equally from the two modalities.

Helpers also want to know, "Which approach to helping is most efficient?" The efficiency of helping modalities speaks to the issue of the utilization of resources, such as the number of helper hours required to bring about change in clients. If efficiency is defined solely as the number of helper hours required to assist clients achieve their goals, group approaches are by far the most efficient of the two approaches. Small helping groups range from 8 to 12 participants in size and group meetings typically last for 1.5 hours. Over the course of 12 weeks, the amount of helper time invested in a single client is 12 hours if an individual approach is utilized. Over the same 12 weeks, 1.8 hours (18 total hours divided by 10 clients in the group) of helper time is invested in each individual in the group. This figure probably exaggerates the differences in efficiency between the two treatment modalities, however. In all likelihood, the group leader would have spent 3 hours prior to the beginning of the group screening potential group members to determine their suitability, which increases the amount of time spent for each client to 2.1 hours. Nevertheless, group approaches to helping are demonstrably more efficient than individual approaches.

Finally, when evaluating helping modalities it is also important to ask, "Are there setting or institutional issues that influence the feasibility of using various helping modalities?" Group sessions, like individual sessions, have to be scheduled, and the problems of coordinating the schedules of ten group members versus one person in individual helping are evident. These problems become greater when helping occurs in schools, community colleges, and universities due to the difficulty of matching the schedules of the helpers, who typically have 8:00 A.M. to 4:00 P.M. schedules, to those of their clients who have classes and other commitments. The task of scheduling groups becomes somewhat easier when helpers are available at night and on the weekend.

Factors That Make Groups Effective

Much of Chapter 4 and all of Chapter 7 focused on the factors that make individual helping effective. Communication skills, understanding cultural differences, and caring are important helping skills regardless of the helping modality used. However, in groups the helper becomes a facilitator who uses helping skills to create an environment in which people can develop new interpersonal skills, change their opinions of themselves, and, if necessary, alter their personalities. Yalom (1985) identifies some of the conditions that produce changes. He labels these factors *curative factors.* Yalom's curative factors, as well as others that lead to individual change in a group setting, will be discussed.

Hope

People who come to helpers have varying expectations. Some expect immediate relief and thus have unrealistic expectations of the helping process. Other clients are quite skeptical that the helping process will work at all. One woman the authors knew opened the first group session with the statement, "My husband sent me here, but I know you cannot help me." She had little hope that she would receive help and had come to the session to prove to her husband that she was beyond help. Other clients may tell about their past failures in the helping process as a means of communicating to the group leader that they do not expect to benefit from the process. Still others are less open about their negative expectations, but they are nonetheless skeptical.

How do helpers instill expectations of hope? In some instances, the helper need do nothing. During the early stages of groups, people are encouraged to tell why they came for help and what they hope to accomplish in the group. Because some clients express positive expectations, others in the group become hopeful. However, not all dubious group members are persuaded that they will receive help in the group, making leader interventions necessary. To instill hope in skeptical group members, helpers may wish to tell stories about clients who have succeeded in the past. Leaders may also wish to express confidence in the potential of each group member to benefit from the group or reassure skeptical group members that they will receive help from the group.

Group leaders may wish to use a *paradoxical* approach to instilling hope. Paradoxical techniques involve prescribing the symptom. In the case of group members who are skeptical about the potential of the group to help them with their problem, they are encouraged to maintain their skepticism about the group. Statements such as, "I think it is wonderful that you question whether the helping process will work for you. I want you to maintain your doubtful attitude throughout the group and question everything." Although there is disagreement among helpers regarding why paradoxical techniques work, they are effective in changing the perspective of many clients.

Universality

Clients who have mental health problems are often ashamed of their problems and refuse to discuss them with their acquaintances. As a result, they are unaware that other individuals, sometimes tens of thousands of them, have the same problem. When clients become aware that other individuals have the same problem they do, they often experience a great sense of relief. Clients' realization that they are not alone in their misery is *universality*. In the intimacy that develops in groups, people feel safe enough to talk about the problems they are experiencing. Group helpers often hear the statement, "I feel better already. I thought I was the only one with this problem." One client told her group leader, "I knew this was supposed to be a group, but I was sure that I was the only one who would show up because my problem is so unique."

Trust

All approaches to helping are based on the establishment of trusting relationships. Group approaches to helping, like individual approaches, require clients to disclose ever increasing levels of personal information. In individual helping, trust develops between the helper and the client. In group approaches, clients must learn to trust the helper and the other clients in the group. Because trust is a prerequisite to receiving help, group leaders work very hard to form groups in which members can trust each other. This is done in two ways. First, clients who have a limited ability to trust may be excluded from groups. Before placing an individual in a group, helpers may ask them several questions such as:

1. Do you have trouble trusting strangers?
2. If you are going to be successful in the group, it is likely that you will have to disclose personal information. How do you feel about that possibility?
3. Do you sometimes keep secrets from people who are close to you? What types of information do you withhold?

Test your ability to trust by completing Exercise 9.1.

Second, forming groups that include members who have common backgrounds, interests, and personality characteristics can facilitate the formation of

EXERCISE **9.1**

Assessing Your Trust Quotient

Assess your TQ, Trust Quotient, by answering the following questions with a T if the statement describes you and an F if the statement does not describe you.

_____ 1. Once I get to know people, I generally feel that I can trust them.

_____ 2. I self-disclose to people I trust.

_____ 3. I am a risk taker and typically do not worry whether people can be trusted.

_____ 4. When I am with a group of people I know, I express my thoughts and feelings freely.

_____ 5. I am not afraid to express my opinions, even if they are controversial.

_____ 6. I believe that most people are trustworthy.

_____ 7. When I have been hurt as a result of trusting someone, I have concluded that the person was the problem, not that most people are untrustworthy.

_____ 8. I am a trustworthy person.

_____ 9. I have been told that I am too trusting, but if I have to err, I want it to be on the side of being too trusting.

_____10. My philosophy is that if a person who I trust turns out to untrustworthy, it is more their problem than mine.

trust. As will be shown later in this chapter, successful group leaders also use techniques to facilitate the development of trust and to intervene when trust issues arise in the group.

If you marked all ten statements as true, you are likely a highly trusting person. If you marked five or less of the foregoing statements as true, you may have difficulty trusting other people.

Helpers in training sometimes ask why people do not trust each other. In many instances there are legitimate reasons why people never learned to trust or lost their ability to trust. Children who were physically, sexually, or emotionally abused by their parents learned early on that people who should be most trustworthy cannot be trusted. Some people, who learn trust as children, invest that trust in relationships that betray and emotionally scar them. Other individuals lose their ability to trust people after traumatic accidents or events that literally destroy most of their beliefs about the trustworthiness of their worlds, for example, a soldier who returned from the Vietnam War to find his beloved wife living with another man.

Cohesion

Cohesion, based partially on trust, is a feeling of "we'ness," of belonging to the group. When it develops, group members are more likely to come to the group on time, may be reluctant to leave the group when it is over, and may make verbal statements such as "This is a great group" or "I can't imagine a better group of people." In addition to trust, interpersonal attractiveness of group members to each other is an important factor that contributes to cohesiveness. People tend to be attracted to people like themselves, that is, people who are from the same socioeconomic background who have similar values and interests. Generally speaking, groups should be made up of people who have similar problems, but who have dissimilar approaches to working on their problems. Later in this chapter, the matter of selecting group members who are likely to form cohesive groups will be discussed. One last feature that contributes to group cohesiveness is inclusion. When a group begins, it has the potential to remain a series of individuals, to form into subgroups, or to become a cohesive group unit. When all people feel included in the overall group, the likelihood that the group will be cohesive is enhanced.

Imparting Information

The process of giving information may not be seen as a curative factor by some helpers, but authorities on groups have historically stressed the importance of providing information. One way of imparting information is through the strategic use of written information to assist clients overcome their problems; this is called *bibliotherapy*. Bibliotherapy is a deliberate part of the helping process that is used by helpers to facilitate the curative process. When parents get a divorce, child psychologists may help children to understand their feelings about what is occurring by having them read books that describe the feelings of other children who have had common experiences. Adults who have panic attacks are often asked to read books that assist them in understanding the factors that precipitate a panic attack, the physiological reaction that occurs during the process, and the steps they must take to control the physical changes that occur when they do have an attack. Bibliotherapy is often used in groups, but information is also imparted through a variety of verbal processes, including the personal disclosures of other individuals, and mini-lectures by the helper.

Altruism

Many clients come to groups with the expectation of receiving help with their problems. Few come with the idea that they may become helpers and contribute to the welfare of others in the group. Effective group leaders make it explicit to clients in the group that they are to call on their own personal resources to help others in the group. By helping others, clients learn to transcend their own weaknesses and act altruistically to benefit others. By helping others, clients learn that they are not powerless.

The Corrective Recapitulation of the Primary Family Group

Yalom (1985) believes that the reason that people come to groups, particularly therapy groups, is because of faulty parenting. Although not all authorities in the area of group approaches to helping agree with this assumption, it is the case that groups offer a rich learning environments that cannot be matched in individual helping sessions. Children can learn to deal with their peers assertively instead of aggressively attacking them. Adolescent girls can master strategies to prevent date rape, and veterans can acquire the skills needed to deal with their recurring nightmares. Individuals who have developed obsessive-compulsive disorder can learn to interrupt the obsessive patterns that trigger their compulsive behavior as a result of their interactions with the group leader and group members. Groups can provide supportive environments in which clients feel safe enough to try new behaviors. However, few group helpers attempt to recreate the original family atmosphere.

Modeling

Most behavior is developed as a resulting of imitative learning, that is, we observe others and imitate their behavior. Groups, if properly formed, provide members with several models (people who can be imitated). For this reason it is typically a mistake to form groups of individuals who have the same problem and respond to their problems in the same way. Courts often force group helpers to form groups that are too homogeneous. For example, judges often require spouse abusers to attend several sessions of group therapy to learn alternatives to battering when they are attempting to settle marital disputes. Unfortunately, the individuals in these groups, particularly the men, often believe that beating their spouses is an appropriate way to solve their marital problems. Although the helpers who lead these groups do not share the client's opinions about the appropriateness of abusing their spouses, their influence may not be great enough to change the behavior of the clients because of the beliefs of the members.

Social Skills Development

Many people who come for help lack social skills. In group settings they can receive feedback regarding their skills and develop new ones. People who dominate will sooner or later be told that they talk too much, just as the aggressive individuals will learn that they are overbearing. The passive person will be encouraged to be more assertive, and the shy person be helped to become more self-confident. In sum, new social skills will be learned, even if this is not one of the primary purposes of the group.

Catharsis

Typically individuals come to helpers after they have decided that they cannot solve the problem confronting them without assistance. This decision often has many emotionally laden components. Imagine that you have drawn one of the following conclusions regarding yourself:

1. I may be homosexual, and the people around me despise gay and lesbian persons.
2. I have a serious mental health problem that is going to limit my future.
3. I cannot control even the most basic processes of my body. Every panic attack reminds me of my weakness.
4. I'm crazy. Only a crazy person would have the thoughts I do.
5. I am weak. If I were strong, I would be able to control my fears and anxieties.

Catharsis, at least initially, is dumping the emotional load being carried by sharing the thoughts and feelings that have developed. As the group progresses, catharsis may involving sharing pent up feelings about other group members and, in so doing, learning to express feelings rather than holding them inside.

Feedback

Occasionally, most of us wonder how we are perceived by other people. In a group setting, clients can ask and receive feedback about themselves. Once clients receive feedback about their personal mannerisms, communications styles, and the impression they make on other people, they have the opportunity to improve the way that they relate to others.

Existential Factors: Coming to Terms with Our Existence

The existential factors in groups relate to helping clients develop a sense of their humanity, their relationships to others, and their importance in the overall scheme of things. Dying persons in a hospice support group may be helped to come to grips with two of the great truths of human existence: life is not fair and that death is an inevitable result of living. The 17-year-old probationer who blames others may learn to accept the idea that each person has to take responsibility for his or her behavior. All clients may come to realize that the trivialities of life need to be set aside in favor of the more important aspects of their life if they are to finding meaning in their existence. Groups can also be useful to individuals who are seeking some sense of their overall place in the cosmos, their relationship to nature, and for some, their relationship to God.

Self-Understanding

Most approaches to helping have a common objective: to facilitate self-understanding. In a group setting, clients have the opportunity to talk about themselves, receive feedback from others about the way that they function, compare their personal philosophies and values with those of others, and examine the contradictions in their thoughts and behavior. In this process, clients have the opportunity to identify unwanted parts of themselves and to initiate change.

Although helpers understand that self-understanding is rarely curative in and of itself, it can contribute to the overall process of change and growth.

Stages of Groups

Group approaches to helping, like individual approaches, move through stages. The reader may recall that individual helping begins with the development of a relationship and moves from that point to exploration and identification of the presenting problem, goal setting, intervention, evaluation, and termination. Groups move through analogous, but somewhat more complex, stages (Corey, 2000; Tuckman & Jensen, 1977):

Stage 1: Pregroup

Stage 2: Formation and Orientation (Forming)

Stage 3: Norming

Stage 4: Working (Performing)

Stage 5: Termination (Adjourning)

Stage 1: Pregroup

Technically, anything that happens prior to the beginning of a group is not a stage through which the group passes. However, it is a truism that many groups are doomed to fail because of errors committed by group leaders before the first group meeting. To put it differently, no amount of skills or judicious selection of group leadership techniques can salvage a group that is poorly planned. Although group helpers must attend to a number of details as they plan for groups, including scheduling and selecting a time and place for the group to meet, the most critical task to be carried out at the pregroup stage is the screening and selection of group members. Earlier in this chapter, it was pointed out that groups with members who have common characteristics are more likely to become cohesive, and that cohesive groups are more likely to succeed. However, there are times when group helpers must form groups of clients who are quite heterogeneous. When the socioeconomic backgrounds, values, and personality characteristics of group members are dissimilar, leaders must plan exercises and activities that will help the members of the group break down their stereotypes, engage in cooperative activities, and allow for expression of common values and beliefs.

Screening Interview.   The screening interview is used to collect information that can be used to make a judgment about the compatibility of prospective members. However, there are other tasks that must be accomplished during screening. Two of these are to make prospective group members fully aware of the purposes of the group and to apprise them of the techniques that will be employed to accomplish these purposes. For example, if clients are expected to participate in leader-directed fantasies (see Exercise 9.2) and describe their reactions to their experience, they should be apprised of this fact. In so far as possible, group leaders must remove the element of surprise from group experiences. Another issue that can be addressed during the screening interview is to make helpers aware of the rules that govern the group. Most group helpers have expectations regarding regular attendance, punctuality, treating other group members with respect, and so forth. The screening interview is also a good time to tell prospective members that, in addition to working on their own concerns, they are expected to be supportive of other group members and help them when possible. In this way, the curative factor of altruism can be set into motion.

Another task that needs to be completed during the screening interview is the assessment of the motivation of prospective group members. Voluntary clients, that is the people who agree to participate without coercion, may appear to be highly motivated, when in fact they are not because they are skeptical about the outcomes of the group experience. As was noted earlier in this chapter, one of the leader's tasks is to instill hope in clients, and this process can and should begin in the screening interview. Many nonvoluntary clients must be included in groups. Clients who are ordered to engage in group experiences—for instance, by the courts—are one type of involuntary group member. Some institutions, such as correctional institutions and custodial hospitals, require participation in group activities on an ongoing basis. Another possible type of involuntary clients

---

E X E R C I S E **9.2**

A Leader-Directed Guided Fantasy: Self-Exploration

Begin by filling your lungs: inhale, filling your lungs as completely as possible. Now hold that breath—hold it—hold it. Now exhale very slowly. Repeat by filling your lungs completely, holding your breath as you count 1001, 1002, 1003. Again, exhale very slowly. Repeat this process one more time, and as you fill your lungs close your eyes and allow yourself to relax completely.

Relax and allow your mind to become a blank screen. Think of nothing but how well you feel as you relax. Now join me on an imaginary journey of self-exploration, a journey to find out more about yourself. Imagine that you can go any place and do anything, and you want to find out more about yourself. Imagine yourself entering your brain to find out what makes you tick. Look around. Try to find that part of your brain that stored the messages of self-doubt. When you find it, identify the self-doubts and erase them from your memory banks. You don't need them anymore. Now go to the part of the brain where the positive self-statements are stored. What do you say to yourself to make you feel strong and capable? Make those positive self-statements stronger and more self-affirming, and feel yourself grow stronger.

Now it is time to leave your brain. Slowly leave your brain and begin to imagine yourself sitting in your chair. Try to remember this room. Feel the pressure of your chair. Slowly open your eyes.

is incarcerated felons who "volunteer" because they have learned that engaging in group activities enhances the likelihood that they will be paroled. Although the assessment of motivation requires a high level of experience and clinical skill in some instances, one simple technique can also be quite enlightening to group helpers of all experience levels. This technique involves asking prospective clients to rate their motivation to participate in the group that is being formed on a 1 to 10 scale, with a 1 indicating that they have very low motivation and a 10 meaning that they have very high motivation. People who have motivation ratings of less than 5 should be asked to clarify their reasons for wanting to participate in the group and perhaps be excluded from the group altogether.

The final task to be accomplished in the screening interview is to determine if there are people in the community or institution that should not be included in the same group as the person being screened. This is ascertained by asking, "Is there a person or are there persons in this community or institution that you would not like to have included in your group?" The individual being screened may also be told that it is generally unwise to be in groups with relatives (marriage and family groups are an obvious exception), best friends, and enemies as a means of eliciting a list of people who should not be included in the group if the individual being interviewed is selected for the group.

Who Should Be Excluded from Groups?   The major purpose of screening is to identify groups of people who can work together harmoniously and productively. From this point of view, almost anyone who is a candidate for a group could be ruled out as a prospective client because of the nature of group members who are included. However, there are some individuals who should probably be excluded from all groups because they have characteristics that make them not well suited for effective group work. Unfortunately, not all of these clients can be identified in a brief screening session. However, when identified, the following people often should be excluded from groups.

Marginally Functioning Persons.   This includes people who have severe psychological problems that are not controlled to some degree by medication. The authors are reminded of two graduate students who were assigned to lead an outpatient group for ambulatory schizophrenics. Two of the group members often failed to take their medication and would occasionally have rather severe reactions to their hallucinations. These reactions, when they occurred, typically eliminated the possibility of progress for that session. Individuals who are low functioning intellectually also may not succeed in most groups. Individuals who are borderline mentally retarded, however, can benefit from and be beneficial to others in most groups. Clients who are mentally retarded can benefit from many types of groups, particularly social skills and support groups, but they may not benefit from traditional therapeutic groups.

Dominating Individuals.   Dominating individuals monopolize the group verbally. Often, when they are not talking, they disregard the communications of others. The nature of group approaches requires that there be opportunities for all people in the group to share their thoughts and feelings. Dominating individuals may demand more "air time" than is rightfully theirs. The result is often resentment, and, ultimately, conflict disrupts the workings of the group.

Verbally Aggressive Individuals. The verbally aggressive individual confronts, challenges, and at times abuses others through the use of insults, sarcasm, and verbal put downs. All approaches to helping require the development of a positive atmosphere. The verbally aggressive person is one who continuously violates the rule of treating others with respect and who raises resentment in the process.

Very Shy Individuals. Very shy individuals lack self-confidence and social skills and are unlikely to self-disclose or be supportive of others. Although it may seem odd, other group members begin to resent their silence for two reasons. First, when most members are beginning to take risks and talk about themselves and their problems, the shy member is not similarly inclined. At this point, the clients in the group begin to question the shy person's commitment to the group and, sometimes, question why the individual is in the group. This obviously subverts the group process. Second, painfully shy people fail to provide the support that others need as they attempt to wrestle with the concerns that brought them to the group. Again, resentment may result. However, the most compelling reason for not including very shy people in group approaches to helping is that they are unable to take advantage of the group to get the help they need. These individuals should probably be placed in individual treatment until they have the self-confidence and social skills needed to interact in a group setting.

Passive Aggressive Individuals. Passive aggressive individuals have two aspects of their functioning that can be quite disruptive in groups. One of these is their apparent willingness to listen to feedback and advice from the leaders and other clients. However, after the advice or feedback has been completed, the passive aggressive individual engages in a classic "yes, but" reaction. They may say, "That is really valid feedback, but I'm not sure you got the whole picture" or "That is great advice, but I have already tried it and it didn't work." Unfortunately, the harder the group and the leader try, the more the passive aggressive individual resists attempts to help. Needless to say, this tends to frustrate leaders and members. Passive aggressive individuals also may form coalitions with other group members to disrupt the group or to subvert the leader's influence. They may encourage group members to resist the leader by providing conflicting advice or feedback to reinforce conflict with the leader or join silent members in pacts of nonparticipation. Unfortunately, even the most experienced leaders are often unaware that a member is passive aggressive until after the group begins.

Stage 2: Formation and Orientation (Forming)

Although there are many critical points in the life of a group, none is more important than the first session. Clients come to the group with varying expectations of what will occur, even though they have been oriented to the group during the screening session. Many clients are quite anxious because they are unsure of their roles in the group and how they are supposed to interact with the leader and other group members. Some authorities have referred to this particular stage of the group as the *dependency phase* because group members are dependent on the leader for direction and support. The leader's first task is to allay the anxieties of the clients by (1) reiterating the rules, (2) clarifying the roles of group members, and (3) facilitating self-disclosure.

The rules of the group are the same as those laid out in the screening group. As the group progresses, rules may be clarified or made more specific. For example, if group members were told that they were to treat individuals in the group with respect, this might be clarified to include listening while others are speaking. Generally, the roles of the group members are also the same as those laid out during screening: to get and give help. Again, some clarification of these roles may be necessary as the group progresses. Because clients may not understand what is involved in getting or providing help, explanations may be necessary. For example they may be advised that discussing their problems and receiving feedback from other clients is a step that they may wish to take. Finally, in this phase of the group it is important to begin the process of self-disclosure. Initially this is done by having group members introduce themselves. This can be done by conducting rounds. Rounds involve going around the group and having people in the group tell about themselves. It may also be done by forming dyads in which each member of the dyad takes five minutes to tell the other about him- or herself. When the dyads return to the group, they introduce their partners instead of telling about themselves.

After the first session, the group helper works to facilitate the self-disclosure process in a number of ways. One of these is through simple reinforcement of risk-taking behavior that involves talking about oneself. Effective group helpers realize that talking about one's problems and weaknesses takes courage, and they regularly express appreciation when clients do so. Another strategy for encouraging clients to self-disclose is through leader self-disclosures. For example, helpers who are leading groups of recovering drug abusers might tell about their struggles to free themselves from drug addiction. One additional technique that a group helper might use to facilitate self-disclosure is through the use of exercises. One of the authors' favorites is to have clients talk about the family members whom they most and least resemble. The result is that clients disclose much information about themselves, albeit indirectly, as they talk about their relatives.

The major barrier to self-disclosure is distrust. Skilled group helpers recognize the resistance that grows out of distrust and intervene. One technique for making this intervention is to place people who appear to distrust each other in dyads that require them to be dependent on each other. The trust walk, for example, requires a blindfolded client to take a walk with another client who guides the walk. After a few minutes, these roles are reversed. Another technique for dealing with distrust is to have clients tell each member in the group why they trust or distrust them. Often, when clients attempt to verbalize their reasons for distrusting others, they find that they have no clear rationale for their feelings and begin to trust others. In other situations, the reasons for the distrust are tangible and need to be dealt with in the group. It is not unusual for group members to distrust people who break the rules of the group or who have shown lack of respect for one or more people in the group. Another reason why some people distrust some or all of the people in the group is that they do not feel included. In some instances, this may have occurred as a result of being cut off during group discussions or for more illusory reasons. Typically what is required to allay this concern is that persons who feel excluded need to be reassured that they are valued group members. Usually, when the issues that are keeping group members from trusting each other are disclosed, they can be handled in the context of the group. Once trust and other related issues are resolved, cohesion develops.

Stage 3: Norming

Neophyte group helpers often mistakenly believe that the comfort with, and positive statements about, the group are sure signs that the group is on its way to positive outcomes. This will be true only if the group adopts a working norm. A *norm* is a rule that governs the behavior of the group. As strange as it seems, some groups adopt an informal agreement that they will not address the problems that brought the members to the group in the first place. Effective group helpers remind group members to work on their problems, encourage risk taking so that the process of working on problems can occur, and ultimately, confront the group about its failure to move on to problem solving.

It is also worth noting that working norms, once established, may change. For this reason, the norming phase of groups has been likened to a swinging door. Groups may make their way through the swinging door to working, but events in the group may cause them to return to a nonworking posture. Groups often reverse themselves and return to the norming stage when an unresolved trust issue surfaces or when one member fails to keep the disclosure of other members in confidence. Group leaders need to be mindful that trust is a major issue that either facilitates or retards movement to the adoption of a working norm. Trust is an issue because group members do not wish to feel vulnerable to real or imagined threats when they lower their personal barriers and disclose their innermost feelings. It is the leaders' responsibility to create a safe environment to make sure that their clients' fears will not be realized.

When members are distrustful, passive aggressive, or engaged in power struggles with people outside the group who are trying to force them to change when they do not wish to do so, hidden agendas develop in groups. A hidden agenda is a plan by an individual to accomplish a goal that is unspoken and is often contrary to the overall goals of the group. For example, a client may try to dominate a group to keep it from moving into the working stage. The group leader is often forced to identify these hidden agendas, bring them to the group's attention, and get agreement that the agenda will be abandoned by the individual in order to promote movement.

Stage 4: Working (Performing)

The working stage of the group, as the name implies, is the point in the group that clients actively engage in working on the problems or issues that caused them to join the group. During the working stage, groups resemble individual counseling sessions but in a group setting. The problem experienced by each group member is unique. Group leaders who fail to acknowledge the particular nature of each group member's concern will fail.

Many factors influence the strategies that are used in the working stage. Leaders' theoretical positions will be a major factor in the strategies they use. Behavioral group helpers believe that inappropriate behavior is either the result of faulty learning experiences or lack of opportunity to learn appropriate ways of behaving. Accordingly, they will try to provide learning situations that will allow clients to either learn new behaviors or unlearn maladaptive behavior. Other group helpers will try to assist clients to identify irrational thoughts, alter those thoughts, and use their new ways of thinking to change their lives. Needless to say, there are literally dozens of theoretical approaches that can be used as the basis for interventions in group settings.

Finally, the strategies chosen by the helper must be tailored to the cultural background of the client. For example, in many instances it would be inappropriate to teach an Asian American assertive behavior or to expect Native Americans to disclose their deepest feelings. The gender of the clients, their age, and their socioeconomic status are other factors that may influence the types of interventions used.

Stage 5: Termination (Adjourning)

The final stage of any group is termination. The termination date of groups with closed membership (no new members may be added once the group begins) may be established before the group begins. In closed membership groups, the termination date is determined based on the progress of the clients in the group. In these groups, termination occurs when the majority of the clients have accomplished their goals. Those clients who have not completed their work at the time of termination are seen individually, included in another group, or referred to another helper. Open-ended groups have rotating members and have no preset termination date. These groups, which are typically found in mental health and inpatient settings, operate continuously. When clients who are participating in the group are discharged from the facility, other clients are incorporated into the group. Although the continuous change in group membership poses a number of problems for the group helper, these groups can be quite successful.

One of the tasks of group facilitators at termination is to determine the progress of members and help those who need more work find new sources of assistance. Another important task that must be addressed during this stage is to facilitate the process of saying goodbye. Some group members will experience separation anxiety as they anticipate functioning without the support of the group.

Others will experience a sense of loss and begin to mourn the loss of their relationships with other clients and the leader. Still others will eagerly anticipate the ending of the group because of their newfound attitudes and skills. If the group has been successful, most clients will feel some or all of these feelings. Although most clients will want to move on because they have accomplished their purposes for being in the group, they realize that leaving the group represents a significant loss. Leaders can facilitate the termination of the group by summarizing the entire group experience, calling attention to the progress that individuals have made, encouraging members to implement what they have learned, and saying individual goodbyes. Perhaps most important, farewell exercises that allow all clients to express their thoughts and feelings about the group experience and to say thanks to individuals who have been particularly helpful can aid clients to sever their ties to the group.

Types of Groups

Helpers employ many different types of groups in their work. Jacobs, Harvill, and Masson (1998) identify several distinct types of groups including support groups, educational groups, discussion groups, task groups, personal growth groups, counseling and therapy groups, and family therapy groups. Four of the groups in addition to social skills development groups will be discussed here since they are formed for the purpose of helping. Family groups will not be discussed here because they have been discussed elsewhere in the book.

Support Groups

The purpose of support groups is to provide emotional support for people who have experienced, or are currently experiencing, stress or trauma. The groups, if properly managed, can (1) reduce stress, (2) prevent stressful situations or traumatic events from precipitating more serious psychological problems, and (3) enable clients to cope with difficult situations. Support groups are typically offered in the following agencies and with the following clients:

- Hospitals for patients or their relatives
- Public schools for children whose parents are getting a divorce, learning disabled students, underachievers, and pregnant teens
- Colleges for gays and lesbian students who are "coming out," doctoral students who are experiencing problems with their research, and undergraduates who are away from home for the first time
- Community mental health agencies for rape victims, victims of violent crimes, abused spouses, and people suffering from debilitating mental health problems
- Drug and alcohol rehabilitation agencies for people who are recovering from addiction problems

- Veterans' facilities for veterans with post-traumatic stress disorder and individuals who have debilitating physical illnesses and injuries as a result of their military careers
- Alcoholics Anonymous, Narcotics Anonymous, and AlaTeen for recovering substance abusers and their families
- Correctional institutions and agencies for probationers and parolees
- Hospices for the dying and their friends and loved ones
- Parent groups such as Parents without Partners for single parents and stepparents
- Outplacement firms for workers who have lost their jobs
- Businesses and organizations for people who need to manage their stress and prevent burnout
- Nursing homes to help residents deal with aging and the loss of independence

Educational Groups

As the name suggests, the purpose of educational groups is to provide information in much the same way teachers helps student gain knowledge about history and mathematics. Educational groups, like many of the groups discussed in this section, are offered widely. Some examples of the institutions and agencies that offer educational groups and the types of groups offered include:

- Schools and colleges teach study skills and resume development.
- Health educators teach good-touch/bad-touch classes to elementary school children to prevent sexual abuse. They may also teach human sexuality classes as one means of preventing problem pregnancies.
- Rehabilitation counselors teach adaptive strategies to handicapped persons who are entering the workplace.
- Rape crises centers teach young women how to avoid date rape.
- County health departments hold classes on the proper use of contraception and on safe sex techniques.
- Rehabilitation agencies teach amputees how to use wheelchairs and prosthetic devices.
- DARE public safety officers teach elementary students about the dangers of drug use.

Social Skills Groups

Social skills groups are formed to assist clients in learning specific social skills such as making friends. Social skills groups have become increasingly popular because research has consistently demonstrated that they can be used to assist a wide range of clients in a relatively short period of time. People who come to these groups are usually self-referred because they believe they have social skills deficits. Some examples of the institutions and agencies that offer social skills groups and the audiences to which the groups are offered include:

- Schools offer friendship skills development groups to elementary school students, conflict management skills groups to middle school students, and job interviewing skills groups to high school students.
- College counseling centers offer assertion-training groups. Career planning centers help students prepare for contacts with employers.
- Community colleges offer parenting skills classes.
- Churches offer marital enrichment classes that emphasize communication and negotiation skills.
- Rehabilitation agencies offer work-related social skills groups to clients with mental disabilities.
- Community agencies help welfare recipients prepare for the labor market by teaching workplace etiquette.

Personal Growth Groups

These groups are developed to help people function more effectively. People admitted to these groups are typically relatively free from psychological problems and not undergoing any major life changes such as divorce. Personal growth groups are not as popular as they were 25 years ago, but they are still offered widely. People who come to these groups wish to improve their relationships, their personal functioning, and their overall satisfaction with their lives. They are likely to be found in the following settings:

- Members of the clergy and private practitioners offer marriage enrichment groups to couples who wish to improve their healthy marriages.
- Private practitioners offer weekend growth groups to individuals who wish to function more effectively.
- College counselors offer personal growth experiences for student leaders and others who are attempting to improve their interpersonal relationships.
- Consultants to businesses offer seminars on gender and cultural relationships.

Counseling and Therapy Groups

The purposes of counseling and therapy groups vary widely depending on the theoretical orientation of the helper who leads them. Solution-focused groups have as their primary purpose the resolution of immediate problems that are causing anxiety, stress, or some other unpleasant emotional reaction. They may begin the problem-solving portion of a group by asking, "If your problems were resolved, how would your life be different?" The objectives of Rational Emotive Behavior Therapy groups are to assist clients identify their irrational thoughts ("I must be perfect"), reduce or eliminate those thoughts, and learn new ways of behaving. Other types of therapy groups have seemingly more ambitious aims such as the restructuring of personality or the improvement of clients' self-concepts. Counseling and therapy groups are offered on a more limited basis because of the training required to lead them. However, some of the examples of institutions and agencies that offer these groups follow:

- Public schools offer groups to students who have chronic anger problems.
- College counseling centers and community mental health centers offer group counseling and therapy to students with a wide range of mental health problems including obsessive-compulsive disorders, eating disorders, depression, phobias, and panic attacks.
- Private practitioners offer counseling and therapy groups to clients who have a wide range of problems.
- Drug and alcohol treatment centers, hospitals, and mental health agencies offer group therapy to drug and alcohol abusers.
- Hospitals offer therapy groups to psychiatric inpatients as a part of the overall treatment process.
- Veterans' organizations offer group therapy to veterans suffering from post-traumatic stress disorder and other battlefield-related mental illnesses.

Skills of Effective Group Helpers

Although group approaches to helping are as effective as individual approaches and can be conducted more efficiently, individual approaches to helping are still preferred by many helpers. Why? Many helpers have not developed the complex skills required for effective group leadership. In this section the skills needed to facilitate groups will be examined and compared to the skills required to be proficient in individual helping. This comparative analysis of the skills needed in individual and group helping will be done on a stage by stage basis. Each stage will be introduced with an insert containing a listing of the skills required to facilitate groups at this stage. This insert will be followed by a description of the group skills and, if necessary for clarification, the individual helping skills as well.

Pregroup Stage

As can be seen in Table 9.1, the major difference between the skills required for individual and group helping lies in practitioners' ability to select group members who are compatible. As noted earlier, the group leader must consider age, gender, socioeconomic status, intellectual functioning, mental health status, values, and personality variables in the assessment of an individual's compatibility with other group members.

TABLE 9.1   Skills Required at the Pregroup and Preindividual Helping Stages

Skills Required	Group Helping	Individual Helping
Determining individuals' readiness for helping	Yes	Yes, but this often occurs in the first session
Determining individuals' "fit" with other clients	Yes	No
Explaining purpose of helping and techniques to be used	Yes	Yes, but this often occurs in the first session
Explaining confidentiality and its limits	Yes	Yes
Coordinating group schedule	Yes	No
Conducting first group as screening session	Yes	Yes, if intake procedure is used to determine assignment

Orientation and Formation Stage

The information in Table 9.2 illustrates the point made in the introduction to this section: facilitating groups requires a wider variety of skills than does conducting individual helping sessions. An examination of the techniques that are unique to facilitating groups follows.

Linking.   One of the bases for cohesion in groups is member similarity. The skilled group helper facilitates the recognition of similarities among members by using a technique that is not unlike reflection of content and feeling called *linking*. Consider the following series of communications:

> CARL: You know what I hate most about this place—no privacy. I can't do anything without someone watching.
> LJ: Yeah! Those bastards watch you like a hawk on visiting day. I'd like to have five minutes with my wife.
> JORGE: (Laughs) I know what you got on your mind. (Group laughs)
> LEADER: Okay, okay—Carl and LJ are making the same point. They are frustrated because of the lack of privacy.

Cutting Off.   The idea that a leader would interrupt a group member who is dominating a group surprises some helpers who are beginning their group training. However, in the early stages of a group it is important for all clients to have an opportunity to talk about themselves. A dominant member can take up too

TABLE 9.2 Skills Required at the Orientation and Formation Stage and the Relationship Stage of Helping

Skills Required	Group—Orientation and Formation	Individual—Relationship Development
Active listening; basic communication skills	Yes	Yes
Using culturally appropriate verbal and nonverbal communication skills	Yes	Yes
Designing exercises to promote getting acquainted and working toward self-disclosure	Yes	No
Linking communications of members	Yes	No
Visually scanning group to read nonverbal reactions	Yes	No, the focus is on the nonverbal behavior of one person
Cutting off members who talk too much	Yes	No
Rounds	Yes	No
Drawing out; encouraging shy individuals to self-disclose	Yes	Yes, but the need for this skill occurs less frequently
Asking open-ended questions	Yes	Yes
Processing group interaction to clarify meaning	Yes	No
Increasing the specificity of communication by use of minimal encouragers and questions	Yes	Yes
Managing conflict and protecting weaker members	Yes	No
Identifying and eliminating intra-group trust issues through the use of exercises and other means	Yes	No
Promoting inclusion of all group members	Yes	No

much "air time" and eliminate this opportunity. The process of cutting off a group member is illustrated below:

> **MYKALA:** (She has been talking about her marital problems several minutes and shows no sign of stopping; she continues) . . . and all I can say is that I made a mistake. I regret the day I married Jerald, but I'm not sure what to do about it.

LEADER: (Holds up hand to signal stop) Mykala, I need to stop you at that point. I hear your frustration with your marriage, but I want to hear from everybody before the session ends. (Leader then reassures Mykala) I promise you that we will get back to your concerns.

Designing Exercises to Facilitate Self-disclosure.   Group leaders often use exercises called ice breakers in the early stages of a group. One of these is called, "What's in your wallet or purse?" Individuals in the group are asked to select an item from their wallets or purses that tells something about them and to show the item and to explain its significance. One man showed his gold credit card and explained that all his life he had worked to be financially secure and he had arrived at that point. He went on to say that although his gold card had a credit limit of $50,000 and he could buy almost anything that he wanted, there was something still missing from his life. A woman showed her driver's license and explained that it represented the ultimate in frustration. She explained that although she had a driver's license, her panic attacks kept her from driving because she was afraid she would be trapped on a bridge, in a tunnel, or a major traffic jam.

Rounds.   Rounds involve taking turns talking about a particular issue. For example, the leader may ask group members to tell a little about themselves at the start of a group to start the process of self-disclosure. This can be done by asking for volunteers or simply saying, "Let's use rounds, starting with Sara." If this technique is used often, leaders should start each round with different clients.

Visually Scanning Group.   While only one person can talk at a time in a group setting, all clients can communicate simultaneously using nonverbal communication. Head nods indicate agreement or disagreement with the speaker. Turning out of the group may mean that an individual is becoming alienated from the group. Doodling may mean that a member is getting bored. Effective leaders continuously scan the group for nonverbal communications and respond to them. For example: Jalen has been talking about his lack of assertiveness with professionals and several other group members are nodding in agreement. The leader says "I can tell that you are pretty angry with yourself because you feel abused by doctors, and I can see that Kristen, Lance, and Consuela are feeling the same way."

Drawing Out.   Group helpers are constantly on the alert for clients who, for whatever reasons, are not participating verbally in the group. One strategy for recognizing their communication is to respond to their nonverbal communications. However, from time to time leaders must invite quiet members to participate through the use of leads such as, "Kevin, I would really like to hear from you. I'm sure you have some valuable input on this topic." When the low participator does respond, the leader should immediately reinforce the verbalizations by saying things like, "It was great to hear from you."

Processing Group Interactions to Clarify Meaning.   Processing is a high level group leadership skill that requires the group leader to identify problems in the group process, call these to the attention of the members, and, with the members, correct the problem. An example of the use of processing is described in the following vignette.

> SECOND GROUP MEETING: So far 45 minutes have elapsed in this 90-minute session. To this point in the meeting only the three verbal members have spoken, and it is clear that the other members are frustrated, but they are unsure what action to take to assert themselves. The group helper uses processing to intervene.
>
> LEADER: I think we have a problem in our group. I'm wondering if I am the only one who thinks so.
>
> CAROL: (One of the talkative members) I'm not sure what you mean.
>
> JANE: (One of the quiet members) I think we may have a problem.
>
> LEADER: (Using a minimal encourager) Tell us what you are thinking.
>
> JANE: Several of us haven't talked at all. It started last week in our first session.
>
> CAROL: (Defensively) What's stopping you?
>
> LEADER: What about the rest of you? Is there a problem?
>
> JILL: Yeah. It's my own fault I know, but I feel like, well you know, that some people in the group really don't care whether I participate. (Several others shake heads in agreement)
>
> LEADER: For our group to be successful, all clients need to have an opportunity to talk, and it seems that several of you think that is not occurring now. How can we deal with this problem?
>
> Group continues discussion and agrees that (1) quiet people should be more assertive and (2) talkative people need to be more sensitive. This action repaired the faulty process that has developed in the group.

Managing Conflict and Protecting.   Conflicts are inevitable in groups, and it is the helper's responsibility to assess the nature of the conflict and either intervene or allow the people involved in the conflict to resolve the matter themselves. The principle that should guide the helper's decision about intervening is that, if the conflict threatens the success of the group or the welfare of an individual in the group, intervention is required. Conflict between or among group members would normally be allowed to run its course, that is, be resolved by the protagonists, if neither of these threats is present.

In the previous section dealing with processing, the leader intervened by focusing on the faulty group process. In other instances the leader will intervene by reminding the clients of the rules of the group, particularly the rule of treating others with respect. In some situations, leaders must actually remove a client from the group to restore harmony. Expulsion from the group typically occurs when clients are aggressive or disrespectful. However, clients are not asked to leave the group until after the inappropriateness of the client's behavior is pointed out and one or more attempts are made to reduce the conflict in the group.

Once conflicts are identified and the leader decides to intervene, the following steps should be taken:

1. Identify the nature of the conflict. To do this, have each person in conflict state his or her perception of the reasons why there is a conflict in the group.
2. Conduct empathy training. Have each person involved in the conflict take the points of view of the other people in the conflict.
3. Brainstorm solutions to the conflict.
4. If individuals in conflict cannot agree on a solution, work on a compromise solution or rotate solutions so that several solutions are tried.

Promoting Trust.   As was noted in the section on trust, there are several ways of promoting trust such as trust walks and direct expressions of trust or distrust. However, the most difficult aspect of promoting trust is discerning when trust is an issue in the group. Some of the indicators that there is a lack of trust are subtle. For example, when personal disclosures contain only "name, rank, and serial number information" or some members of the group do not participate, trust is probably an issue. Occasionally, when a member of a group commits a particularly egregious act such as telling what others have said outside the group, trust issues result in open disputes. When trust is developing, the leader can use processing, for example, ("It seems to me that we may have a trust issue in our group"), strategies such as trust walks, and feedback among the group members to each other about their perceived trustworthiness. However, more dramatic and immediate action is required whenever a breach in confidence can occur. The leader should begin by asking members for solutions. The leader may also suggest the following alternatives: (1) the offending client may be allowed to stay in the group if he or she pledges not to violate the rules of the group in the future or (2) expel the client who has broken the rule. After a discussion, the members should decide what to do with the member who has broken the rules, but this is not the case where the majority rules. The decision to allow a client to continue participating in the group must be an unanimous vote. If one person has serious reservations about the person who broke confidentiality staying in the group, the member should probably be taken out of the group.

Promoting Inclusion.   Making sure that all people feel as though they are valued members of the group requires a combination of leadership techniques that have already been discussed. Shy or nonassertive members must be encouraged to participate by drawing them out, by cutting off verbose clients, and by protecting them from the verbal assaults of other members. They must also be verbally reinforced when they take risks and self-disclose. Rounds is another excellent technique for promoting inclusion.

In some instances, exercises may be employed to promote inclusion. One such exercise begins when the leader identifies a group member who feels excluded, confirms that this is the case by asking them if they feel as though they are an important part of the group, and designs a "breaking in" exercise. In this exercise, all members of the group except the one who feels excluded stand, link arms facing outward, and physically resist the entrance of the member into the inner part of the group without injuring anyone. Most clients who feel excluded strain vigorously to unlock the arms of the members of the group or try to go under the group. One young woman approached one of the male members of the group, unzipped his fly, and when he dropped his arms to restore his zipper to its proper place, calmly walked into the group. Needless to say, her act generated a great deal of discussion.

Norming Stage

This is the stage in the development of the group in which decisions are made, sometimes implicitly, whether to move on to the working stage. In a sense, there is no analogous stage in the individual helping process, but individual helpers do face a parallel problem: resistance. The strategies used in group and individual helping to move clients to the working or problem-solving stages are shown in Table 9.3.

As Table 9.3 shows, the techniques needed at the analogous stages in group and individual helping are the same. The main difference is that group leaders will be using the techniques with 8 to 12 clients as opposed to one.

Working (Performing) Stage

Both group and individual helping have working stages that are characterized by clients being actively engaged in resolving the issues that brought them to the helper. Although the specific techniques employed will vary based on the theoretical orientation of the helper, some techniques that are used by helpers with various theoretical orientations will be discussed here to illustrate the advantages of group over individual helping. The intervention strategies that will be discussed are listed in Table 9.4.

TABLE 9.3   Skills Used during the Norming Stage

Technique	Group	Individual
Confrontation	Yes	Yes
Assessment of goals	Yes	Yes
Immediacy; focusing on the relationship	Yes	Yes

Role Playing. Role playing, which is sometimes referred to as behavioral rehearsal, is used in both group and individual interventions. It involves practicing social skills such as making friends, acting assertively with bosses, acting appropriately with coworkers, refusing offers to take drugs, solving conflicts, and decision making. The advantage that group leaders have in the use of this technique is their ability to create role playing involving more than two people (the helper and the client) and the opportunity to involve clients in the process of providing feedback about the appropriateness of the social skills used by the clients who are role playing. In reality, clients in the group may have more influence than the leader in the process of shaping new behavior.

Homework Assignments. Homework assignments, as the name suggests, involve activities conducted outside the helping process. In the working stage of groups, these acts typically involve problem-solving activities. Group helpers can create buddy systems that can enhance the opportunity that homework assignments will be carried out successfully. The smoker who is enrolled in a stop-smoking group may need emotional support from time to time, which can be obtained by calling his or her buddy from the group. Recovering alcoholics might be assigned to visit a popular restaurant that serves alcohol in pairs for the same reason. Children may be asked to observe the efforts of other children in the group to make friends and provide feedback about their efforts. In fact, the possibility for enhancing the outcomes of homework is unlimited in group situations.

Guided Imageries. Guided imageries are used during the helping phase of a group to suggest new options. For example, a high school counselor developed a graduation imagery for a group of prospective dropouts so they could "experience" the thoughts and emotions they would feel when they graduated. People with phobias are often exposed to guided imageries in which they "experience" snakes, heights, tests, public speaking, and so forth. Although guided imagery can be used in individual helping, the richness that results from a group experience cannot be duplicated. For example, when one claustrophobic client reports that he or she has successfully taken the elevator to the fifteen floor without getting off at every other floor, this encourages people who have failed to get on to the imaginary elevator to try again. Moreover, the encouragement that comes when

TABLE 9.4   Techniques Used during the Working Stage

Techniques	Group	Individual
Role playing	Yes	Yes
Homework assignments	Yes	Yes
Guided imagery	Yes	Yes
Logs and diaries	Yes	Yes

one client tells another, "If I can do it, so can you" is impossible to duplicate in an individual session.

Logs and Diaries.   Logs and daily diaries of activities, thoughts, or reactions are often used in individual and group helping to promote introspection, to keep records of successes and failures, and to identify targets of interventions. For example, cognitive therapists such as Beck (Beck et al., 1979) ask depressed clients to keep a log of their activities, which are typically very limited, and, once a baseline is established, make homework assignments to get them to alter what are very limited activity schedules. Clients may be asked to get out of bed earlier and stay up later, interact with other people on a regular basis, engage in plea-surable activities, and so forth. When group members share their logs, they can vicariously experience the success of others, get positive feedback when they succeed, and receive support and encouragement when they fail.

Termination (Adjourning) Stage
Exercises That Facilitate Termination.   As was noted earlier, a major advantage of groups is that a variety of exercises can be used to facilitate member growth and change. This advantage extends from the initial stage to termination. Jacobs et al. (1998) outline a particularly powerful exercise called wishes that can help the group commit to continue the change process that they began in the group. In this exercise, the leader asks the members to reflect on the wishes they have for each other's futures now that the group is ending. Very often these wishes are expressions of hope that members will engage in continuing efforts to change and grow. Another exercise that leaders may use to get closure at the end of groups is to use rounds and have members respond to open-ended sentences such as:

> The most important thing I learned was . . .
> The highlight of the group was . . .
> My greatest regret is . . .

Group Celebrations.   Although many clients will approach the end of a group with anxiety and a touch of sadness, the completion of a successful group is cause for celebration. These celebrations may include toasts using nonalcoholic bever-ages where members drink to the success of the group. They may also be quiet gatherings where people have an opportunity to interact and say their goodbyes.

Summarization by Members.   Although it is common practice for leaders to summarize what has transpired in groups as well as in individual work, using rounds as a strategy involves all clients and puts a final exclamation point on the importance of all group members.

TABLE 9.5   Techniques Used during the Termination Stage

Techniques	Group	Individual
Exercises that facilitate termination	Yes	No
Group celebration	Yes	No
Summary by members using rounds	Yes	No

Factors That Keep Groups from Succeeding

Neither group nor individual helping is universally successful. In this final section of the chapter, factors that can lead to group failures will be outlined. Many of these factors have been alluded to throughout the chapter, but prospective group helpers may benefit from one final reminder that many things can go awry. Groups are likely to fail if the helper:

- Has poor group facilitation skills
- Is aggressive and establishes a negative atmosphere in the group
- Fails to adequately inform members about the nature of the group process
- Fails to select compatible group members
- Fails to properly assess the motivation of clients, which results in numerous dropouts
- Fails to intervene in group processes that preclude the development of trust and open communication
- Fails to deal with hidden agendas that subvert the group process
- Fails to deal with dominating clients, aggressive clients, very quiet clients, or other types of clients who find successful group work difficult
- Fails to successfully deal with member behavior that results in mistrust such as breaking the confidence of another group member
- Fails to recognize that the group is not moving through the norming stage to the working stage
- Fails to craft interventions that will facilitate growth and change of the individuals in the group
- Acts unethically

Summary

When compared to individual approaches, group helping has many advantages and a few disadvantages. The major advantage of groups is that they are more efficient than individual counseling. The chief disadvantage is that helpers need to develop a complex set of skills to be successful group leaders. Groups, like individual approaches to helping, move through discernible stages that are in many ways analogous. The group stages that have been identified here include pregroup, formation and orientation, norming, working, and termination. At each of these stages, the group helper has certain critical tasks that must be accomplished to maximize the probability of the group being successful. Certain factors, such as failure to select compatible group members and inability to intervene in critical group processes, may doom groups to failure.

CHAPTER 9 EXIT QUIZ

Answer each of the following questions with a "T" if it is true and an "F" if it is false.

_____ 1. Group approaches to helping are generally more effective than individual approaches.

_____ 2. Most authorities on groups agree that pregroup is a stage in group process.

_____ 3. One of the major tasks of the group leader during screening is to fully assess the nature of each prospective group member's problem.

_____ 4. For some group helpers, the first group meeting is actually a screening meeting.

_____ 5. In screening group members, a rule of thumb for including people in groups is that they should be similar, but not identical, in values, personality characteristics, and socioeconomic background.

_____ 6. Groups that have members with similar ethnic characteristics do better than groups that are dissimilar in this regard.

_____ 7. It is probably a bad idea to include people in a social skills group that have the same approach to dealing with the problem at hand.

_____ 8. Rounds involves people taking turns as they talk about a problem.

_____ 9. When group leaders use processing, they are analyzing alternative processes that can be employed to solve group members' problems.

_____10. When groups become highly cohesive, the members are more likely to be on time.

_____11. It is almost a certainty that groups that become cohesive will move to the working stage of the group.

_____12. The factors that typically must be addressed in establishing cohesiveness are inclusion, trust, and self-disclosure.

_____13. Effective groups, regardless of the type, work because of the presence of the same therapeutic factors.

_____**14.** Becoming aware of the reality of death as an inevitable result of living is a therapeutic factor know as universality.

_____**15.** Group leaders should be prepared to protect weaker group members from verbal assaults.

_____**16.** Leaders should expect group members to cut off clients who talk too much.

Answers:

1. F; 2. F; 3. F; 4. T; 5. T; 6. F; 7. T; 8. T; 9. F; 10. T; 11. F; 12. T; 13. F; 14. F; 15. T; 16. F.

SUGGESTED LEARNING ACTIVITIES

1. Begin by asking each person in the class to select a partner that he or she did not know before the class began. Ask these dyads to get to know each other as well as possible within a ten-minute period. Tell them that when they return to the group they are to formally introduce their partners to the group by providing the class as much information as possible.

2. What each person in the group says influences his or her feelings as well as the emotions of other people in the group. Use rounds to demonstrate this point by doing the following:
   a. Have each person in class state his or her name and favorite color.
   b. Next, have each person tell what makes him or her happy.
   c. Conclude the self-disclosure by asking each person to tell something that makes him or her sad.

   Allow people who have difficulty with this exercise to pass. Process this exercise by asking about the emotions that each person experienced as they disclosed information about themselves. Then ask if any of the disclosures of others influenced their emotions.

3. Many groups, including some classes, are characterized by one-way communication. To illustrate why this is effective, whisper a message into the ear of the person next to you. That person is to whisper what they heard into the ear of the person sitting next to them and so on around the circle until the message returns to you. No one may ask for clarification of the message they heard. Repeat the message that was sent and the message that came back to you. Normally they will be very different.

4. Divide the class into two groups. Group 1 will be observers and group 2 will role-play a group. One person from group 2 is selected to be the leader and he or she, group 1, and all of group 2 except three students are dismissed from the room. The remaining members of group 2 are told that they are going to participate in a task group in which there are hidden agendas. The task is to design a new student lounge for the department. Student A is selected and assigned the role of trying to ingratiate himself or herself with the leader by agreeing and supporting

the leader while pretending to support the group decision-making process. Students B and C are asked to support B's plan while pretending to support a group decision. They are then given a few minutes to develop a plan for the lounge.

Students who have been outside the room are asked to return. The leader is then told that his or her task is to facilitate a task group that is to plan a new student lounge for the department. The students in group 1 are assigned the task of observing the group process with the objective of determining the communication patterns in the group.

After 30 minutes, debrief the groups by asking all students except A, B, and C the following questions:
a. What was your overall reaction to the group process?
b. Were there things about the group that made you uncomfortable? Frustrated you?
c. If there were problems, did you agree with the way they were handled by the leader? How would you have handled the problems that you perceived?

The final step is to talk about the negative impact of hidden agendas on groups.

5. Leading groups effectively requires helpers to scan the group with their eyes and respond to the emotions displayed by the group. They must also learn to interpret and deal with negative verbal behavior. Divide the class into groups of four. Have group members alternate leading the groups during a series of 15-minute role-playing exercise that addresses the topic, "Solving the Problems in Our Society." Leaders are told that they are to scan the group for nonverbal behavior and respond to it using the following approach: "I can see that you . . ." (identifies the feeling implicit in the nonverbal behavior). At the beginning of each role play, hand each member a slip of paper that contains the emotion they are to portray nonverbally during the discussion.

Role Play 1: Negative Nonverbal Behavior
a. Yawns and shows other signs of boredom
b. Shows anger when a person asks a question or responds to another
c. Shows disgust by turning out of the group abruptly when a member comments

Role Play 2: Positive Nonverbal Behavior
a. Shows approval by touching a group member on the arm, patting on the back, or nodding
b. Shows interest by leaning or turning toward a speaker
c. Shows appreciation by smiling

Role Play 3: Mixed Nonverbal and Verbal Behavior
a. Person is cold and aloof; obviously doesn't care
b. Throws up hands in disgust
c. Sneers in anger at a speaker

At the end of each role play, leaders should be given feedback about the accuracy of their response to verbal and nonverbal behavior by group members.

REFERENCES

Beck, A.T., Rush, A.J., Shaw, B.F., & Emery, G. (1979). *Cognitive therapy of depression*. New York: Guilford.

Corey, G. (1995). *Theory and practice of group counseling* (4th ed.). Pacific Grove, CA: Brooks/Cole.

Gladding, S.T. (1991). *Group work: A counseling specialty* (2nd ed.). Columbus, OH: Merrill.

Jacobs, E.E., Harvill, R.L., & Masson, R.L. (1998). *Group counseling: Strategies and skills* (3rd ed.). Pacific Grove, CA: Brooks/Cole.

Tuckman, B.W., & Jensen, M.A. (1977). Stages in small group development revisited. *Group and Organizational Studies, 2*, 419–427.

Vander Kolk, C.J. (1985). *Introduction to group counseling and psychotherapy*. Columbus, OH: Merrill.

Wheelan, S.A. (1994). *Group processes: A developmental perspective*. Boston: Allyn and Bacon.

Wilson, R.R. (1987). *Breaking the panic cycle: Self-help for people with phobias*. Baltimore, MD: Anxiety Disorders Association of America.

Yalom, I.D. (1985). *The theory and practice of group psychotherapy* (3rd ed.). New York: Basic Books.

10 Working with Communities

WHAT YOU WILL LEARN

1. How to view an entire community as the "client"
2. How behavioral theory can be applied to helping communities
3. Ways to assess the problems and needs of communities
4. Advocacy roles for helpers in supporting community development
5. How to link the efforts of individuals, families, and community agencies
6. How to use volunteers to strengthen community services

For several decades, various groups have devised criteria for rating the livability of communities. For example, Oxford, Maryland, on the eastern shore of that state posted billboards advertising Oxford as "the 8th most livable small city in America." Retirees and others sometimes make decisions regarding where they will live based on such ratings.

For any community to be rated highly as a livable community depends on the criteria used. The most common criteria for comparing the livability of communities include:

- Safety: measured by crime statistics, especially the incidence of violent crime;
- Health care: the proximity of hospitals, mental health and medical specialists;
- Housing: in particular, the availability of affordable homes and apartments;
- Employment: a favorable local job market;
- Educational system: the availability of quality schools and academic programs for people of all ages;
- Recreation: access to leisure activities such as parks, swimming pools, athletic fields, nearby resorts, ski areas, lakes, and streams;
- Cultural events: the presence of the arts, such as a symphony, the opera, theater, and other cultural events;
- Transportation: the availability of public transportation and easy access to a major airport;
- Overall cost of living: the price of utilities, property taxes, and insurance rates.

The same criteria can be used to evaluate a community with problems. High crime rates, high unemployment, poor housing conditions, and few recreational opportunities create a dismal environment for people of all ages. This would result in a low livability index. If these factors are combined with inefficient government and the availability of few medical facilities and few human services, the residents of the community have little hope that conditions will improve. While we have listed quite a few factors that define a quality community, the U.S. Office of Management and Budget (OMB), the president's advisor on community needs, identifies the universal concerns of communities as being health, education, and public safety. For more information, access the OMB's Web site at *www.whitehouse.gov/OMB.*

Imagine that a group of the most competent professional helpers move into a community that has a low livability index. How might a handful of effective helpers make an impact in the lives of needy residents in the midst of all the larger community problems? Would it be effective to ignore all of the larger community problems and focus only on the individual concerns of clients coming to a clinic or agency? Sometimes helpers commit to improving the health of the community at large in addition to their commitment to individual clients.

Making a Commitment to the Community

When you are employed as a helping professional, you are most likely to work for an employer in the community in which you live. The livability and health of that community affects you as a person as much as your clients. The changes you might like to see take place in your community can benefit your clients as much as you. An important part of professionalism is a commitment to citizenship, a commitment to serving the community, both inside and outside your specific job duties. Complete Exercise 10.1, p. 220, to determine where you might begin.

Volunteer activities supply important human resources to the community. Discuss with other class members some of the volunteer activities that you have participated in. Think back to your childhood and some of the volunteers who organized and maintained programs that were important to you. How would your community have been without these programs?

Looking at volunteer service as an indicator of a person's commitment to a community adds to our understanding of what a community really is. At times we think of a community in terms of a geographic area or locale. At other times a community is not a physical place but an emotional bond, a sense of togetherness among people. The most complete notion of community combines both ways of understanding what a community is. It is a physical place where people feel united and committed to each other.

EXERCISE **10.1**

Community Roles for Volunteers

Aside from their job duties specified by their employer, professional helpers are encouraged to serve the community as volunteers. Listed below are volunteer activities that attract many professional helpers in their capacity as committed citizens. Check the volunteer activities that you are both interested in and qualified to perform.

Activity	Interested	Qualified
1. Disaster relief work with the Red Cross.	_____	_____
2. Coach an athletic team for youth.	_____	_____
3. Raise funds for a local charity.	_____	_____
4. Tutor children after school at home.	_____	_____
5. Help beautify and clean up local parks.	_____	_____
6. Work a local soup kitchen for homeless.	_____	_____
7. Attend planning meetings for local events.	_____	_____
8. Run for a political office (for example, city council).	_____	_____
9. Visit the elderly at local nursing homes.	_____	_____
10. Provide services off hours at a free clinic.	_____	_____
11. Organize a letter-writing campaign for a cause.	_____	_____
12. Join a political campaign for a local candidate.	_____	_____
13. Help staff a youth recreational center.	_____	_____
14. Be a scout leader or church or synagogue group leader.	_____	_____
15. Write media scripts to advertise community programs.	_____	_____

Assessing the Needs of a Community

Identifying the problems and needs of a community is a sizeable task if care is taken to avoid bias in the results. Well-meaning helping professionals have alienated the very communities they wanted to serve by limiting input into the needs assessment process. Local citizens can provide important insights into the needs of the community. However, this input often is not easy to obtain, especially the input of representative citizen groups. For example, a group of social workers advertised a meeting they were holding to assess the needs of an inner-city neighborhood. The meeting was held in one of the churches and was well attended. The social workers realized that those in attendance were much better educated, in better health, and of a higher income bracket than the average resident of the neighborhood. The social workers decided that they needed to canvas the homes of residents either unable to attend meetings outside their home or too uncomfortable to speak out in public. Using the telephone to interview did not seem to be a good idea, since many of the poor in the neighborhood were without phone service. Also, residents of this high crime area were hesitant to open their doors to a stranger. This would severely limit the response to door-to-door interviewing. Because the social workers were new to the community, they had not yet built good, trusting relationships with residents. Had they, they could have enlisted the help of local residents to canvass the neighborhood. The social workers had to rely on other sources of information to assess needs. Here are some frequently used sources of information on community needs:

- Government statistics: Federal, state, and local government agencies compile a great deal of useful information. Examples of information useful in assessing community needs are census data, crime statistics, health statistics from the national Center for Disease Control or a state agency, and economic information on employment and income brackets.
- Utilization rates for local services: Local services used at hospitals, homeless shelters, the Salvation Army, churches, and schools indicate community need.
- Anecdotal information from community workers: Long-term community workers often know about needs that do not get reported and therefore are not reflected in statistics or official reports.
- Surveys of the general population: This can be accomplished by paper and pencil surveys completed in interviews with researchers assessing needs household by household. Surveys can be mailed to residents. Surveys can be completed in community centers, on street corners, and over the phone.
- Comparisons of services among communities: The services offered by one community can be compared to the services offered by another. Comparisons of numerous communities can help to establish a standard, and judgments can be made if a community falls below that standard.

These different needs assessment strategies demonstrate two basic approaches to identifying needs. One is to strive for strict objectivity that eliminates bias in the views reported and provides a representative sample of outcomes of community member action. This is the social science approach. A contrasting strategy is to understand the internal experience of community members by immersing oneself in the community to get the "feel" of what it is like to cope with the existing problems and to understand the aspirations and hopes of community members. This is a cultural, ethnographic approach. Both approaches are valuable in understanding the community (Wilber, 1996). The social science approach is objective and empirical; it is good at summarizing the concrete, material components of the community. The cultural approach accesses the inner experiences of people, their values, and how they are affected by what happens.

Understanding How to Help a Community: A Behavioral Analysis

Most college students are familiar with modern learning theory, which includes both classical and operant conditioning as its central concepts. Students probably have studied the work of Ivan Pavlov in classical conditioning and the work of B.F. Skinner in operant conditioning. In addition, the contributions of Albert Bandura and others may have been studied prior to reading this text. As a refresher for those who have previously studied learning theory and as an introduction to those who have not, we will review key learning concepts from important behavioral theorists as we apply behavioral learning theory to helping communities.

Summarizing Major Learning Theories

Classical Conditioning.   Ivan Pavlov believed that people developed behavior initially as a way to meet their biological needs such as for food and water.

Operant Conditioning.   B.F. Skinner believed that people's behavior is shaped through what he termed *environmental contingencies,* which are rewards and punishments. Behaviors that are rewarded are strengthened and more likely to occur in the future. Behavior that goes unrewarded extinguishes and does not occur in the future. Behavior that is punished occurs less frequently, but only if the individual who provided the punishment is present. The best way to illustrate this latter point is to consider what happens to driving behavior on the freeway when a police car is present. The traffic slows, at least until the police car exits from the freeway. Skinner did not believe that punishment is an effective way to develop new behavior.

Social Learning Theory.   Albert Bandura took a very different view than Skinner about the way that new behavior is developed. Although he did not totally reject the idea that the environment shapes some behavior, he said that most new behavior is developed by imitating models. Children imitate the behavior of other people for the most part, which explains how we develop complex behaviors such as language. Children often receive rewards for the imitations they do in the form of hugs, pats, and attention of other types. Adolescents and adults also imitate the behavior of others, but written material, movies, and television programs also serve as models. As people acquire new behavior, they use it if they feel confident that they can perform the behavior and if they feel performing the behavior is important. Students who are confident that they can learn math because they have learned it in the past may not necessarily do well in math because they may feel math is unimportant.

Applying Behavioral Theory to Communities

Modern learning theory has numerous advantages for understanding how communities can become more livable. It does not use too many ideas that overcomplicate the way forces inside and outside the community shape the behavior of citizens. The ideas used seem sensible and straightforward. They can be easily understood and applied to everyday situations.

In using behavioral ideas in creating livable communities, we can begin by recognizing that both the physical and social environment help determine how community members behave. The behavior of people in the community creates the social environment, and behavior that is rewarded in some way will reoccur. What constitutes a reward will vary among different people, but all rewards share the common feature of reducing such biological survival drives as hunger, thirst, and sex. Because people are very social and can only survive as part of a group, often something that reaffirms their social position becomes rewarding. For example, a smile, some words of praise, and other messages that say "you fit in, you have a place among us" are rewards. Rewards or reinforcements are powerful determiners of behavior.

If prosocial behavior is rewarded, a community will become filled with inhabitants responding to each other in positive ways. Rewards turn occasional responses into habits. Rewards will maintain desired responses.

We also know that responses of community members do not have to be rewarded each time for them to continue. A schedule of reinforcement that is intermittent (reward not given every time) actually will make a response more resistant to extinction. Negative behavior in communities often receive intermittent reinforcement. For example, fighting is not always rewarded. At times, injury is the result of fighting rather than some positive outcome. However, a street gang may reward a member with praise and privileges for assaulting a member of a rival gang, even if the assault resulted in physical injury to the gang member. Sometimes a community may punish someone, thinking it will deter negative acts, while the punishment *is* the incident that becomes rewarded by another source, such as a newspaper article. A police unit might come into a neighborhood to disrupt the activities of a street gang. In doing so, the police may be physically abusive. The gang rewards the victims of this abuse immediately after the police leave.

Rewards may occur in a community only when certain conditions are present. For example, many positive actions are not rewarded unless a person able to provide a reward is present. The person being present often becomes a reinforcing stimulus, that is, many citizens may not respond unless the reinforcing person's presence signals citizens to respond. We call the combination of the stimulus condition, behavior, and reward as the *reinforcing event*. Reinforcing events often are not the same for everyone in a community. High status citizens may earn rewards when low status citizens do not.

Communities commonly use both rewards and punishments to attempt to manage the behavior of their citizens. Considering both the value of obtaining rewards and the value of avoiding punishments constitutes what is called *contingency management*. It is more effective in communities when individuals and groups of citizens learn to manage contingencies rather than when a handful of authorities (for example, police and elected officials) try to manage them.

In addition, contingency management will be more effective for individuals and groups of citizens if rewards and punishments are equally distributed across the community (fair), the conditions surrounding the reinforcing event are clear, and when the contingencies are mostly positive. Also, it seems that contingency management works better if individuals control their own rewards, rather than the rewards being controlled by others. It is better for community leaders to teach all their citizens contingency management than have the leaders manage the contingencies. If this occurs, citizens can arrange for their own rewards.

These simple ideas can be used to diagnose community problems. The community may be relying on punishment rather than reward to shape citizen behavior. A community may not be very livable because there are few rewards present. Problems may exist because some citizens are rewarded for behavior that makes the community unlivable. For example, a family in the inner city who has prospered economically may move to the suburbs. The inner city has lost a talented and resourceful family that could add to an inner-city neighborhood. It has become less livable by them leaving. The family was rewarded for moving to the suburbs with lower taxes, greater physical safety, and more pleasant surroundings.

While contingency management may sound simple, when applied to people's lives it becomes more complex. Often a community member must perform a series of acts or responses in combination to achieve a reward. If the entire sequence or combination does not occur, neither does the reward. This is true for most social behavior, which usually is complex. For example, to have a successful first date, one must link together many different social exchanges over at least several hours.

Learning complicated social behaviors would be difficult, especially if each behavior in the complex series had to be rewarded to gradually shape the more complex behavior. Behavioral shaping using rewards for behavior as it progresses has been demonstrated. Many excellent videos show animals being trained to do very complicated sets of tasks. However, complex social learning seems to be more easily learned through imitation or modeling. If a person is interested in becoming a public speaker, the person could watch videos of successful public speakers. The same is true of learning how to sell merchandise to customers. Most of us realize this and have used models for goals such as improving our game of tennis or our golf swing.

In a very livable community, many excellent models reside who can teach by example how to serve a community. Communities with many problems often lack adequate models to show others how those problems can be solved. For example, high school graduates from remote, impoverished rural communities may have more difficulty learning how to compete for college scholarships. They may be the first in their family to apply to college. The college-attending rate also may be low in their rural area with few college graduates working nearby. School counselors may need to provide special access to online resources that guide students through the college application process. Special programs may need to be developed to bring role models to the school to demonstrate the attitudes and strategies that achieve success in the college application process.

From a behavioral learning perspective, a community that is unable to solve its problems need not be labeled as disordered or pathological, implying that the situation is hopeless. Rather, the community simply needs to be exposed to experiences that provide members the opportunities to learn the skills needed to solve community problems. Communities can solve other problems through their members unlearning negative responses by removing their rewards. For example, the reporting of violent crime in the media has been lessened in some communities to deprive the perpetrator the recognition of the act, a reward sometimes sought by the one committing the crime. Instead alternate, prosocial behaviors receive rewards. In this way, a learning perspective is very optimistic, always seeing learning opportunities as important answers to the community's problems. Case Illustration 10.1, p. 226, shows how students from a local university applied some of the principles just described to a community and its problems.

Advocacy as a Tool for Community Development

In Chapter 1, advocacy was described as one of the primary strategies used by helpers to deal with the complex problems faced by their clients. Often clients do not possess the knowledge and skill needed to deal with educational, governmental, or social service agencies. The helper represents the client to the institution or agency for clients to receive benefits for which they are entitled. At the same time the helper works to empower clients to better represent themselves with social service agencies or health care systems. Examples include helping a recent immigrant with language difficulties understand how to receive medical services or helping an elderly person document a disability.

The idea of empowerment is associated with the advocacy process. The advocate works with a client with the goal to no longer be needed. The person in need gradually is able to advocate for him- or herself. Being empowered to advocate for oneself is described by Miller and Keys (1996) as a four-step process of (1) gaining awareness of societal discrimination, (2) recognizing individual rights and strengths, (3) taking action through participation in community groups, and (4) working in collaboration with supportive advisors.

Poindexter, Valentine, and Conway (1999) identify the type of advocacy illustrated so far as *case advocacy*. Helpers have intervened for the benefit of an individual, a couple, or a family. They describe a second type of advocacy, *class advocacy*, as planned effort toward changing organizations and communities in order for entire populations and subpopulations to have their needs better met. Class advocacy helps clients by attempting to change dysfunctional systems and to help them operate more effectively. In this case, advocacy seeks systemic change so services to clients will be more appropriate, more adequate to meet needs, and more accessible to all who need the services the system provides.

History contains some excellent examples of class advocacy. In the 1950s and 1960s, especially during the time of John Kennedy's presidency, there was a strong belief among socially conscious individuals that government and other social institutions could be changed to create a great society full of opportunity and justice. For example, class advocates worked toward correcting racial injus-

C A S E   I L L U S T R A T I O N   **10.1**

Mayfield State University

Mayfield State University is a small school with a strong commitment to service learning. This is illustrated by numerous projects designed by the allied social science departments that teach students important skills while the community benefits from the effort students make.

The community of Mayfield suffers from many social and economic problems, which are researched by Mayfield State students. The professors directing this research have an ongoing arrangement with the local newspaper to publish preliminary results of research projects before they are finally submitted to professional journals. These studies have identified the problems and needs of Mayfield. Students also research how other communities solve the problems faced by Mayfield. Seniors at Mayfield State have been interns in the community with the city council, the park board, and numerous social service agencies. They and their supervising professors have helped local government and service agencies write state and federal grants to fund special programs. A street fair and banquet culminates the effort of students and community at the end of the school year. Students and model programs receive public recognition in the newspaper and at public events.

Other Mayfield State students volunteer in the Big Brother and Big Sister programs and other youth-oriented programs. Merchants in the community provide Mayfield State students who complete at least one hundred service hours with a discount card that can be used each Tuesday to lower the cost of purchases students make. Mayfield State University has data on the placement of its graduates that show an increase in starting salary and a shorter job search duration since community service-learning programs became operational. Enrollment at this small state school has remained steady while that in similar schools in the state has shown a decline. A loss in enrollment of one hundred students to a school such as Mayfield State reduces the school's budget by hundreds of thousands of dollars.

Both students and the community have been rewarded for their efforts. The community has attracted several new employers who relocated their businesses because of the cooperative relationships across the community. Joblessness has declined. New construction in Mayfield has replaced some of the dilapidated structures in the community, making Mayfield physically more attractive. A greenspace coalition begun by students and professors has tripled the outdoor recreation available within the city limits. Faculty have been role models for university students in caring about what happens to Mayfield. In turn, Mayfield State students have been prosocial models for the youth in the community. Community citizens have learned from students how to address problems through both research and service.

---

tices. Especially in the South, voter registration drives were conducted to increase the political power of African Americans. Following nonviolent strategies popularized in India by Mahatma Gandhi, social or class advocates protested injustices via demonstrations and civil disobedience to bring attention to unjust civil laws. They refused to abide by the racial segregation laws of the time. Challenges to racial injustice took place in the courts as well as the streets, at political conventions, and through the media. Awareness of racial injustice may not have been as rapid and complete in the 1960s if television did not exist. Class advocates began to realize how powerful media attention could be in setting the stage for important social changes.

More recently court action taken against the tobacco and automobile industries demonstrate class advocacy for the health and safety of every citizen. The legal judgments rendered in such cases document how violation of rights go beyond an individual or small group.

These past and present events characterize many of the means used by class advocates to help create more kind and friendly communities. While this may be the goal, the advocate realizes that challenge and confrontation may be a necessary part of the process that leads to achievement of the goal. Read over the list of advocacy actions below; which ones do you feel comfortable with and capable of doing?

- Discuss with your friends some of the social inequities among groups in your home community and what might be done to correct them.
- Write a letter to an elected official to identify a community problem and to suggest how it might be corrected by governmental action.
- Write a letter to the editor of the local newspaper to advocate for an issue.
- Join the political campaign of a candidate who is committed to social change.
- Join an activist group that protests inequities in the community and promotes social change.
- Participate in a street demonstration protesting what you consider to have been an illegal action by an institution or agency.
- Organize a group of disadvantaged citizens in order for them to have a stronger voice in the community.
- Travel to the state legislature to meet with representatives to advocate passage of legislation that will help underserved citizens.
- Reinforce others who have taken action for the welfare of others and, in doing so, may have encountered risks and dangers.

The above list does not exhaust the many ways that the larger community problems, those that affect many citizens, can be given attention and resources gathered for their solution. There are so many groups of citizens that have major difficulties that require the mobilization of costly resources. Exercise 10.2, p. 228, lists some of these groups.

Communities in Action: Illustrations

Both case and class advocacy are important aspects of the work performed by Caritas House in Morgantown, West Virginia. This facility and its over seventy volunteers are committed to serving people affected by HIV and AIDS and to stopping the spread of HIV infection (Litten, 1999). In 1998, Caritas House merged

EXERCISE **10.2**

Community Groups

Consider each community group below. Rate the degree to which your home community advocates for them. Rate each group from 1 to 5 with 1 = very low to 5 = very high. After you have completed your ratings, your instructor may suggest that you discuss your ratings with other class members in small groups. Try to identify the reasons one class member's community may advocate for a particular group and another's community may not.

Community Group	Degree to Which Home Community Advocates for the Group				
HIV and AIDS patients	1	2	3	4	5
Alzheimer's patients and their families	1	2	3	4	5
Children with profound disabilities	1	2	3	4	5
Chronic mentally ill	1	2	3	4	5
Homeless people	1	2	3	4	5
Chronic pain patients	1	2	3	4	5
Victims of domestic violence	1	2	3	4	5
Victims of sexual abuse	1	2	3	4	5
Paroled sex offenders	1	2	3	4	5
Pregnant unmarried teenagers	1	2	3	4	5
Victims of natural disasters	1	2	3	4	5
Cancer survivors	1	2	3	4	5
Gay and lesbian citizens	1	2	3	4	5
Gifted children	1	2	3	4	5
Street prostitutes and their children	1	2	3	4	5
Adults with mental disabilities	1	2	3	4	5
Migrant workers	1	2	3	4	5
Recent immigrants and refugees	1	2	3	4	5

with the Mountain State AIDS Network and serves twenty-one counties in West Virginia. During that same year it was involved in numerous community education events from an African American Awareness Summit to seminars in alcohol and drug treatment centers. The organization recruited two therapists to lead support groups for no fee. Besides direct care giving to HIV and AIDs clients, Caritas House volunteers raise money for medications, supplies, rent, utilities, and travel expenses for medical care. They advocate for clients who are homeless, in prison or jail, in psychiatric facilities, hospitals, transitional housing, or living with relatives or friends. Almost one-half of the volunteers are young adults between the ages of 18 and 30. Caritas House continues its work because of grant-writing and support from the Robert Wood Johnson Foundation and the Claude Worthington Benedum Foundation. Caritas House is a member of the National Federation of Interfaith Volunteer Caregivers (IVC). Its board president is an attorney, former Peace Corps volunteer, and for a time a professional singer in a rock group with a hit record. Other volunteers are involved in activities that include client transportation, shopping assistance, meal preparation and delivery, laundry and house maintenance, personal care, fundraising, clerical assistance, education, and outreach support.

Bernier and Seigel (1994) describe how treating the whole social system can be useful in helping families who have a member with attention deficit hyperactivity disorder (ADHD). From this combined case and class advocacy approach, often called an *ecological systems* perspective, social workers address child and family needs through case work, legislative lobbying, community organizing, and advocacy. Central to the ecological model is the importance of simultaneous interventions at multiple levels within society.

Social workers in a rehabilitation hospital in Canada established the Amp Reach Program with the help of volunteers who themselves had an amputation (Wells et al., 1993). This collaborative partnership provides emotional support, information, and affirmation to the new amputee. In a similar way, medical professionals and volunteers play important complementary roles in providing hospice care for children. Together they can reach out to the child, the grieving parents, surviving siblings, and school friends of the dying child (Armstrong-Dailey & Goltzer, 1993). Volunteer, paraprofessional advocates often play an important role with difficult treatment populations, such as high-risk alcohol and drug-abusing mothers. The volunteer is more likely to share the cultural background of the persons needing help and to develop a long-term relationship with them because of a strong belief in the client's promise for the future (Grant, Ernst, & Streissguth, 1999).

One controlled research study demonstrated the power of advocacy. In this investigation, 278 battered women were randomly assigned to a control group or a treatment condition that involved ten weeks of contact with trained advocates. The battered women worked one on one with the advocates to obtain maximum access to community resources. Overall, the treated women experienced less violence with twice as many women in the advocacy group being subjected to no violence at all across a two-year follow up (Sullivan & Bybee, 1999).

The use of volunteers as advocates and the collaboration of agencies for the coordination of services is absolutely necessary in today's climate of doing with less government (Bailey & Koney, 1996). There has been a major structural change in U.S. society since the 1980s with political emphasis now on decentralized and fewer government functions. Communities must rely on consumers as well as helping professionals to set the agenda for social change and service provision in the community. This can result in a closer community that develops a strong incentive to cooperate in the development of strategies that help needy people and make communities more livable. The illustrations provided demonstrate ways citizens are at work helping their communities.

Summary

In this chapter, we examined the factors that make some communities more livable than others and how helping professionals work together with citizens to help communities become livable. We applied behavioral learning theory to community life to better understand how changes take place that make communities more or less livable. The use of both case and class advocacy were examined along with the general empowerment process that enables communities and their members to advocate for themselves. Finally, examples of community programs that utilize both helping professionals and volunteers to improve community life were examined.

CHAPTER 10 EXIT QUIZ

Answer the following with a "T" if the answer is true and "F" if the answer is false.

_____ **1.** Helping professionals treat not only individuals and families but entire communities as well.

_____ **2.** Economic factors play an important role in the degree to which a community is livable.

_____ **3.** Negative behavior is never reinforced by public policies.

_____ **4.** Role models are just as available in a depressed community as in an affluent one.

_____ **5.** Contingency management is based on the principle that universal rewards exist that influences everyone's behavior.

_____ **6.** Case advocacy is demonstrated by a social worker teaching an elderly person how to write a complaint letter to a government agency.

_____ **7.** A group working to change voter registration laws demonstrates class advocacy.

_____ **8.** Empowerment is a process that can lead to self-advocacy.

_____ **9.** There is no research evidence that demonstrates the effectiveness of volunteer advocates.

_____**10.** The trend to reduce the role of government in the lives of citizens has increased the need for greater cooperation among providers and consumers of social services.

Answers:

1. T; 2. T; 3. F; 4. F; 5. F; 6. T; 7. T; 8. T; 9. F; 10. T.

SUGGESTED LEARNING ACTIVITIES

1. List at least five community organizations or agencies in your community that you believe provide important services. Select one of these organizations or agencies for volunteer work. Provide your reasons for this decision.

2. Attend a meeting of a service organization on campus. Write a brief summary of what was discussed during the meeting.

3. Search the Internet for funding opportunities for private, nonprofit community organizations.

4. Have a panel discussion on the pros and cons of volunteer service. Try to reach agreement on what is needed for optimal use of volunteers who work in conjunction with helping professionals.

REFERENCES

Armstrong-Dailey, A., & Goltzer, S. (1993). *Hospice care for children.* New York: Oxford University Press.

Bailey, D., & Koney, K. (1996). Interorganizational community-based collaboratives: A strategic response to shape the social work agenda. *Social Work, 41*(6), 602–611.

Bernier, J.C., & Siegel, D.H. (1994). Attention-deficit hyperactivity disorder: A family and ecological systems perspective. *Families in Society, 75*(3), 142–151.

Grant, T.M., Ernst, C.C., & Streissguth, A.P. (1999). Intervention with high-risk alcohol and drug-abusing mothers: Administrative strategies of the Seattle model of paraprofessional advocacy. *Journal of Community Psychology, 27*(1), 1–18.

Litten, J.P. (1999). *Annual report.* Caritas House, Inc.

Miller, A.B., & Keys, C.B. (1996). Awareness, action, and collaboration: How the self-advocacy movement is empowering for persons with developmental disabilities. *Mental Retardation, 34*(5), 312–319.

Poindexter, C.C., Valentine, D., & Conway, P. (1999). *Essential skills for human services.* Pacific Grove, CA: Brooks/Cole.

Sullivan, C.M., & Bybee, D.T. (1999). Reducing violence using community-based advocacy for women with abusive partners. *Journal of Consulting and Clinical Psychology, 67*(1), 43–53.

Wells, L.M., Schachter, B., Little, S., & Whylie, B. (1993). Enhancing rehabilitation through mutual aid: Outreach to people with recent amputations. *Health and Social Work, 18*(3), 221–229.

Wilber, K. (1996). *A brief history of everything.* Boston: Shambhala.

11 Helping on the Internet

W H A T Y O U W I L L L E A R N

1. The ways that the Internet can be used to help
2. The ethical and practical guidelines for offering helping services on the Internet
3. The location and content of several helpful Internet Web sites
4. Some of the potential uses of the Internet in training helpers

The Internet has made a significant impact on everything from buying presents to communicating with family members. (Test your knowledge of Internet jargon in Exercise 11.1. The answers are at the end of this introduction.) Many people now provide email addresses instead of post office boxes and bypass their stockbrokers to purchase securities online. Although many households still do not have access to computers and the World Wide Web, recent technological advances are placing both within reach of more people. These advances include the development of inexpensive, powerful computers; software that makes access and use of the Internet relatively easy; inexpensive access to the Internet through large Internet Service Providers (ISPs), and the evolution of search engines that hasten the users' access to information. However, the best is probably ahead for this 25-year-old technological marvel. Miniature cameras have already been developed that will increasingly allow helpers and clients to meet "face to face" in cyberspace without leaving their offices or homes.

Using the Internet as a means of providing helping services is a recent phenomenon. However, the use of computers to deliver helping services is not new, particularly in the area of career counseling. As early as the 1960s, Computer Assisted Career Guidance Systems (CACGS) were used to simulate the work of career counselors. CACGS are designed to elicit information, administer interest inventories and aptitude tests, and use the information gained from the process to identify relevant careers. These programs also contain large amounts of information about careers and training institutions that can be used to assist clients (Isaacson & Brown, 2000). The difference between using CACGS and the helping process described in this chapter is that clients interact with computers when they are using CACGS instead of human beings. For example, a client who logs on to a CACGS will be presented with a menu of options that allows the user to

EXERCISE **11.1**

Test Your Knowledge of the Internet

Answer each of the following questions with a T if you believe the statement is true and an F if you believe the statement is false.

_____ 1. Every Web site has an address called a Uniform Resource Locator (URL).

_____ 2. Documents placed on the Internet are known as pages.

_____ 3. When an address on the Internet ends with *.org*, it is a commercial site.

_____ 4. *Downloading* is a process of taking information from the Internet and storing it in a computer.

_____ 5. There is a directory of many of the Internet Web sites much like the yellow pages.

_____ 6. A keyword search is one approach to search for information on the Internet.

_____ 7. The Internet contains tens of millions of documents.

_____ 8. Government permission is required before information can be placed on the Internet.

_____ 9. Web addresses on the Internet are not case sensitive, which means that letters can be entered in upper or lower case.

_____10. Internet addresses almost always begin with *http://*, which stands for hyper-text transfer protocol.

_____11. A Web site contains all information available on the World Wide Web about an individual or organization.

_____12. A Web site is called a *clearinghouse* when the home page contains a comprehensive set of links to other related Web sites with similar information.

_____13. The difference between the Internet and the World Wide Web is that the Internet was established for the transfer of information while the World Wide Web allows the transfer of text, audio, graphics, and video from computer user to computer user.

go directly to sources of educational and occupational information contained in the program, take test and inventories, use a self-assessment device to identify potential career options, or enter assessment data. These options are not unlike the alternatives that are provided by career counselors when they begin the helping process.

It should also be noted that helping services have been delivered via telephones for several decades. The best-known telephone helping services are probably the crisis hotlines that are operated in most cities. However, some helpers in private practice have used the telephone regularly with clients. These helping sessions are conducted in much the same manner as person-to-person in-office helping sessions with the obvious difference being there are no visual cues to the client's verbal responses. Because there is no visual dimension in the helping process, helpers must be able to ascertain the client's reactions by their vocal responses. Although telephones can be used as a basic means of delivering helping services, other helpers use telephones as an adjunct to their person-to-person services. For example, one psychologist who specializes in helping people who are afraid to come out of their houses talks to them on a cellular phone as they drive to his office. This helps them control their fear of open spaces, traffic jams, bridges, tunnels, and so forth. Currently, the Internet offers few advantages when compared to telephones. The addition of a visual dimension to communication on the Internet that uses relatively inexpensive technology and transmission costs will give this medium a distinct advantage when compared to telephones. However, the Internet offers helpers other advantages that will be discussed later in this chapter.

Understandably, many helpers have become excited about the potential of the Internet to provide efficient services to clients who either do not have transportation or must travel long distances to receive services. Others are enthusiastic about using the Internet to assist clients who are homebound because of psychological and physical disabilities. Still another group of helpers, many of whom are in private practice, see the Internet as a means of expanding their practices to people who were heretofore unreachable. Enthusiasm for Web counseling abounds in many parts of the helping community. However, other helpers have reservations about the use of technology because they fear that this high tech approach will result in the loss of the personal touch that characterizes most approaches to helping. It should be noted that that many of the same fears being voiced today surfaced in the 1960s when the use of computers in the helping process first began. Today millions of people use computer-assisted approaches to get information about career and educational opportunities, assess their strengths and weakness, and make tentative career choices. Other helpers are not as concerned about the use of technology as they are the misuse of it. They are concerned that unethical helpers will use the Internet to offer unregulated services to unsuspecting clients.

In this chapter, the current and potential use of the Internet to provide helping services will be explored. Additionally, guidelines for offering helping services on the Internet will be provided. Some of the Web sites that contain information and services that may be useful to helpers will be also explored and uses of the Internet to provide preservice and in-service training to helpers will be examined.

Answers for Exercise 11.1

■ Questions 3, 5, 8, and 9 are false. All other answers are true. The correct answers for the questions that are false are:

   3. If *.org* appears on the end of an Internet address it indicates that the address is for an organization such as a professional organization. If *.com* appears at the end of an address, it is likely that it is an address for a commercial business. Other common endings are *.edu* (educational organization) and *.gov* (governmental organization).

5. There is no single directory for the Internet, and it is unlikely that one will develop. Specialty directories may be developed in the future.

8. Anyone can place information on the Internet without permission. That explains why there is a great deal of pornography and other controversial material on the Internet.

9. Although some addresses are not case sensitive, many are. When entering an address on the Internet, it is wise to use the same case listed in the address.

10. This statement is true, but Internet addresses may also begin with *ftp://*, *gopher://*, or no prefix at all.

Using the Internet in Helping

Helpers with Internet access have several options available to them. They may use electronic mail (email) to instantaneously correspond with their clients. Email messages allow helpers to provide information and encourage clients who are struggling with serious personal issues. Email also allows helpers to request information from clients on aspects of helping such as their success in completing homework assignments. Helpers may also interact with clients in chat rooms. Communicating in chat rooms is an interactive process that simulates to some degree the type of conversation that one might have in a person-to-person session. The process begins when one person, perhaps the helper, types a question or statement. Others who are visiting the chat room then may type in responses to what was typed by the first person. Chat rooms have the advantage of allowing one or more others to join the session. For example, it is often useful to have clients interact with people who have their same concerns to learn how they deal with the problem. This has led some helpers to form support groups for people who have certain types of mental health problems such as obsessive-compulsive disorder. In these instances, chat rooms are scheduled for regular meetings and people simply log on and participate. Arranging chat rooms and schedules can be difficult. However, schedules and distances are much easier to accommodate when the interaction occurs online. The obvious drawbacks to the use of chat rooms to provide helping is that neither helpers nor clients has visual or auditory contact during the helping session. Also, confidentiality becomes an issue unless participants use pseudonyms.

In addition to using email and chat rooms, helpers can develop Web sites on which various types of information can be posted. For example, information can be posted that relates to the types of problems being experienced by the people who come to the agency. The use of information in the helping process is called bibliotherapy, which is nothing more than reading materials that teach clients about their problems and strategies for managing them. Sampson (1998a, 1998b) suggests that information posted on Web sites can also play an invaluable role in the assessment process. Information orienting clients to tests and inventories can be posted on the helper's Web site, and clients can access it prior to taking assessment devices. Chat rooms and Internet connections, such as those already discussed, can also be used in the orientation of clients to assessment devices.

Some of the inventories that helpers use are online and may be taken directly on the Internet. In some instances, people taking inventories on the Internet can also receive computer-generated interpretations. Helpers can also interpret tests and inventories using the Internet. Sampson (1998a) suggests that one issue that remains in the interpretation of inventories is when the results contain information that may be interpreted as bad news by the client. The suggestion that the authors offer is not to use the Internet to interpret test and inventory results that may be construed in a negative way by clients.

Web sites can be used to facilitate the operation of a human resource agency or a private practice. One example of this is to use the Web site as the basis for scheduling appointments. Each client could be assigned a code so that confidentiality could be guaranteed. Then, clients who wish to make appointments could access a master schedule that shows available time slots and email the time that they wish to be seen. Clients who have forgotten the time of their appointment could also get that information from the Web site address. In the future, Web sites will be interactive and appointments will be made directly on the Web site by entering an identification number. Additionally, reminders will be sent to clients regarding their appointments automatically by email based on the schedule on the Web site. Another type of information that can be posted on a Web site is disclosure statements. Helpers are normally required to provide clients with disclosure statements that include a description of the services offered, the cost of the services, and confidentiality information. Disclosure statements can be made available on the helper's Web site as well as in traditional forms.

Finally, Web sites can be developed that provide hyperlinks to other useful sites. Hyperlinks, also referred to as hot buttons, are icons or symbols on Web sites that, when clicked, transport the person immediately to another Web site. There are many Web sites on the Internet that may be useful to clients. For example, tests and inventories can be taken online simply by going to the Web site of the publisher of the assessment device. Helpers pay for these inventories with a credit card in most instances. Other inventories are available at no charge. Helpers interested in having their clients take these tests and inventories should begin by identifying the types of assessment devices they wish to use, locate them on the Internet, and place hyperlinks to the sites where they are located in their Web sites. Hyperlinks to sources of information relevant to clients and to the Web sites of agencies that may provide assistance to them can also be inserted into helpers' Web sites. Some examples of useful Web sites will be presented later. Adding hyperlinks to the helper's Web site makes access to other Web sites much easier for clients and may reduce the number of trips clients make to see their helpers.

Helpers can also use the modems on their computers to link themselves to their clients. This can be done by developing a directory and having the computer dial the client instead of using the telephone. This helping process is almost exactly the same as the telephone approaches to helping described in the introduction to this chapter, particularly with regard to the absence of visual cues. One difference, at least to this point, is that the cost of providing helping services on the Internet is lower than providing services via the telephone.

The final use of the Internet to be discussed here has already been mentioned, Web counseling using visual images. Web counseling, which will be referred to as *virtual helping*, has been defined as helping involving traditional processes, as well as information that occurs when helpers and clients are in different locations and use the Internet for communication (NBCC, 1997). Because the images and sound quality of this medium are potentially quite good, the virtual helper–client interaction approximates that of an in-office session. Although meeting clients in cyberspace has many advantages, questions remain about its utility. For example, one question that is frequently asked is, "What happens if the client cries or becomes hysterical?" The underlying issue behind this type of question is the concern many helpers have about being unable to touch clients during virtual helping sessions. Anyone who has been confronted with a grieving or hysterical relative or friend during a long distance telephone call probably has a sense of the concern being raised by these helpers. When people are in distress, and clients often are, one way of calming them is to touch them by patting their shoulders, holding their hands, or giving them a reassuring hug. Touching is not an option in virtual helping, so soothing upset clients must be done verbally. It should be pointed out that not all helpers are concerned about their inability to touch their clients. Some helpers do not touch their clients for fear it will convey the wrong message or because their approach to helping requires them to avoid intimate contact with clients. It seems likely that the issue of touch is one that will need to be resolved for some individuals by experience. Other helpers have put these concerns aside, and are using it.

The development of Web sites as adjunct to the helping process has many possibilities, but there are also some downsides. One is that Web sites must be constructed and maintained. Some helpers are using available software to construct their own Web sites, but most hire people who have technical skills in this area to construct them. Webmasters also charge fees for maintaining the Web sites, as do ISPs that offer Web sites with their services. Moreover, because Web sites typically include email addresses that allow the persons who visit the site to contact the person or agency who own the site, helpers may find themselves highly involved in answering email. One way to minimize responding to email is to ascertain the types of questions that prospective clients and others may pose, develop answers to the questions, and post the answers on the Web site. Regardless of the downside of Web sites, it is likely that most agencies and many individuals in private practice will have Web sites in the near future.

Guidelines for Internet Use

Concerns about the misuse of the Internet by helpers have resulted in the generation of standards for helpers who deal with mental health issues. In 1998, the National Board of Certified Counselors (NBCC) published core standards and ethical guidelines for the use of the Internet. Although the ethical standards that should guide most of the activities engaged in by helpers will be discussed later, those standards that are associated with the use of the Internet will be presented in this chapter. They are included at this point because in many ways they shed more light on the practice of virtual helping than do the core standards. Moreover, even though the two statements were meant to address separate issues, they overlap. The core standards for using the Internet are paraphrased below.

1. Helpers should work to develop research-based guidelines for Internet practice. Helpers should make certain that the use of the Internet does not interfere with their relationship with clients.

2. Confidentiality of client information should be maintained in so far as possible. Helpers must take care to document their contacts with clients via the Internet so that the basis for treatment plans and recommendations can be documented and communicated to others when appropriate.

3. When the helping process occurs on the Internet, clients should be fully informed of the risks and benefits, as well as their rights and the helper's responsibilities to them. The safety of clients must be of utmost importance. Therefore, adequate referral resources in the clients' geographic regions must be maintained so that when emergencies do arise they can be managed successfully.

4. When referral to other helpers becomes necessary, helpers who use the Internet must be prepared to provide referral resources to their clients. Location-specific and cultural issues should be taken into consideration when using the Internet in the helping process.

There are several implications of the standards for Internet users advanced by NBCC. One of these is that helpers must work to maintain the therapeutic relationship that is essential to helping. One practical implication of the use of Internet resources is that helpers may have to offer clients the option of person-to-person helping because of the likelihood that some clients might be alienated by the use of online approaches. A predictable implication of the NBCC standards is that helpers must take all reasonable steps to insure that information transmitted on the Internet remains confidential. Advances in technology are making this easier and it is likely that this continue to be a major issue in the future. Also, helper's responsibilities for their clients are reaffirmed in the NBCC statement. Their safety and well-being must be assured regardless of the approach utilized. Finally, NBCC warns that helpers who use the Internet must use culturally sensitive approaches. Unfortunately, we know nothing about cultural implications of the use of technology in the helping process at this time. Perhaps this is the reason that NBCC suggests that helpers need to develop empirical guidelines for their Internet practices.

The Standards for the Ethical Practice of WebCounseling (NBCC, 1997) are meant to serve as a supplement to the codes of ethics of helpers because most groups of professional helpers have not adopted specific ethical guidelines for virtual helping. It seems likely that all groups of helpers, including counselors, will amend their codes of ethics to incorporate guidelines for the use of the Internet in helping. NBCC set forth thirteen ethical guidelines for helpers who engage in virtual helping. These are paraphrased below. Helpers should:

1. Review all legal and ethical guidelines that might pertain to the practice of virtual helping, such as the age at which children can engage in the service without parental permission, whether the practice is permitted under state regulatory statutes, and whether the practice is covered by liability insurance carriers.

2. Make clients aware of the security strategies used to insure confidentiality and the limits of those strategies.

3. Make clients aware of the amount of time information about the helping process is maintained.

4. Use code words or other means in place of names when clients log on to the helping sessions so that security can be maintained.

5. Verify consent when parental or guardian consent is required.

6. Secure appropriate consent to release the data when information about virtual helping is released.

7. Make sure that clients who are working on the Internet have the same information about the helper as is presented to other clients.

8. Make clients aware that they have rights and provide hyperlinks on Web sites of ethics committees, licensing boards, and other regulatory bodies.

9. Arrange for backup helpers who can provide assistance if the helper cannot be reached because of technical failures, and provide the client with information about how to reach the backup.

10. Make sure that clients have means of contacting helpers when they are offline.

11. Post on Web sites the types of helping that is appropriate and inappropriate for virtual helping.

12. Make sure that clients understand that technical problems can occur and discuss the implications of these failures when there are failures.

13. Discuss the possibility of misinterpretation due to lack of visual cues when using chat rooms and other procedures that do not provide visual images.

With the exception of number 13, the aforementioned ethical standards presented simply warn helpers that they have unusual responsibilities when using the Internet in the helping process. These unusual responsibilities have to do with anticipating technical breakdowns, making contact when not online, checking on legal limitations and guidelines of virtual helping, and confirming consent when minors are involved and information is to be released. Guideline 13 suggests that helpers may have to adopt one or two new helping strategies. For example, clients may be told that they need to ask more questions to clarify the helper's intent because of the lack of visual cues. However, it is more likely that helpers will have to continuously check with their clients to see if their meaning has been fully understood. Clearly, concerns about visual cues will be less of an issue when video is added to Internet helping.

Some Useful Web Sites

As was noted earlier, helpers may wish to develop Web sites that contain hyperlinks to sites that are useful to their clients. They may also wish to develop a list of Web sites that can be duplicated and handed to their clients to encourage their exploration of their problems and solutions to them. In this section, a few of the hundreds of thousands of Web sites available to helpers and their clients will be explored. This presentation will include the topic and address of the Web site and a brief description of the information found on the site. Since Web site addresses change from time to time, Internet users should learn to use search engines to identify sources of information. An exercise at the end of the chapter deals with this issue.

National Organization on Disability *http://www.nod.org/*

People who access this site can get information about successful programs for the disabled as well as links to publications, press releases from the organization, and to related sites.

Mental Health Net: Depression *http://depression.mentalhelp.net/*

This site contains information about depression and its treatment. Links are provided to information about the symptoms of depression, its treatment, research on depression, and other online resources. People who access this site can take a free screening device to help them determine whether they are suffering from depression.

People Who Are Substance Abusers

The site for the National Center on Addiction and Substance Abuse at Columbia University is located at *http://www.casacolumbia.org/publications1456/publica-tions.htm.*

After accessing this site, dozens of publications regarding substance abuse can be ordered online. This site may be more helpful to helpers than to clients, but there are publications available that will be useful to clients.

Senior Citizens

The home page of *http://agepage.com/articles.htm* is called, appropriately enough, AgePage. It provides information and hyperlinks to a host of information ranging from the management of arthritis to the utility of massage therapy. Information regarding income taxes, medications, nursing homes, and much more is available on this site.

Victims of Domestic Violence

The site at *http://incestabuse.miningco.com/msubsdv.htm* will take the client to the home page of Mining Co.com. This clearinghouse provides a vast array of information about domestic violence, incest, and abuse material that is of potential interest to both helpers and clients. There were many other reports, papers, and statistical abstracts available on the Web site that may be useful to helpers.

Teenage Pregnancy

A portion of the Web site at *http://www.ripnroll.com/teenpregnancy.htm* is devoted to providing statistics that may be interesting to helpers such as the fact that 560,000 teenage girls give birth in the United States. However, there is also information dealing with the health risks to pregnant teenagers and their babies as well as advice for avoiding these problems.

Another site that deals with teenage pregnancy is *http://www.fnoapp.org/anaswer.html*. This is the home page of a group of Florida agencies that are designing and implementing teenage pregnancy prevention programs. It has a feature that is found on some other sites, the "question of the week." The question that was posed at the time of this writing was, "Do teen births vary by race and ethnicity?" The answer provided was "yes," Asians and Pacific Islanders had the lowest rate in 1995 (25 births per 1,000 15- to 19-year-old females) and Hispanics had the highest rate (107 births per 1,000 15- to 19-year-old females).

People Who Are Engaged in Self-Exploration

The site at *http://www2.ncsu.edu/unity/lockers/users/l/lkj/* where two versions of the Career Key are located, one for middle school students and the other for adolescents and adults. Both of these interest inventories can be taken online. They are automatically scored and career options explored. A hyperlink is provided to the *Occupational Outlook Handbook* so that people who take the inventory can go immediately to this important source of occupational information to get job descriptions, salary information, educational requirements, and projections regarding the demand for workers in particular occupations.

Evaluating Web Sites

As noted at the outset, the Web Sites presented in this chapter are but a sampling of the sites available to helpers and clients. To find sites that are related to specific interests, a search of the Internet should be conducted. An exercise at the end of this chapter will provide an introduction to search strategies. However, not all Web sites are useful and some may contain inaccurate or misleading information. Before developing hyperlinks to a Web site, the content of the site should be evaluated by asking the following questions:

- When was the site last updated? This information usually appears on the home page.
- Who developed and maintains the sites?
- Can this person be contacted via email so that questions can be asked?
- Are the sources of the information on the Web site reputable? For example, are they excerpts from professional journals or government publications?
- Is the reading level of the material appropriate for the clients who will access it?
- Can the material on the Web site be accessed easily? For example, are there buttons that allow easy return to the home page?
- Are hyperlinks to other useful Web sites available?

Ultimately, helpers should visit each Web site and use it in much the same way that one of their clients would. If using a Web site is frustrating or the information is out-of-date or inaccurate, the Web site should not be used.

The Internet as a Training Tool

Most two- and four-year colleges and universities have embarked on preservice efforts that they term *distance learning* involving the Internet. In some instances, these are highly sophisticated efforts involving the delivery of information to people in off-campus sites using electronic classrooms. In these efforts, each student can view and be viewed by the instructor, and, because students have their own microphones, they can interact with the instructor in much the same way that they do in a typical classroom. In other instances, the distance learning program simply involves posting assignments and course syllabi on the instructor's Web sites. Students then download these and work on the assignments. Some helper training programs are beginning to use the Internet as a tool in their supervision to save both the supervisor and the student the time and expense of commuting to campus. Other efforts are underway in many colleges and universities to deliver in-service training to helpers using the Internet. Again, the primary motive driving these efforts is to use trainees' and instructors' time and energy wisely. Without question, the use of the Internet in training and supervision will accelerate, particularly as video is linked to the audio component. The reader may wish to assess his or her own technological skills in this area by completing Exercise 11.2.

Summary

The Internet has great potential for delivering helping services, but its use is not without problems. Helpers who use it must take extraordinary care to protect the confidentiality of their helpers, prepare for technological breakdowns, and provide for emergency services when the occasion demands it. They must also be prepared for "low touch" when using this technological development in their work. Some specific uses of the Internet include providing individual helping, orienting clients to the services that an individual or agency provides, administering assessment devices, and delivering information that can be used in biblio-

EXERCISE **11.2**

Testing Your Technology Skills

Answer each of the following questions by checking yes, no, or uncertain. You may wish to seek training or hands-on experiences with computers to enhance skills that you do not have or that you are uncertain about.

Yes	No	Uncertain	Item
_____	_____	_____	1. I can use a computer to access the Internet.
_____	_____	_____	2. I can use email as a communication medium.
_____	_____	_____	3. I can evaluate the quality of a Web site.
_____	_____	_____	4. I can find information useful to my clients on the Internet.
_____	_____	_____	5. I can use chat rooms as a means of communication.
_____	_____	_____	6. I can construct Web sites using available software.
_____	_____	_____	7. I understand the pros and cons of using the Internet in the helping process.
_____	_____	_____	8. I understand the ethical issues involved in using the Internet in the helping process.
_____	_____	_____	9. I can interpret tests and inventories using the Internet.

therapy. There are literally thousands of Web sites that can support various aspects of the helping process, a few of which were reviewed in this chapter.

CHAPTER 11 EXIT QUIZ

Answer each of the following questions with a T if the statement is true and an F if the statement is false.

_____ **1.** Although the Internet is 25 years old, it has only recently been viewed as a tool by helpers.

_____ **2.** Computers have been providing helping services for nearly 40 years.

_____ **3.** The concern that some helpers have that the use of technology will make helping less personal has no basis in reality.

_____ **4.** Chat rooms are potentially useful for support groups.

_____ **5.** Although disclosure statements are infrequently required, the authors believe that they should be given to every client.

_____ **6.** One of the major advantages of establishing a Web site is that it can ease clients' access to information if they have a computer and Internet access.

_____ **7.** The NBCC standards for core providers and ethical practice in Web counseling cover very different areas of practice on the Internet.

_____ **8.** Perhaps the best way to summarize the NBCC ethical standards regarding counseling is that helpers must take extraordinary care to protect the rights of the client when using the Internet.

_____ **9.** Websites found on the Internet regarding mental health and human resources issues can typically be trusted to contain accurate information.

_____**10.** In 10 years, the technology to link video to audio will be available to helpers who wish to use the Internet.

Answers:

1. T; 2. T; 3. F; 4. T; 5. F; 6. T; 7. F; 8. T; 9. F; 10. F

SUGGESTED LEARNING ACTIVITIES

1. To develop some sensitivity to the problems involved in conducting interviews without visual cues, conduct one of the following exercises paired with another student:
   a. Role-play a helping interview in a telephone conversation. Make sure that the client has a subtle, but emotionally laden issue to discuss.
   b. Blindfold the helper in a role-playing exercise. Then reverse roles. In each case, discuss your reactions to helping without visual cues.

2. Conduct a keyword search on the Internet using one of the following topics (not all of these searches will yield useful information, so be forewarned).

Personality assessment	Physical disabilities
Mental health problems	Poverty
Mental health counseling	Human resource workers
Correctional institutions	Juvenile crime
Teenage pregnancy	Senior citizens
Mental retardation	Learning disabilities
Abused children	Spouse abuse
Hunger in America	Substandard housing
Medicaid	Medicare

1. Get online and click on the Internet access button.
2. Begin by entering one of the terms listed above in the search box. Then click Search or Go depending on your software. This will initiate an all word search, that is, a general search that tries to identify Web sites that are related to all the words entered.
3. After this is complete, look at the topic generated, and then click Back, which will be at the top left part of the screen. This will return you to the original screen where the search began. This time look at the pull-down menu under the phrase you have entered and click on Exact Phrase or Exact Word Search. Then click on Search or Go. This will give you a much more limited and typically more useful list of Web sites to explore.
4. A third option offered by some search engines is to switch to another search engine. For example Mindspring, an Internet Service Provider, uses HotBot as its primary search engine. This produces a list of Websites that are related to your search. However, at the end of each list you are given the option of clicking on Lycos and using that search engine to look for information related to your topic. Try searching your topic using a second or third search engine.

REFERENCES

Isaacson, L.E., & Brown, D. (2000). *Career Information, Career Counseling, and Career Development* (7th ed.) Boston: Allyn and Bacon.

NBCC (1998). Core standards for Internet mental health providers. Greensboro, NC: Author.

NBCC (1997). Standards for the ethical practice of webcounseling. Greensboro, NC: Author.

Sampson, J.P., Jr. (1998a). Using the Internet to enhance test selection, orientation, administration, and scoring. Paper presented at the American Association for Assessment in Counseling Convention, Indianapolis, IN, March.

Sampson, J.P., Jr. (1998b). Using the Internet to test interpretation. Paper presented at the Assessment '98 Conference, St. Petersburg, FL, January.

12 Ethical and Legal Issues in the Helping Professions

WHAT YOU WILL LEARN

1. The ethical principles that guide the behavior of professional helpers
2. How ethical principles are used to help professional helpers make decisions
3. How legal and ethical issues interact to influence helping practices
4. The legal and ethical consequences of unethical helping practices

Ethics are moral principles that guide behavior. As individuals mature and develop values systems, they develop a set of moral standards that determine how they will conduct their personal lives. Similarly, as helping professionals progress through the training process, they learn and internalize the values of their profession and begin to use these to govern their professional behavior. Values and the ethical behavior stemming from them have always been at the forefront of thought and debate among professional groups. The result of these debates has been the generation of codes of ethics based on the values of each group of helping professionals. As would be expected, these codes of ethics have many similarities, but there are some differences as well. These similarities and differences and the principles that have grown out of the codes of ethics of helping professionals will be discussed in detail in this chapter.

As just noted, ethical principles evolve from values. What are values? They are the core beliefs held by an individual, a professional group, or a society. Values, once developed, are experienced as standards or moral imperatives. It is the goal of every program that trains helping professionals to inculcate a set of professional values into each trainee. Cottone and Tarvydas (1998) and Kenyon (1999) suggest that the core values of the helping professions are fidelity (being loyal, honest), beneficence (doing good for others), nonmaleficence (doing no harm to others), justice (being fair), finality (taking action that supercedes law and social custom), respect (honoring the rights of others), gratitude (repaying for a good), reparation (making up for a wrong), and autonomy (honoring the rights of individuals to make their own decisions). As will be discussed later, some authorities suggest that helpers need to rethink their endorsement of some of these values.

The codes of ethics of helping professionals are designed primarily to guide their professional practice, not their personal behavior. However, there are exceptions to this rule, particularly at those junctures where professional and personal lives intersect. As will be shown later, some friendships and sexual relationships are regulated by codes of ethics. Also, the boards that credential helping professionals may revoke their licenses to practice if they engage in certain illegal behavior in their personal life. Helpers who commit felonies such as tax evasion or vehicular homicide may find that they are no longer allowed to work in their chosen profession.

Another implication of some codes of ethics is that they may specify that helpers must hold themselves to a higher standard than other workers. First, just because something is legal does not mean that is ethical. It is legal to engage in sexual reorientation therapy, that is, therapy that focuses on helping homosexuals adopt a heterosexual sexual orientation, but it is unethical in many of the helping professions. Second, following the policies of one's employer may be classified as unethical if it violates ethical standards. Some agencies do not fully inform their clients of the nature of their services, a practice that is unethical. These and other issues will be addressed in the section dealing with ethical codes and decision making.

Why have helping professionals adopted such rigorous moral standards? First, and foremost, professions exist for the purpose of serving the public. When a professional group adopts and enforces a code of ethics, it assures members of society that its members are acting in their best interests.

Second, for an occupational group to be recognized as a profession, they must have and enforce a code of ethics. Medicine, the oldest profession, has a well-known code of ethical standards known as the Hippocratic Oath. Although few people in the general public are aware of the standards set forth in the Hippocratic Oath, they are aware that it exists and that it is generally aimed at protecting their welfare.

The third reason for having and enforcing a code of ethics is that it is a preliminary step to occupational self-regulation. All fifty states have psychological licensing boards that determine the requirements for the practice of psychology in their states and issue licenses to people who meet their requirements. Additionally, these boards have the power to revoke licenses if psychologists act unethically, fail to follow the rules established by the boards, or violate a legal statute, as failure to report child abuse. These boards have some nonpsychologists on them, but psychologists dominate them. Most states have similar licensing boards that regulate the practice of social workers, counselors, marriage and family therapist, and other helping professionals. The major implication of the establishment of these boards is clear. Legislatures in states with licensing boards have concluded that the helping professions are capable of self-regulation. Self-regulation is a prerequisite for legislative recognition.

Fourth, codes of ethics are designed to provide helping professionals with guidelines that can be used to make decisions regarding complex matters. For example, what should a helping professional do when confronted with a suicidal client or one that intends to murder his teacher? Or how should a helping professional handle the revelation that one of his or her clients who has AIDS is having unprotected sex? When looked at superficially, the answers to these problems may seem simple, but they are not. Ethical standards provide much-needed guidelines that can be used to make decisions in these and other situations.

Fifth, and finally, ethical standards have increasingly become necessary to assist helping professionals avoid malpractice suits. Many of the latest codes of ethics set forth both ethical principles and standards of practice. The American Psychological Association's (APA, 1992) Ethical Principles of Psychologists and Code of Conduct has 6 principles and 102 ethical standards that are more specific guides to behavior. The Code of Ethics and Standards of Practice of the American Counseling Association (ACA, 1997) gives more attention to ethical principles, but it also includes fifty-one standards of practice. Standards of practice are very important in malpractice suits against helping professions. Two questions that are raised, in addition to others, are (1) did the person practice ethically, and (2) did the helper follow the standards of practice of her or his profession? The area of malpractice will be explored in more detail later in this chapter. However, that discussion will be preceded by a discussion of the principles of ethical practice, the use of ethics in making professional decisions, and the relationship between legal and ethical issues.

Ethical Principles

Although the ethical principles of the various groups of helping professionals are unique to some degree, they are organized around six general areas: responsibilities and obligations to (1) clients, (2) society, (3) the professional group, (4) other professionals, (5) employers, and (6) themselves.

Obligations to Clients

Perhaps the most notable things about the codes of ethics of helping professionals is the emphasis they place on protecting the welfare of the individual. The APA's (1992) Ethical Principles and Code of Conduct has the following statement in its preamble: "It [the code] has as its primary goal the welfare and protection of the individual and groups with whom psychologists work." Section A.1 of the ACA Code of Ethics and Standards of Practice contains a similar statement. It reads: "The primary responsibility of counselors is to respect the dignity and promote the welfare of clients." NOHSE's (1995) Ethical Standards of Human Service Professionals contains this statement: "Human services professionals respect the integrity and welfare of the client at all times. Each client is treated with respect, acceptance, and dignity." The general statements quoted here set the tone for the ethics behavior of helping professionals. However, it is necessary to explore some of the subprinciples of the ethical codes to fully appreciate the depth to which helping professionals should go to promote the welfare of their clients. The subprinciples that will be discussed here include competence, confidentiality, prohibitions against sexual intimacy, informed consent, dual relationships, and prohibition from abandonment.

Competence. The codes of ethics of helping professionals make it clear that practitioners are to enter their respective fields as skilled professionals and maintain their skills during their careers. Moreover, the American Association of Marriage and Family Therapists (AAMFT, 1991) Code of Ethics makes it clear that competence means more than possessing the skills to practice. Competency to practice includes getting help for personal problems when they arise so that the client's concerns can be addressed with vigor and objectivity. Under Professional Competence and Integrity (section 3.2) the following statement appears: "Marriage and family therapists seek appropriate professional assistance for their personal problems or conflicts that may impair work performance or clinical judgement." Other codes of ethics, in addition to admonishing helping professionals to gain and maintain the skills they need to deliver high quality services, have similar statements regarding the necessity for helping professionals to maintain their mental heath.

Suppose that a helper in a college counseling center was assisting a nineteen-year-old male to choose his major. At the beginning of the second session the client confided that he did not really come to the center for help with his major. He disclosed that he had become involved in several homosexual relationships, but that he continued to be sexually attracted to women and was confused. The helper had no training in helping clients who were experiencing sexual identity problems. What should he do?

The obvious answer to this professional dilemma is to refer the client to a qualified helper. However, none was available, and the client wished to proceed. Codes of ethics make it possible for helpers such as the one in this vignette to proceed so long as they are under the supervision of a qualified professional. That is what happened in this case. The outcome of helping was that the client decided that he was bisexual.

Confidentiality. If helpers are to be successful, they need the trust of the people they are helping. In no small measure this trust develops because helpers assure their clients that *almost* anything they say during the helping process will not be disclosed to other people. This protection from disclosure is called *confidentiality.* There are three reasons that the foregoing statement contains the word *almost.* The first of these is that at times helpers must break confidentiality to protect clients from suicidal impulses. Second, helpers must disclose what they have learned to protect others from harm when clients disclose that they are planning to harm others. Case Illustration 12.1 outlines an example of this. Third, many states have laws that require helpers to disclose certain types of information that may be gained during helping, such as child abuse. Helpers who fail to comply with these laws will in all likelihood lose their license to practice and be prosecuted. The National Organization for Human Services Education's (NOSHE, 1995) state-

CASE ILLUSTRATION **12.1**

An Intended Homicide

Julia, a 10-year-old girl, disclosed to her school counselor that she was planning to kill her 13-year-old stepbrother. She had been planning to kill him since he raped her and her parents had done nothing about it. She was going to use her father's handgun, which she had been taught to use, to kill him the first time their parents left them alone.

Two issues in this situation warrant disclosure of the information. The most immediate of these is the danger to the stepbrother. The second issue is the failure of the parents to take corrective action after a rape, which constitutes child abuse in most states. The school counselor immediately called the parents and the Department of Social Services. The stepbrother was sent to live with his mother and was required to undergo evaluation and treatment.

ment regarding confidentiality adds one dimension to the limitations on confidentiality. Statement 3 in their code of ethics reads: "Human services professionals protect the client's right to privacy and confidentiality except when such confidentiality would cause harm to the client or others, *when agency guidelines state otherwise* [italics added], or under other stated conditions [for example, local, state, or federal laws]." The provision in the NOSHE ethical standards that agency guidelines may supercede practitioners' obligation to protect the privacy of their clients is unique.

The foregoing discussion focuses on the confidentiality of verbal disclosures that occur in the helping process. However, helpers do not restrict their data gathering to interviews. Much of the information gathered in the helping process is done using data sheets, tests, inventories, and other assessment devices. These devices become a part of the client's records and are also protected from disclosure. Helpers and the agencies that employ them have developed elaborate procedures to make sure that records do not fall into the hands of people who should not have access to them.

It is the professional helper's responsibility to fully inform clients about their obligation to hold information, including information such as test results, in confidence. They should also make clients aware of the limits of their confidentiality. Table 12.1 contains a list of situations in which a helper might not hold information in confidence. Failure to do so is a breach of ethics. The Association for Specialists in Group Work (ASGW, 1989) makes an usual statement about confidentiality: "Group counselors take steps to protect members by defining confidentiality and the limits of confidentiality." The code continues: "Members are made aware of the difficulties involved in enforcing and ensuring confidentiality in a group setting." The latter statement has been inserted because group helpers are aware that clients who participate in groups do sometimes talk about

TABLE 12.1   Limits of Confidentiality

Situations When Helpers Will Not Keep Information Confidential

1. When child abuse is suspected
2. In some states, when elder abuse is suspected
3. When clients are a danger to themselves
4. When clients are a danger to others
5. When the helper receives a court order to disclose information
6. When the client waives confidentiality via a signed consent form
7. When the client is under the supervision (for example, by a probation officer) and there is a prior agreement regarding disclosure
8. When it is necessary to consult with another helper to maximize the likelihood of success of the helping process
9. When institutional (typically correctional or mental heath facilities) policies require the sharing of the information with others
10. When the client attorneys subpoena the helper to testify in some type of litigation
11. When the client is a minor as defined by state statute and is not protected by privileged communication laws

Source: Adapted from: Arthur, G.L., & Swanson, C.D. (1993). *Confidentiality and privileged communication.* Alexandria, VA: American Counseling Association.

their group experiences to others not involved in the group. The point of these guidelines, and those contained in other codes of ethics, is that helpers have the ethical responsibility to take all reasonable steps to inform their clients about the types of information that can be held in confidence and what types cannot.

Prohibitions against Sexual Intimacy.   All of the codes of ethics of helping professionals prohibit sexual intimacy between helpers and clients and sexual harassment of clients by helpers. Almost all of the codes go one step further. They (e.g., ACA, 1997; APA, 1992; NASW, 1996; NOSHE, 1995) preclude sexual intimacy between helpers and clients for at least two years after the termination of their helping relationship. This may seem unnecessary to the novice, but there have been a number of well-documented cases of manipulation of clients because of the nature of the professional relationships that were established, including the use of the relationship to gain sexual favors during and after the helping relationship.

Informed Consent.   Helpers have a responsibility to fully inform clients of the techniques they will be using in the helping relationship as well as the procedures they will encounter when they volunteer to participate in research studies. In short, there should be no surprises in the helping or research processes. The statement in section 12.C of the Clients' Rights in the American Mental Health

Counselors Association (AMHCA, 1987) summarizes this position: "Clients have a right to clear statements of purposes, goals techniques, rules of procedures, and limitations as well as potential dangers of the services to be performed."

Dual Relationships.   A dual relationship exists when a helper is involved in a helping relationship with a client at the same time that he or she has a personal relationship with the client. For example, a helper who provides any helping service to a friend or family member is involved in a dual relationship. Similarly, a helper employed in a mental health agency who attempts to provide marriage and family counseling to a colleague is engaging in a dual relationship. Groups of professional helpers are concerned about dual relationships because the objectivity of the helper may be diminished as a result of being a friend, relative, or coworker, and this may limit the helper's effectiveness in the helping relationship. However, it is interesting to note that, while codes of ethics do warn against engagement in dual relationships, they do not prohibit them. The Ethical Standards for School Counselors published by the American School Counselors Association (ASCA, 1992) suggest that a counselor "avoids dual relationships that might impair his/her objectivity and/or increase the risk of harm to the clients. . . . If a dual relationship is unavoidable, the counselor is responsible for taking steps to eliminate or reduce the potential for harm."

There are times when dual relationships are unavoidable. Social workers, school counselors, child psychologists, human services workers, psychiatrists, nurses, and others who work with children often find that, in addition to their individual work with the children, they are engaged in providing counseling, therapy, or consultation to parents or teachers. Although these situations contain several pitfalls, one of the biggest problems is that helpers will inadvertently disclose information gained in the helping relationship as they consult with parents or teachers. This inadvertent disclosure might damage the relationship with the child or adolescent.

Prohibitions against Abandonment.   Abandonment in this context means that helpers terminate services with clients without assisting them to secure the help they need. If helping professionals abandon their clients, one of the primary purposes of professional groups—promoting the welfare of the client—is not being realized. Abandonment occurs for a number of reasons. One of these reasons is that helpers terminate their services when clients can no longer pay for the services. Another reason for terminating services occurs when helpers find that they have exhausted their expertise and feel that they cannot provide the services required. Although helpers are acting ethically when they do not provide services that exceed their capabilities, their obligation to clients does not end at that point. Abandonment may also occur when helpers decide to discontinue or relocate their practices. However, according to current codes of ethics, there are no defensible reasons for abandoning clients. Standard of Practice Seven from the American Counseling Association Code of Ethics spells out helpers' responsibilities: "Counselors must assist in making appropriate arrangements for the continuation of the treatment of clients, when necessary, following the termination of counseling relationships." The National Association of Social Workers Code of Ethics (NASW, 1996) contains a similar statement: "Social workers should take reasonable steps to avoid abandoning clients who are still in need of services."

Advocacy. Advocacy is the process of acting for or with clients to protect their welfare. Helpers often find themselves offering services to clients who are unable to represent themselves to landlords, governmental agencies, educational institutions, and so forth. For example, some clients speak little or no English and are thus unable to adequately deal with the Department of Social Services or the local employment office. Other clients have limited intellectual capacity and may not fully understand the complex issues involved in making sure that schools provide all the services to which they are entitled. Other factors such as reading proficiency, physical limitations, and lack of experience in dealing with various issues make it impossible for some clients to act independently. In these cases some, but not all, codes of ethics require the helper to take on the role of advocate. Only one group, rehabilitation counselors, has a well-articulated standard in this area. Canon Three of the Code of Professional Ethics for Rehabilitation Counselors (CRCC, 1995) contains an extensive set of advocacy responsibilities when rehabilitation counselors engage in helping clients who have disabilities. These include promoting physical access to buildings and educational opportunities, the elimination of attitudes that may limit the opportunities of individuals with disabilities, and representing clients with disabilities to agencies that routinely provide services to them to ensure that the services are made available. The Code of Ethics of the National Association of Social Workers (NASW, 1996) provides guidelines regarding advocacy that are similar to those found in many other codes. For example, when social workers take action on behalf of their clients who lack the capacity to make informed decisions, they should "take reasonable steps to safeguard the interests and rights of those clients." Case Illustration 12.2 offers an example of client advocacy.

Obligations to Society

Helping professionals have obligations to society, and, like their obligations to individuals, these are embedded in their codes of ethics. Section C.5 of the American Counseling Association's code (ACA, 1997) identifies several societal obligations. These include nondiscrimination, avoidance of sexual harassment (included elsewhere in some ethical statements), the importance of making accurate reports to groups such as the courts and health insurers, the necessity to provide accurate statements to the media, and the importance of not using their status as counselors to secure "unjustified personal gains." The APA (1992) code of ethics identifies many of the same areas, but it goes one step further. It indicates that any type of harassment of others (including sexual harassment) is a societal obligation. Therefore, harassing coworkers because of their age, gender, or sexual orientation would be unethical.

CASE ILLUSTRATION **12.2**

A Victim of the System Gets Help Because of Advocacy

MiKindra, an African American, was partially paralyzed at birth, abandoned by her mother because of the physical disability, and raised by her grandmother. She graduated near the bottom of her class and narrowly missed being placed in the class for students with mental retardation. Her caseworker referred her to the state Division of Vocational Rehabilitation (DVR) for testing and placement in a training program. Once again she was classified as low functioning and was to be placed in a community college training program for nurse's aides. However, she confided to her social worker that she had difficulty seeing some aspects of the test and that she had similar problems in high school. MiKindra, now 19, had never had an eye examination. An examination arranged by the caseworker revealed that MiKindra had extremely poor eyesight and glasses were prescribed. MiKindra asked to be retested by DVR. They refused. The caseworker administered a simple intelligence test that suggested that MiKindra's assessment results were an underestimate of her ability. She and MiKindra presented the results to DVR and insisted that she be retested. The new test results agreed with the caseworker's test results. Consequently she was placed in a training program to learn computer operation skills. She graduated with all A's and B's and teaches in that school today.

Finally, one of the major societal responsibilities of helping professionals is known as "the duty to warn." This principal evolved from a famous court case in which a psychologist failed to provide adequate warning to a young college student (Ms. Tarasoff) after one of his clients threatened to kill her. Subsequently, the client killed Ms. Tarasoff. The example in Case Illustration 12.1, had many of the same elements as those in the Tarasoff case. The 10-ten-year-old girl presented a credible threat to her stepbrother. The helper's responsibility was clear: take action to prevent harm to the brother. Helpers are ethically bound to report potential homicides and other events such as bombings that would endanger the welfare of the general public.

Obligations to One's Professional Group

Although helping professionals have many obligations to their profession, participation in the enforcement of the ethical standards, including cooperation with ethics committees if a helper is charged with unethical behavior, is a very high priority. The International Association of Addictions and Offenders Counselors operates under the ACA Code of Ethics and Standards of Practice (ACA, 1997). They therefore subscribe to the idea that it is the helper's responsibility to (1) fully understand the code of ethics, (2) approach other helpers who may be functioning unethically and attempt to resolve the problem informally, and (3) if informal approaches to resolution of the ethical problem are unsuccessful, report the misconduct to the appropriate ethics committee. The ACA (1997) code of ethics does not go as far as either the APA (1992) or AAMFT (1991) codes of ethics in specifying the degree to which helpers must comply with an ethics committee investigation of allegations of unethical conduct. All three codes (and the others mentioned here) specify that helpers are to cooperate with the investigation. This means that helpers must answer questions and provide data or be out of compliance with their codes of ethics. However, the APA (1992) and AAMFT (1991) codes of ethics specify that helpers who are being investigated may not resign during the investigation process.

Being charged with unethical behavior is one of the feared events in a professional's life. However, being charged with unethical behavior is very much the same as being charged with a crime. Helpers are innocent until proven guilty. Because charges of unethical behavior have been used by some helping professionals to harass others, it is now unethical to file complaints against others for the purpose of harming their reputations.

Helping professionals have obligations to their professional group other than those associated with participation in the enforcement of ethical standards. For example, many professional groups have developed guidelines for the use of technology in their work that have not yet been included in codes of ethics. Helping professionals are expected to be aware of these guidelines and incorporate them into their work. They are also expected to take the matter of cultural differences and other individual differences into consideration in their work. Finally, although it was stated in the beginning of this chapter that codes of ethics have been developed to provide guidelines for work-related issues, it was also stated that the helping professions tend to hold their members to a higher standard. The APA (1992) code of ethics indicates that the morals of helpers in that profession are a personal matter except they should conduct themselves in a manner that does not harm the reputation of psychology or other psychologists.

Obligations to Other Professionals

Guidelines for interacting with people from the same professional group as well as professionals from other groups are included in the codes of ethics of helping professionals. As has been noted throughout this book, there are many types of helping professionals. Partly because of past animosities among these groups, authors of codes of ethics have taken great care to provide ethical guidelines for helping professionals' interactions with other professional groups. For example, Principle 7, Professional Relationships (subsection b of the AMHCA Code of Ethics, 1987) reads: "Mental health counselors know and take into account the traditions and practices of other mental health professionals with which they work and cooperate fully with such groups."

As noted above, the ethical codes of helping professionals provide guidelines for interacting with people within one's own professional groups. These guidelines pertain to working relationships with supervisors and colleagues and deal with factors such as sharing of information, cooperation in managing helping relationships, and consultation regarding problems encountered in helping relationships. For example, helping professionals are advised to consult with other professionals, both within and outside of their own group, when confronted with difficult situations. In the section on competency a vignette regarding an unprepared helper was presented. This helper elected to continue with the case under the supervision of a colleague, which is an acceptable option under the codes of ethics of professional helpers. The ACA (Section B.2.a) (1997) code states that "Counselors may chose to consult with any other professionally competent person about their clients."

Obligations to Employers

Generally, the codes of ethics of helping professionals take similar approaches to dealing with various areas of professional behavior. However, in the matter of dealing with employers, the codes diverge. The ACA (1997) code of ethics indicates that, if a counselor accepts employment, they are in fact accepting the policies of the employer. The NOSHE (1995) code of ethics states a similar stance. Statement 32 in that code reads: "Human services professionals adhere to commitments made to their employers." However, the NOSHE code recognizes that conflicts may occur and recommends that employers and human services professionals work together to manage the conflict. The APA (1992) code of ethical standards does not assume that psychologists will honor the policies of the employer. Psychologists are simply told that when discrepancies between their code of ethics are encountered, they are to adhere to their code of ethics.

Obligations to Themselves

As noted earlier, these ethical guidelines are developed primarily to provide standards for the practice of helping services. Therefore, there are few statements that are directed at individual functioning. However, the NOSHE (1995) code of ethics suggest that human services professionals strive to display those characteristics associated with helping professionals such as empathy and respect for others. Some of the codes also warn that the commission of a felony may lead to the loss of their license to practice (e.g., APA, 1992) as noted in the introduction to this chapter. Additionally, as was noted in the section dealing with competency, all the codes of ethics of helping professionals contain pointed statements admonishing helpers to monitor and deal with personal problems that may interfere with their professional relations with clients and colleagues. One code, the NASW Code of Ethics (1996), does not address this area specifically.

Take a moment to complete Exercise 12.1 to test your understanding of helping professionals' ethical behavior.

Enforcing Codes of Ethics

Each group of professional helpers has established mechanisms for dealing with helpers who are charged with violating their codes of ethics. However, the indi-

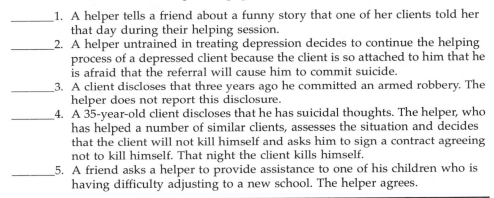

EXERCISE **12.1**

Ethical or Unethical

In the spaces below, indicate whether you believe that the helper is acting unethically or ethically by placing a U or E before each statement. Please note that you have not been given specific information that pertains to each situation described. Your task is to take the information you have learned and generalize to these situations. The answers are found at the end of the chapter on page 266.

_____1. A helper tells a friend about a funny story that one of her clients told her that day during their helping session.

_____2. A helper untrained in treating depression decides to continue the helping process of a depressed client because the client is so attached to him that he is afraid that the referral will cause him to commit suicide.

_____3. A client discloses that three years ago he committed an armed robbery. The helper does not report this disclosure.

_____4. A 35-year-old client discloses that he has suicidal thoughts. The helper, who has helped a number of similar clients, assesses the situation and decides that the client will not kill himself and asks him to sign a contract agreeing not to kill himself. That night the client kills himself.

_____5. A friend asks a helper to provide assistance to one of his children who is having difficulty adjusting to a new school. The helper agrees.

vidual helper is the most important link in the enforcement of ethical standards. The individual has two roles: (1) identifying unethical behavior in colleagues and resolving the violation informally, and (2) if the problem cannot be resolved informally, reporting the violation to the appropriate ethics committee. Although the ethical behavior of others is important, the most important role individuals play in the enforcement of their code of ethics is to monitor their own behavior and function.

Adequately monitoring one's own ethical behavior requires each helper to have a clear understanding of his or her own moral standards. Codes of ethics are not substitutes for personal morality, only supplements to them. Self-monitoring also requires that helpers commit their ethical standards to memory so they can accurately judge whether they are acting responsibly. Although it is probably the case that more breaches of ethics occur because of ignorance than because of deliberate misconduct, ignorance is no defense. Ethics committees charged with investigating violations of ethical standards will find both helpers who violate their codes of ethics deliberately and those who engage in misconduct out of ignorance guilty of unethical behavior.

As would be expected, reports of unethical behavior often come from members of the helper's professional group. However, they may come from other professionals or members of the general public. In some instances, charges of unethical behavior surface as a result of lawsuits against helpers. Complaints of unethical conduct may be directed to several enforcement committees. For example, all state licensing boards have the legal authority and the professional obligation to investigate charges of unethical behavior. State and national professional organizations also have ethics committees that are charged with adjudicating ethical complaints against their members.

Once an ethics committee receives a complaint of ethical misconduct, it will initiate an investigation. If the complaint is received from another professional, the committee may request that the complaint be made in writing if it was a verbal report. The committee is also likely to ask the professional who lodged the complaint to identify the specific ethical principles that the helper is accused of violating. If the complaint comes from a member of the general public, the committee may collect information from the people involved in the incident to identify the specific standards that have been violated.

Once the specific nature of the charge has been clarified, the helper who has been accused of ethical misconduct will be advised of the charges and asked to respond to them. As was pointed out earlier, helpers must respond to the requests of the ethics committees for information or be in violation of their code of ethics. The ethics committee may also elect to collect information from others via written statements or oral testimony. The purpose of this process is to develop a full understanding of the situation that gave rise to the charges and to determine the guilt or innocence of the helper. Once all pertinent information has been collected, the ethics committee renders a verdict. This verdict may be shared with people other than the accused if the committee decides that the helper is guilty. For example, the decision by the ethics committee of a state professional organization that one of their members is guilty of violating their code of ethics will be shared with the national organization and the state licensing board. Some groups may also publish decisions that an individual is guilty of unethical conduct in professional publications.

Most of the actual consequences of being found guilty of ethical misconduct are related to the seriousness of the offense. However, the embarrassment of being found guilty of being unethical is likely to be great regardless of the other penalties that are imposed. One of the mildest penalties for acting unethically is a warning to the helper to be more careful in the future. If a warning is issued, the helper will in all likelihood be placed on probation for a period of time. Another penalty that unethical helpers may incur is expulsion from professional organizations for periods ranging from a few months to permanent expulsion. By far the most serious penalty that can be levied against a helping professional for unethical conduct is the suspension of the license to practice, even if the suspension is for a short time. For most helpers this means that they can no longer make a living using their professional skills, and it may also impair their ability to get a job if their license is reinstated.

Before reading further, complete Exercise 12.2, which shows how complex penalizing unethical behavior can be.

EXERCISE **12.2**

Society's Moral Dilemma

Dr. Jack Kevorkian has assisted in the suicides of dozens of people. Although the termination of a life violates his professional code of ethics, the Hippocratic Oath, he has not yet lost his license to practice medicine. He has been charged with unethical conduct and breaking state laws, and he may eventually lose his medical license. However, there seems to be a reluctance to suspend his license to practice medicine. In the spaces below, list the pros and cons of helping people who are terminally ill and often in pain take their own lives.

Pros of Assisted Suicide

_____

_____

_____

Cons of Assisted Suicide

_____

_____

_____

Do you believe that doctors should be allowed to assist terminally ill people commit suicide? Yes_____ No _____. Why did you respond as you did?

_____

_____

You have just made a moral decision. Was it an easy decision? Many ethical decisions are difficult, which is one reason formal codes of ethics have been developed.

Why do you think physicians have been slow to find Kevorkian guilty of unethical behavior? See page 267 at the end of the chapter for possible explanations after you have considered this question.

Decision-Making in Helping: Ethical and Legal Factors

As has already been shown, both ethical and legal guidelines influence helpers' decision making. All states have laws requiring helpers to report child abuse. Some states have adopted similar laws that require helpers to report elderly abuse. Reporting that their clients are HIV positive or have AIDS even if they are having unprotected sex is prohibited by law in some states. Other states leave the matter of reporting that clients are endangering others to the discretion of the helper. Some laws, such as those dealing with reporting child or elder abuse, work in concert with codes of ethics. Others impair helpers from serving and protecting the public. The legal prohibitions against reporting that an individual has AIDS and is having unprotected sex conflict with helping professionals' duty to warn. The question is, "Which takes precedence, legal guidelines or ethical principles?"

Cottone and Tarvydas (1998) note that different codes of ethics take on the issue of whether to follow legal or ethical guidelines. Clearly, the APA (1992) code of ethics requires helpers to follow their ethical guidelines and ignore the law. On the other hand, the ACA (1997) Code of Ethics and Standards of Practice and the CRCC (1995) Code of Professional Ethics for Rehabilitation Counselors give precedence to the law. Other codes of ethics (e.g., AAMFT, 1991; ASCA, 1992) do not address this issue.

Thompson (1990) suggests that six types of interactions between legal and ethical standards may occur. The two most common situations confronting helpers involve ethical dilemmas only. In these situations, the helper may choose to violate or follow the ethical standards of their professions without concern for the legality of their action. For example, the APA (1992) code of ethics contains a number of principles and standards regarding the use of test results. A helper who follows those guidelines is in no ethical or legal jeopardy. Helpers who violate these standards are in jeopardy of being charged with unethical behavior, but they are not in danger of criminal prosecution because there are no laws prohibiting the misuse of test results. The third type of situation that helpers encounter occurs when there are legal and ethical constraints on their behavior, but by acting ethically they are also in compliance with the law. An example of this type of situation is the reporting of child abuse. A fourth type of interaction between ethical and legal constraints on helpers' actions occurs when helpers violate both their ethical standards and the law. Helpers who provide marijuana to clients because they believe that it is therapeutic are examples of these professionals. Some helpers who belong to the American Counseling Association face this issue on an ongoing basis. Some of them regularly ignore laws that preclude the identification of clients who have AIDS and run the risk of being charged with both unethical and illegal behavior, depending on the states in which they practice. This risk occurs because the ACA (1997) code of ethics defers to legal standards. The fifth, and most difficult, situations for helpers involves being ethical and obeying an unjust law such as laws that preclude identifying people with AIDS regardless of their sexual habits. Members of the American Psychological Association (APA, 1992) might very well find themselves in this situation because their code of ethics holds them to the higher standard, the welfare of their clients. The sixth situation identified by Thompson involves acting ethically and at the same time being out of compliance with the law, which poses problems for some helpers. He indicates that placing an advertisement that contains testimonials from clients violates only some codes of ethics but is an illegal practice according to the Federal Trade Commission. Because of the risks involved, few helpers will opt to place such potentially ethical but illegal advertisements.

Although ethical and legal guidelines are of primary consideration when decisions are being made about course of action to be taken, Cottone and Tarvydas (1998) point out that institutional policies must also be considered in the decision-making processes of helping professionals. As was shown earlier, in some codes of ethics (e.g., ACA, 1997) helpers are presumed to agree with the policies of an institution or agency if they accept employment. Cottone and Tarvydas (1998) developed a four-stage decision-making model that can be used by helpers, a simplified version of which follows:

Stage 1. Identify the Ethical Problem

a. Does it involve a conflict between legal and ethical issues? If yes, what are the ethical principles and legal issues involved? If no, proceed to the next stage.

Stage 2. Identify Potential Solutions to the Ethical Problem

a. Are there institutional policies involved that should be considered? If yes, list them. If no, proceed.
b. In light of the legal, ethical, and institutional policies involved, what courses of action are possible?
c. Which of these solutions appears to be best for the client? For members of society?
d. Is consultation required at this time? If no, proceed. If yes, consult.

Stage 3. Make a Preliminary Selection of a Course of Action

a. Consider the consequences of the decision for the client.
b. Consider the impact on:

1. Client
2. Helper
3. Colleagues/Profession
4. Institution

Stage 4. Implement Course of Action Selected

a. Identify a sequence of activities, including barriers that must be overcome.
b. Carry out course of action, being careful to document what is done and to evaluate the outcomes.

Source: Adapted from Tarvydas, V.M. (1998). Ethical decision making. In Cottone, R.R. & Tarvydas, V.M. (Eds.), *Ethical and professional issues in counseling* (pp. 144–155). Columbus, OH: Merrill.

Legal Threats to Helpers

To this point in the chapter the focus has been primarily on codes of ethics and how legal issues sometimes interact with ethical issues to influence the decision-making processes of helpers. Thus far the discussion of legal issues has focused on the criminal consequences of violating the laws. The aim of this section is to make helpers aware of the civil legal entanglements that may occur if they fail to heed their codes of ethics. We live in a litigious society. The result is that all helping professionals carry professional liability insurance that typically amounts to a million dollars or more. Liability insurance is a necessity for helping professionals for two reasons. First, defending one's self against an unsuccessful lawsuit, that is, one that results in a verdict that the helper is innocent of any wrongdoing, can cost in excess of $25,000 in legal fees. Second, awards to plaintiffs when helpers have been found guilty have exceeded $500,000 in some cases.

Earlier the authors (Brown & Srebalus, 1996) identified a number of areas in which helpers are vulnerable to legal action if they act unethically or fail to follow the standards of practice of their profession. A standard of practice is an accepted way of conducting the helping process. Although codes of ethics set forth standards of practice for dealing with ethical issues, they do not identify accepted ways of helping. These standards can be found in authoritative books and in the practice of seasoned practitioners. What follows are discussions of areas of practice that may lead to successful lawsuits if helpers violate the standards of their professions.

Malpractice Liability

Helpers may be found guilty of malpractice if (1) they have a duty to a client to offer services that requires a standard of skill or care, (2) they are derelict in the provision of the care, (3) there is harm, injury, or loss to the client, and (4) a causal link can be established between the client's loss and the dereliction of duty by the helper (Anderson, 1996). The case of *Tarasoff v. the Regents of the University of California* was mentioned earlier. In this case, the courts decided that the psychologist had a duty to warn Ms. Tarasoff and her parents of the impending danger from Mr. Podar. It should be pointed out that the psychologist did notify the campus police of the threat to Ms. Tarasoff's life and Mr. Podar was brought in for questioning and psychiatric evaluation. However, the psychologist's duty was not satisfied by the act of notifying the police. Of course, the loss in this case was Ms. Tarasoff's life.

Many of the lawsuits returning the largest awards involve suicide and homicide. This is the reason that groups of professional helpers have included the duty to warn prominently in their codes of ethics. That is also why helpers are typically provided with extensive training in suicide and homicide management. In a successful suit against a Mississippi helper, it was learned that she had received little in the way of ethics training and risk management. The plaintiff then sued the trainers, accusing them of dereliction of duty.

Recently, malpractice suits have been lodged against school counselors who, according to the suits, have failed in their duties to help students gain admission to prestigious schools. At this time these suits are being contested on two grounds. The first of these challenges the idea that it is the role of school counselors to help students gain admission to prestigious undergraduate institutions. These defenses hold that getting students into the college of their choice is not a duty.

The second defense against these suits challenges the assumption that students suffer losses because they do not get into the colleges of their choice.

Another area that has yielded large awards to clients involves sexual intimacy between helpers and clients. In these cases, the duty is clearly to provide helping services that do not include sexual contact. The breach of this duty has come through sexual intercourse during therapy, sexual relationships soon after the termination of therapy, or other forms of sexual contact. The losses in these cases are more difficult to establish, but in some instances clients have claimed the loss of self-esteem, loss of other relationships, or the development of psychological problems such as depression or anxiety. One spouse was awarded $500,000 because he claimed that his wife's sexual involvement with her therapist resulted in the termination of their marriage. Even though the actual losses are hard to establish in these cases, it is even more difficult to defend helpers' behavior given the strong ethical taboos against sexual contact between helpers and clients. Some malpractice insurers will not defend their policyholders who are accused of sexual misconduct.

Another area where legal action against helpers has been successful is in the area of informed consent. Informed consent can only be given by adults who are intellectually and psychologically competent. Moreover, to give informed consent, clients must have enough information to make a judgment about whether they wish to participate in the helping process or the research. As was noted in the section on ethics, helpers are admonished to fully inform clients who come for help or who are involved in research projects. Clients have successfully claimed that they have suffered losses because of unexpected therapeutic interventions and manipulation during research studies. This latter area, harm that may occur as a result of participation in research, has been particularly troublesome for researchers who are attempting to follow ethical guidelines and maintain the integrity of their research at the same time. To deal with this issue, research is often conducted without full informed consent, and subjects are "debriefed" after the study to provide more information about the research.

Informed consent is also an issue in invasion of privacy suits. Many helpers are routinely involved in collecting information about clients. Invasion of privacy occurs when information about the clients is gotten without the clients' knowledge or consent. It can also occur when information is obtained from minors or intellectually or mentally impaired individuals without the consent of parents or guardians. Finally, the privacy of a client can be violated when negative information given to a helper under conditions of confidentiality is provided to others.

Finally, an area of growing concern is failure to provide services. In many situations, the roles of helper are poorly defined. Additionally, when their roles are defined, they may not be permitted to fully deliver the promised services by managers and administrators. One example of the latter situation occurs regularly in health maintenance organizations (HMOs). Policies in HMOs limit the number of sessions that helpers can spend with clients and, in doing so, may limit their effectiveness. One group of helpers has started an aggressive legal campaign against the HMOs, but no case law has yet emerged from this effort.

Privileged Communication

The term *confidentiality* was used in the section on ethics to describe the ethical duty of helpers to keep information gained in the helping process a secret. *Privileged communication* is a legal term. In some instances, legislators determine that it is in the best interest of clients to award them privileged communication that guarantees them that the information that they provide to some helpers cannot be divulged without their consent. One of the best-known example of privileged communication exists between members of the clergy and their parishioners. However, many people are granted privileged communication in their dealings with lawyers, doctors, and helping professionals.

When considered alongside failure to warn or violating a standard of care, disclosing privileged information is not a major issue. Awards in these cases are likely to be much smaller than the others discussed thus far in this chapter. However, disclosure of privileged communication has consequences that go beyond civil lawsuits. Disclosing privileged information is a misdemeanor and opens the helper up to criminal prosecution. Additionally, professional helpers who disclose privileged communications are violating one of the major ethical principles of their codes of ethics: confidentiality. Therefore, the consequences of disclosure of this type of information are likely to be considerable. Helpers can avoid suits charging them with violations of privileged communication by requiring permission slips before any information is released.

Defamation

Defamation of clients generally means writing or saying something about the person that is untrue with the intent to harm them. Put somewhat differently, defamation occurs when information passed on by a helper results in embarrassment, contempt, or financial loss. Anderson (1996) indicates that helpers may be open to defamation suits if they (1) provide false information that a client has committed a crime, (2) erroneously report that a client has a sexually transmitted disease, (3) provide faulty information that negatively affects the occupational status of a client, or (4) incorrectly indicate that a female is promiscuous. Of these areas, the one in which helpers are most vulnerable probably relates to disclosures of inaccurate information regarding the occupational qualifications of clients. Many helpers in schools, community colleges, universities, welfare-to-work programs, and other agencies are asked to write recommendations for clients and could easily err in this process.

The best defense against defamation is accuracy. However, even if accurate information is provided, the interpretation placed on it in the courts may result in a successful suit. Although it may not be an entirely acceptable approach to dealing with the problem of suits coming from recommendations, some helpers either refuse to write some recommendations or they write three types of recommendations: great, greater, and greatest. In sum, they write nothing in a recommendation that could be construed as negative.

A summary of steps helpers can take to avoid malpractice suits follow:

1. Know your code of ethics and follow its guidelines.
2. Use a written disclosure form to tell clients what to expect. Surprises are not acceptable in the helping process.
3. Use tried and true approaches in the helping processes. Innovations that have not been accepted by your profession will be hard to defend in court.
4. Get signed releases before talking to anyone about your clients or releasing information about them.
5. Avoid any hint of sexual harassment or contact.
6. If you are unsure about a course of action to take in helping, consult with others and make a record listing whom you consulted and what you discussed.
7. Report any suspicion of child and elder abuse.
8. Consider any threat of suicide or intent to commit a homicide as a genuine threat. Investigate thoroughly. Consult with colleagues. Keep good case notes.
9. Exercise your duty to warn if the threat of suicide or homicide appears credible. Remember, the duty to warns means taking all reasonable steps to insure that the homicide or suicide does not occur.
10. Never try a new technique until you have received instruction and supervision in its use.
11. Stay current. Don't let your knowledge or your skills deteriorate.

Summary

Professions have well-developed codes of ethics that are routinely enforced. Helping professions are no exception. Understanding and applying the ethical principles of one's professional group is an essential prerequisite to success as a helping professional. However, practicing ethically is not enough. Helping professionals must understand the legal issues that interact with and limit the extent to which ethical principles can be applied. The consequences of practicing either unethically or illegally are severe.

CHAPTER 12 EXIT QUIZ

Answer each of the following questions with a T if the answer is true and an F if the answer is false.

_____ 1. Codes of ethics are developed primarily for the purpose of persuading legislators to recognize the various groups of professional helpers.

_____ 2. Increasingly, codes of ethics contain standards of practice.

_____ 3. Codes of ethics are approximately the same as good common sense and set forth guidelines that most moral people follow.

_____ 4. Helpers, unlike business leaders, have as their first responsibility the protection of the welfare of society.

_____ 5. When a helper talks to a client about confidentiality, he or she must also discuss the limitation of what they can keep confidential.

_____ 6. Of the many subprinciples regarding relationships to clients, the one that is not emphasized in all codes concern dual relationships.

_____ 7. A dual relationship occurs naturally when a helper is seeing a couple in the helping process.

_____ 8. Of major concerns to almost all groups of helping professionals is that unethical members will resign while they are being investigated for unethical conduct.

_____ 9. One of the most important obligations to society that helpers have is reporting events that might lead to loss of human life.

_____ 10. The most difficult ethical decision for helpers to make is when their actions are ethical but illegal.

_____ 11. Most codes of ethics suggest that the first line of defense against unethical behavior is informal action taken by practitioners.

_____ 12. Some codes of ethics for professional helpers suggest that by taking a job in an agency or institution helpers are agreeing to the policies of that employer.

_____ 13. Divulging privileged information after receiving a court order is ethical.

_____ 14. Conviction of illegal activities is likely to result in charges of unethical behavior.

_____ 15. Failure to secure informed consent is a major factor in invasion of privacy lawsuits.

Answers:

1. F; 2. T; 3. F; 4. F; 5. T; 6. F; 7. F; 8. F; 9–15. T.

ANSWERS TO QUIZ IN EXERCISE 12.1

1. Unethical: The possibility exists that the person to whom the story was told might repeat the story in another setting where the client was present and tell the source of the story. The client might conclude that other information had been disclosed as well, thus damaging the helping relationship. This helper has violated her promise of confidentiality.

2. Unethical: The decision to proceed is based in faulty logic on several levels. However, lack of competence in treating depression represents the most serious ethical breach.

3. Ethical: Unless there is clear evidence that the person is about to commit another armed robbery, there is no reason to disclose this information.

4. Ethical: The helper followed the correct procedure. Helpers are not expected to be infallible.

5. Ethical: Although the helper may not have used the best judgment in this situation because of the dual relationship involved, this situation probably can be managed.

EXERCISE 12.2

Some thoughts on why Dr. Jack Kevorkian may not have been found guilty of unethical behavior. There are at least two possible explanations. First, the societal standard regarding assisted suicides for people who are beyond medical help is changing. Some state legislatures are considering laws that would allow assisted suicides. Second, recent surveys of physicians have revealed that a sizeable minority of doctors admit to having assisted in the deaths of one or more of their patients. Doctors may be reluctant to charge and convict one of their own who is engaging in an activity that they condone or have practiced. However, on March 26, 1999, a jury found Dr. Kevorkian guilty of second-degree murder because he actively engaged in helping a person commit suicide.

SUGGESTED LEARNING ACTIVITIES

Each class member should interview a member of one of the following groups of helpers to determine how ethical and legal concerns influence their decision making when they enter a helping relationship and in their day-to-day activities: clinical psychologists, school counselors, mental health counselors, social workers, psychiatric nurses, psychiatrists, probation and parole officers, rehabilitation counselors, career counselors, or another helping profession. The results of these interviews should be reported to the class.

REFERENCES

American Association of Marriage and Family Therapists (AAMFT) (1991). *American Association for Marriage and Family Therapist code of ethics.* Washington, DC: Author.

American Counseling Association (ACA) (1997). *American Counseling Association code of ethics and standards of practice.* Alexandria, VA: Author.

American Mental Health Counselors Association (AMHCA) (1987). *American Mental Health Counselors Association code of ethics.* Alexandria, VA: Author.

American Psychological Association (APA) (1992). *American Psychological Association ethical principles of psychologists and code of conduct.* Washington, DC: Author.

American School Counselors Association (ASCA) (1992). *American School Counselors Association ethical standards for school counselors.* Alexandria, VA: Author.

Anderson, B.S. (1996). *The counselor and the law* (4th ed.) Alexandria, VA: American Counseling Association.

Arthur, G.L., & Swanson, C.D. (1993). *Confidentiality and privileged communication.* Alexandria, VA: American Counseling Association.

Association for Specialists in Group Work (ASGW) (1989). *Ethical guidelines for group counselors: Association for Specialists in Group Work.* Alexandria, VA: Author.

Brown, D., & Srebalus, D.J. (1996). *Introduction to the counseling profession* (2nd ed.). Boston: Allyn and Bacon.

Commission on Rehabilitation Certification (CRCC) (1995). *American Rehabilitation Counselors Association/National Rehabilitation Counselors Association/Commission on Rehabilitation Counselor Certification code of professional ethics for rehabilitation counselors.* Chicago, IL: Author.

Cottone, R.R. & Tarvydas, V.M. (Eds.). (1998). *Ethical and professional issues in counseling* (pp. 144–155). Columbus, OH: Merrill.

Kenyon, P. (1999). *An ethical case workbook for human services professionals.* Pacific Grove, CA: Brooks/Cole.

National Association of Social Workers (NASW) (1996). *National Association of Social Workers code of ethics.* Washington, DC: Author.

National Organization for Human Services Education (NOSHE) (1995). *Ethical standards of human services professionals.* Tacoma, WA: Author.

Tarvydas, V.M. (1998). Ethical decision making. In R.R. Cottone & V.M. Tarvydas, (Eds.), *Ethical and professional issues in counseling* (pp. 144–155). Columbus, OH: Merrill.

Thompson, A. (1990). *Guide to ethical practice in psychotherapy.* New York: Wiley.

13 Becoming Employed and Advancing in a Helping Career

1. The career cycles of helping professionals
2. The entry requirements for helping professionals
3. Some secrets to becoming employed as a helping professional
4. The requirements for maintaining your status as a helping professional
5. The types and purposes of professional organizations and a rationale for involvement in them

Helping professionals, like all workers, pass through certain stages as they enter into and advance in their careers. You may have passed through the first stage of the typical helping professional's development: exploration of the career options available. For the typical college student, the exploration stage is characterized by a great deal of uncertainty and perhaps some anxiety. It is the norm for individuals at this stage to try to collect as much information as possible about their career options so that they can narrow their choices. In some instances, this search for information simply adds to the confusion because many of the people who are consulted for career information have biases that they freely share. For example, one psychology major shared with her advisor that she was considering entering school counseling only to be told "that would be a waste of your intellect. You should be a clinical psychologist."

People who leave college and enter the world of work in other occupations often have different exploration stage experiences. Their career exploration process begins when they realize that they are unhappy in their current jobs and need to seek new alternatives. One life insurance salesperson confided that he slowly began to realize that the only part of his job that he enjoyed was meeting with clients face to face and helping them plan their futures. He also came to the realization that the large income that he made as a successful salesperson was unimportant and that helping people was what he wanted to do. It is not unusual to see people who have worked for many years in occupations that were not fully satisfying return to school to explore training to become helping professionals.

The exploration stage culminates in the identification of a career option within one of the five helping professions. These professions are psychology, social work, counseling, marriage and family therapy, and human services. Of these professional groups, marriage and family therapy is the narrowest because it focuses on one type of activity: providing therapeutic services to couples and families. Nursing, which is not generally considered in the same category as the other professions, does offer prospective helpers one career option: psychiatric nursing. Therefore, some prospective helpers consider nursing as an option. Although students may choose to become a counselor or a psychologist, they must also decide which of the specialties within these broad professions they will enter. Some of the specialties within each of the major professional helping groups are listed in Table 13.1.

The second stage in the career cycle of helping professionals is preparation. As noted in Chapter 1, a major consideration in choosing a helping career is the amount of training one wishes to pursue. Students who are choosing training programs often look closely at a number of variables including cost, location, length of the training program, and their own interests. However, more and more students are aware that they must look at a very critical variable, the accreditation of the program. The Council for Standards in Human Services Education sets standards and recognizes preparation programs that meet those standards in the training of human services professionals. The American Psychological Association (APA) and the National Association of Social Workers (NASW) accredit programs that prepare psychologists and social workers, respectively. The Council for the Accreditation of Counseling and Related Educational Programs (CACREP) accredits many different types of counselor education programs, and the Council of Rehabilitation Education Programs (CREP) accredits programs in rehabilitation counseling. The American Association of Marriage and Family Therapists (AAMFT) is responsible for accrediting marriage and family therapy training programs, but not marriage and family counseling programs. Although this maze of accrediting agencies can be confusing, many students prefer to graduate from accredited programs in their professional area.

The last three stages of the typical helping professional's career will be the primary focus of this chapter. These stages are gaining employment, advancing in one's chosen field, and withdrawing from it.

Becoming Employed: Required Professional Credentials

In the latter stages of completing a training program, trainees begin to turn their attention to the employment process. This includes setting up placement files in their institutions' career planning and placement agencies, developing resumes, perhaps attending sessions to learn job interviewing skills, and investigating state credentialling laws.

The credentials required for becoming a practicing professional varies tremendously from state to state. Let's look at North Carolina as an example. Psychologists and masters' level social workers (MSWs) must obtain licenses before

TABLE 13.1 Major Groups and Specialties of Helping Professionals

Group	Specialty within Group
Counseling	School
	Rehabilitation
	Mental Health
	Substance abuse
	Gerontological
	Career
	College
	Pastoral/religious
	Employment
	Offender
	Marriage and Family
	Grief
	Military
Psychology	Clinical psychology
	Counseling psychology
	School psychology
	Organizational/industrial psychology
	Rehabilitation psychology
Social Work	Medical social work
	Drug and alcohol
	Individual/group
	Marriage and family
	Macro-option (community orientation)
	Micro-option (psychotherapy)
	Community agency (e.g., case worker)
Human services	Hospice specialist
	Retardation specialist
	Drug and alcohol treatment specialist
	Gerontological specialist
	Mental illness specialist

they can practice at any level. Private practitioners, government employees, and employees in business and industry must be licensed or must be gaining the supervision needed to become licensed. In psychology, there are two licenses: Licensed Practicing Psychologist and Licensed Psychological Associate. Licensed Psychological Associates must work under the supervision of a Licensed Practicing Psychologist if they are engaged in psychotherapy or certain types of assessment work. A Ph.D. in clinical, counseling, school, rehabilitation, or organizational/industrial psychology is required for licensure as a practicing psychologist. A 60-semester hour masters degree in one of those areas is required for licensure as a Licensed Psychological Associate. The standard for licensure as a Licensed Clinical Social Worker is a 60-semester hour MSW. Counselors do not have to be licensed to work in business and industry or in government positions such as those in rehabilitation and employment agencies. School counselors must be licensed by their state department of public instruction. Additionally, counselors in private practice must hold the Licensed Professional Counselor Credential, a license that requires the completion of a 48-hour masters degree program. For the most part, human services professionals do not have to be licensed in North Carolina. One exception to this would be human services professionals who expect to work in drug and alcohol treatment centers in the direct provision of services such as evaluation or treatment of users. These people would have to be licensed as substance abuse counselors, a credential that requires a baccalaureate degree. In almost all cases, the laws that led to the licenses referred to here, as well as those in other states, originated after professional groups lobbied the state legislature for their passage. We will comment more on this issue later in the chapter.

The foregoing example of the licensure jungle in North Carolina cannot be generalized to any other state with one exception. Counselors who work in schools must hold the appropriate credential for their states. However, several states do not have licensure laws to regulate the practice of counselors and social workers. Further, a few states allow masters' level psychologists to become Licensed Practicing Psychologists, which allows them to offer a full range of psychological services. However, although each state has a different set of credentialling laws to regulate the practice of helping professionals, there is one generalization that any helping professional who is entering the field can make. This generalization is that there will be increased emphasis on credentialling in the future. This increased emphasis on credentialling will result in higher standards for obtaining credentials and increased numbers of credentials. Therefore, helping professionals who are entering their respective fields at this time should get all of the licenses to which they are entitled and maintain them throughout their careers. Failure to do so may result in the need to retrain at some point in the future because the standards for credentialling have escalated.

Locating Job Openings

Sources of information about jobs vary tremendously depending on the profession and the employer advertising the job. Some jobs, particularly those in government and other public agencies, are advertised in newspapers, posted on Web sites, listed with institutional placement offices, and sent directly to training programs where they are often posted on bulletin boards. Other types of jobs may not be advertised so widely. They may be advertised in professional publications such as newsletters and word-of-mouth solicitations at professional meetings and elsewhere. Jobs in business and industry are almost always posted first on the businesses' Intranet or other job posting service. If they are not filled as a result of the internal search, personnel officers and others make individual contact with people they know and solicit nominations. Rarely are these positions advertised in the same manner as those in public agencies, leading some career counselors to refer to jobs in the private sector as the "hidden job market." The primary way that a helping professional learns about jobs in the hidden job market is through a process called *networking*. Networking involves meeting people who have knowledge about job openings and making them familiar with your qualifications. Helping professionals who are actively engaged in networking always have a business card and a resume ready to hand to people who may help them locate a job vacancy.

Another approach to locating job openings is by making "cold calls" to agencies that may have job openings or by sending "leadless" letters to these agencies. A leadless letter is so named because the person who is sending it has no information that there is a job opening in the agency to which the letter is sent. Cold calls are visits to agencies that have not advertised job vacancies. When job seekers use cold calls or leadless letters, they hope they will locate a job that has either escaped their attention or that has not yet been announced. These approaches can be successful, but job seekers must have realistic expectations about their results. The following note appeared on a bulletin board in a community college in Florida:

> Sent: 200 letters to employers
> Received: 20 replies
> Had: 6 interviews
> Result: 2 job offers

The job hunt for helping professionals is made more difficult by the variety of agencies in which helpers are employed. Here is a partial list of agencies that might be contacted during the job hunt:

- career development services on college campuses (for example, career planning and placement)
- child guidance clinics
- community mental health centers
- correctional facilities
- counseling centers (colleges and universities)
- departments of social services
- elementary, middle, and high schools
- employment assistance programs in businesses
- family planning centers
- group homes for the people with mental retardation
- halfway houses for substance abusers and psychiatric patients
- health maintenance organizations (HMOs)
- hospices
- human resources agencies (businesses, universities, and government)
- job placement offices, private and public
- military bases (exit and reenlistment)

- private practice groups
- psychiatric hospitals
- rehabilitation agencies
- religious counseling services
- retirement facilities and nursing homes
- shelters for battered individuals
- substance abuse centers in hospitals and elsewhere
- university counseling centers

Job announcements, whether they be in newspapers, on the Internet, or on a company's Intranet, typically include a job description, the nature of the training required, and certificates or licenses required. They often specify that candidates from accredited training programs are preferred or only candidates who have graduated from an accredited program will be considered. As noted earlier, people entering training programs for helping professionals increasingly want to enter programs that are accredited by the appropriate accrediting agency so that they are competitive in the job market. For example, read the following sample job posting:

> SUBSTANCE ABUSE COUNSELOR to provide direct treatment and supervise a residential program for adolescent males experiencing substance abuse issues. Counselor would facilitate daily groups, conduct individual and family therapy, and supervise group home programming and staff. Certified Substance Abuse Counselor preferred. Minimum requirements: MA in human services field and one-year supervised experience in the substance abuse field.

Once a job opening is located, the most important aspect of the job search occurs: the interview. Bookstores are filled with how-to guides for interviewees, and at least one of these probably should be read before interviewing for a job. However, it is far more important to enroll in a short course on interviewing skills prior to the first interview. These courses, which are typically offered by career planning and placement centers, cover everything from dressing appropriately to responding to difficult questions. You can assess your job hunting skills by completing Exercise 13.1.

After Employment: The Role of Professional Organizations

Professional organizations were mentioned in three contexts in the previous section: the influence they bring to bear on the accreditation of training programs, their lobbying for licensing laws that regulate practice, and their role in the job hunt. However, the importance of professional organizations goes far beyond these three roles. In this section, the professional organizations often joined by

---

EXERCISE **13.1**

Assessing My Job Hunting Skills

Job Finding

Job Hunting Skills	Yes	No	Unsure

1. I have good networking skills.
2. I can use the Internet to conduct a job search.
3. I understand the workings of the institutional placement office.
4. I subscribe or have access to professional publications that list jobs.
5. I can write convincing letters to employers about my qualifications.
6. I have the skills needed to make a favorable impression when contacting an employer by telephone.

Job Getting Skills

Job Getting Skills	Yes	No	Unsure

1. I can prepare a professional-looking resume.
2. I can post a resume on the Internet.
3. I have good job interviewing skills.
4. I can be convincing when interviewing on the Internet.
5. I have the skills to write an appropriate note after the interview.

---

helping professions will be listed and some additional roles that professional organizations play in the lives of helpers discussed.

There are dozens of professional organizations for helpers, a few of which are listed in Table 13.2. Organizations sometimes compete with each other for members. Helping professionals must often choose which organizations are most attuned to their interests and which will facilitate the attainment of their career goals. Each of the organizations listed has qualifications for membership. Interested readers may contact these organizations directly at the Web site addresses listed.

The organizations listed in Table 13.2 provide a number of services to the practicing professional. One of the most important of these is continuing education. Although most helping professionals breathe a sigh of relief at the end of

TABLE 13.2 An Abbreviated List of Professional Organizations

Organization	Helpers Who Belong
American Association of Marriage and Family Therapists *http://www.aamft.org/*	Marriage and family therapists
American Counseling Association *http://www.counseling.org*	All counselors
American Mental Health Counselors Association *http://www.amhca.org/home2.org/*	Mental health counselors
American Psychological Association *http://www.apa.org*	All psychologists
American Rehabilitation Counselors Association *http://www.nchrtm.okstate.edu/arca/links.html*	Rehabilitation counselors
American School Counselor Association *http://www.edge.net/asca*	School counselors
National Association of Alcoholism *http://www.naadac.org*	Substance abuse counselors
National Association of School Psychologists *http://www.naspweb.org*	School psychologists
National Association of Social Workers *http://www.naswdc.org*	Social workers
National Career Development Association *http://129.219.88.111*	Career counselors and career development facilitators and specialists
National Organization for Human Service Education *http://www.nohse.org*	Human services workers
National Rehabilitation Counseling Association *http://www.nationalrehab.org*	Rehabilitation counselors

their formal training, the fact is that the learning process has just begun. The credentials discussed earlier must be renewed periodically, and it is generally the case that several hours of continuing education hours are required before a credential can be renewed. For example, counselors, psychologists, and social workers typically have to complete twenty hours per year of continuing education to renew their licenses. These hours can be earned by attending sessions at annual conventions, enrolling in workshops, and completing correspondence courses offered by professional organizations in addition to taking formal courses that are offered at two- and four-year colleges and universities.

Professional organizations are also responsible for initiating optional credentialling efforts. Unlike the licenses discussed earlier, optional credentials are not sought by helping professionals because they are a prerequisite to employment. For example, social workers who work in states that do not require licensure for practice may wish to become a Certified Clinical Social Workers (CCSW) to show that they have gone beyond the requirements in their states. The CCSW is offered by the National Federation of Societies for Clinical Social Workers (*http://www.nfncsw.org*) to social workers who complete a rigorous training program, undergo the required supervision, and pass an examination regarding their knowledge of social work. Similarly, the National Board for Certified Counselors (NBCC) (*http://nbcc.org/index.htm*) offers the NCC (National Certified Counselor) certificate, as well as a host of specialty certifications for people in gerontological counseling, substance abuse counseling, school counseling, career counseling, mental health counseling, and other specialty areas.

Another major role of professional associations is to represent their members in the "turf wars" that occur among various professional groups. The jousting that occurs for the right to practice helping skills originated with battles between psychiatry and psychology. It continues today on a variety of fronts. For example, in at least one state, New York, state psychologists are lobbying against licensing laws for counselors. In another state, California, the licensing law for child and family counselors has recently been changed to focus on marriage and family therapy. The result will be that individuals who were licensable prior to the amendment to the law will no longer be able to become licensed to practice. These battles among helping professionals became so fierce in Florida at one time that, in exasperation, the legislature threw out all licensing bills. After the warring groups agreed to cooperate in the area of legislation that licensed and regulated the practice of helpers, licensing laws were reinstated.

Because the struggles listed above represent the types of battles that occur regularly in most states, organizations that represent different groups of helping professionals regularly engage in lobbying efforts to make sure that their members are protected from efforts to limit what is termed their *scope of practice*. One of the "hot button" issues at this time is an effort by some psychologists to preclude other helping professionals from administering all types of psychological tests and inventories. One implication of this effort, if it is successful, is that school counselors would be unable to give scholastic aptitude tests and inventories. Additionally, social workers, human resources professionals, and substance abuse counselors would have to call on licensed psychologists to administer the screening devices that they now routinely use in their practices. Moreover, personnel officers and others would be unable to administer tests and inventories routinely used in the screening of employees, and many other professionals would be unable to administer psychological tests and inventories. Other turf wars that are ongoing include third party payment for mental health services (whether health insurers will pay for counseling and psychotherapy delivered by some groups of professionals), the rights of some helpers to own and operate businesses that offer mental health services (in some states, only physicians and psychologists can own these types of businesses), and so forth. These are obviously serious issues that have a tremendous impact on the lives of helping professionals.

Finally, professionals associations do more than represent their members. They are at the forefront of efforts to expand the services to their clients. Often professional associations join forces to lobby for changes in legislation that will influence the welfare of children, the elderly, and people with psychological and physical disabilities, homeless individuals, and many other groups. Many helping professionals are unaware that their rights to practice and the opportunities available to them are threatened by the efforts of other groups. Others who are aware of the issues choose to let others within their professional groups represent them in efforts to protect and expand the services they offer. A few, typically a relative handful of members of each organization, carry the brunt of the burden to represent the professional group. Our advice is to become heavily involved in the efforts of your professional associations and to shoulder some of the responsibility for its efforts to promote your profession.

Getting More Education

A major decision in the life of many helping professionals has to do with the amount of education they need to deliver helping services. As noted in Chapter 1, the amount of education required to function in the helping professions ranges from the associate's degree to the doctorate. Some of the factors to consider when selecting a graduate program will be taken up in this section. However, as individuals make this decision, they should ask themselves, "Do I want to be an independent practitioner or am I content working under the direction of another professional?" If the answer is, "I want to make my own decisions about my clients," then training beyond the baccalaureate is required in most instances. The question that must be answered is, "Which graduate program should I choose?" Normally this question is answered in a three-stage process in which the student considers two sets of overlapping variables. During the first stage, the student answers the following questions:

1. What helping profession do I wish to enter or continue in?
2. What geographic locations am I willing to consider?
3. How much money am I willing to spend on my education?
4. What are the entry requirements of the programs of interest, and can I be admitted?

After these four questions are answered, prospective graduate students may consult directories of training programs such as those listed below to get additional information. They may also get information from college catalogs or from their Web sites. Some training programs have their own Web sites that include information about admission requirements, the background of the faculty, and nature of the programs offered. Some programs go so far as to post their course outlines on their Web sites.

Counselors
Council for the Accreditation of Counseling and Related Educational Programs

5999 Stevenson Avenue
Alexandria, VA 22304
703.823.9800
Council on Rehabilitation Education, Inc.
POB 1788
Champaign, IL 81824
217.333.6688
Association for Clinical Pastoral Education, Inc.
1549 Clairmount Road, Suite 103
Decatur, GA 30033
404.320.1472

Psychologists

American Psychological Association
1200 17th Street, NW
Washington, DC 20036
202.955.7600

Social Workers

Council on Social Work Education
1600 Duke St. Suite 300
Alexandria, VA 22314
703.683.8080

Marriage and Family Therapists

Commission on Accredited Marriage and Family Therapy Programs
1717 K St. Suite 407
Washington, DC 20006
202.429.1825

Human Services Professionals

Council for Standards in Human Services Education
North Essex Community College, Mental Health Technology Program
Elliot Way
Haverhill, MA 01830
http://www.nohse.com

Once prospective students have narrowed their search for training programs to a few schools and they are ready to apply, another set of criteria comes into play in their search for a graduate-training program. It is useful to use a grid such as the one presented in Exercise 13.2 to compare programs that are being considered.

The third stage in the choice of a graduate program occurs after the programs to which students have applied make their decisions. If an individual is admitted to only one program, the third stage actually involves a decision to accept the program's offer to attend or to reject it and reapply at a later time. If a student is admitted to more than one program, then most of the criteria that were considered in stages one and two are reviewed and a decision is made. For example, a student may have decided that he or she will spend up to $20,000 on his or her graduate education, but he or she is admitted to two schools, one that costs $10,000 and the other that costs $20,000. At this point, the student must consider whether it is worth an additional $10,000 to get the education he or she desires when both programs will provide the training sought. Many students elect to spend the additional money to attend the more expensive program, typically because of intangible variables.

Advancing in Your Field and Retirement

The amount of training completed is directly related to career advancement in the helping professions, but training alone is not the only factor that determines advancement. Other factors that will influence the helper's career include keeping

---

EXERCISE **13.2**
Comparing Prospective Training Programs

Criteria to be Considered	School 1	School 2	School 3
Is the program accredited?			
How long will it take to complete the program?			
Have recent graduates gotten jobs?			
What is the nature of the field placements (e.g., the client group served, location, supervisory ratio)?			
Will I be qualified for the licenses and other credentials I need when I complete the program?			
What degree will I receive? (e.g., MA, M.Ed.)			
What is the faculty–student ratio?			
How large is the institution in which the program is located?			
What is the theoretical orientation of the program faculty?			
Will I qualify for financial aid?			
Are there intangibles such as cultural programs, sport teams, and other factors that are important?			

up-to-date through continued participation in in-service training, time management and other work habits, professional attitude, networking, and getting a mentor.

A mentor is an older or more experienced person who teaches, advises, opens professional doors, and encourages fledgling professionals (Brown & Srebalus, 1996). As the definition of a mentor suggests, mentors work in the same setting as the new professional and have learned how to deal with the issues in the workplace. Some agencies assign each new employee a mentor. If this does not occur, new hires should identify persons who know the workplace and have a personal style that is compatible with theirs and ask them to assist them become an effective employee. The benefits of being mentored are numerous. At a minimum, people who receive mentoring in the workplace adapt more quickly to the setting and feel more comfortable in their jobs. Other benefits may include quicker advancement in one's job, social support in the workplace, and greater access to the agency's resources such as travel funds.

In a sense, the selection of a mentor is the first step in the networking process. Networking is a systematic process of connecting with other people who can facilitate one's career advancement (Brown & Srebalus, 1996). However, networking is not limited to the current workplace. Skillful networkers build a series of contacts both inside and outside of their workplaces who can assist them to identify job openings, lobby on their behalf when jobs are available, and provide them with feedback about their credentials and prospects for getting jobs. Although most professional helpers network to some degree, few do it systematically. Those who do use different approaches. Some create a file of names and addresses of people they meet who work in agencies or settings of interests. One way of getting this type of information is to ask for other professionals' business cards. The networkers provide their own business card to others when they meet them. They also follow up first contacts with notes, telephone calls, or email messages. Another approach involves being remembered positively. Following up initial meetings with calls and email messages is one way of doing this. Another is to provide work samples or other materials that might be of interest to the helping professionals met. People who network do not want to be remembered as not following through or as procrastinators. They volunteer to work on committee and projects in professional associations and elsewhere. People who engage in successful networking select committees that will give them maximum exposure to influential people. They have excellent interpersonal skills, the most important of which is that they are good listeners.

Mentoring and networking can accelerate advancement in one's career. However, success in any career begins in the workplace. Successful workers are positive and have professional attitudes. People who are positive compliment others on their work, make positive statements about the organization or agency, and avoid complaining about the agency or their jobs. People with professional attitudes follow the policies of their agencies as well as the ethical and legal guidelines governing their behavior. Successful workers use their time effectively and do their jobs well. Time management is not merely working all the time. It involves setting goals that are related to organizational and personal timeliness and pursuing those goals in a dedicated fashion. People who advance in their careers are assertive. Most workers find themselves in situations in which they are underpaid or have not been promoted in a timely fashion at some point in their career. At this point they must forcefully but tactfully make their grievances known to their supervisors or leave their positions if the inequities are not corrected. Powerful mentors and a well-developed network of influential people can be particularly useful to helpers who find themselves in situations requiring remediation or the need to pursue a new job.

Finally, advancing in one's career requires that helpers provide high-quality services on an ongoing basis. In some instances, this can be accomplished by simply building on what was learned in the initial training program. In other instances, comprehensive retraining is required to learn new strategies and techniques. For example, in Chapter 11 helping on the Internet was discussed. Few helpers have been trained to use computers and Internet technology as a tool in the helping process. As the potential of this technology grows, many helping professionals will be expected to retool so that they can use the Internet in the helping process.

Retirement seems decades away for most students who are entering the field, but in our plan-ahead society wise workers in all fields look at the benefits afforded them by their employers so that retirement is a possibility when the time comes. Interestingly, many helpers elect to leave their agencies and private practices to offer helping services on a volunteer basis to people who otherwise would not have access to helping services.

Summary

Helpers, like other workers, pass through certain stages in their careers. For helpers at the beginning of their careers, many important steps lie ahead. One of these steps may involve deciding whether to go directly to work or to pursue more education. If the decision is to get a job, the job search must be pursued with skill and vigor. If advanced training is sought, there are many decisions that need to be made very carefully. Helping professionals must also decide to what degree they will become involved in professional organizations. As noted in this chapter, professional organizations play a key role in all phases of the helping professionals' careers, beginning with finding a job. Ultimately, each helping professional will withdraw from his or her career, and even though retirement is years in the future, it deserves some consideration at the outset of a helper's career.

CHAPTER 13 EXIT QUIZ

Answer each of the following questions with a T if the answer is true or F if the answer is false.

_____ 1. Students and workers in other occupations often come to the conclusion that they wish to change careers and become helping professionals.

_____ 2. The numbers and types of credentials required for helping professionals varies from state to state.

_____ 3. The National Board of Certified Counselors offers credentials required in many states.

_____ 4. Most states require psychologists to have a doctorate before they can practice independently.

_____ 5. Cold calls and leadless letters have little in common as job hunting strategies.

_____ 6. The most important part of getting a job is the interview.

_____ 7. Generally speaking, organizations representing helping professionals have common views on matters such as licensing and scope of practice of each group.

_____ 8. Graduating from an accredited program is increasingly important in the job search.

_____ 9. In the future, it is likely that there will be less emphasis on credentials and more emphasis on skills among employers.

Answers:

1. F; 2. T; 3. F; 4. T; 5. F; 6. T; 7. F; 8. T; 9. F.

SUGGESTED LEARNING ACTIVITIES

1. Have small groups of students conduct a search of the Web sites listed in Table 13.2. Have them report on what they find at each site.

2. Invite politically active psychologists, social workers, counselors, and human resource workers to class to discuss the legislative efforts that their groups are promoting. Ask them about differences that exist among the four groups with regard to key professional issues.

3. Have each student visit the Web site of a university to determine the requirements for admission to the graduate school and to get information about one of the training programs for helpers offered by that university. For example, a student might look at the Social Work program and another might look at the Clinical Psychology program. This search may be initiated in at least two ways. Students who wish to look at one college or university should go to the search option on their Internet browser, type in the name of the college or university that they are exploring, use the pull-down menu to click on Exact Phrase/Word Search, and then click on Search. This will normally locate the home page of the college or university. A second way to conduct this search is to go to the home page of CollegeNet (*http://www.collegenet.com/*) and click on Four-Year College Search. Next

click on the state in which college or university is located and then click on the name or college or university when it appears in the list presented. This latter method is preferred if the programs at several universities are to be explored because it saves time.

4. Have several representatives from different types of training programs visit the class to discuss their training programs and the admission processes leading to them.

5. Each student should contact America's Job Bank (*http://www.ajb.dni.us/*) and register as a job seeker by posting their resume on this Web site. They may then conduct a job search on this same sight by following the directions that appear after they register.

REFERENCES

Brown, D., & Srebalus, D.J. (1996). *Introduction to the counseling profession* (2nd ed.). Boston: Allyn and Bacon.

14

Maintaining Your Physical and Mental Health

W H A T   Y O U   W I L L   L E A R N

1. How to assess both internal and external demands that can increase stress
2. How to assess stress and burnout in oneself and in others
3. How to identify stressors in everyday life
4. Ways of managing stress and burnout
5. How to understand health as composed of physical, emotional, cognitive, and spiritual components
6. How to design a lifestyle that leads to greater health as a helping professional

Being a member of a helping profession can be an exciting and challenging experience. From the challenges of helping people one can develop a deep sense of personal satisfaction, an increase in self-confidence, and an overall sense of well-being. This usually occurs when the challenges faced are within our capacity to meet them. When the balance shifts toward the demands placed on us becoming greater than our capabilities to meet those demands, rather than feeling good our experience changes to feeling overwhelmed. With it confidence decreases, anxiety rises, and our ability to perform often becomes impaired. This chapter is about meeting the challenges of being a helping professional, facing the risks involved, avoiding lasting damage from the stress of helping, and achieving a sense of satisfaction and meaning from what we have done.

We all know about challenges and demands and the pressures of meeting them. Exercise 14.1, p. 286, lists some of the demands college students face. Some of the demands will be familiar to students who have left home to go to school, while others will be more familiar to individuals who have attended school in their own community.

Coping with demands from our environment will be made easier or more difficult depending on how we perceive and interpret those demands. Here are some attitudes and assumptions that guarantee that even a moderate life challenge will become a stressful experience:

- Believe that you have to be all things to all people
- Insist on always being right

EXERCISE **14.1**

College Pressures

Check the items below that apply to you. Leave blank those items that are not relevant. Each item describes a challenge or demand associated with attending college.

_____ 1. Deciding which college to attend
_____ 2. Paying for college expenses
_____ 3. Leaving pets behind
_____ 4. Maintaining friendships with distant friends
_____ 5. Maintaining a long-distance dating relationship
_____ 6. Picking a college major or career
_____ 7. Deciding where to live, on or off campus
_____ 8. Getting along with roommates
_____ 9. Not having a dating relationship with someone
_____10. Coping with family problems, such as parent troubles
_____11. Finding time to both study and socialize
_____12. Finding time to both study and work to support oneself or one's family
_____13. Spending time with both one's studies and one's family or partner
_____14. Making decisions about sex and the use of alcohol or other chemicals
_____15. Storing your belongings in a safe place
_____16. Eating nutritious foods that taste good
_____17. Maintaining a car and finding parking on campus
_____18. Deciding about home visits or whether to live at home
_____19. Deciding about where to live during the summer vacation
_____20. Feeling good about how you look, what you wear, and how it matches with what others are doing
_____21. Having backups for homework and computer files
_____22. Having money for leisure activities and extras, such as CDs and concerts
_____23. Deciding on a career and how it will fit with your parents' expectations
_____24. Dealing with unreasonable and unfair professors
_____25. Finding quiet places to study and relax

- Expect others to take care of you and make you happy
- Not satisfied unless you get everything you want
- Don't expect others or yourself to make mistakes
- Hold grudges and brood on how others have offended you
- Expect others to read your mind and be disappointed when they don't
- Only feel happy when everything is just right; let one flaw ruin everything
- Never learn to say "no"
- Assume the worst so you will never be disappointed

Meeting everyday demands is often difficult for individuals who lead complex lives. Having more to do than time to do it and having tasks that are too difficult contribute to work overload. Having difficulty meeting these external demands makes one miserable enough, but combining external demands with a tendency to be self-critical leads one to be punished from both internal and external forces.

We are describing how individuals become stressed. Stress is the response of our bodies to demands. For example, if we are confronted with a dangerous situation—for example, someone that may want to harm us—numerous bodily changes occur. Our hearts begin to beat faster, our blood pressure rises, and we begin to feel generally more tense and alarmed. In the course of this arousal, many chemicals manufactured by our brain and glands rush through our body to prepare us to meet the danger. This arousal prepares us for basic defenses: to fight or flee. At first glance, this may seem very adaptive. While this is true, modern life seems to keep us too annoyed with both big and little things, too irritated, too busy, too much on the go, too much in a state of almost continual arousal.

Medical science has demonstrated that exposure to stressful stimuli or stressors over an extended period of time wears at our bodies and causes eventual physical damage. The most common example of this is heart disease. Stressed people often have damaged arteries that are susceptible to deposits of cholesterol around the damaged areas. This buildup of cholesterol or plaque in the coronary arteries can block blood flow, resulting in a heart attack. Thus, managing stress is not simply a matter of just feeling good. It is a matter of slowing destructive forces that can hasten our deaths.

How to Assess Stress

Individuals who are especially good at listening to their bodies and monitoring their cognitions and emotions can determine whether they are excessively stressed. Exercise 14.2, p. 288, contains some of the common physical, emotional, and cognitive signs of stress.

After completing Exercise 14.2, you could go back and check the items that indicate how stress leads to physical changes, and other items that show emotional and cognitive changes. In general, exposure to stressors over time leads to significant and mostly negative changes. However, it seems impossible to completely avoid stressful situations. In fact, not all stress is viewed as bad. Hans Selye, the scientist most responsible for our understanding of stress (Selye, 1976), divided stress into positive stress or eustress and negative stress or distress. When life demands add excitement, challenge, and opportunity while staying within the reach of our abilities, we achieve eustress. When the demands signal danger and overtax our adaptive abilities, they lead to distress. Case Illustration 14.1, p. 289, may be a reminder of some of the distress common among college students.

Paul is stressed by the difficult challenges he is facing, in raising his GPA and gaining admission into law school. His social support system is also under stress, and he may not be coping as well as he could with the demands facing

EXERCISE **14.2**

A Simple Stress Test

Some of the most significant indicators of stress are changes people observe in their life situation that signal increased pressures or demands. Take a few minutes to read the items below. Check the items that apply to you.

_____ 1. Considerable worry over small matters

_____ 2. Sudden and inappropriate anger over minor issues

_____ 3. Becoming less friendly and interested in being around loved ones

_____ 4. Getting sick more often; having more colds and other medical problems

_____ 5. Having more trouble forgetting mistakes

_____ 6. Beginning to make more mistakes; starting to worry about being accident-prone

_____ 7. Feeling tired often without having a good reason for feeling so

_____ 8. Spending long periods brooding over things

_____ 9. Becoming less productive in work and less engaged in play

_____10. Beginning to feel empty and helpless

_____11. Seeing others as less kind and considerate

_____12. Becoming less interested in sex and sharing affection

_____13. Experiencing increased problems with indigestion, headaches, and muscle pain

_____14. Having more difficulty with sleep, either getting to sleep or sleeping too much

_____15. Becoming more forgetful, missing appointments, having difficulty concentrating

_____16. Becoming more cynical, suspicious, and distrustful

_____17. Being less giving, volunteering for fewer activities

_____18. Feeling too tired to go out with friends

_____19. Having trouble relaxing and taking things as they come

_____20. Seeming to be more callous toward others, less sensitive to their needs

_____21. Increasing the use of alcohol and tobacco

him. He may be making things more difficult for himself by procrastinating on important tasks, brooding over his shortcomings, and trying to self-medicate his distress with alcohol.

Stress, Burnout, and Becoming a Professional Helper

Learning how to manage stress is a very important part of preparing for a career in one of the helping professions. The work that helping professionals do is often very challenging. We have known for decades that stress incurred from work,

CASE ILLUSTRATION **14.1**
Paul

Paul has been in college for four years and may graduate in three more semesters. He started as a freshman at another school, sat out a semester, and transferred to his current school. His first semester was a disaster with a cumulative GPA of 1.67. Since transferring, Paul's grades have improved, but he still believes them to be too low to get into law school. Paul has always been disappointed with his performance on standardized tests and is worried about taking the LSAT in the future. He has purchased some study guides for the admission examination but has not opened them. The guides seem to stare at him from his bookshelf.

Paul is an officer in his fraternity that has had charges filed against several of its members for a hazing incident. In addition, the house is under investigation for violations of the college alcohol policy.

Final examinations are two weeks away; Paul has to complete several research papers, and he is doing poorly in his business statistics class. When he goes home over Christmas, he realizes that he needs to break off his relationship with his girlfriend, telling her that he is dating someone else. His old girlfriend's parents are close friends of his parents.

In the midst of social and academic pressures Paul finds it difficult to sleep, to find time to eat well, and to relax. He is on edge with trouble controlling his already short temper. He has had several recent arguments with his new girlfriend, both times after he had had too much to drink.

occupational stress, is one of the most serious health problems facing society next to infectious diseases and environmental pollution (Kasl, 1978). Thus, the habits developed to manage stress while in school will be extremely beneficial in the future.

Occupational stress associated with the helping professions is manifested by a phenomenon called *burnout.* This is a good name for this stress condition because its key symptom is work-related exhaustion, both physical and emotional (Freudenberger, 1974). However, burnout is defined as a syndrome or combination of symptoms specifically evident among human service professionals (Spicuzza & DeVoe, 1982). The symptoms are physical (exhaustion), emotional (depression and irritability), and cognitive (lost idealism and negativity toward clients). To give you an idea of the significance of burnout among helping professionals, over 2,500 books and journal articles were written about it between 1974 and 1990 (Kleiber & Enzmann, 1990).

The background of the burnout concept is interesting. Freudenberger was a clinical psychologist working in New York and was the first to use the term in 1973 (Gold & Roth, 1993). At that time, helping professionals often described chronic users of drugs as "burned out." Freudenberger thought there was a parallel in the chronic symptoms of these drug users and the more temporary symptoms he frequently observed among overworked human service workers.

In the decades that followed Freudenberger's early observations, we have come to understand that burnout can develop when helpers are exposed for prolonged periods to personal and work-related stressors in conjunction with the perception that there are inadequate resources to cope with those stressors (Maslach, Jackson, & Leiter, 1996).

Because burnout leads to cynicism, lowered confidence, withdrawal, and disturbances in interpersonal relationships, one's effectiveness in working with people is reduced. Burnout has a constricting effect, limiting the flexibility so important to being successful in the helping professions. Thus, burnout changes the picture we have of careers in the human services. Rather than observing the beginning helper increasing in effectiveness over time, the helper's ability to respond to the needs of clients is reduced because of burnout. Thus, novice helping professionals at times are more effective than the veterans. This challenges helping professionals to pay careful attention to the first signs of burnout and to take measures to reduce it so their service to clients is not reduced.

Recipe for Burnout

What do the thousands of articles and books say about how to guarantee that professional helpers will develop burnout? Here is the recipe: Give trainees a glamorized image of the helping professions. Make sure they are naive about the risks and dangers of the work in the real world so they will be unprepared to cope with them. Never give a realistic job preview.

When they enter a helping profession, make sure they are given a large number of very difficult clients. Make the helper work long hours in unpleasant physical surroundings. Be sure that administrators and support staff are punitive and nonsupportive. Make the cost of mistakes very high. Have the administrators make it clear that the helpers are never doing enough, that more is always expected.

Above all else, never make supervision available. Pile on the paperwork, especially that which is trivial. Make sure that the work routine is the same, day after day and year after year. Above all else, be sure that the helpers are paid poorly, and that there is little opportunity to learn about the effect of their effort. Isolate them as much as possible, making sure communication is difficult among peers and among workers and administrators. If even half of these conditions occur, in a very short period, professional helpers will burn out.

How to Manage Stress

What Your Employer Can Do.   Hopefully we demonstrated how employers can help induce burnout among its workers. By reversing the actions just described, we can understand how the work environment can be designed not to eliminate stress and burnout but to buffer or reduce the impact of unavoidable stressors. Look for the following in an agency:

- Recognition for accomplishment and hard work
- Pleasant physical surroundings that make work more enjoyable
- Friendly supervisors and support staff
- Mandatory time away from work to replenish energy
- Variety in a work assignment with the opportunity to rewrite one's job description
- Enforced limit on the number of difficult clients on one's caseload
- Comp time for working overtime and flexible scheduling that recognizes responsibilities to family and friends
- Many opportunities for continuing education to increase professional skills

What You Can Do. While your future employer can help you manage stress and burnout in the ways described, there are many practices individuals can adopt that make them both less susceptible to stress and burnout and more likely to recover quickly when they do experience episodes of burnout. The practices we will discuss include cognitive restructuring, time management, relaxation, and social support. These practices put individuals more in charge of their experience and help buffer them from stressors. Because student life is stressful (Bowman, Bowman, & DeLucia, 1990), and because transitions from the classroom to applied settings such as internships can be stressful (Mitchell & Kampke, 1993), there is no better time to learn stress management than when one is in school.

Cognitive Restructuring. Chapter 7 provided a brief description of Rational Emotive Behavioral Therapy (REBT). Cognitive restructuring has similarities to REBT in that the assumption is that distress is in part the result of dysfunctional thinking. Stressors increase in intensity by the way the individual thinks about them. Stress can be managed better by examining basic assumptions, seeing how in practice they make the situation worse, and finally replacing the assumptions or thoughts with ones that enable one to cope with the stressors more effectively. Complete Exercise 14.3, p. 292, to gain a better understanding of this principle.

Time Management. Time pressure produces stress in most people. Meeting deadlines, getting everything done, especially the important things, haunt many of us. When we miss deadlines for important projects, our need for better time management becomes obvious. However, a more common complaint is not that things do not get done, but that what gets done is less important than the things we would like to accomplish. Most of us find it easier to complete small tasks every day. More difficult to achieve are long-range goals, especially with respect to large projects. And long-term satisfaction and our sense of self-worth are attached more to the larger goals of our lives.

Because more is at stake with these larger goals, people tend to get more anxious when they even think about them. To avoid the anxiety attached to important life objectives, many of us substitute working on more immediate, less significant tasks. Having trouble getting started on a task and substituting trivia for the important are two common examples of procrastination.

Time management is a label for a variety of strategies that help us overcome procrastination. The emphasis in most time management approaches (Covey, 1990; Lakein, 1973; Mackenzie, 1972) is on identifying goals, prioritizing goals, identifying activities that waste time, and planning workspace and time. The emphasis is not only on what one should do but also on what one should avoid doing. When these strategies work, people waste less time being involved in what they find insignificant and unsatisfying and more involved in what they see as truly important. In doing this, they "work smarter, not harder" (Lakein, 1973).

Let us look at some examples of this in the lives of college students. Many students can get to class and complete brief homework assignments. More difficult are larger class projects, research papers, and studying for comprehensive examinations. For graduate students, the most difficult part of a degree program is the completion of a thesis or dissertation. Each extends over an extensive period of time, involves many steps, and requires planning and perseverance.

But it is not just students who procrastinate. Take this author as an example. Too many times has he sat down and stared at the screen of his computer, feeling anxious about the book manuscript deadline, waiting for moments of inspiration that rarely, if ever, came. Sometimes he just began writing, editing, rewriting, editing, and rewriting again and again. At other times he left the computer, made a cup of coffee he did not need, decided to check his email, and remembered he needed to call someone about some trivial issue. He found a lot of things to do except work on his book chapter. When the chapters did not get written, he felt

---

E X E R C I S E   **14.3**

Stress Enhancing Beliefs

Immediately following Exercise 14.1 was a list of beliefs that can intensify the distress individuals experience in everyday events. For example, one of the items was: "Don't expect others or yourself to make mistakes." This is a belief that you must be perfect. Ask yourself, does this increase or decrease the distress one would feel after someone did not anticipate what might happen and something goes wrong? If we research most people's actions, no one is ever mistake-free. To expect to be perfect places extra strain on oneself. If the data gathered supports this, then changing the expectation seems appropriate. A more adaptive way to think about mistakes might be: "Everyone makes mistakes. Try not to make too many, but when they happen, learn from them, forgive yourself for the mistake, and move on with your life."

Go back to pages 285–286 and review the other beliefs listed. Examine the consequences of each in everyday life. Write down an alternative way of thinking about the issue that would be more adaptive. Discuss these changes with others in class.

bad and saw himself as letting down his beloved co-author. No matter what the context may be, procrastination always sounds all too familiar.

Suggestions for Better Time Management

- Time spent planning saves time. Write down life goals, especially the long-term ones.
- Prioritize your goals. First categorize them as of high, medium, and low importance. In each category, rank order each goal with the most important being first.
- Write down deadlines for projects related to goals. Use a time planner to record assignments, important dates, and events.
- Use "to do" lists, and check them often.
- For big projects, spend time breaking them down into their component parts. Make the big project a sequence of smaller, more achievable ones.
- Get organized. Plan your workspace. Eliminate anything that distracts you from your work. If needed, find a quiet place to work where others cannot locate you.
- Understand what makes you the most productive. If you are a morning person, use that time of day to get things done. If you are a night person, use that time to work on important tasks.
- Identify time wasters and limit exposure to them.

Time wasters deserve a bit more discussion. Most of us regret time spent chatting on the telephone, watching TV, and daydreaming. We often judge these activities to be time wasters afterwards. Other activities may be necessary for everyday maintenance but are rarely very satisfying. Some examples include doing the laundry, cleaning, changing the oil, and so forth. Sometimes such tasks can be combined. Why not give yourself a manicure or pay bills while watching TV? How about writing a letter or studying while in the laundermat?

When people devote time to what is important to them, they feel less distressed. They get rid of responsibilities; they eliminate the risk of failure. Finally, time management involves not doing some things. Removing oneself from tedious and unfulfilling tasks reduces our exposure to stressors.

Relaxation. If stress is a form of arousal intended to prepare us to deal with challenges, demands, dangers, and threats, then the opposite of stress is relaxation. Benson (1975) wrote an enormously popular book entitled *The Relaxation Response.* In it he argues that fast-paced modern life has led to the loss of the natural antidote to the arousal response of stress—the ability to relax. Benson argues that most people today need to relearn how to calm themselves. Earlier generations, less harried than ours, instinctively knew how to relax, but over the past century this capacity has been lost. He proposed systematically relearning relaxation, especially a deep calm that is achievable through meditation. (See Exercise 14.4.) Others have recommended learning other techniques that help one to progressively relax muscle groups until the entire body in a state of deep relaxation.

Learning meditation, yoga, and deep relaxation techniques indeed are worthwhile goals that can be accomplished over time. Other relaxation techniques that require less training and time to master might be considered. Here are several:

- Simple quiet times, sitting alone in a pleasant place with the purpose of simply being there.
- Taking a walk or going on a run without a radio or CD player. On the walk, just look around and observe; see the layers of leaves in the trees, notice what you are often too busy to see.
- Taking a long, soaking bath, enjoying the warmth of the water and the privacy of the bathroom.
- Going to an art museum just to look, just to sit, and just to stroll through the rooms of paintings and sculpture.
- Visiting a church to look at the stained glass windows, possibly to sit, to pray.
- Building a campfire to watch the flames and glowing coals.
- Sitting quietly, listening to your breathing, and beginning breathing more deeply.

For many it is difficult to do the things just listed. If they sit quietly, quickly they begin to feel guilty that they are not doing something "productive." They

---

EXERCISE **14.4**

Breathing to Control Stress

One of the things that happens when your body becomes stressed is that breathing changes in two ways. The first of these is that you begin to breathe too rapidly. Second, your breathing shifts to the upper part of the chest (the thorax) from the lower part or the diaphragm. To slow your breathing and return it to a normal pattern, do the following:

1. Force yourself to take a deep breath.
2. Hold that breath as long as you can.
3. When you must exhale, purse your lips as though you are kissing someone on the cheek and exhale very, very slowly.
4. Avoid inhaling as long as possible, then take another deep breath, and hold your breath as long as possible.
5. Purse your lips and exhale slowly again.
6. Repeat this process 10 to 12 times. Your body should feel relaxed and your stress level will be back to normal.
7. Check to see if you are breathing normally by placing your hand on your stomach. If it moves in and out slowly, you are breathing normally.

feel uncomfortable with silence; they need to have sounds around them. It seems that Benson may have been right; today we do find it difficult to relax.

The importance of relaxation is that it is good for our health. Taking time away from the demands of school and work can act as a buffer from stress. Periods of relaxation can replenish lost energy and enthusiasm, increasing the efficiency of scheduled work times.

Social Support.   Positive relations with supervisors, coworkers, spouses, and friends have been shown to be important buffers in the management of burnout (Cohen & Wills, 1985; Corrigan, Holmes, & Luchins, 1995). It is easy to see that a positive relationship with a supervisor will help make the stressful work of a helping profession less punishing. Being able to vent frustrations to others, especially a boss, relieves pressure.

Supportive relationships among coworkers are also important. Groups of workers create the environment in an office as much as do managers. Often helping professionals work in isolation. Their relationships with clients are confidential. The clients themselves often are so needy that there is never much thought about the needs of the helper. Coworkers can compensate for the often one-sided nature of helper–client relationships.

Stressful human services work can be destructive to the personal lives of helpers. The most common reason for therapists to seek professional help for themselves is a troubled marriage (Deutsch, 1985). It makes sense that helpers may have little energy left for relating to their families after being depleted by the demands of their clients. Those helpers that maintain the support of their loved ones find the effort worth it because it inhibits burnout. Often maintaining good relationships with others involves paying as much attention to little things as to big issues. Case Illustration 14.2 offers an example of this.

Developing a Healthy Lifestyle

In recent years it is difficult to avoid hearing about the extensive effort of employers to keep their employees fit and healthy. It makes good sense. Both business and government have invested a great deal in their workers. Besides salary and benefits, employees have been given extensive training. With experience, employees become increasingly more valuable. To replace many of these employees would be extremely expensive, so employers are motivated to protect this investment by encouraging workers to develop good health habits.

A concept that underlies this health promotion is "wellness." Myers (1992) connects wellness with the fostering of a healthy lifestyle, not just in the present but throughout one's entire career. Wellness is not just relevant to physical health but also to psychological and spiritual fitness, family and work adjustment, as well as effective use of leisure time and stress management.

We are bombarded in the media with information on healthy living. Few of us today are ignorant of the fact that smoking is one of the most serious risks to good health. Most of us also are aware that diet is important, not simply to

CASE ILLUSTRATION **14.2**
Celeste and Marvin

Celeste and Marvin have been together for three years. Both have demanding work schedules. Celeste is a protective services supervisor, and Marvin is a computer systems manager. Each morning they set their alarm twenty minutes early so they can snuggle through two snooze alarms and each give the other a brief back rub before getting out of bed. Before they leave for work, they try to share coffee and review their plans for the day. A week never goes by without numerous email messages being exchanged, from forwarding jokes to simple messages each might think the other would enjoy. They coordinate evening work so there can be more nights a week that they can both be home together.

At work Celeste is the person in the office who gets everyone to sign a birthday card for one of the staff. As a supervisor she makes it a point to drop by "just to visit." She works hard to remember the names of spouses and children of the other workers. At the end of the day, when workers are returning from home visits and investigations, she considers her time debriefing workers, helping them cope with the frustrations of the day, as her most important duty.

Celeste has several close friends who also work for the Department of Human Services. When they get together at one another's home or meet for an event, they have a standing rule: "No shop talk."

Marvin and Celeste plan at least one event every month that they can look forward to as special. It might be a drive to the mountains to look at the colorful leaves in the fall. It might be weekend trip to the city that includes a stay at a nice hotel.

---

avoid becoming overweight, but because healthy eating increases vitality. It provides energy that can be invested in both work and leisure.

Eating vegetables and whole grains, reducing the intake of fats and refined sugar seem to many of us a sacrifice. It is more like dieting than a healthy diet. Others have learned that some of the most prized, delicious foods in the world are in fact very healthy. For many it would be a treat to eat foods from Japan, from the Provence of France, and other areas of the Mediterranean. These foods are rich in flavor. People living in those parts of the world cook with little meat and lots of vegetables, fruits, and seafood. More recently, these cuisines have reduced the use of fats and today represent some of the best opportunities for people who love food but desire to eat healthy.

Besides diet, exercise is a key element in wellness (Romano, 1984). One's endurance, strength, and flexibility determine the degree of physically fitness. Exercise develops them. McCullagh (1984) notes that involvement in "lifesports" is one of the best ways to achieve fitness. Lifesports include swimming, racquetball, running, bicycling, and other sports that do not require the formation of teams. They can for the most part be done alone or with a friend. These activities are enjoyable and often become habitual while they promote cardiovascular fitness. Because work in the helping professions for most is sedentary and indoors, other activities that take one outside and provide exercise promote stress reduction, overall better health, and variety to one's weekly schedule.

Finally, a healthy lifestyle includes restrictions in the use of alcohol and other substances. In our culture, the use of alcohol is sanctioned as part of a celebration, and moderate drinking in the company of friends is acceptable. Alcohol use is a problem when it becomes a form of self-medication to cope with stress and hardship. It is one thing on Friday to celebrate the end of the week with a couple of beers with friends and another to drink several straight shots of vodka to control anxiety before a blind date. The abuse of alcohol is one of the common problems of distressed helping professionals (Deutsch, 1985). Learning to cope with stress through the avoidance of stressors, relaxation, cognitive restructuring, and social support are more effective and extraordinarily less dangerous.

Getting in Touch with One's Spirituality

Spirituality is the acceptance of the idea that human beings are a part of something that is greater than themselves that cannot be explained rationally or with words. For some this means the acceptance of certain religious beliefs. Others see their spirituality as rooted in their relationships to people. They often subscribe to the idea that it is important to be sensitive to the needs of others and to lead one's life by placing the welfare of others ahead of their own. Still others find spiritual meaning in their relationship to nature and find solace in the beauty and continuous rebirth that occurs in natural events. People who have discovered the innermost part of themselves understand their most basic beliefs and values and allow their lives to be guided by them. This gives them a sense of purpose and allows them to live a life based on reflective morality, that is, a life based on thoughtful, deliberate decisions. Without an understanding of one's values, it is likely that decisions will be made spontaneously, often without concern for their consequences (Kenyon, 1999). People who make spontaneous decisions often allow themselves to be influenced by the people around them instead of their core beliefs.

In the literature on helping, there is also a distinction made between being spiritual and being religious (Shafranske & Maloney, 1990). A religious person is one who belongs to an organized church and accepts the dogma of that church. A spiritual person commonly has a belief in a higher power that is benevolent in nature. That benevolent higher power can be called on to influence human affairs in a positive manner. Establishing an intimate relationship with this higher power is the ultimate goal of spiritual development.

Summary

In this chapter, we examined many of the health threats helping professionals face. Underscored was the hope that one's career as a helper would be more of a satisfaction than a danger. Both external and internal sources of stress were examined along with ways of coping with them. Occupational stress in the helping professions was described as burnout. Its nature was examined along with strategies to manage it. Finally, stress management was put in the context of a healthy lifestyle. Designing such a lifestyle included consideration of exercise and diet in addition to the health strategies previously discussed.

CHAPTER 14 EXIT QUIZ

Answer the following questions with a T for true and an F for false.

_____ 1. Little can be done as a student to prepare oneself to cope with the stress one will face as a helping professional.

_____ 2. Perfectionists are better able to manage stress than are more easy-going individuals.

_____ 3. *Stress* is just another term for *nervous tension*.

_____ 4. A supervisor plays an important role in how much stress a helping professional experiences.

_____ 5. Time management is intended to help individuals feel less stressed by helping them cope with procrastination.

_____ 6. Because stress is a form of arousal, relaxation is an antidote to stress.

_____ 7. Because burnout can strain a helper's relationships with loved ones, it is especially important to consciously work at developing social support.

_____ 8. Diet is especially important for helping professionals because so many are overweight.

_____ 9. Alcohol and other substances are not effective in managing stress.

_____10. Managing stress and burnout is better achieved by a combination of strategies rather than any single strategy.

Answers:

1. F; 2. F; 3. F; 4. T; 5. T; 6. T; 7. T; 8. F; 9. F; 10. T.

SUGGESTED LEARNING ACTIVITIES

1. Think of the people you know well and ones you think are overly stressed. Make a list of the things they do and the attitudes they have that you think contribute

to their stress. How do you compare to these people, and which items on the list you have made apply to you?

2. Make a list of the things you do not like about your current life. Rank order your complaints from worst to least. This list can translate into important stressors in your life. Reducing their impact will lessen your stress.

3. Make another list of the most serious time wasters for you. Consider how you might avoid them.

4. Answer the following questions: When during the day do you get the most done? If you exercise regularly, what form of exercise do you do? Can your approach to being fit continue to be something you can do for a lifetime?

5. Divide the class into groups of four to six. Share in the group times when you or someone else did something big or small that was kind and thoughtful. It could be something as insignificant as placing a candy kiss on someone's desk. Have each group share their list of thoughtful deeds with the class.

- Discuss how students can be more supportive of one another.
- Get back into small groups and make lists of what professors can do to reduce student stress. Show how these actions parallel what supervisors at work in the future can do to reduce the stress of helping professionals.
- Discuss how class members as individuals can maintain and increase support from their families.
- Discuss the added difficulties a psychologist or social worker would encounter if he or she had a marital or drinking problem. How would being a distress helping professional affect getting assistance for a problem?

REFERENCES

Benson, H. (1975). *The relaxation response.* New York: Morrow.

Bowman, R.L., Bowman, V.E., & DeLucia, J.L. (1990). Mentoring in a graduate counseling program: Students helping students. *Counselor Education and Supervision, 30*(1), 58–65.

Cohen, S., & Wills, T. (1985). Stress, social support, and the buffering hypothesis. *Psychological Bulletin, 98*(2), 310–357.

Corrigan, P.W., Holmes, E.P., & Luchins, D. (1995). Burnout and collegial support in state psychiatric hospital staff. *Journal of Clinical Psychology, 51*(5), 703–710.

Covey, S.R. (1990). *The seven habits of highly effective people: Restoring the character ethic.* New York: Simon and Schuster.

Deutsch, C. (1985). A survey of therapists' personal problems and treatment. *Professional Psychology: Research and Practice, 16*(2), 305–315.

Freudenberger, H.J. (1974). Staff burnout. *Journal of Social Issues, 30*(1), 159–165.

Gold, Y., & Roth, R.A. (1993). *Teachers managing stress and preventing burnout.* London: Falmer Press.

Kasl, S.V. (1978). Epidemiological contributions to the study of work stress. In C.L. Cooper & R. Payne (Eds.), *Stress at work* (pp. 219–226). New York: Wiley.

Kenyon, P. (1999). *An ethical casebook for human services professionals.* Pacific Grove, CA: Brooks/ Cole.

Kleiber, D., & Enzmann, D. (1990). *Burnout: 15 years of research: An international bibliography.* Gottingen: Hogrefe.

Lakein, A. (1973). *How to get control of your time and your life.* New York: New American Library.

Mackenzie, R.A. (1972). *The time trap.* New York: McGraw-Hill.

Maslach, C., Jackson, S.E., & Leiter, M.P. (1996). *Maslach burnout inventory manual.* Palo Alto, CA: Consulting Psychologists Press.

McCullagh, J.C. (1984). *The complete bicycle fitness book.* New York: Warner Books.

Mitchell, M.L., & Kampke, C.M. (1993). Student coping strategies and perceptions of fieldwork. *American Journal of Occupational Therapy, 47*(6), 535–540.

Myers, J.E. (1992). Wellness, prevention, development: The cornerstone of the profession. *Journal of Counseling and Development, 71*(2), 136–139.

Romano, J.L. (1984). Stress management and wellness: Reaching beyond the counselor's office. *Personnel and Guidance Journal, 62*(9), 533–537.

Selye, H. (1976). *The stress of life.* New York: McGraw-Hill.

Shafranske, E.P., & Maloney, H.N. (1990). Clinical psychologists' religious and spiritual orientations and their practice of psychotherapy. *Psychotherapy, 27*(1), 72–78.

Spicuzza, F.J., & DeVoe, M.W. (1982). Burnout in the helping professions: Mutual aid groups as self-help. *Personnel and Guidance Journal, 61*(2), 95–99.

15 Becoming a Helper: Some Issues That Influence Practice

WHAT YOU WILL LEARN

The major issues confronting new professional helpers and how these will influence their functioning

In the preceding fourteen chapters, a number of issues have been addressed ranging from the skills of the helper to getting a job and advancing in one's chosen field. In this section, a brief overview of the societal context in which helpers function will be presented. The rationale for this presentation rests on two ideas. First, the social policy of the moment (for example, welfare reform) has a tremendous impact on the functioning of professional helpers. Second, as was pointed out in Chapter 14, many students hold altruistic attitudes about the helping process that must be tempered by real world considerations of what is possible. Our clients may, and often do, need long-term help, but case loads, agency policies, and insurance companies make giving them this help increasingly difficult. What follows are some of the major issues that will greatly influence the manner in which professional helpers implement their skills in the future.

Workfare and other Welfare Reforms

Human services workers, social workers, and others who staff the agencies who serve people on welfare have faced a tremendous challenge during the last few years, a challenge that is likely to last into the foreseeable future. This challenge was precipitated by welfare reform that, although it took many forms, dictated that able-bodied welfare recipients who are free from mental health problems must seek employment. The impetus to reform the welfare system had many sources, not the least of which was concerns about the abuse of welfare funds. Although concerns about abuse of funds were decidedly distorted, particularly when compared to the abuse of "welfare funds to farmers and businesses" such as subsidies to tobacco farmers, the results of the reforms have changed the manner in which helpers must deal with welfare recipients. With the possible exception of the physically disabled, few recipients of welfare funds can count on long-term financial support from the welfare system. Rather, they are expected to develop job skills and enter the workforce. Welfare agencies have teamed with other organizations such as state employment offices to develop programs that provide career development activities aimed at assisting welfare recipients make informed career choices and develop strategies for acting on those choices. In some instances, this involves entering job training programs, while in other cases people are helped to develop employability skills including completing job applications and interviewing skills. In spite of efforts by advocates for the poor to turn back the clock, it seems likely that some welfare recipients will continue to

- receive no or reduced benefits when they have additional children,
- be forced to take jobs that pay less than their welfare benefits,
- be forced into community jobs to receive welfare benefits when no other jobs are available,
- be required to enter career development and job training programs,
- go to work even when they have young children at home, and
- be faced with limitations on the number of years they can receive benefits (Schmolling, Youkeles, & Burger, 1997).

Managed Health Care

Many clients need relatively long-term counseling and psychotherapy. Some health insurance companies, health maintenance organizations (HMOs), and other health insurers limit the number of sessions that they will underwrite to six or less. Those companies that do pay for longer-term care (sometimes up to twenty-four or more sessions) require periodic reviews of the client's progress before authorizing additional sessions. These limitations placed on services have caused helpers generally to limit the goals that they establish with clients and to adopt brief therapeutic approaches such as solution focused brief therapy (SFBT) (Berg, 1995). A helper who utilizes SFBT begin with so-called magic questions such as, "If your problems were solved, what would your life be like?" Once the client answers this question, the helper works with the client to construct the solution identified. Although SFBT and other brief therapies have the advantage of reducing the time spent in the helping process, their effectiveness is largely untested.

Managed health care companies are having a tremendous impact on the approaches used by helpers. They are also impacting the helping process by increasing the emphasis of pharmacological approaches to treating mental health problems. Although it is undoubtedly the case that the treatment of serious mental disorders such as clinical depression, schizophrenia, manic-depression, and others has been greatly aided by the use of drugs, it is also the case that many mental health problems such as simple phobias and panic disorders can be successfully treated using traditional approaches. Managed health care companies have seen pharmacological approaches as more efficient than traditional counseling and therapy without considering that many clients do not wish to rely only on drugs and the possibility that drugs and traditional approaches together may be better solutions. Without intervention from professional organizations, their emphasis on the use of drugs to treat psychological problems is likely to continue. One group, clinical psychologists, has elected to lobby for prescription privileges so that they can become more actively involved in the treatment of their clients. Although others may follow this path, it seems likely that all professional helpers are faced with learning more about the interaction of their approaches to treatments with the impact of drugs as well as the strengths and weaknesses of pharmacological approaches to treating mental health problems.

Outpatient Care of People with Chronic Mental Health Problem

Outpatient treatment of serious mental health problems is not a new phenomenon, but it is more widespread than ever before, primarily because of the development of the pharmacological drugs mentioned in the foregoing section. The result has been the gradual closing of thousands of inpatient treatment centers, a move that has been endorsed by many mental health professionals. However, not all clients with chronic mental health problems respond to drugs. Some psychiatrists estimate that nearly one-third of all people who are treated with drugs are not greatly helped by them. No reliable statistics were found regarding the impact of drugs on the functioning of the chronically mentally ill. However, if anecdotal reports are to be believed, some people who do either do not respond to treatment or fail to get adequate care end up as homeless individuals while others turn to illegal drugs and alcohol as forms of self-medication. One result is addiction and the subsequent need for treatment. Professional helpers in a variety of community agencies will come into contact with the chronically mentally ill and be forced to develop strategies to assist them develop the best possible quality of life given the limitations they bring to the helping process.

Deemphasis on Rehabilitation of Criminals

Crime is a major issue in our society in spite of the fact that the incidence of violent crime has declined in the last few years (FBI, 1998). Although violent crime such as murder and rape are on the wane, we have record numbers of prisoners in our local, state, and federal correctional institutions because of numerous efforts aimed at increasing the punishment criminals receive. One of these efforts has resulted in the passage of numerous laws that limit the power of judges to take mitigating circumstances into account in sentencing criminals by requiring a minimum amount of time served. For example, in North Carolina an individual who is convicted of armed robbery must serve a minimum of seven years in prison. Other laws allow teenagers and children to be tried as adults in some instances and sentenced to long prison terms. Given the current attitudes toward people who break the law in our society, this seems likely to continue.

Another impact of the more punitive societal attitude toward criminals is a reduction in efforts to rehabilitate offenders, both while they are incarcerated and afterwards. Prison guards who once received training in basic helping skills are less likely to receive this training today. Correctional officials have been accused of running "country club" institutions where prisoners are coddled with libraries, gymnasiums, and cable television. As a result, institutions have become more sterile. Probation and parole officers still have the responsibility of helping the offenders with whom they work, but their traditional roles as law enforcement officers have been reinforced and increasingly emphasized.

The Rights of the Handicapped

Throughout this book, we pointed out that advocacy is one of the roles of professional helpers. We also noted in the section on ethics that only rehabilitation counselors have advocacy as an ethical responsibility *at this time.* There is little question that this will change in the very near future. The increased emphasis on advocacy among helpers has been partially the result of the multicultural movement. The leaders of this movement have made it clear that helpers must go beyond their passive roles to more active roles to help people who have been disenfranchised by decades of neglect and outright discrimination. However, legislation establishing the rights of handicapped persons has probably been even more influential in forcing helpers to look at their obligations to their clients. It is probably no accident that rehabilitation counselors were the first, and at this time only, group to develop ethical principles regarding advocacy. The first law regarding the rights of the handicapped was passed in 1973 and was titled the Rehabilitation Act of 1973. However, more recent legislation, the Americans with Disabilities Act passed in 1990, has more far-reaching implications for helpers. This act and companion legislation preclude discrimination in housing, transportation, educational opportunities, access to recreational activities, and access to jobs for persons with physiological disabilities; cosmetic disfigurement; neurological, musculoskeletal, or sense organs difficulties (including speech difficulties); mental and physical disorders; emotional or mental illness; or specific learning disabilities. Ethical considerations aside, it is illegal to offer services that fail to advance the cause of the handicapped. Educators, employers, and others are ignoring the laws that have been passed when they ignore these legal mandates. And, if current deliberations within the American Counseling Association (ACA) and other professional organizations are any indication, it will be unethical not to act as an advocate for the handicapped (as well as for some other protected groups, such as racial minorities).

Advocacy for people with disabilities includes helping them in all aspects of their lives. However, one area that deserves particular attention is assisting handicapped persons improve their educational attainment. As Day and Curry (1998) observe, by increasing educational attainment, workforce participation can be enhanced for handicapped people regardless of the extent of their disabilities.

Currently, high school and college completion rates for this population are substantially below those of non-handicapped persons. For example, college graduation rates for handicapped persons are only one-third of those for nondisabled individuals.

Changing Population Demographics

Chapter 3 noted that the minority population is an increasing portion of the U.S. population. This change is occurring because of differences in the birth rates among various ethnic and racial groups and the expectation that approximately 820,000 people will immigrate to this country each year into the foreseeable future. However, the increase in the number of minorities is not the only significant population trend that will influence the functioning of helpers. The most obvious and immediate change in the population will be the increase in the number of older persons due to the highly publicized arrival of the "baby boomers" at retirement age. Because life expectancy is expected to rise from its current age of 76 to 86 in the next 50 years, the need for services to people over 65 will continue into the foreseeable future. In 1995, there were 33.5 million people over 65. By 2050 this number will increase to more than 67 million. Although the increase in the number of elderly people has received much attention, services to the under-17 population will also need to be increased. Currently, there are 70 million people in this age group, a number that is projected to increase to 96 million by 2050 (U.S. Bureau of the Census, 1996). Agencies and the helpers within them will be forced to reinvent themselves to provide high quality services to an ever changing client population.

Economic Risk and Hispanics

As the economy of the United States has shifted from manufacturing to services producing, the skills needed to fill the new jobs have increased. Fortunately there has been a concurrent rise in the high school graduation rates of all groups but one: Hispanics. Only about 31% of foreign-born and 57% of native-born Hispanics have completed high school as compared to 90%, 88%, and 86% of Asians, whites, and blacks respectively (Day & Curry, 1998). Low educational attainment and poverty have always been linked, and thus it seems likely that Hispanics face increased risk of being left behind economically. This is particularly troublesome when one considers that after 2020 Hispanics are expected to add more people to the U.S. population than any other group. Helpers must work to develop creative new strategies that will encourage Hispanics and others to complete their education and to gain the technical skills required in an economy that will increasingly emphasize the need for technical, problem-solving, and communication skills.

Summary

Helpers moving into positions confront an interesting and at times overwhelming array of difficult problems. Those problems change from time to time as social policy relating to target groups is altered to attain certain types of societal goals. The recent alteration of welfare policy is a prime example of how new roles and challenges can be thrust on helpers. However, social policy is not the only factor that influences the functioning of the professional helper. Economic shifts and population changes must be attended to if the needs of client groups are to be adequately met. Changes in the economic climate influence such factors as the availability of jobs and the wages paid. Individuals who live on the edge of poverty can suddenly find themselves in need of a number of types of assistance ranging from financial to psychological support. Changes in the economic climate can also influence the amount of money available to provide services to client groups. Finally, immigration, longer life expectancy, and birth rates influences have profound effects on the make up of the client groups served by professional helpers. Some of the changes in clients will require that helpers learn new skills and approaches as well as new theoretical and philosophical approaches to helping.

CHAPTER 15 EXIT QUIZ

Answer each of the following questions with a T if the statement is true and an F if the statement is false.

_____ 1. One group that will double in size by the year 2050 is the under-17 group.

_____ 2. The group that is of greatest risk is Hispanics because of their immigration status.

_____ 3. Managed health care has increased the emphasis on group counseling and therapy.

_____ 4. Approximately 75% of the persons who suffer from chronic mental illnesses are helped by pharmacological drugs.

_____ 5. The most far-ranging legislation in terms of the rights of the disabled was the Americans with Disabilities Act of 1990.

Answers:

1–4, F; 5, T.

SUGGESTED LEARNING ACTIVITIES

1. Invite representatives from a number of social agencies to discuss the changes that they expect to make in the near and long term as they adapt to social policies, economic changes, and population shifts.

2. Send teams of students to interview people from various groups of helpers. Ask the helpers to detail the changes they have made in their practice since they became practitioners. Also ask them to outline what new skills they have acquired since they entered their helping profession.

3. Have a panel of helping professionals discuss the topic "What frustrates me about my practice today." Make sure that students ask questions about the helpers' visions of practice when they were students and the realities they encountered.

REFERENCES

Berg, I. (1995). *Solution focused brief therapy.* Videotape. Bowling Green, KY: CMTI Video Series.

Day, J.C., & Curry, A.E. (1998). Educational attainment in the United States. Washington, DC: U.S. Department of Statistics Administration, Census Bureau.

FBI (1998). *Crime in the United States.* Washington, DC: Author.

Schmolling, P., Jr., Youkeles, M., & Burger, W.R. (1997). *Human services in contemporary America* (4th ed.). Pacific Grove, CA: Brooks/Cole.

U.S. Bureau of the Census (1996). Resident population projections of the United States: Middle, low and high series, 1996 to 2050. Washington, DC: U.S. Government Printing Office.

INDEX

JSC Willey Library
337 College Hill
Johnson, VT 05656